British Social Attitudes

Attitudes

the
12th report

Social and Community Planning Research (SCPR) is an independent, non-profit social research institute. It has a large professional staff together with its own interviewing and coding resources. Some of SCPR's work - such as the survey reported in this book - is initiated by the institute itself and grant-funded by research councils or foundations. Other work is initiated by government departments, local authorities or quasi-government organisations to provide information on aspects of social or economic policy. SCPR also works frequently with other institutes and academics. Founded in 1969 and now Britain's largest social research institute, SCPR has a high reputation for the standard of its work in both qualitative and quantitative research. SCPR has a Survey Methods Centre and, with Nuffield College Oxford, houses the Centre for Research into Elections and Social Trends (CREST), which is an ESRC Research Centre. It also houses, with Southampton University, the Centre for Applied Social Surveys (CASS), an ESRC Resource Centre for training in survey methods.

The contributors

Daphne Ahrendt
Project Manager, International Survey Research Limited

Lindsay Brook
Research Director at SCPR and Co-director of the *British Social Attitudes* survey series

Ed Cape
Principal Lecturer, Faculty of Law, University of the West of England

John Curtice
Senior Lecturer in Politics and Director of the Social Statistics Laboratory, University of Strathclyde

Lizanne Dowds
Research Fellow at the School of Psychology, The Queen's University of Belfast

Geoffrey Evans
Fellow in the Centre for European Studies, Nuffield College, Oxford

Anthony Heath
Official Fellow in Sociology at Nuffield College, Oxford

Roger Jowell
Director of SCPR and Co-director of the *British Social Attitudes* survey

series; Visiting Professor at the London School of Economics and Political Science

Alison Park
Senior Researcher at SCPR and Co-director of the *British Social Attitudes* survey series

Nirmala Rao
Lecturer in the Department of Social Policy and Politics at Goldsmiths' College, London

Chris Rootes
Senior Lecturer in Sociology and Director of the Centre for the Study of Social and Political Movements at the University of Kent at Canterbury

Peter Taylor-Gooby
Professor of Social Policy, University of Kent

Katarina Thomson
Research Director at SCPR and Co-director of the *British Social Attitudes* survey series

Ken Young
Professor of Politics and Vice-Principal, Queen Mary and Westfield College, University of London

British social attitudes; ed. by
Roger Jowell, John Curtice and Alison
Park. 12th ed.

Jan 96   301.5423

185521606X 3 237 81

s/o

British Social Attitudes

the
12th report

Edited by
Roger Jowell
John Curtice
Alison Park
Lindsay Brook
& Daphne Ahrendt
with Katarina Thomson

Dartmouth

SOCIAL & COMMUNITY
SCPR
PLANNING RESEARCH

Published by
Dartmouth Publishing Company Limited
Gower House
Croft Road
Aldershot
Hants GU11 3HR
England

Dartmouth Publishing Company
Old Post Road
Brookfield
Vermont 05036
USA

ISSN 0267 6869
ISBN 1 85521 606 X

Printed and bound by Athenaeum Press, Ltd.,
Gateshead, Tyne & Wear.

Contents

Introduction

The purpose of this volume, like that of its eleven annual predecessors, is to take a first look at the findings of the latest survey in SCPR's *British Social Attitudes* series. These surveys are designed to chart, describe and analyse trends in public attitudes over the years. On certain topics, we now have a formidable time-series upon which to draw. They include the public's attitudes towards subjects as diverse as crime and punishment, health, social security, politics, relations with Europe, civil liberties, the environment and a wide range of moral issues such as abortion and racial prejudice. On other topics, such as euthanasia and censorship, we have only just begun to create what we hope will become an equally robust set of measurements.

Thanks to the support of our many funders, the series itself is secure for at least the next few years. We owe an immeasurable debt to the Sainsbury Family Charitable Trusts - and in particular to their retiring Director, Hugh de Quetteville - for their continued provision of core funding for the survey. This funding has not only sustained the series since 1984 but, above all, helps to maintain its independence and high standards, both of which are, we believe, valued as much by the survey's other funders as by the research team and those who use the data.

The core funds do not, however, cover the bulk of the survey's costs. These are often met in the form of earmarked funds for several annual rounds of the survey. In particular, we are grateful for long-term support of this kind from numerous government departments including the Employment Department and the Department for Education (now largely merged), the Home Office, the Department of Health, the Department of Social Security and the Department of the Environment. The Countryside Commission also generously provides regular funds of this kind, as do a

number of charitable foundations such as the Charities Aid Foundation, the Nuffield Foundation and the Leverhulme Trust. In the same vein, we continue to receive considerable support from the Economic and Social Research Council (ESRC), not only for a number of different modules of questions, but also to finance the project's participation in the International Social Survey Programme (ISSP).

We are very fortunate to have so much generous and loyal support from such a diverse range of sources, all of whom are content to accept the series' 'rules of engagement' which explicitly place final control over all matters of content and dissemination in the hands of the project team.

The strength of the support given to the series allowed us to increase the survey's sample size in 1994 in order to ease pressure on questionnaire space. We now interview around 3,500 randomly chosen adults each year and field *three* versions of the questionnaire, each administered to one-third of our respondents. Previously we had administered two versions, each to one-half of a smaller sample. However, some modules of questions continue to be asked of *all* respondents and others of two-thirds.

The central feature of the *British Social Attitudes* series continues to be an annual survey among a probability sample of British adults. Most questions are asked 'face-to-face' by interviewers using lap-top computers, but some are contained in a self-completion questionnaire which is collected or posted back later.

This core activity is now supplemented by relationships with two parallel surveys among different populations which the survey series has spawned, two cross-national ventures to which the survey acts as British host, and two other major academic time-series.

The link with other academic time-series is secured through the work of a five-year old ESRC Research Centre based at SCPR and Nuffield College, Oxford. Recently funded for a further five years under its new name, the Centre for Research into Elections and Social Trends (CREST), the Centre links the *British Social Attitudes* series with the *British General Election Studies* and with the newly established *British Election Panel Surveys*. Thus these three time-series, each concentrating on different but overlapping subjects, have for some time been able to 'feed' off each other -to their mutual advantage - borrowing questions, developing standardised attitudinal scales and testing methodological innovations.

The first of the two parallel surveys spawned by *British Social Attitudes* is the *Northern Ireland Social Attitudes* (NISA) survey series, already in its sixth year and now funded by all the Northern Ireland Departments. Conducted among a probability sample of around 1,400 Northern Irish respondents per year, fieldwork is carried out to very high standards by our colleagues in the Central Survey Unit of the Policy Planning and Research Unit (PPRU) in Belfast. The survey uses substantially the same questionnaire as in Britain, but with certain additions of particular local interest.

Some of the differences in social attitudes between British and Northern Irish respondents are regularly reported in these volumes (see, for example,

Chapter 7), but more comprehensive accounts are to be found in the NISA series of reports, the fourth and most recent of which was published earlier this year.[*]

The latest parallel survey to have emerged, conceived and designed in collaboration with colleagues at Barnardos, is the 1994 *Young People's Social Attitudes* survey. One of Barnardos' purposes as a charity is to influence social welfare policy in relation to children, young people and their families, and this survey is designed to bridge a gap in our knowledge about young people's attitudes towards a range of issues from fear of crime to racial prejudice, from moral issues to children's rights and education. Around 600 12 to 19 year olds who lived in the households of *British Social Attitudes*' respondents were interviewed (see Appendix 1 for details of sampling). Around half of the questions we asked of the teenagers were identical to those we asked of adults, allowing fascinating comparisons to be made across the generation gap, while the remainder were tailor-made. A first look at some of the findings appears in Chapter 3 of this volume, but a fuller report edited by our colleagues at Barnardos will appear in spring 1996, examining young people's attitudes to moral issues, education, crime, and so on.[**] Funding for future rounds of this survey will be sought to ensure the continued availability of data about the views of young people.

The main cross-national venture in which the *British Social Attitudes* series is involved is the International Social Survey Programme which SCPR helped to found in 1984 and then chaired for its first seven years. Now comprising 25 member nations spanning four continents, the ISSP coordinates the development and technical standards of a mutually-designed annual questionnaire module which is then administered to at least 1000 adults in each member country. The latest module, to be reported in a future volume in this series, concentrates on aspects of 'national identity', a topic especially timely in view of developments in Eastern Europe, separatist pressures in countries as disparate as Canada, the UK and Spain, and the continuing debate in Britain over its role in the European Union.

The second cross-national grouping in which we participate is the European Consortium for Comparative Social Surveys (COMPASS). Formed in 1993 by SCPR and social research organisations in four other nations (Germany, the Irish Republic, Italy and The Netherlands), COMPASS has received two grants from the European Union. The first was to carry out a cross-national comparative study of environmental behaviour and policy preferences. The second comes under the European

[*]   Breen, R., Devine, P. and Robinson, G. (eds.) (1995), *Social Attitudes in Northern Ireland: the 4th Report*, Belfast: Appletree Press.

[**] Roberts, H. and Sachdev, D. (eds.) (1996, forthcoming), *Young People's Social Attitudes*.

Union's Human Capital and Mobility Programme and requires us to develop proposals for European-wide training in survey methods.

These international ventures provide the *British Social Attitudes* series with immense added value. In particular, by enabling British attitudes and behaviour to be compared with those in other countries, we can begin to discern in what ways, if any, British values are distinctive and why this might be so.

Several new developments will, in due course, enrich the series further:

- Thanks to a recent grant from the ESRC, awarded jointly to the Family Policy Studies Centre and SCPR, we are now able to repeat a module of questions first asked in 1986 on people's family networks and social support systems;

- A further recent ESRC grant, awarded to us in collaboration with Jacqueline Scott of Cambridge University, is enabling us to conduct further analyses of the 1988 and 1994 ISSP modules on family and gender roles;

- New funding from the Nuffield Foundation has allowed us, in collaboration with David Donnison of the University of Glasgow, to develop and run a module of questions on attitudes to euthanasia;

- In the same vein, further ESRC funding has been allocated to us, in collaboration with Arthur Gould of Loughborough University, to devise and run a new module of questions on attitudes to illegal drugs;

- The ESRC has also funded us, in collaboration with the Institute for Fiscal Studies, to develop and run a module of questions on attitudes towards taxation and public spending;

- Extra funding from the Charities Aid Foundation has allowed us to include in the 1995 survey a special module of questions examining the impact of the National Lottery on patterns of charitable giving;

- The British Board of Film Classification, the Broadcasting Standards Council and ICSTIS (The Independent Committee for the Supervision of Standards of Telephone Information Services) have jointly funded us, in collaboration with Steven Barnett of the Centre for Communication and Information Studies at the University of Westminster, to develop a new module of questions on censorship and the proper boundaries of 'taste and decency' in the mass media.

Many of the early findings of these new developments will be reported in next year's volume.

Meanwhile, this volume covers an equally wide terrain - spanning politics to prisons, and working mothers to the welfare state - each chapter containing a wealth of new material about changing values and behaviour. To the extent that there is a consistent theme in the various chapters here, it is the exploration of a growing public concern - sometimes approaching distrust, or even fear - about aspects of Britain's social and political condition.

One of these concerns is about the nation's political system. John Curtice and Roger Jowell consider the decline in the public's trust and confidence both in politicians and in the capacity of central government to respond to the nation's needs. Ken Young and Nirmala Rao examine the health of local democracy and the concern that growing control by central government is eroding support for local government. Alison Park addresses the concern that Britain's next generation of citizens, its teenagers, are disillusioned with and uninterested in politics. And Geoff Evans concentrates on public anxiety and ambivalence about Britain's future role in Europe.

Meanwhile, other chapters examine fears about the future of the welfare state. Peter Taylor-Gooby looks at the problems for welfare that are posed by claims of growing social and economic division in Britain. Katarina Thomson focuses on the problems of childcare faced by the growing proportion of mothers who go out to work. And Chris Rootes and Anthony Heath examine whether the expansion of universities has been accompanied by a diminution of public support and of confidence in their value.

Fear itself is the theme of the chapter by Lizanne Dowds and Daphne Ahrendt. They examine the reported growth in the public's fear of crime and the sources of these fears, real and imagined. Finally, Lindsay Brook and Ed Cape examine the related issue of how society should treat its criminals and the conflicts that exist between law enforcement and civil liberties.

Although all nine chapters collectively draw on public concern about one issue or another, the picture is nonetheless far from uniformly pessimistic. True, some recent changes may have left scars on the national psyche, but fear that Britain's public institutions may be about to collapse under the weight of public criticism or social division appears to be misplaced. Support for the welfare state seems undiminished, while greater scepticism about Britain's political institutions may well be no bad thing. Britain may not be a nation at ease with itself, but nor is it a nation in despair.

As always, several chapters reveal the way in which self-interest tends to influence people's attitudes. Thus, for instance, the poor are keener than the rich to see an increase in social security spending, just as parents of young children tend to opt for more education spending. But by no means all the social divisions we uncover are based on self-interest. Others reflect differences in resources. So, as we discover in Chapter 7, the better educated are more inclined than others to participate in politics and, as

Chapter 3 reveals, the foundations for this tendency seem to be laid very early.

The number of colleagues who contribute critically to this enterprise gets larger each year. Within SCPR we are particularly indebted to all our interviewers and area managers for their consistently high standards in coping with an ever-growing and ever more complicated survey, and to our colleagues in the office whose unenviable task it is to supervise the fieldwork, data preparation and data processing. As we go to press we wish once again to record our appreciation to Lis Box for producing the camera-ready copy from our messy (and numerous) drafts.

Outside SCPR we owe an immense debt to Ann Mair of the Social Statistics Laboratory at the University of Strathclyde. Without her annual efforts to produce a meticulous SPSS system file and cross-tabulations, we would never be able to fulfil our commitments. Much the same tribute is due to the staff of Dartmouth Publishing, and to Sonia Hubbard in particular, not only for their endurance in producing twelve volumes and a number of companion volumes in as many years, but also for doing so within ever-shrinking deadlines.

As usual, however, we reserve our most heartfelt vote of thanks for the 4,000 or so respondents - from 12 years old upwards - in England, Scotland and Wales and the further 1,400 or so in the six counties of Northern Ireland. They all gave their time without reward save for making their voices heard. If any of them should dip into this volume, we hope they will feel that their time was well spent.

                                                                        The Editors

1 Comfortable, marginal and excluded

Who should pay higher taxes for a better welfare state?

Peter Taylor-Gooby [*]

Welfare in Britain has undergone substantial changes since the first *British Social Attitudes* survey was carried out in 1983. Government has sought to retrench on welfare spending, reducing some benefits, uprating some by less than price increases and making others more difficult to get. At the same time the demand for welfare has increased. People are living longer, increasing the demand for health care and pensions. A growing proportion of children are being brought up in single-parent households. High unemployment has become a permanent rather than a temporary feature of the economy, and more and more people are working in insecure temporary or part-time jobs. As a result of these and other pressures, the proportion of the population in poverty has risen from around seven per cent to 24 per cent between 1977 and 1991 (Hills, 1995: 33).[1]

These developments have engendered a lively debate about the future of the welfare state. More than one commentator has suggested that the welfare state's role needs to change, while at the same time expressing doubt about the willingness of the public to accept such change. This chapter examines whether trends in public attitudes towards the welfare state do in fact pose a dilemma about its future, paying particular attention to two influential but rather different theses about the likely future social basis of support for welfare.

The first thesis emerged in the late 1980s and early 1990s, most notably in the writings of Field (1989) and Galbraith (1993). Both argue that society is becoming increasingly divided into two very unequal parts. By far the larger proportion forms a comfortable and contented majority.

---

[*] Professor of Social Policy, University of Kent

However, there is also a minority 'underclass', bearing the brunt of high rates of unemployment and cuts in social benefits. Welfare ought to be directed at the latter, but this is frustrated by the political opposition of the contented majority which feels it has increasingly little need for the welfare state. Thus Galbraith argues, "government ... is accommodated not to reality or common need but to the beliefs of the contented, who are now the majority of those who vote" (1993: 10). The result is an unequal but stable society, where the sharp end of social change is directed exclusively at those who lack the political power to redress their situation.

More recently this thesis has been challenged by Hutton (1995) with his notion of a 40:30:30 society. Hutton argues that important divisions are emerging within the comfortable mass. Only a fortunate minority (that is, Hutton's 40 per cent) feel that it is **never** likely to need the safety net provided by the welfare state. The rest of the supposedly comfortable mass, employed in sectors of the labour market previously regarded as secure, cannot now be confident that they will not need help from government at some stage in their lives. They form a new middle group which, while enjoying full-time work, is continually subject to the uncertainty of wage restraint, temporary contracts, short-time working or redundancy. "...the unpredictability of that income leaves them at a disadvantage" (Hutton, 1995: 193). Meanwhile, those in the bottom 30 per cent are, like Field and Galbraith's underclass, the subemployed and unemployed whose experience is one of marginality and exclusion.

A variety of policies have been canvassed suggesting how governments ought to respond to the 40:30:30 society. They range from greater reliance on community values and individual responsibility (for example Etzioni, 1993) to an emphasis on the role of welfare spending as a means of investing in a civilised and cohesive society (for example OECD, 1994a; European Union, 1994). All these policies imply that the traditional welfare state is obsolete. No longer should governments provide a wide range of services from which virtually all citizens can expect to benefit at some point in their lives. Rather, 'new welfare' requires an increasingly flexible system of governmental provision which is directed specifically to the needs of unemployed and marginally employed groups. At minimum, this means better unemployment and income support benefits. More broadly, it requires an expansion of training and job opportunities.

But do the social divisions within the 40:30:30 society make this possible? The answer is maybe. It is argued that the impact of greater insecurity permeates the whole of society. "Not merely the economy but society has been 'marketised' with an increase in anxiety, dread of the future and communal breakdown. The impact is nearly universal ..." (Hutton, 1995: 197). In particular, the insecure middle 30 per cent fear they will descend to the condition of the bottom 30 per cent and are acutely aware that the state safety-net allows more to slip through it. As a result they may help form the basis for a new majority that will support fresh directions in welfare policy.

Both theses concerning the future of the welfare state argue that the welfare state itself needs to change. However, Galbraith, together with Field, believes that the contented majority will block change. Hutton, in contrast, believes that a new insecure middle group could form a majority coalition together with the underclass which supports change. Our survey enables us to examine whether or not current attitudes do have the potential to unite an increasingly divided society. We shall discover that less seems to have changed than either of these arguments might suggest, and that the future is more hopeful than they imply.

Support for welfare - the long-run trends

On our evidence, the first impression is that the British public does not want either to abandon the welfare state or to recast it into 'new welfare'. People remain firmly wedded to the traditional welfare state, the bulk of whose resources are sunk into health, education and pensions - services from which all can expect to benefit at some stage in their lives.

Support for higher levels of welfare spending, at the cost of higher taxes, grew between 1983 and 1993. True, the level of support for more spending fell back slightly in our most recent survey, possibly in response to the bitter debates about VAT increases that took place early in the year. But even so, in contrast to the 1980s, a clear majority - nearly six in ten - are in favour of more spending even if this means higher taxes. It is too early to say yet whether the pressure for more welfare spending has now reached a plateau, or whether it will increase further still in future.

Trends in attitudes towards taxes and spending

If the government had to choose, it should ...	1983 %	1986 %	1990 %	1993 %	1994 %
... reduce taxes and spend *less* on health, education and social benefits	9	5	3	4	4
... keep taxes and spending at the *same* level as now	54	44	37	29	33
... increase taxes and spend *more* on health, education and social benefits	32	46	54	63	58

When asked about specific services, support for increased spending on health, education and pensions remains undiminished from the high levels of the mid-1980s. Nearly nine in ten would like more spending on the health service and over three-quarters support more expenditure on education and pensions. In contrast, support for more spending on unemployment benefits is lower and has been more variable over time. Indeed, it fell by no less than ten points over the last year, most likely

because of the drop in the level of unemployment during this period. We asked:

Listed below are various areas of government spending. Please show whether you would like to see more or less government spending in each area. Remember that if you say 'much more', it might require a tax increase to pay for it.

	1985			1993			1994		
	More	Same	Less	More	Same	Less	More	Same	Less
	%	%	%	%	%	%	%	%	%
Health	87	11	1	87	9	1	88	11	5
Education	74	22	2	79	16	1	76	23	2
Pensions	74	23	1	78	17	1	78	21	1
Unemployment benefits	30	38	19	48	39	8	38	44	18

Similarly, health and education topped people's preferences, and social security[2] was a lower priority, when we asked:

Here are some items of government spending. Which of them, if any, would be your highest priority for extra spending? And which next?

There have been some minor fluctuations in support for specific areas over the years, but enthusiasm for extra spending on health and education has not diminished. Indeed, it is noticeable that the recent gradual decline in the popularity of health as a priority - a decline accompanied by increasing satisfaction with the health service (Bosanquet, 1994) - has been reversed over the last year. Controversy concerning the new funding arrangements may have begun to take its toll.

% giving first or second priority to	1983	1986	1990	1993	1994
Health	74	81	70	60	72
Education	49	57	60	57	60
Housing	20	21	20	20	19
Help for industry	29	16	6	14	11
Social security	12	12	13	13	12
Police and prisons	8	8	4	11	12

Support for 'old welfare' remains strong, the most likely explanation being, as Lipsey (1994) argued, 'enlightened self-interest'. People support the welfare state not out of altruism, but because they realise that they might need services which government can provide cheaply and - in most cases - 'on demand'. National Insurance, for all its faults, is the insurance provider

least likely to go bankrupt. Even if Britain does have a contented majority, part of its contentment lies in some of the services provided by the welfare state.

This self-interest is apparent when one looks at how support for more spending varies amongst different groups. Older people are especially likely to support spending on health care while people with young families are particularly concerned about education. But the most marked differences are to be found in attitudes towards social security benefits. Over one in five of those in households in the lower half of the income distribution put benefits as their first or second priority for extra spending, whereas only five per cent of those in the top half of the income distribution do so.

Of course, one might ask whether the public is prepared to put its vote where its mouth is. The long-run trend towards support for more spending on welfare would appear to be at variance with the fact that the party most committed to tax cuts and least identified with welfare provision has won the last four general elections. But as Lipsey (1994) pointed out, elections are not won and lost primarily on welfare issues: tax policies appear to be much more salient in current political struggles. Further, we have to remember that the Conservatives won the support of only just over four in ten of the voters in each of their election victories; their majority in the House of Commons reflects the way the electoral system works rather than public opinion.

Although attitudes towards welfare spending may not determine how people vote, there are some clear differences between each party's identifiers. Even among Conservative identifiers, nearly half now favour more spending and higher taxes compared with just a quarter in 1983. But at the same time, the gap between the proportion of Conservative identifiers favouring more spending and the proportion of Labour identifiers doing so, has widened somewhat from 18 points in 1983 to 23 points now.

Attitudes to tax and spending by party identification

If the government had to choose, it should ...	Conservative			Alliance/ Liberal Democrat			Labour		
	1983	1989	1994	1983	1989	1994	1983	1989	1994
	%	%	%	%	%	%	%	%	%
... reduce taxes and spend *less* on health, education and social benefits	10	3	4	6	2	2	8	3	4
... keep taxes and spending at the *same* level as now	63	46	47	54	29	30	46	25	24
... increase taxes and spend *more* on health, education and social benefits	24	48	46	36	65	65	42	68	69

Further, although health and education are the top two priorities for extra spending amongst all parties' identifiers, Conservative identifiers are less

likely to nominate social security or housing than are Labour identifiers. This underlines the more contentious nature of those welfare services which are directed at the disadvantaged minority.

Spending priorities and party identification

% giving first or second priority to	Conservative	Liberal Democrat	Labour
Health	68	77	75
Education	61	65	58
Housing	13	14	25
Help for industry	16	11	8
Social security	6	11	17
Police and prisons	17	11	10

Two points emerge from our findings so far. First, far from wanting to see a diminution of the welfare state, the majority of the British public not only wants to see it maintained, but expanded - even if this means paying higher taxes. Secondly, this support is predominantly based on self-interest. There is consistent and strong support for more spending on health and education, areas from which everyone can hope to benefit. Support for benefits enjoyed by more specific groups, such as Unemployment Benefit, is, in contrast, more limited and variable. Thus, although the contented majority may not have turned its back on the welfare state, it is also far from clear that it would tolerate a redirection to the greater benefit of an increasingly excluded minority. Before we accept this conclusion, however, we need to look more closely at attitudes towards this poor minority.

Attitudes to the poor

Poverty in Britain has increased sharply over recent years as a result of "increased earnings dispersion, higher unemployment, polarisation between two earner and no-earner couples, rising self-employment and investment incomes, the declining relative value of cash benefits and discretionary tax changes" (Hills, 1995: 62). The most recent official Department of Social Security review shows that the incomes of all social groups rose in real terms over the period 1979 to 1991/92 - except those of the poorest ten per cent. Their income fell by no less than 17 per cent once housing costs are taken into account. Further, amongst those groups that did experience a rise, that rise was greater the higher the initial level of income[3] (DSS, 1994). Admittedly, recent analysis of spending data indicates that poorer groups were able to maintain their spending levels during this period - presumably by borrowing, the sale of assets and access to types of income not recorded in income surveys. But over the same period, the spending of the better off rose sharply, with the result that, over the past fifteen years, inequality in

living standards has widened almost as much as inequality in incomes (Goodman and Webb, 1995).

Public perceptions of poverty

But how does the public perceive poverty? Does it accept the approach adopted by most social scientists and implicit in the previous paragraph that poverty is a relative concept - that it means not having what most other people have? Or does the public adopt a more basic notion - that poverty exists only when people do not have enough to buy some absolute minimum level of necessities? This view follows the lead of the government which has argued that, as living standards throughout society are rising, increasing inequality does not automatically result in growing misery. Or perhaps the public adopts an even more restrictive notion, poverty simply meaning not even having enough to eat.

As the following table shows, only around a quarter of people think of poverty in relative terms. In contrast, over half accept a basic - or absolute - notion of poverty. It is only when we adopt a highly restrictive definition of poverty that near unanimity about the existence of poverty can be achieved. There has been little change in these figures since we first asked the question in 1986.

Popular conceptions of poverty

% would say someone in Britain was in poverty if...	1986	1989	1994
... they had enough to buy the things they really needed, but not enough to buy the things most people take for granted	25	25	28
... they had enough to eat and live, but not enough to buy other things they needed	55	60	60
... they had not got enough to eat and live without getting into debt	95	95	90

At first sight this seems to suggest that the majority of people in Britain adopt such a restrictive notion of poverty that they would be deaf to any pleas made by the country's excluded minority. However, despite holding such a restrictive notion, nearly seven in ten believe that poverty has increased over the past ten years - and over half believe that it will increase further in future. As the table below shows, these figures represent a considerable increase on the comparable data from the 1980s. The public is apparently unconvinced by official claims that the poor are benefiting from rising living standards and is, in fact, aware of the growth of inequality over the last decade. Indeed, over half of Conservative identifiers accept that 'there is quite a lot of real poverty in Britain today'.

Perceptions of the level of poverty

	1986	1989	1994	1994 Party Identification		
	All	All	All	Conser-vative	Liberal Democrat	Labour
	%	%	%	%	%	%
There is quite a lot of real poverty in Britain today	55	63	69	54	67	79
Poverty in Britain has been increasing over the last ten years	51	50	68	50	75	78
Poverty in Britain will increase over the next ten years	45	44	54	35	57	64

Why people are in need

Of course, a recognition that poverty exists does not - in itself - imply support for more welfare spending on the poor. It may be, for instance, that people feel the poor themselves are responsible for the situation in which they find themselves. To examine this possibility we asked respondents to choose which of four possible reasons came closest to their view as to why some people 'live in need'. Only 15 per cent thought this stemmed from 'laziness or lack of willpower', while virtually an identical proportion took the fatalistic view that it was just 'bad luck'. In contrast, nearly one in three explicitly endorsed the notion that it was due to 'injustice in our society'. The remainder adopted the somewhat vaguer view that it was 'an inevitable part of modern life', a view which also avoids laying blame at the door of the poor themselves. This distribution of opinions is little changed from that of the 1980s.

Causes of need

% who think there are people who live in need because...	1986	1989	1994	1994 Party Identification		
	All	All	All	Conser-vative	Liberal Democrat	Labour
... they have been unlucky	11	11	16	17	16	14
... of laziness or lack of willpower	19	19	15	18	12	12
... of injustice in our society	25	29	29	16	29	40
... it's an inevitable part of modern life	37	34	32	39	31	29

Even amongst Conservative voters, only 18 per cent believe that people are in need because of laziness or lack of willpower. Instead, they are most likely to take the view that poverty is inevitable whereas, unsurprisingly, the most common view amongst Labour voters is that it is the result of injustice.

Images of state welfare

The majority of people do not, therefore, see the poor as responsible for their own plight. However, there is another possible reason why simply recognising the existence of poverty might not necessarily translate into support for more welfare spending. If people have a negative image of the impact of welfare upon who receive it, then they are unlikely to be enthusiastic about increasing social spending. It is true that nearly half believe that the welfare state makes people 'less willing to look after themselves'. However, only one in three thinks that the welfare state encourages people 'to stop helping each other'. The image of the welfare state in this respect has improved somewhat in recent years. Furthermore, around half believe that people receiving social security are 'made to feel like second-class citizens' - implying a dissatisfaction with the way the welfare system operates rather than with its impact on clients.

Images of welfare

	% agreeing		
	1983	1987	1994
The welfare state makes people nowadays less willing to look after themselves	52	52	46
The welfare state encourages people to stop helping each other	37	40	32
People receiving social security are made to feel like second-class citizens	48	50	51

Of course, the image of the welfare state is rather more negative among some groups than others. Conservative Party identifiers are roughly twice as likely as Labour Party identifiers to adopt an anti-welfare position, with Liberal Democrats falling somewhere in the middle. Older people are also more likely than younger people to see benefit claimants as undeserving and to believe that the welfare state is creating a dependency culture and discouraging self-help. But the differences in attitudes between different social classes and income groups are much less marked than differences associated with age or political preference. In short, for the most part, the image of the welfare state is not itself a major impediment to the better off being prepared to use it to help the poor.

The picture now looks a little more mixed. Concern about spending levels focuses mainly on education and health services that serve mass needs,

rather than on the benefits specifically directed at poorer groups. However, there is also a growing recognition of the existence of poverty and its likely increase in the future. Furthermore, most people do not believe that the poor should be blamed for their condition or that state welfare is damaging to the social fabric. So although the contented majority appears most concerned to pursue its self-interest, it is by no means clear that it would be entirely adverse to changes that would give greater help to the excluded minority.

Indeed, perhaps what we have here is evidence supporting Hutton's view that the majority is *not* contented. It may be that insecurity has encroached sufficiently upon the lives of the middle mass of the population to have resulted in increased awareness of poverty and inequality, even if this group is not immediately experiencing such problems. Consequently, this middle group may well be more favourably inclined towards policies to mitigate those risks and disasters of modern life to which they feel increasingly vulnerable.

The notions of insecurity and uncertainty are not easy to glean from survey data. But in the next section we explore two different ways of identifying Hutton's 40:30:30 society, to try and see whether we can find evidence of a middle group whose welfare agenda is closer to that of the poor than to that of the contented majority.

Insecurity and the welfare state

Subjective measures

Our first approach is a subjective one. It uses answers to a question which asked people how well they were coping on their current household income. Only a small proportion (seven per cent) reported that they found it 'very difficult on their present income', but more than twice as many (16 per cent) said that they found it 'difficult'. In contrast, just under half said that they were 'coping' and just over a quarter reported 'living comfortably'. The pattern of these answers mirrors those obtained a decade ago. People might be more aware of poverty in society, but their immediate experience of managing on their income has not changed greatly over the years.

Feelings about household income

	1984	1994
	%	%
Living comfortably on present income	24	28
Coping on present income	50	49
Finding it difficult on present income	18	16
Finding it very difficult on present income	8	7

We also asked respondents:

> *Looking back over the **last year** or so, would you say your household's income has ... fallen behind prices, kept up with prices, or gone up by more than prices?*

> *And looking forward to the **year ahead**, would you say your household's income will ... fall behind prices, keep up with prices, or go up by more than prices?*

Answers to these questions correlate well with respondents' feelings about their current household income. Around four in five of those who reported difficulties in living on their present income considered that their household income had fallen behind prices over the past year, and over seven in ten expected the same thing to happen over the next twelve months. Similarly, over three-quarters of those who said they were living comfortably on their income reported that it had either kept up with or outstripped prices over the previous year. It would thus seem likely that people's feelings about their current household income reflect, to a reasonable degree, their overall feelings of economic security or insecurity.

However, as the next two tables show, there is little relationship between security of income as measured by these questions and attitudes towards either overall levels of spending on the welfare state or priorities for welfare spending. For example, those who are currently 'finding it difficult' living on their income, those who are 'coping' and those who are 'comfortable' are all almost equally keen on increased welfare spending and higher taxes to pay for it.

Attitudes towards taxes and spending by feelings about household income

If the government had to choose it should ...	Feelings about household income		
	'Comfortable'	'Coping'	'Difficult'
	%	%	%
... reduce taxes and spend less on health, education and social benefits	5	3	5
... keep taxes and spending at the same level as now	32	37	29
... increase taxes and spend more on health, education and social benefits	60	55	57

There are some differences in the degree to which the three groups place their emphasis on health or education spending. But these are largely explained by the age profile of particular groups. For instance, those who say they are 'coping' on their household income are disproportionately

young - a group for whom, as we noted earlier, education is a particularly high priority. More interesting is the fact that those who are 'finding it difficult' to live on their household income are three times as likely to regard social security as a priority as those who are living comfortably. But there is little support for Hutton's thesis since members of the middle group - those who are 'coping' on their current income - have similar views on this subject as those who are 'comfortable'.

Spending priorities and feelings about household income

% giving first or second priority to	Feelings about household income		
	'Comfortable'	'Coping'	'Difficult'
Health	75	50	67
Education	66	81	57
Housing	15	21	21
Social security	7	11	21

Objective measures

Our second approach to assessing Hutton's 40:30:30 society thesis was to use a variety of largely objective information available from the survey that seemed likely to capture the divisions implicit in his thesis. In the bottom group, designed to contain Hutton's excluded 30 per cent of welfare recipients, we included those on Unemployment Benefit or on Income Support. We also included in the bottom group pensioners whose household income fell into the lowest third of the pensioner income distribution. The middle group included those whose household derived most of its income from employment but who had experienced at least one month's unemployment in the last five years, as well as those who anticipated losing their job due to redundancy or firm closure in the next year, or were so low paid that they received means-tested Family Credit. In this insecure middle 30 per cent we also included pensioners on middle incomes. The top 40 per cent was made up of those whose household income depends on employment and who have less fear of losing their job in the next year, together with higher income pensioners.

Although this strategy produces a 20:30:50 division of our sample rather than 30:30:40, it conforms to the main thrust of Hutton's argument. More important than the proportions in each group is whether we can ascertain a potential coalition of interests between the middle and bottom groups that sets them apart from the top one. In practice, as we found earlier with our subjective measure, so far as attitudes towards taxes and spending are concerned, this is clearly not the case. Indeed, the three groups have very similar views.

Attitudes towards tax and spending, by objective Hutton group

If the government had to choose it should ...	Objective 'Hutton Group'		
	Excluded	Insecure middle	Top
... reduce taxes and spend *less* on health, education and social benefits	7	4	3
... keep taxes and spending at the *same* level as now	26	32	34
... increase taxes and spend *more* on health, education and social benefits	61	59	59

However, our measure does succeed in capturing some sharp differences in attitudes towards spending priorities for the welfare state. Nearly a quarter of the excluded regard social security as a priority, compared with just one in fourteen of the secure top group. Similarly nearly a third of the excluded make housing a priority compared with just over one in seven of the top group. Most interestingly, the attitudes of the insecure middle group are half way between those of the other two groups.

Priorities for spending, by objective Hutton group

% giving first or second priority to	Objective 'Hutton Group'		
	Excluded	Insecure middle	Top
Health	63	71	79
Education	49	53	67
Housing	32	24	15
Social security	24	15	7

This provides some marginal support for Hutton's thesis. However, we should bear in mind that health and education are still the top priorities for all three groups. And the three groups have largely similar views both about what constitutes poverty and on its incidence. Such evidence hardly suggests that Hutton has identified a major fault-line in British society.

This is confirmed by the answers to those questions introduced earlier which asked respondents whether they wanted more or less spent on a number of the main welfare areas. There is a clear difference here between the excluded group - no less than two-thirds of whom would like more money spent on unemployment benefits - and the top group, of whom only just over a quarter want more such spending. But, since just under four in ten of the insecure middle group want more spending on unemployment benefits, they are much closer to the top group in their attitudes than to the excluded bottom.

The evidence so far

Britain is becoming a more unequal society. However, on our evidence, this has not undermined collective support for the provision of high quality mass services like health and education. The poor may be getting (relatively, at least) poorer, but they generally want the same kinds of services as their neighbours. In contrast, there is rather more disagreement about those benefits which are specifically directed at the poor themselves. This disagreement would appear to be captured better by the Galbraith and Field model of 'contented majority and excluded minority' than by the Hutton 40:30:30 model of 'comfortable top, insecure middle and excluded bottom'. There are signs that insecurity has had some impact on the attitudes of the middle group - but these indications are, so far, limited. As a result, there are no grounds for believing that the majority would support a substantial redirection of welfare spending towards the excluded and impoverished minority. However, at the same time, the majority's recognition of growing poverty does not suggest that they think the poor should be forgotten either.

So far we have focused primarily on the output of the welfare state in terms of benefits and services, as well as the needs that these services are designed to meet. But if more money is to be spent on health and education, then arguably someone has to pay. This begs an obvious question: will the majority really be prepared to pay more in taxes? As we pointed out earlier, some commentators have suggested that the public sings a different tune when faced with the bill for the improved social provision it says it wants. We move on to look more closely at attitudes towards taxation.

Fairer taxes?

The British government takes a smaller proportion of the Gross National Product (GNP) in tax than any other European Union country apart from Portugal (OECD, 1994b, chart 1). The total British tax bill amounts to about 35 per cent of GNP as against an EU average of 41 per cent, an average which will probably rise when the three most recent member states (Austria, Finland and Sweden) are included in the statistics. Further, in common with most other countries, direct tax rates have been cut, most markedly for those on higher incomes.

This change has not gone unnoticed. We repeated a series of questions first asked in 1983 about the appropriateness of current levels of taxation for different income groups. So far as taxation of those with low incomes is concerned, little has changed. Just over three-quarters believe that they pay too much tax. But when it comes to middle and high income earners, there has been a marked change of attitude. In 1983 well over four in ten thought that tax on middle income groups was too high; now only just over a quarter do so. Meanwhile, well over half now think that taxes on

people with high incomes are too low compared with just one in three in 1983. The public mood would thus seem to endorse a more progressive tax strategy than is currently in place.

Perceptions of tax levels for different income groups

	% saying that taxes are...					
	... too low		... about right		... too high	
	1983	1994	1983	1994	1983	1994
For those on high incomes	32	56	36	32	29	12
For those on middle incomes	4	8	50	66	44	26
For those on low incomes	3	3	16	21	79	76

These results prove even more interesting when examined by the income level of the respondent's household. To achieve this we divided our sample into three roughly equal groups, representing those on low, middle and high incomes. This exercise reveals an extraordinary consensus about who is, and is not, paying too much in taxes. The majority of all three groups believes that those on low incomes are paying too much and those on high incomes too little. Meanwhile, those on middle incomes are thought to be paying about the right amount.

Comparison between the 1994 figures and those from 1983 shows that the fall in the proportion believing those on high incomes pay too much tax has been greatest precisely among those who are themselves on high incomes. The majority of this group now believes that people on high incomes should pay *more* in taxes. Similarly, the fall in the proportion who believe middle income groups pay too much in taxes has been greatest among those with middle incomes. Among this group the majority now thinks they pay the right level of taxes.

In short, it seems that the expressed wish of the public for more spending on mass welfare services cannot simply be dismissed as a hope that they might be able to get something for nothing. The public's opposition to tax increases has mellowed in line with its wish to see more spent on welfare services - and on health and education in particular. Most notably, there seems to be a widespread acceptance that those on high incomes *could* pay more in taxes, not least amongst those who earn such incomes themselves.

Perceptions of tax levels by household income groups

	1983			1994		
	% saying that tax levels for those with *high* incomes are					
Household income group	Too low	About right	Too high	Too low	About right	Too high
Low	38	37	26	58	28	14
Middle	34	38	28	59	32	10
High	30	36	34	51	36	13
	% saying that tax levels for those on *middle* incomes are					
	Too low	About right	Too high	Too low	About right	Too high
Low	6	55	39	8	63	29
Middle	3	51	47	8	70	22
High	3	51	46	7	67	27
	% saying that tax levels for those on *low* incomes are					
	Too low	About right	Too high	Too low	About right	Too high
Low	5	13	82	5	17	78
Middle	3	16	82	2	20	78
High	2	21	78	2	25	72

Conclusion

This chapter makes sanguine reading for welfare state optimists. Despite recent claims that growing social divisions threaten the stability of welfare in this country, there is little sign of this in our data. True, support for those benefits which are more specifically directed at the poor is variable, but this is nothing new. At the same time there is a growing recognition of the existence of poverty in Britain, despite the fact that most people adopt a restrictive definition of what poverty means. Theorists have also argued that the welfare state needs to move away from the provision of mass services and towards more flexible forms of provision clearly directed at the disadvantaged. We have detected little wish that this should happen either. If public opinion has its way, then both rich and poor alike would prefer the structure of the welfare state to remain largely as it is, with the bulk of its resources devoted to mass services from which all can benefit. The only change they would like is to have more of the same.

Indeed, despite the fact that - as yet - the growing insecurity of the labour market appears to have had little influence on attitudes towards welfare spending, it would seem that the foundations of public support for the welfare state have never been more solid. The image of what the welfare

state does for its recipients has improved. Not only do people say they would pay more taxes to finance more welfare spending, but only a minority now believes that those on high and middle incomes can claim to be overburdened with tax.

In one respect, however, both Galbraith and Hutton are right. Public attitudes towards the welfare state are coloured by self-interest rather than altruism. Popular support for 'old welfare' has proved to be robust because it is rooted in the self-interest of Britain's contented majority. It is something that politicians - of any party - tamper with at their peril.

Notes

1. Poverty is here defined as having an income below half the average, after allowing for housing costs.
2. The term 'social security' in the technical sense refers not only to targeted benefits like Unemployment Benefit and Income Support, but also to universal benefits like Child Benefit, pensions and Statutory Sick Pay. However, given common usage of the term 'social security', it would seem reasonable to assume that most respondents will have taken it to mean mainly Unemployment Benefit and Income Support. This is supported by the results in the previous table, which show that pensions receive a similar level of support to education, while unemployment benefits are less popular.
3. Of course, official statistics do not trace groups of people over time; nor do they necessarily show that it is the *same* people whose incomes are rising or falling.

References

Bosanquet, N. (1994), 'Improving health' in Jowell, R., Curtice, J., Brook, L. and Ahrendt, D. (eds.), *British Social Attitudes: the 11th Report*, Aldershot: Dartmouth.

Crompton, R. (1993), *Class and Stratification*, Cambridge: Polity Press.

Department of Social Security (1994), *Households below Average Incomes, 1979-1991/92*, London: HMSO.

Etzioni, A. (1993), *The Spirit of Community*, New York: Crown.

European Union (1994), *European Social Policy: a Way Forward for the Union*, Luxembourg: EU.

Field, F. (1989), *Losing Out - the Emerging British Underclass*, London: Blackwell.

Galbraith, J.K. (1993), *The Culture of Contentment*, London: Penguin.

Goodman, E. and Webb, S. (1995), *The Distribution of UK Household Expenditure, 1979-92*, London: Institute for Fiscal Studies.

Hills, J. (1995), *Joseph Rowntree Foundation Inquiry into Income and Wealth*, Vol. II, York: Joseph Rowntree Foundation.

Hutton, W. (1995), *The State We're In*, London: Jonathan Cape.

Lipsey, D. (1994), 'Do we really want more public spending?' in Jowell, R., Curtice, J., Brook, L. and Ahrendt, D. (eds.), *British Social Attitudes: the 11th Report*, Aldershot: Dartmouth.

Organisation for Economic Co-operation and Development (1994a), *New Orientations for Social Policy*, Social Policy Studies, No. 12, Paris: OECD.

Organisation for Economic Co-operation and Development (1994b), *Revenue Statistics, 1965-93*, Paris: OECD.

2 Fear of crime

Lizanne Dowds and Daphne Ahrendt[*]

The notion that 'fear of crime' - as opposed to crime itself - is a problem in its own right emerged during the 1970s from the results of victimisation surveys carried out in the United States. Such surveys aimed to measure crime rates by finding out how many people had been *victims* of crime, regardless of whether this crime was subsequently reported to the police. But these surveys also identified a large number of people who, though statistically unlikely to experience crime, were quite fearful for their own personal safety - particularly when 'walking alone at night' (a much favoured scenario traditionally used to measure fear of crime). Thus, women were found to be much more fearful than men, and the elderly more fearful than the young, even though the actual chances of either women or the elderly being victims of crime were considerably lower than average.[1]

Such fear of crime by those at low risk was generally regarded by commentators as 'irrational'. Policy makers turned their attention to the issue and, with the sole aim of reducing fear and increasing public confidence, began to encourage different methods of policing and other fear-reduction initiatives (see, for example, Bennett, 1991). Much attention focused on the role of the media, with The Grade Report on Fear of Crime

[*] Lizanne Dowds was formerly a Research Director at SCPR and a Co-director of the *British Social Attitudes* survey series; she is now a Research Fellow at the School of Psychology, The Queen's University of Belfast. Daphne Ahrendt was formerly a Researcher at SCPR and a Co-director of the *British Social Attitudes* survey series; she is now a Project Manager at International Survey Research, London.

(Home Office Standing Conference, 1989) advocating more balanced media coverage to reduce fear.

Against this backdrop, some criminologists began to question the way in which fear was measured and - in particular - the implication that fear of crime among certain groups was irrational. They argued that any interpretation of survey findings should take account of the notion of vulnerability; that is, the fact that groups such as the elderly and women have, perhaps, more reason to fear the *consequences* of crime than others. Feminist criminologists argued that women's fear of crime 'stems from their powerless and precarious position' in relation to harassing behaviour from men (Stanko, 1985).

The questions used to measure 'fear of crime' were also criticised. Some argued that the standard question - which presented respondents with a deliberately threatening scenario of being alone outside at night - was sufficient in itself to induce fear in people for whom this situation would never normally arise as part of their daily lives (LaGrange and Ferraro, 1989). Another common criticism concerned the reliance on general, or global, definitions of crime. These, it was argued, were too hazy and ill-defined: fear or 'anxiety' could be measured properly in surveys only by using questions relating to specific crimes such as burglary. However, this approach has its own problems in that it confuses people's 'fear of crime' and their 'assessment of risk'. Consequently, those who say they are 'very worried' about burglary will include both those who think that burglary is highly likely, but who are not unduly frightened by the possibility, as well as those who think that it is unlikely but remain very frightened by the prospect, however remote.

However, despite their flaws, questions which aim to assess global 'fear of crime' remain useful. For people who spend their lives barricaded behind locked doors, 'fear of crime' is very real. Even those who do not live in fear, but who habitually feel uneasy as they make their way to the local shops, can identify with the concept.

Since much of the research into fear of crime has been associated with research into crime in general, there has tended to be a preoccupation with the link between fear of crime and being a victim of crime. Although fear of crime clearly *is* related to personal experience and will obviously reflect the conditions in which people live, fear also needs to be considered within the context of society as a whole. How, for instance, do broader social attitudes link with our feelings of fear and anxiety about crime? Is fear of crime really a part of wider social attitudes?

One of the most interesting, though infrequently pursued, lines of research centres on this notion - that fear of crime is really a reflection of a more general fear or insecurity about the modern world:

> This general fear...carries with it a lot of baggage which has little or nothing to do with crime as a stimulus and which the police can do little to address. It is as if fear of crime were a lightning conductor

for general frustration or unease about how things are, as well as the way things are going. (Gambles and Tomblin, 1993)

As Chris Hale put it when reviewing the relevant literature:

> There is the consideration of whether 'fear of crime' is simply measuring fear of crime, or perhaps in addition, some other attribute which might be better characterised as 'insecurity with modern living', 'quality of life', 'perception of disorder' or 'urban unease'. (Hale, 1995)

It is this rather neglected line of enquiry which we pursue in this chapter.

Measuring fear of crime

We start by examining two questions which give different measures of fear of crime. The first is the traditional - and much criticised - question used in many victimisation surveys:

> *How safe do you feel walking alone in this area after dark...very safe, fairly safe, a bit unsafe, or, very unsafe?*

The second question was asked on the *British Social Attitudes* survey for the first time in 1994. It attempts to incorporate some notion of the way in which fear can restrict people's lives:

> *Because of worries about crime some people change their everyday life, for example, where they go or what they do. Other people don't change their lives at all. Do worries about crime affect **your** everyday life?*

Figures 1 and 2 compare the responses of men, women and those in different age groups to both the traditional and new measure of fear of crime. On the traditional measure - feeling unsafe walking alone after dark - women are a great deal more fearful than men. Over half of all women, compared with just 16 per cent of men, said that they felt unsafe in this situation. Fear generally tends to increase with age, except that young women are particularly afraid of being out alone at night. On the new measure - worries about crime affecting everyday life - age and gender seem less important. A third of women and a quarter of men say that worries about crime affect their everyday life.

Per cent who feel unsafe 'walking alone in this area after dark'

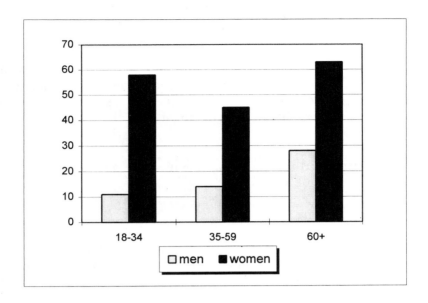

Per cent who feel that worries about crime affect their everyday life

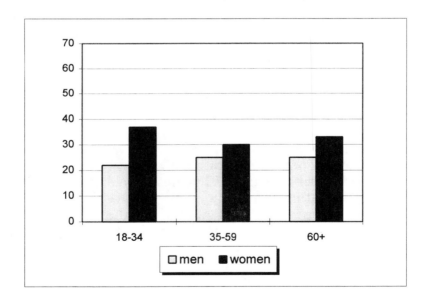

Of course, the two questions do not tap the notion of fear of crime in the same way. 'Worries' and 'fear' are not the same thing, but we thought it desirable to use the less emotional term 'worries', and then reinforce its impact by asking whether such worries were serious enough to affect the respondent's everyday life. The two measures are, in fact, interrelated in

a rather curious way. Over half (58 per cent) of those women who say they feel unsafe at night also say that worries about crime *do not* affect their everyday life. Conversely, about a fifth (19 per cent) of those men who say they feel safe at night still say that worries about crime *do* affect their everyday life.

The ways in which men's and women's worries affect their behaviour differ. Many more women than men say that they avoid going out at certain times or that they don't go out alone. Conversely, men tend to say simply that they are careful to lock up their homes and make sure that other people in the family take precautions - although a substantial number of men do admit that they avoid going to certain places. Part of this difference between men and women may lie in the fact that men are more willing to admit to 'worries' (even if these affect their everyday lives) rather than to feeling 'unsafe'.[2]

	Men	Women
	%	%
I am careful to lock up my/our home (and/or car)	94	95
I don't go out **alone**	3	17
I don't go out **at all**	*	1
I avoid going out at certain times	15	43
I avoid going to certain places	35	44
I avoid public transport	3	7
I carry a personal alarm or a weapon	2	8
I make sure other people in the family take precautions	44	40

* = less than 1%
Note: Figures add to more than 100% as respondents could give more than
      one answer

Fear of crime in relation to social attitudes

When looking at the relationship between social attitudes and fear of crime, it is important to consider other characteristics which might be linked - either to fear of crime or to social attitudes themselves. Many of these characteristics are in fact related. For example, people who live in high-crime neighbourhoods may be more likely than average to be afraid to go out after dark, as might those people who have been victims of crime. But it is also the case that people who live in dangerous neighbourhoods are more likely than average to have been victims. This makes it difficult to establish whether the more important factor in explaining fear of crime is perception of danger as opposed to direct experience of crime. Similarly, it is well known that social attitudes vary between different groups. As a result, it is possible that an apparent relationship between fear of crime and a particular set of attitudes merely reflects a deeper relationship between fear of crime and the social characteristics of those who hold such attitudes.

Such problems can be overcome by using statistical modelling techniques which establish the *independent* importance of relationships between various factors and fear of crime, once the roles of other important factors have been taken into account. The results presented below are based on the use of such statistical modelling (which is explained in more detail in the Appendix to this chapter).

We have seen that fear of crime can vary greatly by age and sex. Correspondingly, both are often included in analyses as 'explanatory' variables; that is, as characteristics which help 'explain' differences between people in terms of their fear of crime. However, this is a rather curious approach as the antecedents of fear among men and women and people in different age groups are likely to be different. Middle-aged men and young women, for instance, might be expected to have quite different worries and fears when it comes to crime. For this reason, we divide our sample into six groups: young men aged between 18 and 34; young women; middle-aged men between 35 and 59; middle-aged women; elderly men aged 60 or over; and elderly women. The relationship between fear of crime and social attitudes is considered separately for each group.[3]

Many social attitudes do prove to be associated with fear of crime. A number fall into distinct categories. Some, for instance, can be seen as reflecting fear of change; others appear to be linked to distrust and authoritarianism. We begin by examining the relationship between fear of crime and a group of attitudes linked to general worries about life.

Life's worriers?

Hough (forthcoming) found clear interrelationships between fear of crime and worries about more general 'mishaps'. The results of our analysis are partially consistent with this. We asked respondents how worried they were about their family, money and health - as well as about more remote world events. It is only among elderly men that such worries are unequivocally related to fear of crime. Worries about their own health were related to feeling unsafe walking alone after dark, while worries about world events were related to allowing worries about crime to affect their everyday life.

We also asked respondents a set of questions about the likelihood of various calamitous events happening in Britain or the world during the next ten years. Again, among elderly men, worries about these events prove to be related to feeling unsafe walking alone after dark. For instance, among those who think it likely that "acts of political terrorism in Britain will be common events", over a quarter (28 per cent) say they feel 'fairly' or 'very' unsafe walking alone after dark. Among those who think that political terrorism is *not* likely, only 11 per cent report feeling unsafe.

Men aged 60 plus

		% feeling 'very' or 'fairly' unsafe alone after dark
Acts of political terrorism in Britain will be common events	Likely Not likely	28 11
Riots and civil disturbance in our cities will be common events	Likely Not likely	28 18
There will be a serious accident at a British nuclear power station	Likely Not likely	33 17
The police in our cities will find it impossible to protect our personal safety on the streets	Likely Not likely	30 14
A nuclear bomb will be dropped somewhere in the world	Likely Not likely	32 18

Among women and younger men there does not seem to be a clear-cut relationship between being one of 'life's worriers' and being fearful of crime. For young women, those who feel disasters are unlikely to happen are actually more likely to feel unsafe walking alone at night. The same is true for those middle-aged women whose worries about crime affect their everyday life.

These results appear contradictory. Why, for instance, is being a 'worrier' linked to fear of crime among older men - whereas among young and middle-aged women, precisely the opposite is the case? One possible answer to this conundrum lies in the fact that fear of crime can take positive and negative forms. Thus for some, fear of crime is linked to passivity and general feelings of anxiousness and helplessness. However, for others, fear can reflect a realistic and active identification of potential problems which need to be addressed (see also Mayhew *et al*, 1988).

Distrust and authoritarianism

A link between attitudes reflecting suspicion or distrust and fear of crime is most evident among middle-aged men, though aspects of it are visible among other groups as well. The *British Social Attitudes* survey series has long included sets of questions designed to measure 'left-right' political leanings and 'authoritarianism'. When considering fear of crime, the 'left-right' dimension proved to be irrelevant; however, authoritarianism did emerge as important.

The use of the label 'authoritarian' requires some explanation. In the context of our survey, to be 'authoritarian' is to have an ideologically consistent set of attitudes which relate to punitiveness, conformity and 'anti-welfarism'. In their work on authoritarianism in Britain, Ahrendt and Young noted the following:

...the authoritarian world-view has been described in part as a reaction against 'unwelcome' social change, a tendency to contrast contemporary problems with a world that has disappeared... (Ahrendt and Young, 1994)

For our analysis, we created an authoritarianism 'scale' based upon questions relating to conformity and punitiveness. We considered 'anti-welfarism' separately.[4]

The results are striking. Among elderly women, feeling unsafe alone at night is linked to strong negative attitudes towards people on social security benefits, whom many seem to regard as welfare 'scroungers'. For instance, among those who think that many social security recipients do not really deserve help, two-fifths (42 per cent) report feeling very unsafe walking alone after dark. Among those who do not hold this view, only one-fifth (20 per cent) feel very unsafe.

Women aged 60 plus

		% feeling 'very unsafe' alone after dark
Many people who get social security don't really deserve any help	Agree	42
	Disagree or neither *	20
If welfare benefits weren't so generous people would learn to stand on their own two feet	Agree	41
	Disagree or neither	22
Around here, most unemployed people could find a job if they really wanted to	Agree	39
	Disagree or neither	25
Most people on the dole are fiddling in one way or another	Agree	38
	Disagree or neither	24
The welfare state makes people nowadays less willing to look after themselves	Agree	36
	Disagree or neither	21
The welfare state encourages people to stop helping each other	Agree	30
	Disagree or neither	29

* This category includes 'disagree' and 'neither agree nor disagree'

Among middle-aged men, fears about crime are related to authoritarian attitudes in general and - in particular - to the belief that immigration should be restricted.

Men aged 35-59

% feeling 'very'
or 'fairly' unsafe
alone after dark

Young people today don't have enough respect for traditional British values	Agree	15
	Disagree or neither	4
Censorship of films and magazines is necessary to uphold moral standards	Agree	12
	Disagree or neither	7
People who break the law should be given stiffer sentences	Agree	14
	Disagree or neither	4
For some crimes the death penalty is the most appropriate sentence	Agree	13
	Disagree or neither	6
Schools should teach children to obey authority	Agree	12
	Disagree or neither	3
The law should always be obeyed, even if a particular law is wrong	Agree	16
	Disagree or neither	8

However, the picture is very different - and contradictory - for young men. When asked about feelings of safety when walking alone at night, those who are most afraid of crime tend to hold distinctly libertarian views.[5] But those young men who report that worries about crime affect their everyday life tend to be *more* authoritarian than average. This discrepancy may relate more to who *admits* to being afraid than who is actually afraid. Many more men admit to having worries about crime which affect their everyday life than admit to feeling unsafe alone at night. Those who do say they feel unsafe at night may therefore be a quite distinctive group - they are certainly more likely than average to be from higher social classes.

Unease within a changing society

In some ways, authoritarianism - and, in particular, distrust of welfare recipients and a desire to restrict immigration - can be interpreted as a more general fear of change. To address this issue more closely, we asked respondents:

Now I want to ask you about some changes that have been happening in Britain over the years. For each one, please tell me whether you think it has gone too far, or not gone far enough:

Attempts to give equal opportunities to women in Britain

Attempts to give equal opportunities to black people and Asians in Britain

The right to show nudity and sex in films and magazines
Attempts to give equal opportunities to homosexuals - that is, gays and lesbians
Providing sites for gypsies and travellers to stay
The right of people to go on protest marches and demonstrations
Laws to make it difficult for people to go on strike
Giving Legal Aid - that is, financial help with the cost of going to court

For some of these items it is arguable whether actual recent changes should be seen as moving in a more or less libertarian direction. But for other items, those who feel that such developments have 'gone too far' can clearly be seen as showing a fear of change that is consistent with an authoritarian world-view. For some, such fear is linked to fear of crime. For instance, among elderly women, the feeling that equal opportunities for homosexuals and the provision of sites for gypsies and travellers have 'gone too far' emerge as independently related to feeling unsafe walking alone after dark. Other items also tend to reflect the same underlying relationship:

Women aged 60 plus

		% feeling 'very unsafe' alone after dark
Attempts to give equal opportunities to women in Britain	Gone too far	48
	About right or not gone far enough	28
Attempts to give equal opportunities to black people and Asians in Britain	Gone too far	41
	About right or not gone far enough	29
Attempts to give equal opportunities to homosexuals - that is, gays and lesbians	Gone too far	36
	About right or not gone far enough	26
Providing sites for gypsies and travellers to stay	Gone too far	52
	About right or not gone far enough	24

Our new measure of fear of crime - whether worries about crime affect everyday life - is also related to this general unease about change. For instance, among elderly women who state that crime affects their everyday life, there is a higher than average tendency to believe that equal opportunities for women have 'gone too far'. Among middle-aged men the key factor is the belief that the right to show nudity and sex in films has 'gone too far'.

Powerlessness

The theme of general powerlessness and apathy emerges most strongly among middle-aged women. Those who feel that "it doesn't matter which party is in power, in the end things go on much the same" are more than twice as likely to feel very unsafe walking alone after dark than those who think otherwise (23 per cent and 10 per cent respectively). Similarly, young women who feel that crime affects their everyday life are much more likely than average to believe that the government is fairly powerless to change things. We asked:

Some people say that British governments nowadays - of whichever party - can actually do very little to change things. Others say they can do quite a bit. Please say whether you think that British governments nowadays can do very little or quite a bit...

Women aged 18-34

	British governments:	% saying that worries about crime affect their everyday life
... to keep prices down	Can do very little	50
	Can do quite a bit	28
... to reduce poverty	Can do very little	47
	Can do quite a bit	31
... to improve the general standard of living	Can do very little	42
	Can do quite a bit	33
... to improve the health and social services	Can do very little	43
	Can do quite a bit	34

However, there is little evidence that feelings of **personal** powerlessness are linked to fear of crime. On the contrary, those who think that they do 'have a say in government' are more likely than average to admit that worries about crime affect their everyday life. This mainly applies to men - both young and elderly. Again, this may demonstrate the way in which worries and concerns about crime can either be associated with passivity and feelings of helplessness or, alternatively, with feelings of positive empowerment.

Awareness of vulnerability

The single best predictor of fear of crime among young women is their attitude towards the availability of sexually explicit pornography. Those women who are most afraid of crime tend to favour limits on the

availability of pornography.[6]   For instance, of those who think that pornographic magazines should be banned altogether, almost half (44 per cent) report feeling very unsafe walking alone after dark. But among those who think that pornographic magazines should be permitted in special adult shops as long as they are not displayed to the public, only a fifth (21 per cent) report feeling very unsafe. The proportion who feel very unsafe at night is lowest of all among those women who are prepared to allow pornographic material to be more widely distributed - only about one in eight (12 per cent) of this group say they feel unsafe walking alone at night.

Because attitudes towards the availability of pornography reflect a number of deeper convictions about the actual causes and consequences of pornography, it may be the case that those who feel that pornography should be banned or restricted do so because of a belief in the potential vulnerability of women to male sexual threats. If so, it is not surprising that those who hold such a view are more likely than average to perceive dangers in walking alone at night. Such an explanation provides some support for the argument advanced by feminist criminologists that women's fears concerning crime are connected to their vulnerability to sexual threats.

Women aged 18-34

	% feeling 'very unsafe' alone after dark
Pornographic magazines and films ...	
... should be banned altogether	44
... should be available in special adult shops but not displayed to the public	21
Other answer (e.g. should be more accessible)	12

The only other group demonstrating this connection between awareness of potential vulnerability and fear of crime consists of elderly men. For this group, their worries about their health are independently related to fears about walking alone at night. On the other hand, elderly men who have a long-standing health problem or disability are significantly *less* likely to say that crime affects their everyday life (perhaps because their life is in any case restricted by health considerations).

The relationship between fear of crime and experience of crime

There are strong conceptual differences between the two measures of fear of crime used in this chapter (on the one hand, fear of walking alone at night and, on the other, having worries which affect one's everyday life). Despite this, whichever measure is used, the same social attitudes consistently emerge as associated with fear. This lends credence to the view that both questions reflect some 'global' fear of crime. However, the other (non-attitudinal) factors related to the two measures differ dramatically in

one respect. Thus, when considering the traditional measure of fear of crime - whether someone feels unsafe walking alone at night - key factors include the extent to which respondents believe they are at risk, signs of disorder (or incivilities) in their neighbourhood, social cohesion among neighbours and housing tenure. But when considering our new measure - whether worries about crime affect the respondent's everyday life - the importance of almost all these non-attitudinal characteristics disappears. All are replaced by a single factor - whether or not respondents have been victims of crime during their life-time. In other words, victimisation is a crucial determinant of whether or not someone worries about crime to the extent that it affects his or her everyday life. The weaker links between an experience of victimisation and feeling unsafe walking alone after dark are not statistically significant once other factors have been taken into account.

		% feeling unsafe alone after dark	
		Men	Women
Assault	Victim	13	63
	Non-victim	16	51
Burglary	Victim	20	54
	Non-victim	13	52

		% saying that worries about crime affect their everyday life	
		Men	Women
Assault	Victim	30	60
	Non-victim	18	32
Burglary	Victim	27	46
	Non-victim	19	30

This finding does much to debunk the thesis that fear of crime is irrational. Fear of crime, if defined as allowing worries about crime to affect the way in which one lives one's life, is strongly linked to personal experience of crime. Furthermore, certain groups appear to be more affected than others by the experience of being a victim - even though they may be less at risk of crime itself. We examined this issue explicitly by asking respondents who had experienced a crime:

> Do you think that as a result of any of these experiences you are now more _aware_ of crime, or has it made no difference?

Those who said that they were more aware of crime as a result of their experiences were then asked:

> And has it actually made _you_ more _afraid_ of crime?

Women and older people were distinctly likely to say that their experiences had made them more afraid. Men were more likely than women to say that experience of crime had made them more 'aware' of crime - but were less likely than women to say that their experiences had made them more 'afraid'. Whether men are less willing to admit to fear or whether they are actually less affected by victimisation experiences is a moot point. However, the pattern of responses among age and gender groups strongly reinforces the notion that, while women and older people may be less at risk of crime, such experiences, when they do occur, are very distressing.

Per cent saying that their experience of crime made them more afraid

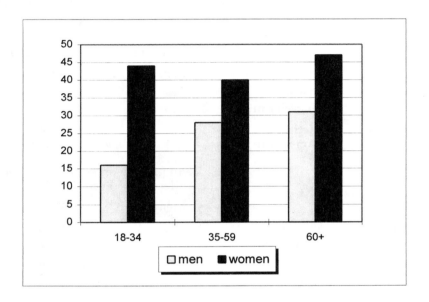

Summary

There is no doubt that social attitudes - even once experience of crime and other characteristics are taken into account - are strongly linked to fear of crime. This, in itself, justifies the case for widening the focus of such research from the confines and constraints of traditional criminological theory. However, it would be unwise to draw any conclusions which imply that certain personality traits 'lead' people towards 'fearfulness'. The *British Social Attitudes* survey measures *attitudes*, not personality traits. Moreover, our analyses do not establish the causality of any relationship between social attitudes and fear of crime. It could be argued, for instance, that the apparent importance of punitive authoritarian attitudes *reflects* fear and anxiety about crime (see also Hough, 1985, and Brook and Cape's chapter for an alternative view).

Despite these caveats, some interesting findings emerge. It is evident that the antecedents of fear of crime are very different for different groups of

people. Thus, one of the best predictors of fears about personal safety among young women is their attitude towards the availability of pornography. Among other groups, however, views on this subject are not at all linked to fear of crime. For elderly women, fear of crime is strongly associated with unease about change in society in general - consistent with the idea that fear of crime is only part of a bigger fear about the disintegration of society. For elderly men, fear of crime is linked to all kinds of other worries - about their health, about things 'happening around the world', about the likelihood of nuclear disasters. There are also general tendencies for fear of crime to be linked with authoritarian attitudes and, among some groups, to attitudes that imply feelings of powerlessness or apathy. On the other hand, the reverse is occasionally true: some of the most worried also appear to feel quite empowered about certain political issues. This is consistent with the view that fear need not always be associated with negative feelings of helplessness - in some cases it can be a positive stimulus to constructive crime prevention measures.

Wider implications can be drawn from the data. For instance, the argument that fear of crime is a problem *in itself* (as opposed to being part and parcel of problems about crime in general or, indeed, a reflection of wider concerns about a changing society) looks uncertain. This casts doubt upon whether reducing fear of crime can be a legitimate or realistic aim of government. Whichever measure of fear is used, strong links exist between fear and social attitudes which have little to do with crime - and still less to do with the arena of government intervention. Furthermore, when one considers our new measure of fear - whether worries about crime affect people's everyday life - it is patently clear that the most important factor associated with fear is actual experience of crime. From this, it seems that the only appropriate way for the government to help alleviate fear of crime among the public is for it to tackle the problem head-on and adopt even more vigorous measures to cut crime. Whether or not this is a realistic aim remains another story.

Notes

1. At least in terms of attacks by a stranger in the street - crimes against women by offenders whom they know are very much more common, while the *overall* violence suffered by women and men may be little different (see for example, Mayhew *et al* 1993).
2. A note of caution should be raised here because of possible context effects in the questionnaire. This new question followed a more traditional BSA question:

   Now, some questions about crime. Do you ever worry about the possibility that you, or anyone else who lives with you, might be the victim of crime?

   In answering subsequent questions a few men may have still been considering their worries about other members of their families. If this is the case it is an interesting question as to whether they could still be said to be fearful of crime.
3. The levels of fear among men and women are so different that different dependent variables were thought to be necessary for the analysis. For men, the dependent

variable used was whether they felt 'a bit unsafe' or 'very unsafe' *versus* any other valid response. For women, the dependent variable was whether they felt 'very unsafe' *versus* any other valid response.

4. Trends in libertarianism and authoritarianism are also considered in the chapter by Brook and Cape.

5. The libertarian-authoritarian scale score is actually of only borderline significance. However, coupled with attitudes advocating more sites for gypsies and travellers and a belief in respondents' own political efficacy, the score makes the fearful in this group distinctly libertarian. Also important in the model is the attitude that change in the law to make it difficult for people to go on strike has 'not gone far enough'. This could be interpreted as either a libertarian or authoritarian view, but again, other variables in the model suggest that it is the former.

6. The question read:

Which of these statements comes closest to your views on the availability of pornographic - that is, sexually explicit - magazines and films?

They should be banned altogether
They should be available in special adult shops but not displayed to the public
They should be available in special adult shops with public display permitted
They should be available in any shop for sale to adults only
They should be available in any shop for sale to anyone

References

Ahrendt, D. and Young, K. (1994), 'Authoritarianism updated' in Jowell, R., Curtice, J., Brook, L. and Ahrendt, D. (eds.), *British Social Attitudes: the 11th Report*, Aldershot: Dartmouth.

Bennett, T. (1991), 'The effectiveness of a police-initiated fear reducing strategy', *British Journal of Criminology*, **31** (1), 1-14.

Gambles, J. and Tomblin, M. (1993), Report prepared for the Metropolitan Police Service Working Group on Fear of Crime, Quadrangle Consulting Ltd.

Hale, C. (1995), 'Fear of crime: a review of the literature', *International Review of Victimology*, **4** (2).

Home Office Standing Conference on Crime Prevention (1989), *Report of the Working Group on the Fear of Crime*, London: Home Office.

Hough, M. (1985), 'The impact of victimisation: findings from the BCS', *Victimology*, **20** (1-4), 488-497.

Hough, M. (forthcoming), 'Anxiety about crime: findings from the 1994 British Crime Survey'.

LaGrange, R. L. and Ferraro, K. F. (1989), 'Assessing age and gender differences in perceived risk and fear of crime', *Criminology*, **27**, 697-719.

Mayhew, P., Aye Maung, N. and Mirrlees-Black, C. (1993), *The 1992 British Crime Survey*, Home Office Research Study No. **132**, London: HMSO.

Mayhew, P., Elliott, D. and Dowds, L. (1988), *The 1988 British Crime Survey*, Home Office Research Study No. **111**, London: HMSO.

Skogan, W. G. (1988), 'Disorder, crime and community decline', in Hope, T. J. and Shaw, M. (eds.), *Communities and Crime Reduction*, London: HMSO.

Stanko, E. A. (1985), *Intimate Intrusions: Women's Experience of Male Violence*, London: Routledge and Kegan Paul.

Acknowledgements

This work was carried out with funding from the ESRC under its Crime and Social Order programme (grant number L210 25 2010). We are grateful to the Council for its financial support. Our thanks are due to Dr. Tim Hope, Co-ordinator of the ESRC programme, and to fellow grant-holders for their comments on earlier drafts of the questionnaire. Space restrictions meant that we could not incorporate all their good ideas.

Appendix: Multivariate models

In order to look at the relationships between fear of crime, social attitudes
and demographic attributes, bivariate analyses were carried out using some
150 variables thought to be associated with fear of crime. Those which
proved significantly related to fear of crime were then entered into
multivariate models for each of the age/gender groups. Other variables
known to be associated with fear were also entered. These included: the
presence of 'incivilities' in the respondent's area (graffiti, teenagers hanging
around, etc.[*]), the respondent's evaluation of their own risk of crime, the
social cohesion of the neighbourhood, respondent's tenure (owning, renting
privately or renting from the council), social class, respondent's ethnic
group, whether the respondent had ever been a victim of (various types of)
crime and whether the respondent had ever known someone else who was a
victim of crime. Also included was a rough measure of the amount of crime
in the respondent's neighbourhood - by summing the number of respondents
within each sampling point who had suffered various crimes.

Linear regression was used to reduce the variables further to the most
important ones. The final models were built using logistic regression, the
results of which are reported below. For this analysis, much of the model
building was done manually rather than using an automated approach.
Weighted data were used, though unweighted data produced much the same
results. Items which met the criteria for reliability were scaled where
possible: scales were constructed for incivilities, respondents' perceived risk
of crime, political apathy, left/right attitudes, liberal/authoritarian attitudes,
welfarist attitudes, trust in the establishment, perceived efficacy of
government, and attitudes to immigration. All of these scales had a
Cronbach's alpha of greater than 0.7.

---

[*] Research such as that of Skogan (1988) indicates that signs of 'disorder', 'broken
windows' or 'incivilities' in a neighbourhood all suggest a local breakdown of social
control; also that this sense of breakdown is the major determinant of fear. The
BSA question was as follows:
*Please use this card to say how common or uncommon each of the following things is in
your area:*

> *Graffiti on walls or buildings*
> *Teenagers hanging around on the streets*
> *Drunks or tramps on the streets*
> *Vandalism and deliberate damage to property*
> *Insults or attacks to do with someone's race or colour*
> *Homes broken into*
> *Cars broken into or stolen*
> *People attacked in the streets*

Table 1 Final model: feeling very unsafe alone at night
(women, aged 18-34)

	R	Significance level
Would limit availability of pornography	-.25	.0003
Believes self to be at risk of crime	-.17	.0060
Incivilities present locally	-.16	.0099
Believes that disasters are unlikely to happen	.14	.0167
Fewer educational qualifications	.12	.0364
Local area is one where people don't help each other	.11	.0418

161 cases in final model
Model chi-Square= 45.3 with 6 df, p<.0000.

Table 2 Final model: feeling unsafe alone at night
(men, aged 18-34)

	R	Significance level
Incivilities present locally	-.23	.0077
Local area is one where people don't help each other	.18	.0226
Believes self to be at risk of crime	-.21	.0128
Higher social class	-.20	.0156
Believes that self does have a say in government	.18	.0226
Believes that changes in the laws to make it difficult for people to go on strike have not gone far enough	.18	.0240
Believes that providing sites for gypsies and travellers has not gone far enough	.16	.0312
Holds non-authoritarian attitudes	.13	.0540

118 cases in final model
Model chi-Square= 57.8 with 8 df, p<.0000.

Table 3 Final model: feeling very unsafe alone at night
(women, aged 35-59)

	R	Significance level
Believes self to be at risk of crime	-.23	.0005
Believes that it doesn't matter which party is in power	-.15	.0139
Feels that local people would not intervene in a burglary	.13	.0265

190 cases in final model
Model chi-Square= 32.2 with 3 df, p<.0000.

Table 4 Final model: feeling unsafe alone at night (men, aged 35-59)

	R	Significance level
Incivilities present locally	-.29	.0004
Holds authoritarian attitudes	-.20	.0080
Victim of burglary	.20	.0087
Believes in restricting immigration	.13	.0405

169 cases in final model
Model chi-Square= 46.1 with 4 df, p<.0000.

Table 5 Final model: feeling very unsafe alone at night (women, aged 60 years or more)

	R	Significance level
Renting accommodation	.28	.0001
Lives in an area where there have been many threats	.20	.0024
Holds negative attitudes towards those on 'welfare'	-.17	.0082
Believes that equal opportunities for homosexuals have gone too far	-.13	.0275
Believes that providing sites for gypsies and travellers has gone too far	-.11	.0409

181 cases in final model
Model chi-Square= 42.0 with 5 df, p<.0000.

Table 6 Final model: feeling unsafe alone at night (men, aged 60 years or more)

	R	Significance level
Renting accommodation	.15	.0295
Believes that disasters are likely to happen	-.14	.0348
Worries about own health	-.13	.0403
Believes self to be at risk	-.13	.0432

113 cases in final model
Model chi-Square= 26.4 with 4 df, p<.0000.

Table 7 Final model: worries about crime affect everyday life
(women, aged 18-34)

	R	Significance level
Believes that giving Legal Aid has gone too far	.13	.0169
Victim of an attack	-.13	.0170
Believes that government is powerless to change things[*]	.10	.0346
Victim of threats	-.10	.0361
Victim of burglary	-.10	.0419

171 cases in final model
Model chi-Square= 30.6 with 5 df, p<.0000.

Table 8 Final model: worries about crime affect everyday life
(men, aged 18-34)

	R	Significance level
Believes that changes in the right of people to go on demonstrations have not gone far enough	-.33	.0001
Believes that respondent has a say in government	-.25	.0024
Age of respondent (older=more fearful)	-.15	.0324
Holds authoritarian values	.12	.0575

140 cases in final model
Model chi-Square= 26.7 with 4 df, p<.0000.

---

[*] The questions read:

Some people say that British governments nowadays - of whichever party - can actually do very little to change things. Others say they can do quite a bit. Please say whether you think that British governments nowadays can do very little or quite a bit...

  to keep prices down
  to reduce unemployment
  to improve the general standard of living
  to improve health and social services
  to reduce poverty
  to cut crime

All the items were included in the constructed scale.

Table 9 Final model: worries about crime affect everyday life
(women, aged 35-59)

	R	Significance level
Victim of car crime	-.16	.0036
Believes self to be at risk	.15	.0059
Victim of an attack	-.10	.0303
Believes that disasters are unlikely to happen	-.09	.0428

189 cases in final model
Model chi-Square= 26.8 with 4 df, p< .0000.

Table 10 Final model: worries about crime affect everyday life
(men, aged 35-59)

	R	Significance level
Victim of theft	-.19	.0013
Believes self to be at risk	.19	.0014
Lives in a locality where there have been many attacks	-.18	.0023
Does not worry about his own health	.14	.0099
Worries about family problems	.13	.0175
Believes that the right to show sex in films has gone too far	.10	.0362

167 cases in final model
Model chi-Square= 38.2 with 6 df, p< .0000.

Table 11 Final model: worries about crime affect everyday life
(women, aged 60 years or more)

	R	Significance level
Victim of burglary	-.12	.0152
Believes that changes in the right of people to go on demonstrations have not gone far enough	-.11	.0220
Believes that changes in equal opportunities for women have gone too far	.11	.0236

238 cases in final model
Model chi-Square= 18.7 with 3 df, p< .0003.

Table 12 Final model: Worries about crime affect everyday life
(men, aged 60 years or more)

	R	Significance level
Worries about things happening around the world	.20	.0073
Believes that respondent does have a say in government	-.16	.0214
Victim of an attack	-.16	.0257
Has no long-term disability	-.13	.0401

136 cases in final model
Model chi-Square= 17.4 with 4 df, $p < .0016$.

3 Teenagers and their politics

Alison Park [*]

In the world of both politics and social surveys, 18 is a highly significant age. Before this age a person is neither eligible to vote nor to participate in many British surveys. Consequently, various interesting questions about teenagers and British politics are seldom addressed.[1] Little is known, for instance, about their knowledge of politics or their interest in the subject. We do not know whether teenagers have distinctive political views - or indeed any political views at all. As people under 18 are not eligible to vote, we are unable to gauge their identification with, or alienation from, politics by measures commonly used for adults (such as their propensity to vote or abstain in elections). Nor, since opinion polls generally omit non-voters from their scope, are we able to discover how much political parties and political debates engage teenagers - or whether British-style adversarial politics as a whole belongs essentially to an arcane world which barely impinges on young people's lives.

These and other questions provided the impetus for the incorporation into the 1994 *British Social Attitudes* survey a *Young People's Social Attitudes* survey, which we designed and developed in collaboration with colleagues from Barnardos. Full details of the sampling are given in Appendix I of this book. In essence, we interviewed all 12-19 year olds living in our adult respondents' households, asking (for comparative purposes) many of the same questions we administered to adults, plus a number of special questions. The topics covered in the *Young People's Social Attitudes* survey

---

[*]   Senior Researcher at SCPR and Co-director of the *British Social Attitudes* survey series.

included political knowledge and interest, education, gender roles, racial prejudice, crime and punishment, and fear of crime.[2]

Since a separate edited book is to be devoted to the overall findings of the *Young People's Social Attitudes* survey (Roberts and Sachdev, 1996, forthcoming) this chapter merely takes a first cursory look at the topic of teenagers and politics. We look at their interest in, and knowledge of, politics. We also consider their allegiance to particular parties. In all cases, we examine sources of differences between teenagers according to age, gender, education level and so on. Where possible, we also compare their answers with those of their adult counterparts in an attempt to establish how much, if at all, teenagers' own political allegiances and interests reflect those of their parents. By doing so we look for clues as to how politically independent the next generation of voters is likely to be.

Political knowledge

The 1994 *Young People's Social Attitudes* survey included a short quiz about politics. It consisted of 10 statements, to which respondents were asked to answer 'true', 'false' or 'don't know'.[3] As can be seen from the table below, the statements were pitched at a fairly unsophisticated level.

Knowledge of whether a statement was correct ranged from 90 per cent to less than 20 per cent. At best, therefore, only one teenager in ten did not know the correct answer. Statements referring to current political issues or personalities proved on the whole to be easier, while those referring to more technical constitutional issues proved more difficult.

The political knowledge quiz

% who gave correct answer:

John Major is the first British male Prime Minister (false)	90
The leader of the Conservative Party is Margaret Thatcher (false)	87
Great Britain is a member of the European Community (true)	84
The Conservative Party won the last general election (true)	80
The president of the U.S.A. is George Bush (false)	77
Northern Ireland is part of the United Kingdom (true)	76
Women are not allowed to sit in the House of Lords (false)	66
Britain has separate elections for the European Parliament and the British Parliament (true)	65
The number of Members of Parliament is about 100 (false)	41
The longest time allowed between general elections is four years (false)	19

More impressively perhaps, despite the marked variations in knowledge that we discuss later, nearly one-half of this national sample of teenagers (46 per cent) gave correct answers to eight or more of the ten quiz questions, while only seven per cent gave three or fewer correct answers.

Political knowledge quiz scores

% of teenagers:

0 or 1 answer correct	2
2 or 3 answers correct	5
4 or 5 answers correct	15
6 or 7 answers correct	32
8 or 9 answers correct	40
All answers correct	5

Who then are the most politically knowledgeable teenagers? As the table below shows, age and educational experience predictably improve knowledge, though not perhaps as much as might be anticipated (Denver and Hands, 1990; Hess and Torney, 1967). Moreover, gender - which has always mattered (Greenstein, 1965; Dowse and Hughes, 1971) - still matters, and perhaps rather more than we might have expected nowadays. In any event, boys are still apparently considerably more politically knowledgeable than girls.

Scores of 8 or more out of ten on the political knowledge quiz

	%
All	46
Age of teenager	
12 to 13	34
14 to 15	48
16 to 17	55
18 to 19	52
Educational status of teenager	
Finished full-time education	34
In full-time education, intends to leave at 18 or earlier	40
In full-time education, intends to leave at 19 or later	58
Sex of teenager	
Female	37
Male	55

Other factors associated with a high knowledge score are a self-reported interest in politics and, more surprisingly, a Liberal Democrat Party identification. Thus, while fewer than half of the teenagers who expressed a Conservative or Labour Party identification obtained a high knowledge score (8 or more out of 10), nearly three-quarters of Liberal Democrat identifiers did, perhaps because their relatively non-conforming political position ties in naturally with greater political interest. In addition, as

expected, the socio-economic group of the teenager's parents is associated with the teenager's (and doubtless his or her parents' own) political knowledge, though this is by no means a linear relationship.

Scores of 8 or more out of 10 on the political knowledge quiz

		%
All		46
Socio-economic group of adult respondent		
I	Professional and managerial	45
II	Intermediate non-manual	58
III	Junior non-manual	50
IV	Skilled manual	49
V&VI	Semi- and unskilled manual	34
Party identity of teenager		
Conservative		48
Labour		47
Liberal Democrat		73
No party identity		38
Political interest of teenager ...		
... a 'great deal' or 'quite a lot' of interest		72
... 'some' interest		55
... 'not very much' interest or 'none at all'		38

As we have suggested, many of the characteristics that are associated with variations in political knowledge may also be closely related to one another. So for instance, though gender and interest in politics are both linked to political knowledge, they may not be *independently* linked. Instead, it could well be that political interest is the *key* determinant of political knowledge and that boys just happen to be more likely than girls to be interested in politics. To disentangle these possible causes and effects, we used a data analysis technique known as 'logistic regression' which enables us to test the independent strength of association between, on the one hand, several different individual characteristics and, on the other, getting a high score (8 or more out of 10) on the political knowledge quiz. All the characteristics are tested, and the one most strongly associated with getting a high score is included in the model. The remaining characteristics are then re-tested, *taking due account of* characteristics already included in the equation, until all those with a significant independent association have been selected.[4]

We initially identified a large number of characteristics with a possible relationship to political knowledge. Some related to the teenager, some to their parent[5] and some to their household as a whole. All those we tested are shown below, the ones which turned out to have a statistically

significant independent association with a high knowledge score being shown in bold. The remainder did not prove to have an independent link with teenagers' political knowledge once the characteristics shown in bold had been accounted for.

Teenage characteristics	*Parental characteristics*	*Household characteristics*
Age	Party identity	Household income
Educational status	Age education ended	**Receipt of benefit**
Gender	Economic activity	
Party identity	(work, unemployment etc.)	
Political interest	Socio-economic group	
	Political interest[6]	

Thus, it proves to be the characteristics of teenagers themselves (such as their age, gender and educational status), rather than those of their parents or households, that have most bearing on their level of political knowledge, as measured by our quiz. The strength of association between each characteristic and political knowledge is shown in the next table.[7] In each case, we give the B coefficient for the association, which may be positive or negative. The higher the B coefficient, the stronger the association of that characteristic with a high political knowledge score. In the event, all the coefficients here are positive, meaning that the characteristics listed are all linked to an increased likelihood of a teenager getting a high score (a negative coefficient would mean there was a decreased likelihood).

Interestingly, gender survives as the strongest predictor of political knowledge. Moreover, we now discover that gender is a key factor *independently* of differences in political interest. Boys are more likely than girls to score highly on the quiz even after gender differences in all the other selected characteristics (including political interest and age) have been taken into account. In other words, among teenagers with the same levels of interest in politics, or among those of the same age, boys continue to be more likely than girls to obtain high scores on the political knowledge quiz.

Educationalists may note with some relief that educational level and intentions are also independently associated with political knowledge. Thus teenagers who are (or expect to be) in full-time education beyond the age of 18 are more likely than those who have left (or expect to leave) full-time education by that age to score highly on the political knowledge quiz. Mercifully, too, political knowledge increases as teenagers get closer to voting age, independently of education. Also confirmed here is the greater likelihood of Liberal Democrat identifiers to score highly on the political knowledge quiz, an attribute that is not associated with Conservative or Labour identifiers for reasons we can only speculate about, as we tentatively did earlier.

Finally, we discover here the first clue as to the influence of household income (or lack of it) on young people's political socialisation. Indeed, it proves to be a more important influence than socio-economic group and,

as we shall see later, is related to political interest too. Having a parent who is unemployed (which would be by far the most common reason for means-tested benefit receipt)[8] turns out to be the *only* parental or household characteristic that has an independent association with political knowledge. This may be a further manifestation of the well-documented absence from democratic participation of those who might rationally be thought to have a special case for *increased* political interest and participation (see for instance Galbraith, 1992). In short, these households seem to have more pressing issues to contend with than taking an interest in contemporary politics.

Getting a score of 8 or more out of 10 on the political knowledge quiz

Characteristic	B coefficient
Teenager male	.73
Teenager in education and expecting to remain until 19 or over	.72
Teenager interested in politics	.56
Household not in receipt of means-tested benefit	.56
Teenager aged 16 or over	.52
Teenager a Liberal Democrat identifier	.40

Political interest

We have seen that political knowledge is linked to political interest. But how much interest in politics is there among teenagers? A popular image of teenagers is of a group disillusioned with conventional politics who have turned either towards unconventional quasi-political credos or who reject politics altogether (Cannon, 1994). In apparent confirmation of this image, we found that, in comparison with adults, teenagers did show precious little interest in politics. Adults as a whole are nearly three times more likely than teenagers to express 'a great deal' or 'quite a lot' of interest in 'what is going on in politics'. But this is only part of the story. In fact, political interest among adults varies markedly with age. Younger adults - those under the age of 25 - are closer to the average teenager in this respect than to older adults. Thus, around one teenager in eight expresses a strong interest in politics, compared with around one in seven of the 18-25 year olds in our adult sample and over one in three of those aged 25 years or over - a very steep gradient indeed.

Teenage and adult interest in politics

	Teenage survey (12-19) %	Adult survey						All adults %
		18-24 %	25-34 %	35-44 %	45-54 %	55-64 %	65+ %	
A 'great deal' or 'quite a lot'	12	15	30	34	37	36	36	32
'Some'	26	44	37	34	36	33	30	35
'Not very much'	32	26	25	23	21	26	29	25
'None at all'	27	15	8	9	6	5	5	8

There are two competing explanations for these differences, with quite different political consequences. The first explanation is that political interest more or less automatically increases with age and that today's teenagers and young adults will consequently acquire more interest in politics as they grow older. In this respect, nothing much will change radically from generation to generation. But a second possible explanation is that today's teenagers and young adults differ fundamentally from their older counterparts, and that they will retain these differences as they grow older. As a result, the present electorate will eventually be replaced by, say, a more disillusioned and apathetic group of voters.

As 1994 marked the first year of the *Young People's Social Attitudes* survey, we do not have the trend data that we need to evaluate these two possible explanations. Nonetheless, we can partly remedy this omission by examining the relationship between age and political interest among 18-24 year olds in previous *British Social Attitudes* surveys and by looking for changes over time.

As the next table shows, young adults have consistently expressed less interest than their elders in politics. Thus, lack of political interest does indeed appear to be related to youthfulness *per se* as opposed to some special force in the 1990s which has precipitated alienation from conventional politics. On the other hand, the gap between the political interest of 18-24 year olds and that of older adults did widen substantially between 1991 and 1994 - from only seven percentage points to a substantial 17 points. This is *solely* accounted for by a sharp drop in the interest of 18-24 year olds, and not by a change among older adults. So, although it is too early to tell, there may also be worrying early evidence here of a 'cohort replacement' model of political change. Could young voters now be plumbing uncharted depths of indifference towards and distrust of contemporary politics? If so, will the future still see the accustomed and democratically healthy rise in political interest with age, or will that process be much less likely in these new circumstances?[9]

Adults with 'a great deal' or 'quite a lot of interest' in politics

	1986 %	1989 %	1990 %	1991 %	1994 %
All adults	29	28	29	32	32
Adults aged 18-24	21	23	19	25	15

Teenagers may, on the whole, be less interested in politics than adults. But are some teenagers more interested than others? As was the case with political knowledge, interesting differences among teenagers do exist in this respect. Logistic regression techniques identified five characteristics that were associated with an interest in politics. As with political knowledge, it was mainly teenagers' own characteristics, rather than those of their parents or household, that proved to be statistically significant.

Not surprisingly, the strongest association is between low political interest and an absence of party identification (both questions measuring much the same phenomenon). As noted in the last section, however, a much less predictable association, and a *very* strong one at that, exists between political interest and household income. Thus, teenagers living in households with gross annual incomes of £20,000 or more are significantly more likely than others to be interested in politics. Once again, just as household receipt of benefit proved in respect to political knowledge, income is a more important source of difference than either parental socio-economic group or the age at which the parent finished his or her full-time education. In this case income proves to be more important than parental economic activity (that is, whether the parent was in work, unemployed and so on). As before then, an absence of financial resources from a household seems to lead its young members away from an engagement with politics - whether temporarily or permanently we do not know.

The other three characteristics we found to be independently associated with an interest in politics - gender, education and age - were all also important as predictors of political knowledge. For instance, even among those of similar age and with similar educational expectations and experience, boys are more likely than girls to express an interest in politics.

Having 'a great deal' or 'quite a lot' of interest in politics

Characteristic	B coefficient
Teenager has no party identification	- 1.28
Household income £20,000 or more	.88
Teenager aged 16 or over	.71
Teenager in education and expects to remain until 19 or over	.65
Teenager is male	.52

Party identification

Interest in party identification, the emotional attachment that an individual has to a particular party, has a long history in electoral theory. It is argued that, from an early age, children are exposed to a variety of forms of political socialisation within the family and thus develop a predisposition towards one party or another. As parties are conceptually quite simple 'objects' to identify with, initial party identification is effectively learned at one's parents' knees (Greenstein, 1965). This is subsequently reinforced by their first voting experience (see Campbell *et al*, 1960; Butler and Stokes, 1969). Naturally some people's party identification changes during their lives, sometimes more than once, but a person's initial party identification nonetheless tends to be a durable adhesive that helps to bind many people to a particular party.

By far the biggest difference between the teenagers' sample and the adult sample is in the proportion of people with *no* party identification (nearly one in three teenagers, as opposed to one in ten adults).[10] In this respect, the 18-24 year olds in the adult sample resemble their elder counterparts much more than they do teenagers. As the table below shows, data from past *British Social Attitudes* surveys have always revealed a lower than average propensity among younger adults to have a specific party identification. After all, many people aged under 24 will not yet have voted in a general election, an event that is recognised in the literature (see above) as helping to crystallise party identification. And the *size* of the gap between the proportion of young and old adults with no party identification has fluctuated trendlessly over the last 11 years, showing no consistent pattern of increase or decrease.[11]

People with no party identity

	1983	1984	1985	1986	1987	1989	1990	1991	1993	1994
	%	%	%	%	%	%	%	%	%	%
All adults	8	6	9	8	8	7	8	7	8	11
Adults aged 18-24	15	9	17	13	17	14	14	10	12	17
All teenagers	n/a	n/a	n/a	n/a	n/a	na	n/a	n/a	n/a	30

n/a = not asked

In order to focus on those with a party allegiance, we exclude from the following table all those who did not express a party identification, basing all percentages only on those who *did* express one.

Nearly half of the adult sample (48 per cent) and a slightly higher proportion of the teenage sample (51 per cent) are Labour Party identifiers. Indeed, it is the similarity of Labour Party identification across all age groups that is most remarkable about the next table, especially when one considers that, for almost all of the teenage sample and most of the youngest adults, anything other than a Conservative government is at best

a distant childhood memory. Liberal Democrat support is also remarkably consistent across all age groups. This is much less true, however, of Conservative Party identification. Among teenagers, for instance, only one in five are Conservative identifiers, increasing to one in four of the youngest adults and one in three of all adults. This is the only occasion on which age seems to be linked to party identification and may partly reflect mid-term government unpopularity, with some people choosing to interpret the question as a measure of current voting intention rather than of long-term party identification *per se*.

Party identification among those who nominate a party

	Teenage survey (12-19)	Adult survey						All adults
		18-24	25-34	35-44	45-54	55-64	65+	
	%	%	%	%	%	%	%	%
Conservative	20	26	28	28	35	44	38	33
Labour	51	48	49	49	44	42	46	46
Liberal Democrat	14	17	17	19	19	13	13	16
Other party	14	9	6	4	2	1	3	4

So the overall teenage sample does differ from the overall adult sample in terms of party identification, but not as markedly as might have been expected. However, the more interesting question in terms of party identification theory is how closely teenagers resemble their own parents in their party allegiances (see Campbell *et al*, 1960; Butler and Stokes, 1969; Greenstein, 1965; Stone and Schaffner, 1988). After all, since the development of party identity is said to begin at an early age and is, above all, influenced by political socialisation at home, the teenagers' party allegiances should be heavily influenced by their parents' allegiances (although in this case the parental data relate only to *one* parent).

And so it proves. As the next figures show, although less than a quarter of teenagers have a Conservative parent, nearly two-thirds of those with a Conservative identification come from a Conservative household. Similarly, while fewer than half of the teenagers have a Labour parent, around three-quarters of those with a Labour identification come from a Labour household. The figures for Liberal Democrat teenagers and Liberal Democrat parents show the same pattern.

% of teenagers with a Conservative parent:	23
% of **Conservative** teenagers with a Conservative parent:	65
% of teenagers with a Labour parent:	46
% of **Labour** teenagers with a Labour parent:	74
% of teenagers with a Liberal Democrat parent:	15
% of **Liberal Democrat** teenagers with a Liberal parent:	50

Having established that parental influence matters, we then constructed a series of logistic regression models in order to discover what other characteristics influence party choice among teenagers. In order to establish the *independent* influences of these factors, we included parental party identification in the model which, sure enough, proved to be the strongest influence.[12]   However, even after taking parents' party into account, a number of other characteristics emerged as important in their own right.

As the table below shows, the working status of the parent (that is whether or not the parent was in paid employment) has a significant relationship with both teenage Conservative and Labour identification. A teenager whose parent was in paid work is *more* likely than one whose parent is not in paid work to be a Conservative identifier, and *vice versa* for Labour identifiers. Parental working status has no significant influence on Liberal Democrat identification.

The age at which a teenager's parent finished his or her full-time education is significantly associated with teenage Labour and Liberal Democrat identification, but not with teenage Conservatives.   Thus, teenagers with a parent who completed his or her education at 18 or above are more likely to be Liberal Democrats (see Heath *et al*, 1985) and less likely to be Labour identifiers.   A teenager's own educational status and intentions also matter.   Thus, those who either are, or intend to be, in full-time education until at least 19 are more likely to be Conservatives.   On the other hand, those teenagers who express an interest in politics are more likely to be Labour identifiers.

So, even after parental party preference is discounted, a number of basic social divisions still appear to influence teenagers' choice of party, suggesting that the classic class-based nature of British politics is likely to persist for some while yet.

Teenage Conservative identification

Characteristic	B coefficient
Adult Conservative identifier	2.39
Adult in paid work	1.26
Teenager in education and expecting to remain until 19 or over	0.72

Teenage Labour identification

Characteristic	B coefficient
Adult Labour identifier	1.78
Adult in paid work	- 0.67
Adult terminal education age 18 or over	- 0.63
Teenager interested in politics	0.62

Teenage Liberal Democrat identification

Characteristic	B coefficient
Adult Liberal Democrat identifier	2.00
Adult terminal education age 18 or over	0.82

As far as those with *no* party identification are concerned, the regression model identified only two characteristics, both anticipated, which predict an absence of expressed allegiance - lack of interest in politics and leaving (or intending to leave) education early. More surprisingly, once these two factors are taken into account, no other characteristic (not even gender or age) had a significant impact.

Conclusion

Teenagers are a good deal less likely than their adult counterparts to be interested in politics or to have formed an attachment to any particular political party. To a large extent, however, this appears to be merely a function of their relative youth rather than of a sudden growth in political apathy or alienation among this particular age group. On the other hand, there is some evidence that younger adults (in particular, new and relatively new voters) *are* rather more disenchanted and disillusioned than their predecessor generation was at the same age. To the extent that this trend persists, it could have serious consequences for British democracy.

Rather depressingly, perhaps, traditional gender images persist among teenagers. Thus, boys are substantially more likely than girls to be interested in politics and to score highly on a political knowledge index. Similarly, teenagers living in low income households are significantly less likely than their wealthier counterparts to develop an early interest in and knowledge of politics. On the other hand, political interest and knowledge do fortunately rise with age and education. As for party preferences, teenagers resemble their parents, much as party identification theory says they are supposed to do, and doubtless just as their parents resembled *their* parents before them.

Notes

1. Throughout this chapter young people aged 12 to 19 are referred to as teenagers.
2. Other data from the *Young People's Social Attitudes* survey will be presented and discussed by Roberts and Sachdev (1996, forthcoming). A brief description of technical aspects of the survey can be found in the Technical Appendices of this report.
3. An eleventh statement in the quiz ("The leader of the Labour Party is John Smith") was omitted after John Smith's sudden death during the early stages of the fieldwork.
4. This procedure shows which characteristics of those considered are significant in their association with a particular event. Two points should be noted. Firstly, significance depends, in part, upon the number of cases included in the analysis, so the fact that a characteristic is not selected by the model does not demonstrate that there is no association whatever between it and the event in question. Secondly, the procedure identifies associations, not necessarily causes.
5. Not all the teenage data could be linked to parental data (for example, in some cases the adult *British Social Attitudes* respondent was a student and the teenager

another student in the same household). These cases were eliminated from the following analyses. The exact number of cases used in the analyses presented in this chapter can be found in the appendix.

6. The political interest question was asked of only two-thirds of the adult *British Social Attitudes* sample. Because logistic regression cannot be run on cases where missing data exist for a single variable, these cases were excluded from analysis, reducing the overall sample size considerably and thus making significance a harder hurdle to clear. For this reason, two analyses were run for each of the models presented in this chapter, one including the adult political interest variable and one excluding it. Since, however, adult political interest was not found to be significant in its association with any of the dependent variables considered in this chapter, the results presented here are based on analyses which excluded this characteristic.

7. More details about each model can be found in the appendix at the end of this chapter.

8. Household benefit receipt, rather than whether the parent interviewed was unemployed, proved to be significant in its association with political knowledge. However, it is still likely that parental unemployment is the key factor at work, since the household benefit question reflects whether *either* parent is unemployed, rather than just the parent who happened to be interviewed.

9. See also Curtice and Jowell in this volume.

10. Party identification is explained fully in Appendix I of this report.

11. As was the case with political interest, this question cannot be properly addressed without longitudinal data. Moreover, since this is the first *Young People's Social Attitudes* survey, we cannot compare these teenagers with previous cohorts.

12. This raises a further question as to whether teenage party identification is influenced more by paternal than maternal party identification. Traditional theories have stressed the importance of paternal party identification, stemming from the observation that, as a result of men's greater politicization, fathers' partisanship is more likely to be visible in the family and hence more likely to influence children (Butler and Stokes, 1969).
   The size of our sample, and the fact that we interviewed only one of the teenager's parents, mean that we cannot address this issue in the detail it properly deserves. Nonetheless, if we examine the congruence of teenage party identification and parental party identification, according to whether the adult interviewed was the teenager's father or mother, there is little evidence to support the notion that paternal party identification matters more.

References

Butler, D. and Stokes, D. (1969), *Political Change in Britain*, London: Macmillan.

Campbell, A., Converse, P., Miller, W. and Stokes, D. (1960), *The American Voter*, New York: Wiley.

Cannon, D. (1994), 'Generation X and the new work ethic', The Seven Million Project Working Paper 1, London: DEMOS.

Denver, D. and Hands, G. (1990), 'Does studying politics make a difference? The political knowledge, attitudes and perceptions of school students', *British Journal of Political Science*, 20, 263-288.

Dowse, R. and Hughes, J. (1971), 'Girls, boys and politics', *British Journal of Sociology*, 22, 53-67.

Galbraith, J. (1992), *The Culture of Contentment*, Harmondsworth: Penguin.

Greenstein, F. (1965), *Children and Politics*, New Haven: Yale University Press.

Heath, A., Jowell, R. and Curtice, J. (1985), *How Britain Votes,* Oxford: Pergamon Press.

Hess, R. and Torney, J. (1967), *The Development of Political Attitudes in Children,* Chicago: Aldine Publishing Company.

Roberts, H. and Sachdev, D. (eds.) (1996, forthcoming), *Young People's Social Attitudes.*

Stone, W. and Schaffner, P. (1988), *The Psychology of Politics,* New York: Springer-Verlag.

Acknowledgement

We wish to acknowledge the close collaboration of Barnardos, with whom the *Young People's Social Attitudes Survey* was conceived and developed.

Appendix

Analysis variables

Analysis variables were derived from a dataset which linked data from the *Young People's Social Attitudes* and *British Social Attitudes* 1994 surveys. Analysis was restricted to cases where the adult *British Social Attitudes* respondent was the **parent** of the teenager. Unless otherwise specified, the following dummy variables were used for the regression analyses discussed throughout this chapter:

Teenage characteristics:

Age: Teenagers aged 16 or over coded 1. Younger teenagers coded 0.

Educational status: Teenagers in full-time education and who expected to stay there until at least 19 coded 1. Teenagers who had left full-time education or expected to leave by 18 coded 0.

Sex: Boys coded 1. Girls coded 0.

Political identity: Four dummy variables were computed with either Conservative or Labour or Liberal Democrat or 'don't know'/none coded 1. All other responses coded 0.

Political interest: Teenagers who had *a great deal* of, *quite a lot* of, or *some* interest in politics coded 1. Teenagers who had *not very much* interest, or *none*, coded 0.

Parental characteristics:

Political identity: Three dummy variables were computed with either Conservative or Labour or Liberal Democrat coded 1. All other responses coded 0.

Terminal education age: Adults who remained in education until at least 18 coded 1. Those whose education ended earlier coded 0.

Current activity: Two dummy variables were computed with either work or unemployment coded 1. All other activity statuses coded 0.

Socio-economic group: Two dummy variables were computed with either socio-economic groups 1 and 2 (professional, managerial and intermediate non-manual) or socio-economic groups 1 to 3 (non-manual) coded 1. All other socio-economic groups coded 0.

Household characteristics:

Household income: Three dummy variables were computed with either £10,000 or more, £20,000 or more and £29,000 or more coded 1. All lower incomes coded 0.

Receipt of benefit: No means-tested benefits received coded 1. Means-tested benefits received coded 0.

The logistic regression models

The development of the various models referred to in this chapter is detailed below. Models were constructed using the *LOGISTIC REGRESSION* function of SPSS.

The following tables define the dependent variable for each analysis - that is, the event that the model attempts to predict. Variables selected as significant in predicting the dependent variable are presented in the order of their selection; the subsequent chi square (-2 log likelihood), degrees of freedom and change in chi square are shown. In all cases, significance was tested at a 0.05 level.

Political knowledge

Dependent variable: getting a score of 80 per cent or more on the political knowledge quiz.

Number of cases included in analysis: 433

	chi square	d.f.	change in chi square
Null model	598.316	432	-
1. Teenager interested in politics	578.052	431	20.264
2. Teenager Liberal Democrat identifier	566.267	430	11.784
3. Teenager in education (and expecting to remain until 19 or over)	556.313	429	9.955
4. Teenager is male	546.088	428	10.224
5. Household receives no benefits	539.237	427	6.851
6. Teenager aged 16 or over	533.632	426	5.605

Interest in politics

Dependent variable: having 'a great deal' of, 'quite a lot' of, or 'some' interest in politics.

Number of cases included in analysis: 433

	chi square	d.f.	change in chi square
Null model	574.265	432	-
1. Teenager has no party identity	540.621	431	33.644
2. Household annual income of £20,000	517.272	430	23.349
3. Teenager aged 16 or over	509.510	429	7.762
4. Teenager in education (and expecting to remain until 19 or over)	501.814	428	7.696
5. Teenager is male	496.308	427	5.506

Conservative identification

Dependent variable: teenage Conservative Party identification.

Number of cases included in analysis: 439

Variables excluded: teenage Labour, Liberal Democrat and 'don't know' identifiers.

		chi square	d.f.	change in chi square
	Null model	378.950	438	-
1.	Adult Conservative identifier	301.780	437	77.170
2.	Adult in paid work	290.901	436	10.879
3.	Teenager in education (and expecting to remain until 19 or over)	285.302	435	5.599

Labour identification

Dependent variable: teenage Labour Party identification.

Number of cases included in analysis: 439

Variables excluded: teenage Conservative, Liberal Democrat and 'don't know' identifiers.

		chi square	d.f.	change in chi square
	Null model	569.637	438	-
1.	Adult Labour identifier	496.937	437	72.701
2.	Adult in paid work	488.084	436	8.853
3.	Teenager interested in politics	481.593	435	6.490
4.	Adult terminal education age 18 or over	476.813	434	4.781

Liberal Democrat identification

Dependent variable: teenage Liberal Democrat Party identification.

Number of cases included in analysis: 439

Variables excluded: teenage Conservative, Labour and 'don't know' identifiers.

		chi square	d.f.	change in chi square
	Null model	286.246	438	-
1.	Adult Liberal Democrat identifier	251.660	437	34.586
2.	Adult terminal education age 18 or over	246.516	436	5.144

'Don't know' identification

Dependent variable: teenage 'don't know' or 'no' party identification.

Number of cases included in analysis: 433

Variables excluded: teenage Conservative, Labour or Liberal Democrat identifiers.

	chi square	d.f.	change in chi square
Null model	518.486	432	-
1. Teenage interest in politics	484.842	431	33.644
2. Teenager in education (and expecting to remain until 19 or over)	480.156	430	4.686

4 Working mothers: choice or circumstance?

Katarina Thomson [*]

Introduction

Women are increasingly likely to go out to work. According to the Labour Force Survey, nearly two-thirds (64 per cent) of women of working age are either in work or are looking for work - compared with 55 per cent ten years earlier. During this period the proportion of men in work or looking for work has fallen. The growth in the numbers of women at work has been particularly evident among mothers with children below school age. No other group's participation in the labour market has grown so rapidly. True, around two in three working mothers opt for part-time rather than full-time work (Sly, 1994). But it is clear that the majority of women with children in Britain no longer pursue motherhood as a full-time vocation. The decisions that they take about whether and when to work are becoming increasingly important to the operation of the country's labour market.

There have been significant calls for measures to increase the participation of mothers in the workforce further still. The Employment Select Committee of the House of Commons has recently recommended making it more attractive for mothers to work (Employment Committee, 1994). One possible reason for doing so, as suggested in a report by the Institute for Fiscal Studies (IFS), is to avoid the loss of skills which can occur when mothers leave the labour force (Duncan, Giles and Webb, 1995). Furthermore, making it easier for mothers to return to work is often

[*] Research Director at Social Community Planning Research and Co-director of the *British Social Attitudes* survey series.

thought essential to the effective promotion of equal opportunities for women - the IFS study was in fact financed by the Equal Opportunities Commission. Meanwhile, recent research suggests that not only nursery education but good childcare outside the home are beneficial for children's development (summarised in Duncan, Giles and Webb, 1995).

Possible influences on whether mothers work

This chapter examines why some mothers go out to work while others remain at home. It also considers why some women work full-time while others work part-time. Many previous studies have focused on *one* possible answer to these questions; in this chapter, however, we look at a range of possible influences and assess their relative importance. In particular, we consider one influence that is often ignored - the attitudes of women themselves towards working mothers. As we discover, these attitudes cannot be disregarded if the participation of mothers in the labour market is to be properly understood.

We look at three main influences on why mothers go out to work. The first includes the economic and demographic circumstances in which a woman finds herself. Will she, for instance, be able to find a job if she wants one? Equally important is how much a job will contribute to the family budget - not just in the short term but also in the long term.[1] The answer to this question depends not only upon the earnings that her skills and experience will dictate, but also upon potential childcare costs and whether her earnings will affect any welfare benefits received by her family.

The second main influence considered concerns the practicalities of childcare. Will she be able to find *suitable* childcare at a price she can afford? Will she be able to cope when the children are ill? What matters here is not simply the childcare arrangements the mother is able to make, but also the degree of flexibility employers are prepared to demonstrate in their working arrangements. Here we build upon earlier analysis of *British Social Attitudes* data (Witherspoon and Prior, 1991).

Finally, there is the question of whether the mother actually *wants* to return to work. This will depend partly upon whether or not she enjoys being at home, and also upon the sort of job she will realistically get. However, her general attitudes towards women and work will also matter - as will the attitudes of her partner, relatives, friends, potential employers and colleagues.

The latest *British Social Attitudes* survey enables us to look at all three sets of influences together. We asked all men and women with children under 12[2] a series of questions about working and childcare last asked in 1990. In addition, we also asked a number of questions which explore attitudes towards women and work.[3] As always, we have a wide range of information on the demographic and economic circumstances of those who took part in our survey.

Who are the working mothers?

Mothers who go out to work are known to have a number of distinctive demographic and economic characteristics.[4] They differ from mothers in general in terms of the number and age of their children, their own age, their educational qualifications and work experience, and their household's economic situation. These characteristics affect both how easy or difficult it is for a mother to *find* a job, as well as how attractive any job might be. Some apply equally to all women (and, indeed, all men) - others are only relevant to mothers with young children.[5]

Family structure

Previous work has shown that the fewer children mothers have, the more likely they are to work outside the home, especially in full-time jobs (Foster *et al*, 1995). Similarly, the older her youngest child, the more likely it is that a mother will work (Harrop and Moss, 1994; Foster *et al*, 1995). This is not surprising - the more children a woman has, the more expensive and complex her childcare arrangements will have to be if she wishes to go out to work. The younger her children are, the more this applies.

These patterns are confirmed by our survey. Of women with three or more children aged under 12, well over half say they 'look after the home' - that is, their main activity is being a 'housewife'. The comparable figure for women with one child is around one in three. Full-time working is virtually unknown among women with three or more children under 12.

Meanwhile, nearly half of those whose youngest child is under five look after the home compared with just a third of those whose youngest child is aged between five and eleven.[6]

Number of children and age of youngest child, by woman's activity[7]

		Full-time employee	Part-time employee	Looking after the home
Number of children under 12:				
None	%	43	19	15
One	%	15	28	33
Two	%	17	28	44
Three or more	%	2	27	56
Age of youngest child:				
Under 5	%	13	25	48
5 to 12	%	16	31	32

Mother's age

Older mothers are more likely to work than younger ones. Among mothers aged below 30, nearly half are housewives - compared with just over a quarter of those aged 40 or over. In fact, women aged 40 or over who do *not* have children under 12 are just as likely to be housewives as those who do have children in this age group. Among younger women, however, mothers of children under 12 are over twenty times more likely to be housewives than are women without young children. In part these differences simply reflect the fact that older mothers are more likely to have older children - and we have seen that such mothers are more likely than average to go out to work. However, the figures also suggest that women who have children later in life are more likely to have the kind of jobs to which they wish to return.

Age by woman's activity

		Full-time employee	Part-time employee	Looking after the home
Woman aged 18-29 who ...				
... has children under 12	%	8	28	48
... has no children under 12	%	58	9	2
Woman aged 30-39 who ...				
... has children under 12	%	18	26	41
... has no children under 12	%	67	10	7
Woman aged 40 plus who ...				
... has children under 12	%	15	33	26
... has no children under 12	%	30	23	23

What sort of job might the mother return to?

Mothers with certain kinds of jobs or work experience are more likely to work than those with different occupational backgrounds. Educational background also matters. Generally speaking, the better qualified the mother, the more likely she is to work - and the less likely she is to look after the home. For instance, among women with children under 12, we found that over half of those without qualifications were looking after the home - compared with just over a third of those with degrees. Recent results from the Labour Force Survey suggest that this gap between better qualified and less well qualified mothers is widening (Harrop and Moss, 1994; Sly, 1994).

Obviously we must remember that occupational and educational background influence the chances of *any* woman being in employment, irrespective of whether or not she has children. As the next table shows,

of those women who do not have children under 12, nearly a third who are without qualifications look after the home, compared with just three per cent of those with a degree. The question, then, is not whether better qualified mothers are more likely to work than less well qualified ones - but whether having qualifications makes *more* difference to the chances of a mother working outside the home than it does to a woman without children. In fact, there is no evidence from our survey to support this claim. For instance, if we look at women with degrees, the *gap* between the proportion with children under 12 who are looking after the home (28 per cent) and the proportion without children under 12 who are doing the same (three per cent) is 25 percentage points. This, in fact, is exactly the same as the equivalent difference among women without any qualifications.

However, we do find that if a better qualified mother does decide to work, she is more likely to work full-time than her less well qualified counterpart - even after we allow for the fact that better qualified women are more likely than average to work full-time. Among mothers with no qualifications, there are ten part-time workers for every one full-time worker. Among mothers with a degree, there are more than twice as many full-time workers as part-time workers.

Highest educational qualification, by woman's activity

		Full-time employee	Part-time employee	Looking after the home
Degree level:				
- has children under 12	%	(38)	(17)	(28)[8]
- has no children under 12	%	66	13	3
CSE to below degree level:				
- has children under 12	%	15	30	37
- has no children under 12	%	48	16	9
No qualifications:				
- has children under 12	%	3	29	55
- has no children under 12	%	25	25	30

As we might expect from the previous evidence on educational qualifications, mothers who are (or were) in manual occupations are less likely than those in other groups to be working outside the home and are more likely to be housewives. It is those in intermediate or junior non-manual occupations (such as teachers, nurses, secretaries and sales assistants) who are the most likely of all to be working, rather than those in professional and managerial occupations. Members of the latter group, however, are much more likely than average to be self-employed. If their numbers are added to the figures shown in the next table, women who are professionals and managers become more likely to be working than those in intermediate or junior non-manual occupations. They are also more likely to be working full-time and less likely to be working part-time. As

the next table shows, only around a third of mothers from professional and managerial occupations are housewives - compared with around four in ten of those from intermediate non-manual or manual occupations. But this pattern also exists among women *without* children under 12. Indeed, within this group, the difference between the proportion with professional and managerial occupations who look after the home (four per cent) and the proportion of those with manual occupations who are similarly engaged (20 per cent) is, at 16 percentage points, larger than the equivalent difference among mothers with children aged under 12 (seven points). In other words, the impact of occupational background is *less* among mothers with children under 12 than it is among women without children of this age.

Socio-economic group of current/last job, by woman's activity

		Full-time employee	Part-time employee	Looking after the home
Professional or managerial:				
- has children under 12	%	23	16	34
- has no children under 12	%	60	5	4
Intermediate or junior non-manual:				
- has children under 12	%	17	34	39
- has no children under 12	%	49	22	13
Manual:				
- has children under 12	%	8	25	41
- has no children under 12	%	30	22	20

We can see that working mothers with children under 12 are clearly atypical in their educational and occupational backgrounds. They are more likely to be educationally well-qualified and employed in non-manual occupations than are their non-working counterparts.[9] But, in general, the social and economic processes which bring this about are at least equally present among women without young children. There is little evidence that such processes have a *particular* impact upon which mothers - as opposed to which women - go out to work.

Household situation

Lone mothers - and their position in the labour market - have aroused particular public concern. If they are unable to work, it is highly likely they will be reliant upon welfare payments as their main source of income. But, in terms of whether or not mothers work, the biggest gulf is *not* between lone mothers and married ones. Rather, in reality, it is between mothers with partners who are in work and those whose partners are not. It is one of the great ironies of the British labour market that women are

more likely to work if their husband or partner is in work than if he is not. Furthermore, the gap between the proportion of these two groups who work has been widening since the early 1980s (Harrop and Moss, 1994; Bartholomew, Hibbett and Sidaway, 1992; Foster *et al* 1995). And, of course, a family where neither partner is in employment is *just* as likely to be reliant on welfare payments as a lone parent family where the mother is not in work.

Two main explanations have been proposed for this phenomenon. The first is that the current benefit system contains *disincentives* to working. Such problems are, to a certain extent, at the root of recent changes to the regulations governing Family Credit. These allow some childcare costs to be deducted when determining whether or not a family's income is sufficiently low for it to be eligible for benefit. The second explanation rests upon the observation that husbands and wives often have similar socio-economic backgrounds, work experiences and, indeed, attitudes towards work itself (Ward *et al*, 1993). Some considerable effort has gone into disentangling these two possible influences on employment (Davies, 1992), but both probably play a role.

The next table compares lone mothers and married or cohabiting mothers. Less than one in three lone mothers work as employees - compared with 45 per cent of married or cohabiting mothers. The table shows clearly that this difference is accounted for by the fact that lone mothers are *mothers* rather than because they are single. Single women without children under 12 are the *least* likely group to be housewives - this applying to barely more than one in twenty.

If a lone mother does go out to work, she is almost as likely to do so full-time as part-time, whereas married (or cohabiting) mothers are twice as likely to be part-time as full-time. Indeed, the proportion of lone mothers employed full-time (13 per cent) is almost the same as the proportion of married mothers working full-time (15 per cent). Doubtless this reflects the need for working lone mothers to earn sufficient income to cover all of their household expenses - including childcare.

The relative importance of whether or not a mother's partner works - rather than whether or not she *has* a partner - is strikingly demonstrated by the fact that a lone mother is *more* likely to work than a mother with a partner who is not in work. Only four in ten lone mothers are housewives compared with no less than two-thirds of mothers with non-working partners. However, the absence from the labour market of mothers with non-working partners seems unrelated to the fact that they are mothers. Their counterparts without children under 12 are also much less likely to work than average. Fewer than one in three of those whose partner is not in work are in employment - compared with seven in ten of those whose partner is in work.

Economic activity of spouse or partner, by woman's activity

		Full-time employee	Part-time employee	Looking after the home
Partner in work:				
- has children under 12	%	16	32	36
- has no children under 12	%	46	25	17
Partner not in work:				
- has children under 12	%	5	17	66
- has no children under 12	%	13	16	36
Not married or living as married:				
- has children under 12	%	13	18	40
- has no children under 12	%	46	10	6

Our findings give some support to the argument that similarities of outlook and experience between husband and wife play at least some role in determining whether or not women go out to work. They may also reflect the importance of economic incentives in determining whether or not mothers work. We can examine this further by looking at whether mothers' *propensity* to work is related to household income.

We asked everyone what their total household income was before tax and, if he or she was working, what his or her own earnings were before tax. From these figures we can estimate what a household's income would be if the woman had no earnings.[10] We might expect that, the lower a household's income without her contribution, the more likely a mother would be to work. However, households with very low incomes are likely to be dependent on benefits, whose loss as a result of a mother's earnings could make the fact of her working of insufficient financial value to be worthwhile.

Both of these economic influences are clearly at work. It is mothers in our 'middle' income bracket who are most likely to go out to work. Just over a quarter of mothers in this group are housewives, compared with over four in ten of those in 'low' income households, and more than half of those in 'high' income households. In contrast, among married or cohabiting women *without* children under 12, there is a weaker relationship between what their household income would be without their earnings and whether or not they are housewives.

Approximate household income without
woman's earnings, by woman's activity

		Full-time employees	Part-time employees	Looking after the home
'Low' income **(less than £10,000)**				
- has children under 12	%	9	27	43
- married/cohabiting and has no children under 12	%	37	22	20
'Middle' income **(£10,000 to £20,000)**				
- has children under 12	%	20	35	28
- married/cohabiting and has no children under 12	%	50	23	16
'High' income **(£20,000 or above)**				
- has children under 12	%	13	21	53
- married/cohabiting and has no children under 12	%	35	26	23

The relative importance of social and economic characteristics

So far we have found a number of ways in which working mothers differ from non-working mothers. They differ in terms of the number and age of their children, their own age, their educational qualifications and work experience, and in the economic situation of their household.[11] But some of these characteristics overlap. For instance, women with a degree are more likely to have professional or managerial occupations and to live in households which would enjoy a relatively high income even if they did not work. As a result, some of the differences we have identified so far may simply be a reflection of other differences. We do not - as yet - know what the *truly* important characteristics are that distinguish working mothers from non-working mothers.

One way of addressing this question is to use a technique called logistic regression. This is a statistical procedure which attempts to predict an outcome (in this case, whether a mother is working or is a housewife) from a set of characteristics about the mother. The advantage of this technique is that, in looking at any one characteristic, the model takes account of all other significant characteristics at the same time. This allows us to disentangle, for example, the relative importance of educational qualifications and occupational status.

The development of the model is explained in more detail in the appendix to this chapter. The characteristics which emerged as having a significant bearing on whether or not a mother worked were (in order of importance):

- Husband or partner is in work
- Mother has educational qualifications (that is, a CSE or above)
- Household income would be under £20,000 without mother's earnings
- Mother is aged 30 or above

In contrast, the following characteristics did not prove to be significant once the others were taken into account:

- Number of children under 12
- Age of the youngest child
- Socio-economic group of current or last job
- Marital status
- Whether there are also secondary school age children in the household

This does not mean that these latter characteristics do not distinguish working from non-working mothers at all - only that they are *less* important than those that were selected. As explained in the appendix, the size of the group we analysed meant that only the most important characteristics had any chance of being statistically significant.

Our results underline the importance of the social and economic interactions between husband and wife. When it comes to whether or not a mother with children under 12 works, the most important characteristic of all is whether or not her husband or partner is in work. It is also clear that mothers work because their families need the income - the third characteristic selected by our model is whether the household's income would be below £20,000 without the mother's earnings. Being over 30 and having educational qualifications also distinguish working from non-working mothers - even once the characteristics already considered are taken into account.

In contrast, occupational status does not enter our model, probably indicating that the apparent differences between working and non-working mothers largely reflect their educational differences. Our results also suggest that marital status (and thus whether someone is a lone mother or not) does not really matter in its own right, once the difference between mothers who have partners that work and other mothers is taken into account.

We shall return to these analyses later in this chapter. For now they have confirmed that the social and economic characteristics of mothers have a considerable influence on her chances of working. We turn next to the question of how far mothers are *impeded* from working by lack of suitable childcare.

How big a problem is lack of suitable childcare?

No mother with pre-school children can return to work without arranging some form of childcare. Furthermore, unless a mother works only a few hours a day, childcare continues to be an important consideration even when children start nursery or primary school.

Forms of childcare used by working mothers

Many surveys have found that, after mothers themselves, relatives and partners are the most important providers of childcare. However, nursery schools are of growing importance for the under-fives (Martin and Roberts, 1984; Witherspoon and Prior, 1991; Bridgwood and Savage, 1993). Nursery schools are likely to become an even more important form of childcare in the future as the Government moves towards its target of making some form of nursery education available to all parents of four year olds. However, nursery school hours are not very long and do not necessarily enable mothers to take up paid work.

These findings are confirmed by our survey. We asked working mothers with children under 12 how they arrange for their children to be looked after while they are at work. Many working mothers, especially those with school age children, do not go beyond the confines of the family in arranging care for their children while they work. Just over six in ten said that a relative or their partner looked after them. Over a third of mothers whose youngest child was aged between five and eleven only worked while the children were at school.

Nursery schools are not a major source of childcare for working mothers. Less than one in ten working mothers with children under five work while their children are at school. Just over one in eight use a day nursery, little more than half the number who use a child minder. Furthermore, comparing the results with those we obtained when we asked the same question four years ago, there is no evidence that day nurseries have become more popular amongst working mothers. Indeed what is most striking is the overall *stability* in the pattern of use. The exception to this is the marked drop (from 11 per cent to four per cent) in the proportion of mothers who expect their children to look after themselves until they get home.

Childcare used by working mothers*

	All		Age of youngest child (1994)	
	1990	1994	under 5	5 to 12
	%	%	%	%
A relative looks after them** (including husband/partner)	57	62	69	57
Mother works only while children are at school	24	23	7	37
Child minder	14	15	25	7
Children look after themselves until mother gets home	11	4	-	8
A friend or neighbour looks after them	10	13	3	23
Day nursery	7	6	14	-
Mother's help or nanny looks after them at home	4	6	9	3
Mother works from home	4	4	2	6
Work-place nursery	1	2	2	1

*   Respondents were asked to mention *all* the arrangements they used, so the
     percentages add to more than 100.
** In 1990 we asked only about relatives. In 1994, two questions were asked,
     one about relatives and one about husbands/partners, the answers to which
     have been combined in this table. Some of the apparent increase from 1990
     to 1994 may be due to this change in question structure.

Are working women happy with their childcare arrangements?

In fact, the pattern of how working mothers care for their children
corresponds closely to what they would *prefer* to do given a free choice
(Witherspoon and Prior, 1991). Well over half say their first or second
preference would be their relatives or partners looking after their children.
Equally, well over half of mothers whose youngest child is between five
and eleven gave as their first or second preference working only when the
children are at school. Overall, no less than seven in ten working mothers
picked as their first or second choice at least one of the forms of childcare
they themselves used. However, the second most popular choice amongst
mothers with children under five was a workplace nursery. One in three
such mothers chose this as their first or second preference and given that
only two per cent actually use a workplace nursery, this suggests one area
where there is clearly unmet demand.

Given the general similarity between the forms of childcare that working mothers use and what they say they want, it is not surprising that a clear majority express satisfaction with their current childcare arrangements. We asked women who use any form of childcare how convenient their arrangements were, and how satisfied they were with them. No less than 62 per cent described themselves as 'very satisfied' while 64 per cent considered their arrangements 'very convenient'. However, some forms of childcare appear to give greater satisfaction than others. In particular, only four in ten working parents who use child minders think their childcare arrangements are 'very convenient' or 'very satisfactory'. Among those who work from home, who only work while their child is at school or who use a relative, partner or nanny the equivalent proportion is never less than seven in ten.[12] It would appear that even among working parents, childcare begins at home.

Would mothers work more if they could find suitable childcare?

The fact that most mothers who work outside the home are satisfied with their childcare does not necessarily mean that *lack* of suitable childcare does not prevent some mothers from returning to work. It may be that those who do not work are unable to gain access to the kind of childcare they would prefer. Alternatively, those who work part-time might be constrained from working full-time because they are unable to find their preferred form of childcare for a sufficient amount of time.

To tap this possibility we asked mothers what they would do if they had access to the form of childcare which they most preferred. Those who currently worked were asked:

> *If you did have the childcare arrangement of your choice, would you prefer to work more hours than now, work fewer hours than now, or are you happy with the hours you work at present?*

Part-time workers who said that they would 'work more hours' were asked whether or not they would work full-time.

We also asked mothers who did *not* work:

> *If you did have the childcare arrangement of your choice, would you prefer to work part-time, work full-time, or would you choose not to work outside the home?*

Given that many working mothers already use the form of childcare they most prefer, it is not surprising that around two in three say they would not change the number of hours they worked. However, among the remainder, there was evidence of a wish to work more hours. No less than a quarter of mothers who worked part-time said they would increase the number of hours they worked if they had the childcare of their choice,

while just one in fourteen would reduce them. Most importantly, no less than four out of five non-working mothers said that they *would* go out to work. On the other hand, nearly a third of full-time working mothers said that they would work *fewer* hours, doubtless a reflection of the fact that, for some mothers, full-time working is the only economically viable option. But, since full-time working mothers form a relatively small group,[15] these figures suggest that, if mothers had access to their preferred form of childcare, the result would be an overall increase in labour market participation.

How women's labour force participation might be affected by having the childcare arrangement of their choice

	%
Full-time employees:	
Would work more hours	7
Would work same hours	62
Would work fewer hours	31
Part-time employees:	%
Would work full-time	17
Would work more hours but still part-time	9
Would work same hours	67
Would work fewer hours	7
Non-working housewives:	%
Would work full-time	24
Would work part-time	55
Would not work	19

This suggests that the lack of suitable childcare *is* a major constraint upon the ability of some mothers to return to work. These results are consistent with recent claims that even a relatively small subsidy for childcare costs could have a very substantial impact on women's participation in the labour market (Duncan *et al*, 1995). However, a note of caution should be sounded. Most working mothers say they would prefer their children to be looked after by a relative or their husbands. The *supply* of such childcare is not inexhaustible. Indeed, it may have already reached saturation point. If so, and if women will not return to work unless they have their preferred form of childcare, then no amount of childcare subsidy will make a difference to them. In addition, there are many women who say that their first or second choice would be to work during school hours or to take their children to a workplace nursery. The behaviour of these women may depend as much on the *availability* of suitable part-time jobs and accommodating employers as on a childcare subsidy.

What help do working mothers get from employers?

However good the childcare that mothers with young children arrange, the practicability of working is at least in part dependent on the availability of flexible working arrangements. Also important is whether or not her husband or partner has access to such arrangements - and whether or not he is prepared to make use of them to help with childcare. We asked *all* employees - those with children and those without - whether the range of arrangements listed in the table below was available to them at their workplace and, if so, whether or not they used them.

Availability and use of flexible working arrangements[14]

	All employees		Women with child under 12		Men with child under 12	
	% who have available	% who use	% who have available	% who use	% who have available	% who use
Part-time working	48	20	84	57	29	6
Time off to care for sick children	45	16	53	41	49	33
Flexible hours	35	27	46	38	39	32
Paternity leave	33	12	n/a	n/a	36	29
Career breaks	27	5	32	9	n/a	n/a
Job-sharing schemes	24	4	33	8	15	-
Working from home	16	12	16	12	23	18
Term-time contracts	14	6	23	15	8	3
Workplace nursery	8	*	12	2	6	-
School holiday care	5	1	9	3	3	1
Allowance towards cost of childcare	3	*	3	1	2	1

* = less than 0.5%
n/a = not asked

One important point quickly emerges. Working mothers are on average far more likely to work for employers who provide flexible working arrangements. No less than 84 per cent of working mothers have access to part-time working, indicating a strong propensity among mothers to congregate in those occupations where such working is an option. Moreover, no less than a third have access to job-sharing schemes, a practice which is most common among clerical and secretarial workers in the public sector (Watson, 1994). In fact, with the exception of working from home, working mothers were more likely than employees in general to have access to all the facilities listed in the table. Consequently, it would seem that the provision of flexible working arrangements might help employers attract

working mothers back into the workplace. In contrast, working fathers are not particularly likely to work for an employer that provides flexible working arrangements, although they are quite likely to use facilities such as time off to care for sick children and paternity leave if these are available to them.

If flexible working arrangements can help attract mothers into the workplace, is there any evidence that employers have become more flexible? Over the last four years there has been a modest increase in the provision of some of the arrangements we asked about. Access to job-sharing schemes, for instance, has increased from 16 per cent to 24 per cent, while the proportion of employees able to work flexible hours has increased from 30 per cent to 35 per cent. Surprisingly, given the interest in 'teleworking' from home (see, for example, Huws, 1994), there is no sign that working some of the time from home has become more common. Neither is there any sign that it is used by working parents more than by other employees.

Unmet demand for flexible working arrangements

The behaviour of working mothers suggests that the provision of flexible working arrangements can help encourage them back into the labour market. By implication, therefore, widening such provision should increase working mothers' labour market participation still further. But what forms of provision are most likely to be effective?

To answer this question we look at those arrangements for which there is unmet demand. We asked respondents who said a particular arrangement was *not* available to them whether or not they would use it if it were available. Of course, this is a hypothetical question and answers may well overstate the use that would in fact be made of such arrangements. In addition, the introduction of some of these measures (particularly allowances towards the cost of childcare) would in fact be tantamount to a pay increase for parents - something they are hardly likely to turn down if offered 'without strings' (Witherspoon and Prior, 1991). Answers may well have differed if such measures were subject to negotiation or were offered instead of another benefit such as increased pay.

But even so, our data can identify those arrangements for which there is a relatively high level of unmet demand. Perhaps not surprisingly, the largest unmet demand proves to be for arrangements which are at present uncommon. For instance, well over half of working mothers say that they would use school holiday care, term-time contracts and workplace nurseries. These are relatively popular among working fathers as well. In contrast, there is relatively little unmet demand for part-time working, which is, of course, already fairly widely available. These findings are very similar to those we established four years ago (Witherspoon and Prior, 1991).

Unmet demand for flexible working arrangements

	All employees	Women with child under 12	Men with child under 12
% who would use if access were available:			
Part-time working	12	10	13
Time off to care for sick children	26	40	40
Flexible hours	43	42	41
Paternity leave	32	n/a	50
Career breaks	30	39	n/a
Job-sharing schemes	21	33	14
Working from home	33	37	31
Term-time contracts	29	58	48
Workplace nursery	28	52	42
School holiday care	31	62	55
Allowance towards cost of childcare	40	82	69

n/a = not asked

Employers may well have an important role to play in attracting mothers back to work. Our data show that mothers are not particularly keen on childcare arrangements which take their children outside the family. Their interest seems to be in changing the world of work so that they have the flexibility to combine working with meeting their childcare responsibilities. On its own, therefore, a childcare *subsidy* may have less impact on changing women's labour market participation than might at first be thought.

Is working the *right* thing for a mother to do?

Childcare subsidies and flexible working arrangements share one important characteristic. Neither will work unless women *want* a job outside the home. We have seen that four-fifths of mothers who are currently housewives would work if they had access to the childcare of their choice. But this still leaves a substantial minority who apparently do not wish to work under any circumstances. Furthermore, a majority of part-time working mothers apparently do not wish to work full-time - and a substantial minority of full-time working mothers would like to work fewer hours. It would seem that not all mothers wish to work as many hours as they can find childcare for - other things in life are important as well.

This suggests that we need to look at the *attitudes* women have to work. Do some women (and others who are important in their lives) believe that it is *better* for the mothers of young children to stay at home, or at least to

keep any employment to a minimum? In contrast, do women who go out to work have an unusually high commitment to work?

Working mothers' job commitment

We look first at the attitudes towards work of those mothers who do work. Do these women work simply because they need the money? Or have they a strong commitment to having a job for its own sake? We asked those in work three questions highly pertinent to this issue (Curtice, 1993; Hedges, 1994). Firstly, we asked about commitment to their current job:

> *For some people their job is simply something they do in order to earn a living. For others it means much more than that. On balance, is your present job just a means of earning a living, or does it mean much more to you than that?*

We then asked about work commitment in general:

> *If without having to work, you had what you would regard as a reasonable living income, do you think you would still prefer to have a paid job or wouldn't you bother?*

Finally, we asked about their feelings towards their current job:

> *Which of these statements best describes your feelings about your job? In my job:*
>
> > *I only work as hard as I have to*
> >
> > *I work hard, but not so that it interferes with the rest of my life*
> >
> > *I make a point of doing the best that I can, even if it sometimes does interfere with the rest of my life*

Working mothers with children under 12 *do* have an unusually high level of work commitment. As far as their current job is concerned, over seven in ten say that it is *more* than just a 'means of earning a living' - compared with around six in ten of men and women without children of this age. Furthermore, part-time mothers (though intriguingly not full-time ones) also demonstrate a higher than average level of commitment to work in general. Nearly eight in ten say they would 'still prefer to have a paid job' even if they did not need the money, compared with just under seven in ten of all the other groups in the table.

Employees' attitudes to work

	Men with no children under 12	Men with children under 12	Women with no children under 12	Women with children under 12	
				part-time	full-time
Present job...	%	%	%	%	%
... is just a means of earning a living	43	39	37	26	29
... means much more than that	57	61	63	74	71
If didn't have to work to have a reasonable living income...					
... would still prefer to have a paid job	67	69	69	78	67
... wouldn't bother	31	29	29	21	32
Feelings about job:					
Works as hard as has to	11	12	8	8	3
Works hard but not so it interferes with rest of life	38	39	48	57	57
Does best even if it does interfere with life	50	50	45	35	40

These results suggest that working mothers work because they believe in the intrinsic *value* of working. However, the answers to our third question indicate that this group is also more likely to balance their commitment to their work with the demands of the rest of their lives. Nearly six in ten full-time and part-time working mothers say that they 'work hard, but not so that it interferes with the rest of my life' (compared with less than half of women without children), with the result that fewer working mothers say that they allow their job to interfere with the rest of their life. In contrast, fathers with young children are no more likely to try to ensure that their job does not interfere with their life than are men without children.

Should mothers go out to work?

So, compared with others, working mothers do appear to have a strong - albeit balanced - commitment towards work. But how do their attitudes towards work compare with those of women who do not work? Specifically, do working and non-working mothers *disagree* about whether or not mothers should work at all? What influence, if any, do the views

of their partner have? The 1994 *British Social Attitudes* survey contained a large number of questions designed to tap attitudes towards women and work.[15] Some examples of the answers we received to these questions are contained in the next table. There are clearly some sharp disagreements between working and non-working mothers. For example, nearly two-thirds of full-time working mothers strongly agree that 'a working mother can establish just as warm and secure a relationship with her children as a woman who does not work', compared with less than one in ten of those housewives who do not work outside the home at all. Part-time employees took a view somewhere in between these two groups.

Attitudes to women and work, by activity of mother

	Full-time employee	Part-time employee	Housewives with no job
% who strongly agree:			
'A working mother can establish just as warm and secure a relationship with her children as a woman who does not work'	(63)	(34)	(9)
% who strongly disagree:			
'A pre-school child is likely to suffer if his or her mother works'	(40)	(21)	(5)
'All in all family life suffers when the woman has a full-time job'	(52)	(17)	(5)

Since we asked a large number of individual questions on this subject, we were able to construct an index - or scale - to summarise our respondents' attitudes. The assumption behind this is that the answers given to individual questions reflect a more general underlying attitude towards the 'proper' role of women. If this assumption is correct, the scores on the index are likely to be a more *reliable* indicator of this underlying attitude than the answer to any individual question.

We constructed an index based on responses to thirteen questions. Further details of this are given in the appendix to this chapter. Scores on the index range from 1 to 5. Those who score 1 are the 'least traditional' - they will tend to support options in favour of women working. Those who score 5 are the 'most traditional' - they will support options in favour of married women staying at home while their husbands go out to work.

Our index confirms the impression we received from looking at some of the individual questions. Full-time working mothers have less traditional views (1.81) than those who work part-time (2.32), who in turn have less traditional views than those whose main activity is 'looking after the home' (2.60). However, this does not prove that working mothers go out to work and non-working mothers stay at home *because* of the views that they hold. It could equally be the case that they hold the views that they do as a *consequence* of their differing work experience. Working mothers might, for

example, hold certain views as a way of justifying their decision to go out to work.

What about mothers' husbands and partners? Do their views matter? We looked at the attitudes of the *men* in our sample who were married or living as married and had children aged under 12. We found that fathers whose wives worked outside the home have less 'traditional' views about women than do men whose wives look after the home. This is consistent with the claim that the attitude of a woman's husband plays a role in her decision about whether to work outside the home. Of course, this may also reflect a tendency for people to form relationships with those who have similar views to themselves - especially on issues as fundamental as the respective roles of men and women.

Index of attitudes towards women and work - average scores

Women with children under 12		Men with children under 12	
Own activity:	score	Activity of wife/partner:	score
Full-time employee	(1.81)	Wife full-time employee	(2.31)
Part-time employee	(2.32)	Wife part-time employee	(2.32)
Looking after the home	(2.60)	Looking after the home	(2.82)
All	2.33	All	2.47

Our index scores suggest that the differing attitudes of working and non-working mothers are not just a form of self-justification. For instance, housewives' attitudes differ according to whether or not they would be prepared to return to work if they had the childcare of their choice. Those who say they *would* be prepared to work full-time are less 'traditional' (with a score of 2.30) than those who say they would work part-time (2.75) who - in turn - are less 'traditional' than those who say they would not work at all (3.08). Similar differences emerge when they are asked what they will do when their children have reached secondary school age. True, this analysis is based on a small number of respondents, but it is consistent with the claim that mothers' willingness to return to work is influenced by their attitudes towards the role of women in the family and at work. If the attitudes of housewives were merely a reflection of their current position in the labour market, the three groups should have identical views.

The attitudes of mothers towards their role in the family cannot be ignored if we are to understand why some work outside the home and some do not. The decisions mothers make about working are not simply determined by economics or the availability of childcare; they should also be seen in the context of mothers' beliefs about their 'proper' role within the family.

What matters most?

So far we have seen that all three of the possible sets of influences which we outlined at the beginning of this chapter apparently have a role in determining whether or not a mother goes out to work. But which of them is the most important? Is the decision to go out to work mainly determined by a mother's economic and social characteristics? Or does it depend mostly on the availability of suitable childcare and flexible working arrangements? Or is a mother's decision to go out to work primarily a reflection of her views about her role in the family?

One way of examining the relative importance of these factors is to see what housewives themselves say when asked *why* they do not work. We asked housewives to say how important a number of reasons were for their not working at all outside the home. The two most commonly seen as being 'very important' were 'it's better for the children if I am at home to look after them' (70 per cent) and 'I enjoy spending time with my children more than working' (68 per cent). This would seem to suggest that, as far as non-working mothers are concerned, their *attitudes* are the most important determinant of their behaviour.

However, this approach relies upon the views of those who are not working. And, in any event, we cannot assume that respondents are necessarily the best judges of the factors that influence their behaviour. An alternative approach is to determine which of our three sets of influences corresponds best with our respondents' labour market behaviour. In short, we need to explore which set of influences seems best capable of distinguishing between working and non-working mothers. To do this we return to the logistic regression model introduced earlier in this chapter. Previously we used this technique to unravel which economic and social differences between working and non-working mothers were most important. Now we widen our model to include not only social and economic characteristics, but also the influence of childcare restrictions and a woman's attitude towards women and work.

The characteristics which we found to have a significant bearing on whether a mother with children under 12 works outside the home are, in order of importance, as follows:

- Obtaining a score of less than 3 on the index of attitudes to women and work (where 1 is 'least traditional' and 5 is 'most traditional');
- Would work the same, or fewer hours, if access were available to her ideal form of childcare (this can be interpreted as meaning that lack of childcare does not currently impose a constraint on her working behaviour);
- Having a husband or partner who is in work;
- The age of her youngest child being between 5 and 11 (rather than under 5).

These results suggest that what *most* distinguishes working from non-working mothers is their attitude towards women and work. The decision made by a mother as to whether or not to go out to work appears - above all - to be an expression of her social attitudes, rather than an instrumental decision driven by economic considerations. Thereafter, the next most important consideration appears to be access to suitable childcare. (We are assuming that those mothers who say they would *not* work more if they had access to their ideal childcare are presently unconstrained by lack of suitable childcare.)

Our model indicates that social and economic characteristics also distinguish working from non-working mothers - but their influence seems to be less important than the attitudinal and childcare factors already discussed. We found that whether or not a woman has a partner in work matters. This means that, even once childcare constraints and a woman's own views on women and work are taken into account, whether or not her partner works is still important. Unlike our earlier model, the educational qualifications of women are not important - it is likely that these are reflected in the views the mother holds about women and work.

Conclusion

Our analysis has important lessons for those who wish to increase the proportion of mothers who return to work. Although we have some evidence that mothers' decisions about whether or not to work outside the home are influenced by their economic circumstances, it is clear that there are many mothers for whom economic instruments (such as childcare subsidies or changes to the benefits system) would not, on their own, cause them to return to the labour market or work more hours. Rather, whether or not mothers go out to work appears to be a social *choice* which reflects women's values about the role of women in work and the family. No policy-maker can hope to change mothers' behaviour without also addressing this ideological dimension. Furthermore, it must be recognised that, even among those mothers who *do* work, many would prefer childcare to take place within the family or at home and may be reluctant to use any subsidy to purchase childcare outside that context. Consequently, if employers want to attract mothers back into the world of work, they must be prepared to adapt this world to the demands of childcare. Given that - in return - they could recruit and retain a strongly committed workforce, such efforts would seem worthwhile.

Notes

1. A recent report by the Central Statistical Office uses data from the British Household Panel Survey to show that "women who take career breaks tend to suffer a loss in status and, although [their status] increases slightly once they return

       to work, on average it does not catch up with their pre-break level. The occupational attainment of women who do not take career breaks continues to increase at roughly the same rate as they get older." It also uses data from the New Earnings Survey to show the effect that this has on women's earnings: whereas men's earnings peak in the forties, those of women peak earlier (Whitmarsh, 1995: 28, 32).

2.   Unless otherwise specified, in this chapter the terms 'mother' and 'mother with young children' refer to women with at least one child under the age of 12.

3.   Many of these questions were asked as part of the *International Social Survey Programme* module on Women and the Family.

4.   The relative rarity of self-employed women with children aged under 12 means that we are not able to look at their attitudes and circumstances, many of which are likely to be quite different from those of employees. Unless otherwise specified, in this chapter the term 'working woman' refers to *employees* who work at least ten hours a week. Housewives are those who say that their main activity in the previous week has been 'looking after the home'. A proportion of this group does, however, have a 'small' job of less than ten hours a week and, occasionally, housewives will be sub-divided on this basis.

5.   For previous work in this area see Sly, 1994; Harrop and Moss, 1994; Sly, 1993; Bartholomew, Hibbett and Sidaway, 1992; Bridgwood and Savage, 1993; Marsh and McKay, 1993.

6.   Although this chapter focuses on women with children aged below 12, the impact of motherhood on the likelihood of a woman working outside the home obviously does not end when her child reaches 12. Among mothers who have at least one child aged between 12 and 15 (and do not have any children aged below 12), 23 per cent look after the home. By contrast, only 14 per cent of women without any children aged below 16 were similarly engaged.

7.   The tables in this section refer to women of working age only. They show full-time employees, part-time employees (working 10 hours or more per week) and those whose main economic activity is looking after the home (with or without a job of less than 10 hours). Included in the base, but not shown in the table, are a number of other activity groups (for example, the self-employed and unemployed). For this reason, the percentages in the tables do not sum to 100.

8.   Figures in brackets in the tables indicate that the unweighted base is less than 50.

9.   However, we should note that, although there are very few in our sample, mothers from skilled manual backgrounds were among those *most* likely to be working, especially as self-employed.

10. The household income, net of any earnings of the woman herself, has been calculated from two *British Social Attitudes* questions:

> *Which of the letters on this card represents the total income of your household from* **all** *sources* **before tax**?

> *Which of the letters on this card represents your* **own** *gross or total* **earnings**, *before deduction of income tax and national insurance?*

In both cases, the information was collected in bands. In making our calculations, we have used the midpoint of each band. For the top band (which is £41,000 or over) we have assumed an income of £42,500. This use of midpoints inevitably means that there is some loss of precision in the estimate. No account has been taken of the effect on benefits of a change in the woman's earnings. In addition, we should bear in mind that there will be some households where the respondent is neither the main income earner nor the main income earner's spouse or partner, for example, where the respondent is living at home with her parents. In these cases the household income may have less relevance to the respondent in deciding whether or not to work.

11. It has also been argued that working mothers differ from non-working mothers in their ethnic background (Harrop and Moss, 1994: 346). This is not examined here because the *British Social Attitudes* survey does not include sufficient numbers of respondents from the minority ethnic groups.
12. In order to secure an adequate number of respondents using each type of childcare, this analysis combines the views of mothers in 1990 and 1994 together with those of fathers in 1994 (the question was not asked of fathers in 1990). For similar reasons, the self-employed and those looking after the home but working less than ten hours per week are also included. However, respondents using *several* types of childcare are excluded as it is not clear which type they are assessing.
13. Indeed, since only 73 full-time working mothers answered this question (unweighted figure), the results should be interpreted with some caution.
14. This table, and all subsequent tables unless otherwise specified, is based on employees of working age who currently work ten or more hours a week.
15. In contrast to the questions on childcare and work commitment, these questions were asked of only a third of the sample. This means that the table which follows is based on relatively small numbers: 27 full-time working mothers, 45 part-time working mothers and 44 non-working housewives (unweighted figures). With such small numbers, differences between the groups should be treated with caution.

References

Bartholomew, R., Hibbett, A. and Sidaway, J. (1992), 'Lone parents and the labour market: evidence from the Labour Force Survey', *Employment Gazette*, **100**, 559-578.

Bridgwood, A. and Savage, D. (1993), *General Household Survey 1991*, London: HMSO.

Curtice, J. (1993), 'Satisfying work - if you can get it', in Jowell, R., Brook, L. and Dowds, L. (eds.), *International Social Attitudes: the 10th BSA Report*, Aldershot: Dartmouth.

Davies, R. (1992), 'The state of the art in survey analysis', in Westlake, A., Banks, R., Payne, C. and Orchard, T. (eds.), *Survey and Statistical Computing*, Amsterdam: Elsevier Science Publishers.

DeVellis, R. (1991), *Scale Development: Theory and Applications*, Applied Social Research Methods Series **26**, Newbury Park, Ca.: Sage.

Duncan, A., Giles, C. and Webb, S. (1995), *The Impact of Subsidising Childcare*, Research Discussion Series No. **13**, Manchester: Equal Opportunities Commission.

Employment Committee Session 1994-1995 First Report: *Mothers in Employment Volume 1: Report and Proceedings of the Committee*, House of Commons Papers 1994-95, 227-I, London: HMSO.

Foster, K., Jackson, B., Thomas, M., Hunter, P. and Bennet, N. (1995), *General Household Survey 1993*, London: HMSO.

Harrop, A. and Moss, P. (1994), 'Working parents: trends in the 1980s', *Employment Gazette*, **102**, 343-57.

Hedges, B. (1994), 'Work in a changing climate', in Jowell, R., Curtice, J., Brook, L. and Ahrendt, D. with Park, A. (eds.), *British Social Attitudes: the 11th Report*, Aldershot: Dartmouth.

Huws, U. (1994), 'Teleworking in Britain', *Employment Gazette*, **102**, 51-59.

Marsh, A. and McKay, S. (1993), 'Families, work and the use of childcare', *Employment Gazette*, **101**, 361-70.

Martin, J. and Roberts, C. (1984), *Women and Employment: A Lifetime Perspective*, London: HMSO.

Sly, F. (1993), 'Women in the labour market', *Employment Gazette*, **101**, 483-502.

Sly, F. (1994), 'Mothers in the labour market', *Employment Gazette*, **102**, 403-413.

Ward, C., Dale, A. and Joshi, H. (1993), 'Participation in the labour market', in Ferri, E. (ed.), *Life at 33: the fifth follow-up of the National Child Development Study*, London: National Children's Bureau and City University.

Watson, G. (1994), 'The flexible workforce and patterns of working hours in UK', *Employment Gazette*, **102**, 239-47.

Whitmarsh, A. (1995), *Social Focus on Women*, Central Statistical Office, London: HMSO.

Witherspoon, S. and Prior, G. (1991), 'Working mothers: free to choose?', in Jowell, R., Brook, L. and Taylor, B. (eds.), *British Social Attitudes: the 8th Report*, Aldershot: Dartmouth.

Acknowledgements

SCPR is grateful to the Employment Department whose financial support for the survey series since 1984 has enabled us to continue to ask questions on labour market and workplace issues, including those on childcare arrangements that are reported here.

SCPR is also grateful to the ESRC for its financial support (via grant M303 253 001) for the Centre for Research into Elections and Social Trends (CREST) which has enabled us to field the *International Social Survey Programme* module on Women and the Family in 1994, and the further grant under the ESRC's Population and Household Change Programme (L315 253 024) for analysis of the *ISSP* data.

Appendix

Index of Attitudes to Women and Work

The 1994 *British Social Attitudes* self-completion Version C contained 24 questions that might be considered directly relevant to attitudes about women and work and which were in the format of attitude statements to which the respondent was invited to 'strongly agree', 'agree', 'neither agree nor disagree', 'disagree', or 'strongly disagree' (with an additional 'can't choose' option) (see Questions C2.01a-g, C2.02a-d, C2.14a-b, C2.24a-b, C2.30a-g, C2.34a-b).

The questions were recoded so that 5 equals the most traditional view and 1 the least traditional view for all items. Answers of 'don't know' or 'can't choose' were recoded as 'neither agree nor disagree'. Cases with missing data were excluded from the analysis.

An exploratory factor analysis was made of the 24 items which showed that one factor was heavily dominant. Items loading by less than 0.5 on the main factor were excluded from the scale. This left 13 items, as listed below. These have a Cronbach's alpha of 0.87, a measure of the reliability (internal consistency) of the scale, which can be regarded as very good for an attitude scale of this sort (DeVellis, 1991: 85). The index score was calculated by averaging the scores for each respondent on each of the thirteen items, giving a maximum value of 5 (most traditional) and a minimum value of 1 (least traditional). The questions included were:

A working mother can establish just as warm and secure a relationship with her children as a mother who does not work

A pre-school child is likely to suffer if his or her mother works

All in all, family life suffers when the woman has a full-time job

A job is all right, but what most women want is a home and children

A man's job is to earn money, a woman's job is to look after the home and family

It is not good if the man stays at home and cares for the children and the woman goes out to work

*Mothers of young children should **not** expect employers to make special arrangements to help them combine jobs and childcare*

The government should provide money for childcare, so that mothers of young children can work if they want to

Women shouldn't try to combine a career and children

In times of high unemployment, married women should stay at home

If a woman takes several years off to look after her children, it's only fair that her career should suffer

Married women have a right to work if they want to, whatever their family situation

Unmarried mothers who find it hard to cope have only themselves to blame

Unfortunately, most of these questions were asked only on Version C of the questionnaire which was administered to just a third of the sample. Further, they were asked on the self-completion questionnaire which has a somewhat lower response rate than the full questionnaire (for further details see Appendix 1 at the end of this book). As a result responses are available for only 946 cases, of which mothers with children are only a relatively small group. Thus, as indicated in the text, some of the analyses based on these questions have to be regarded with caution.

Logistic regression analysis

Logistic regression was carried out on respondents with the following characteristics:

- Women with children under the age of 12.
- Women who answered Version C of the questionnaire (where the attitude questions appeared). Model (i) *could* have been run on the full sample but was restricted to Version C respondents for comparability of significance levels.
- Women whose main economic activity was either working as an employee or 'looking after the home'. The self-employed may have rather different characteristics than employees but, as noted in the chapter, comprise too small a group to be analysed separately. Those neither in work nor housewives were not asked the questions about whether they would work more hours with ideal childcare.

This meant that the sample for the logistic regression was only 126 cases. A further 10 cases were lost in Model (i) and 25 cases in Model (ii) through missing data.

The dependent variable

WORKING2:   1 = woman has any paid job (whether of ten hours or more per week or less than ten hours a week); 0 = woman has no job at all.

The independent variables

Age of woman

AGE1   1 = under 30; 0 = 30+
AGE2   1 = under 40; 0 = 40+

Number of children under 12

NUMCH1   1 = one child under 12; 0 = more than one child under 12
NUMCH2   1 = one or two children under 12; 0 = three or more children under 12

Age of youngest child

AGECH   1 = youngest child under 5; 0 = youngest child 5 - 11

Child of secondary school age

CHSECON   1 = child aged 12-15; 0 = no child aged 12 - 15

Highest educational qualification

QUAL1   1 = degree; 0 = below degree
QUAL2   1 = A level (or equivalent) or above; 0 = below A level
QUAL3   1 = O level (or equivalent) or above; 0 = below O level
QUAL4   1 = any qualifications i.e. CSE (or equivalent) or above; 0 = no qualifications

Current/last job

PROFMAN   1 = professional/manager; 0 = below professional manager/never had a job
NONMAN   1 = non-manual; 0 = manual/never had a job

Approximate household income net of woman's own earnings

NETINC1   1 = <£10,000; 0 = £10,000+
NETINC2   1 = <£20,000; 0 = £20,000+

Marital status

MARLAM   1 = married or living as married; 0 = separated/divorced, widowed, single

Partner's current economic activity

SWORK   1 = partner in paid work; 0 = partner not in paid work/no partner

Attitudes to women and work (Model (ii) only)

SCALE1   1 = score below 2; 0 = score 2 or above
SCALE2   1 = score below 2.5; 0 = score 2.5 or above
SCALE3   1 = score below 3; 0 = score 3 or above
SCALE4   1 = score below 3.5; 0 = score 3.5 or above

Childcare as a barrier to working (Model (ii) only)

WORKMORE   1 = would work more hours than now (or any hours if not currently working) with ideal childcare; 0 = would work same or fewer hours than now or would not work even with ideal childcare

The models

The variables listed below are those selected as significant in predicting the dependent variables. They are shown in the order of selection, with the subsequent chi square (-2 log likelihood), degrees of freedom, change in chi square and the final parameter estimate.

Model (i) - Demographic and economic factors only

	chi square	d.f.	change in chi square	final B coefficient
Null model	141.439	114	-	-2.9180
1. SWORK	128.521	113	12.918	2.2815
2. QUAL4	121.603	112	6.918	1.8998
3. NETINC2	117.071	111	4.533	1.6304
4. AGE1	112.817	110	4.253	-1.1688

(A negative beta denotes an inverse correlation with the dependent variable.)

Model (ii) - Demographic and economic factors plus childcare constraint and attitudes towards women and employment

	chi square	d.f.	change in chi square	final B coefficient
Null model	117.443	100	-	-0.4887
1. WORKMORE	84.917	99	32.526	-3.6033
2. SCALE3	67.703	98	17.214	3.8411
3. AGECH	63.282	97	4.422	-1.4855
4. SWORK	59.248	96	4.034	1.5152

It is interesting that the age of the mother enters Model (i) but that it is the age of the youngest child which enters Model (ii). As noted in the chapter, these aspects are rather closely related and probably reflect two sides of the same coin. The absence of marital status in either model is probably a result of this dimension already being partially taken into account by SWORK (whether the mother has a husband/partner who is in work).

5 Faith in local democracy

Ken Young and Nirmala Rao *

The future of local government in Britain has never looked more uncertain. Concerned with keeping a tight rein on public spending, over the last twenty years central government has brought local councils under its growing control. Yet local government is increasingly being run by central government's political opponents. In the mid-1980s the Conservatives actually abolished some of the most vociferous opponents of their policies - the Greater London Council and the metropolitan county councils. But local government's most traumatic experience has been the replacement of its traditional form of revenue, the rates, by the ill-fated community charge or poll tax - whose failure necessitated the introduction of another new tax, the council tax, within a few short years.

The decision by the Major government to abolish the poll tax in 1991 inaugurated yet another review of the structure and role of local government. A new Local Government Commission was established which placed the structure of local government throughout non-metropolitan England into the melting pot. In Scotland and Wales, the local government system was reorganised directly - without any resort to a commission. Meanwhile, a long-running - and ultimately fruitless - review of the internal management of local government was undertaken, a review which raised

* Ken Young is Professor of Politics and Vice-Principal at Queen Mary and Westfield College, University of London. Nirmala Rao is Lecturer in the Department of Social Policy and Politics at Goldsmiths' College, University of London.

fundamental questions about the ways in which local councils run their affairs.

A nineteenth-century institution which palpably failed to meet the expectations that democratic theory laid upon it, local government often appears to have lost its rationale and sense of direction. A renaissance is regularly predicted; so too is terminal decline. Government action will obviously play a crucial role in determining whether either prediction proves correct, but public attitudes matter as well. Local government will survive the current storm only if there is sufficient public faith in the principles and practice of local democracy. Our aim here is to establish whether or not that faith exists.

Tensions in local government

Underlying the current political vacillations surrounding local government are fundamental questions about its role. Is local government designed to represent the interests - and implement the choices - of local communities? Or is it there simply to deliver national services to the local population *on behalf of* the central government? The answer - in part at least - depends on the views of the public. If we are to argue that local government should be *more* than a local provider of services, then we should be able to establish that the public actually favours local determination of local issues. It should both want local matters to be settled locally - and have confidence in the ability of local councillors to effect and represent their wishes.

This begs the question of how local councillors are to know what their local communities want. One answer, at least, is that they have to secure election. But are local elections seen as meaningful, and voting in them a worthwhile activity? Or do popular expectations of the electoral process fall short of the democratic role accorded to them? A key issue here is the domination of local government elections by national party politics and whether this threatens or enhances the effectiveness of local elections.

Questions about the purpose of local government inevitably raise questions about local councillors. Should a councillor primarily act as an *advocate* for the electors in his or her ward, ensuring that the local bureaucracy is made aware of their problems and difficulties? Or should councillors primarily regard themselves as *managers* of local services, trying to achieve the best deal for their local authority as a whole? A further issue concerns the necessary balance to be struck between a councillor's own personal views, those of his or her party and those of the people he or she represents in the ward or division.

The expectations that we have of councillors have implications for the kind of *person* we think might make a good councillor. For instance, do councillors need to be well-acquainted with the area they represent or does it matter more that they have certain educational or workplace experiences? How far does it matter whether or not local councillors are socially representative of those they represent? There is also the fundamental

question of why so few *aspire* to the office of councillor. Are some discouraged from standing because of the loss of local power to central government - or by the pervasive influence of political parties?

In short, it has never been more important to know what the public expects of local government and how well it thinks it is performing. For some years the *British Social Attitudes* survey has included some questions on local government. In our latest survey, however, we asked a series of questions which provide us with the most wide-ranging exploration of this subject since the survey undertaken for the Widdicombe Committee on the Conduct of Local Government Business in 1985. By comparing our results with those of the Widdicombe survey - and with a similar survey undertaken for the Maud Committee on the Management of Local Government in 1965 - we can establish not only how much confidence the public has in local government today, but whether this has risen or fallen in the wake of the many changes of the last thirty years.

In considering our data we must be aware that - by definition - local government inevitably operates in a wide variety of environments. Effecting local choices or delivering services is a rather different task in Dagenham than in Dyfed. In urban areas councils typically cover a larger population, and their councillors represent more voters, than their counterparts in rural areas. In particular, the importance and prominence of organised party politics vary considerably. The party political label often provides the urban voter with the only practicable means of judging the likely stance of the person who solicits his or her vote, while we can expect personal knowledge to play a greater role in the countryside (Rao, 1994a).

This means that we need to be alert to the possibility that evaluations and expectations of local government differ from one part of the country to another. Equally, of course, matters of local government, like other social and political issues, are capable of evoking very different responses from those in different social positions, for they touch upon underlying values and experiences - of individualism and collectivism, and of participation and quiescence. So we will be looking for signs of social divisions about local government as well.

Supporting local government

The standing of local councils

Perhaps the simplest question is to ask how well the public thinks local government is being administered. We asked our respondents how well they thought a number of British institutions - including local government - were being run. Just four in ten thought local government to be 'very well' or 'well' run. Only the National Health Service got a worse evaluation. On the other hand, things have been worse. Only three in ten thought that local government was well run when we previously asked the question

in 1987. Indeed its current rating is higher than at any time since we first used this question in 1983 (for further details see the chapter in this volume by Curtice and Jowell).

How well-run are Britain's institutions?

% saying 'very well' or 'well' run:

Universities	73
Police	67
Banks	63
BBC	62
Manufacturing industry	59
State schools	51
Trade unions	48
Civil service	48
Press	47
Local government	39
NHS	33

Of course this begs the question of what role the public *expects* local government to perform in the first place. And we do not know whether the public blames local government itself for its inadequacies or whether it believes that responsibility for the situation lies with central government. Interestingly, however, those who appear to have the strongest ties to their locality, that is those who both live and work locally, are somewhat *more* likely to think that local government is well run (44 per cent saying so) than those who live locally but work elsewhere (35 per cent).

What, however, of local government efficiency when it comes to the delivery of specific local services? In the current political climate, this issue might be considered to be a more important and sensitive indicator of public confidence. A key debate in recent years has concerned whether local government itself should deliver local services, as it traditionally has done, or whether it should contract out such delivery to private companies. Since the extension of compulsory competitive tendering under the 1988 Local Government Act, local government has increasingly been required to adopt the latter approach. To tap attitudes towards this debate we asked our respondents whether they agreed or disagreed with two propositions. The first was "private companies can always run things more efficiently than local councils". No less than 45 per cent disagreed with this proposition while only 24 per cent agreed. The second, more specific, proposition was "private companies cannot be trusted to run important public services like rubbish collection and street cleaning". Despite the fact that private companies are already widely responsible for these services, no less than 30 per cent agreed with this statement, while only 44 per cent disagreed.   Certainly, doubt about the current efficiency of local

government does not necessarily translate into enthusiasm for the alternatives.

The central control of local government

What of the central question about the role of local government that we identified at the beginning of this chapter? Does the public want its local government to be *truly* local or to be simply the local provider of national services? For a century or more, there has been a powerful, if somewhat diffuse, consensus that centralisation is antithetical to local democracy. This consensus rested its case on three basic propositions concerning local democracy: that it is associated with more responsive and efficient standards of local service provision than central government could manage to achieve; that it promotes a desirable division of power; and that, as it is closer to 'the people', it is able to express the democratic process more fully. But the vitality of local democracy is a casualty of increasing central government control - and, without local democracy, there remains little to justify local government.

Accordingly, the demonstrable increases in central control of local authorities over the past thirty years have raised concerns about the viability of local democracy and how best it might be sustained. Since the mid-1960s, government-appointed committees have criticised central government control and advocated greater freedom of action for local authorities. The Maud Committee in 1967 argued that too close a control of local authorities by central government would fatally lower their status and responsibility. It pointed to the steady decline in the powers of local authorities and warned that if these trends were not reversed, "people of the calibre required for effective local democracy" will not offer themselves for election. The Widdicombe Committee on the Conduct of Local Authority Business in 1986 concurred.

We tapped public attitudes towards the proper relationship between local and central government by asking:

> Do you think that **local councils** ought to be controlled by **central government** more, less or about the same amount as now?

Although opinion is divided, more than twice as many favour *less* central control than would like to see it increased. Furthermore, attitudes have changed little since we first asked the question in 1983 - the signs of a slight shift towards favouring more central control, evident when we last asked the question in 1990, have been reversed.

Trends in attitudes towards central control

Local councils should be controlled by central government	1983	1984	1985	1986	1987	1989	1990	1994
	%	%	%	%	%	%	%	%
More	13	14	14	15	19	16	20	16
About the same	45	42	46	36	34	37	34	40
Less	34	36	33	37	37	38	35	39

These results seem to endorse the principle of local democracy. However, central government now exercises *greater* control over local government than it did in 1983. If the public's view about the proper relationship between local and central government was unchanged, we would expect there to have been a shift in favour of *less* control in the answers to our question. This has not been the case. If support for local democracy is eroded in tandem with the power of local government - as it appears to have been - then its public foundations are in fact weak.

Furthermore, attitudes towards the relationship between central and local government are not part of a constitutional consensus but are coloured by partisan loyalties. Almost half of Conservative identifiers are content with the *status quo*, while almost a quarter would like to see central control increased. In contrast, nearly half of Labour and Liberal Democrat identifiers favour a reduction of central control - just over one in ten would like central control increased. Further, the partisan divide has widened since the 1980s. Conservatives have become more in favour of central control while Labour supporters have become increasingly hostile.

Attitudes to central control by party identification

Local councils should be controlled by central government	Conservative	Labour	Liberal Democrat
	%	%	%
More	23	12	11
About the same	46	36	39
Less	28	48	46

We also asked our respondents about one very important and tangible issue - local taxation. Since 1979, the Conservative government has gradually reduced local authorities' freedom to determine levels of local taxation. Taxation levels for local businesses are now set by central government - which may also set a limit (or 'cap') on the level of local taxation each authority can levy on its residents. We asked everyone:

> Do you think the **level of the council tax** should be up to the local council to decide, or should central government have the final say?

In earlier years we had asked an identical question about the community charge - and, before that, about the rates. On this issue there seems to be little ambiguity - as many as two-thirds of our respondents favour local determination. However, support is not as strong as it was throughout most of the 1980s. Support for local determination plummeted at the height of the rows about the poll tax in 1990 and has, as yet, not recovered fully to its former level.[1]

Who should decide local taxation?

	1984	1985	1986	1987	1989	1990	1994
	%	%	%	%	%	%	%
Local councils	74	72	71	68	71	56	66
Central government	19	20	19	24	21	35	29
Don't know	7	8	9	8	9	9	5

On this issue there is a noticeable difference in the attitudes of party identifiers. Scarcely more than half of the Conservatives favour local decisions on local finance, compared with three-quarters of Labour supporters. Moreover, Conservatives have moved more rapidly in favour of central determination over the past ten years than have Labour or Liberal Democrat identifiers.

Who should decide local taxation, by party identification

	Conservative	Labour	Liberal Democrat
	%	%	%
Local councils	55	74	69
Central government	42	21	28
Don't know	3	5	4

Our evidence should cause some concern among proponents of local democracy. While there is still greater support for local choice rather than central control, it is by no means clear that such support is as strong as it was a decade ago. In particular, it still seems to be suffering somewhat from the fall-out from the poll tax. Further, both of our indicators suggest that the role of local government has increasingly become a source of partisan contention. One possibility is that because the Conservatives have lost so much ground in local elections, particularly since 1993, they have decreasing interest in defending local government (Young, 1994). It may also be the case that Lady Thatcher's attempts after 1987 to bring about a fundamental shift in attitudes to local government actually had some effect, at least where her own followers were concerned.

The uncaring councillor?

So far we have looked at public attitudes towards local government as an *institution*. But what do people think of their councillors? How effective do they think they are at representing local views? We touched upon one aspect of this issue with two questions - the first dealing with how 'remote' councillors are seen to be, and the second with whether or not councillors are seen as 'caring'. Nearly half agreed that "generally speaking, those we elect as councillors lose touch with people pretty quickly". More than a third agreed that "councillors don't care much what people like me think".

Attitudes towards councillors

		Agree/ agree strongly	Neither agree nor disagree	Disagree/ disagree strongly
Councillors...				
... lose touch with people pretty quickly	%	47	28	23
... don't care much what people like me think	%	36	28	34

It would seem then that local councillors are not held in very high regard. However, as Curtice and Jowell report more extensively in their chapter in this volume, *more* people think that MPs are out of touch. As politicians go, local councillors are held in relatively high regard.

We should also bear in mind that people's answers to these questions are probably influenced by *wider* feelings about the political system than just their views as to the role of councillors. In fact, the two questions considered above are similar to ones that have been asked in previous studies about national politics (see especially Marsh, 1977). There they have both been found to tap people's feelings of *efficacy* about the political system - that is, whether or not they think the system would respond to their demands if they wanted to change something. In this context, feelings of efficacy have proved to be strongly related to a variety of social and economic characteristics. In particular, those with more educational qualifications are more likely to have a strong sense of efficacy than those who are less well educated.

Our questions about councillors demonstrate a similar pattern. There is a strong relationship between the answers given to the two questions. Those who think that councillors "lose touch with people pretty quickly" are also quite likely to think that councillors "don't care much what people like me think". The two questions appear to be tapping the same underlying attitude. Furthermore, the same characteristics which matter when looking at political efficacy in general also matter here. For instance, those with a degree are much more likely to express confidence in their councillors, as indeed are those who express a strong interest in politics.

Thus it seems likely that, in answering our questions, people were only partly influenced by what they think about councillors - they also had in mind their views about the political system in general.

Education and local political efficacy

	Highest educational qualification	
% who agree that:	Degree	None
Generally speaking, those we elect as councillors lose touch with people pretty quickly	23	50
Councillors don't care much what people like me think	15	48

Political interest and local political efficacy

	Great deal/ quite a lot of interest	Some interest	Not very much/no interest
% who agree that:			
Generally speaking, those we elect as councillors lose touch with people pretty quickly	39	49	56
Councillors don't care much what people like me think	29	35	41

Even so, we do have some evidence which suggests that respondents' answers to these questions were also influenced by their local circumstances. Those living in urban areas are somewhat more likely to believe that councillors "don't care much what people like me think" than those living in rural areas. And those who work in the same local authority area as they live were also more likely to give a more favourable response to both questions.

Elections and party politics

As we argued at the beginning of this chapter, if local democracy is to be effective then local elections have to be an effective means of expressing and transmitting local choices. A prerequisite of this is that people actually *participate* in such elections. Indeed, the level of turnout in local elections is generally regarded as a key indicator of the health of local government. By international standards the typical level of turnout in British local elections is - at 40 per cent - on the low side. In France and Germany, for instance, it commonly reaches 70 per cent. Further, as previous surveys have also discovered, our survey demonstrates that those who do vote are not necessarily a wholly representative cross-section of the local population. In particular, older voters and those who have lived longer in the locality

are more likely to vote than younger voters and those who have been more mobile (Miller, 1988).

However, if people believe they cannot achieve very much by voting, even a high level of turnout tells us little about the health of local democracy. Voters are unlikely to support local democracy unless they believe that elections *can* influence local affairs and that they have a real and comprehensible choice between alternative candidates or parties. On these criteria, local elections initially appear to perform quite well. Over half believe that local elections *do* decide what happens in their area; over half disagree that there is "no point in voting in local elections", and nearly half disagree that local elections are too 'complicated'.

The efficacy of local elections

		Agree strongly/ agree	Neither agree nor disagree	Disagree/ disagree strongly
The way people decide to vote in local elections is the main thing that decides how things are run in this area	%	54	26	17
Local elections are sometimes so complicated that I really don't know who to vote for	%	30	20	48
There is no point in voting in local elections because in the end it makes no difference who gets in	%	26	18	54

However, the picture is not so rosy as it first seems. The first two of these three items were asked in the Maud Committee survey of 1965, and were also reproduced in Widdicombe's survey in 1985 (Horton, 1967; Young, 1986a). And if we compare our results with the ones obtained by those surveys we find that, although local elections are not regarded as any more incomprehensible than they were, there has been a substantial decline in the proportion who that think they decide how things are run. Thirty years ago over three-quarters believed that local elections decided things, compared with the 54 per cent who do so now. How far the decline reflects the growing central control of local government, is impossible to say.[2]

Erratum
On page 101, in the second and third tables, replace "disagree" with "agree".

Trends in attitudes towards local elections: 1965-1994

% who agree that ...	1965	1985	1994
... the way that people vote in local elections is the main thing that decides how things are run in this area	77	60	54
... local council elections are sometimes so complicated that I really don't know who to vote for	29	34	30

Source: 1965: Maud Committee Survey; 1985: Widdicombe Committee Survey

Further, belief in the efficacy of local elections is much stronger among some sections of the population than others. First, reflecting their lower propensity to vote in local elections, younger people are less likely to have confidence in the efficacy of local elections than are older people. So far as the *comprehensibility* of local elections is concerned, only the very youngest age group, those under 25, demonstrate a relative lack of efficacy. But when it comes to whether or not elections *decide* things in their area, confidence increases gradually with age.

Age and the efficacy of local elections

	Age group			
% who agree that ...	18-24	25-44	45-64	65+
... local elections decide how things are run	41	48	63	69
% who disagree that...				
... local elections are sometimes so complicated I don't know who to vote for	42	29	27	29

When it comes to education there is a striking contrast. Those with a degree are less likely to feel that elections are complicated than are those with no qualifications. But at the same time they are also more sceptical that local elections are the main factor that decides things in their area.

Education and the efficacy of local elections

	Highest educational qualification	
% who agree that ...	Degree	None
... local elections decide how things are run	42	65
% who disagree that		
... local elections are sometimes so complicated I don't know who to vote for	12	35

There is also some evidence that people living in urban areas are less likely than average to have confidence in the efficacy of local elections. As many as 55 per cent of those living in the most urban areas agreed with the statement "there is no point in voting in local elections because in the end it makes no difference who gets in" - compared with only 45 per cent of those living in the most rural areas.

These findings bring us to the issue of party political involvement in local government. It is in urban areas, of course, that party politics is most prevalent in local elections. We clearly need to take a closer look at its role.

People and party

The tension between locality and party has dogged local government throughout the post-war world, and arguably since its inception (Young, 1986b). Since local government re-organisation in 1974, the spread of party politics has intensified to the point at which it has become an inescapable feature of public life in all but the most rural parts of Britain (Young and Davies, 1990). What are the consequences of this process of 'politicisation' for the health of local democracy?

Previous inquiries into local government have certainly suggested there are drawbacks. Most commonly these have been couched in terms of the deterrent effects of party politics on people who might otherwise be willing to serve as councillors.[3] The Committee on the Management of Local Government observed, on the basis of survey evidence, that "party politics do deter some people from standing for election" (Maud, 1967a: 20). It has been argued that "a number of good men [sic] are permanently kept out of local administration" by the presence of the party (Clements, 1969; Hennock, 1973). For the most part the local studies on which these judgements have been based have generally focused on the local business class. But the Maud Committee also concluded that "professional men, in particular, are deterred from offering themselves for service when it means seeking the support of a political party". Former councillors, in particular, felt that the work of the local authorities could be done better without the influence of party politics (Maud, 1967: 109-110).

A second important stream of criticism of the role of party politics in local government concerns its potential for eradicating the very diversity that local government exists to sustain. Potentially, the rise of partisan politics is as centralising an influence on local government as the controlling impulses of central government. Political parties undertake national campaigns at local election time, thereby encouraging their candidates in different areas to adopt certain common, albeit broad, policy stances. Further, the fate of local councillors appears to depend more upon what is happening nationally than what they may have achieved locally, for most voters vote in local elections on the basis of judgements about national rather than local politics (Miller, 1986). Local elections may then take the

form of a referendum on the current performance of central government rather than be a mechanism for expressing local choice.

The arguments in favour of a role for party politics are three-fold. First, it is argued that political parties enable the electorate to pass a realistic judgement on the performance of their representatives. Secondly, the accountability of government to the electorate is sharpened by offering them clear policy choices. Finally, it is argued that in an age of large-scale and relatively remote government, political parties make elections comprehensible. One of the consequences of local government reform in 1974 was to increase the number of electors each councillor represents - thereby making it difficult to maintain a direct relationship between elector and candidate; political parties, by providing widely understood cues about what candidates stand for, help to restore that link (Sartori, 1968; Rao, 1994a).

The trend towards greater politicisation has occurred *despite* the fact that previous surveys have persistently provided evidence of popular distaste for party politics in local government. Survey research for the Maud Committee in 1965 showed the dislike of party politics to be pre-eminent among the criticisms of the democratic process in local government (Horton, 1967). The survey undertaken for the Widdicombe Committee in 1985 asked more directly whether respondents thought the party system or the non-party system the better way of running councils. It found that over half thought the non-party system was best, while only a third opted for the party system.

We asked our respondents the same question that was asked on the Widdicombe survey:

> *In most areas all councillors come from one of the political parties and councils are organised on party lines. There are some areas where most councillors are independent and the council is **not** organised on party lines. Which do you personally think is the better system ... the party system, or the non-party system?*

The majority in favour of the non-party system appears to have disappeared. Almost exactly the same number of people said that they preferred the party system as the non-party system.

**Trends in attitudes towards party politics
in local government**

	1985	1994
Which do you personally think is the better system?	%	%
The party system	34	34
The non-party system	52	33
Don't know/can't choose	14	33

Source: 1985: Widdicombe Committee Survey

There is however one other marked difference between the pattern of responses we received and those given to the Widdicombe survey. No less than a third of our respondents said that they could not choose which system was best while, in the 1985 Widdicombe survey, only 14 per cent said they did not know which was best. This almost undoubtedly reflects the fact that our question appeared on a self-completion questionnaire with 'can't choose' as a visible option. In contrast, the Widdicombe survey asked the question face-to-face so respondents would have to *volunteer* the fact that they did not know which was best. Even so, the proportion of our respondents who said they could not choose was unusually high even for a question in which a 'can't choose' option was offered.

Still, in so far as the public have noticed, it would seem that the growing politicisation of local government has brought in its wake a growing public acceptance of the role of party politics in local government. Certainly it is true that where party politics is *most* prevalent - that is, in urban areas - there is more support for the party system than there is in rural areas, where the relatively low ratio of people to councillors makes it easier to maintain a more personal, face-to-face style (Rao, 1994a).

Further, the views of party identifiers correspond with the traditional stances of their parties on this issue: Labour has been most closely associated with politicisation; Conservatives have accepted it with reluctance, while Liberals have taken the most independent line. We find that only a quarter of Liberal Democrats prefer the party system, just over a third of Conservatives, but over four in ten Labour identifiers. Meanwhile it is also worth noting that distaste for party politics in local government rises with education, with close to half of graduates preferring the non-party system.

Variations in attitudes towards party politics in local government

| | % preferring | | |
	Party system	Non-party system	Can't choose
Urban/rural[4]			
Very urban	38	25	36
Fairly urban	38	30	32
Fairly rural	30	36	33
Very rural	30	40	30
Party identification			
Conservative	35	39	25
Labour	43	26	31
Liberal Democrat	25	43	32
Highest educational qualification			
Degree	31	48	20
No qualification	35	26	38

Despite the apparent decline in opposition to party politics in local government, the degree to which it has spread still seems rather paradoxical given that there certainly is not any strong enthusiasm for it. The reason, however, is clear. Despite whatever distaste some voters may express for party politics, when asked how they *vote* in local elections, over half say that they vote for a party - irrespective of the candidate standing - while only six per cent say that they vote for a candidate irrespective of their party.

How people vote in local elections

	%
I vote for a party, regardless of candidate	52
I vote for a party, only if I approve of the candidate	28
I vote for a candidate, regardless of his or her party	6
I do not generally vote at all	14

But voters are not entirely inconsistent in their behaviour. Thus Labour identifiers who, as we saw, were most in favour of the party system are also most likely to say they vote for 'a party regardless of candidate', whereas Liberal Democrat identifiers are by far and away the least likely to do so. This is in line with the findings of previous research which suggest that Liberal Democrat candidates and their predecessors are rather more likely to secure support on the basis of their *local* appeal than are Labour or Conservative candidates (Curtice, Payne and Waller, 1983). Equally,

graduates who were also more likely to express a distaste for party politics are less likely to vote for 'a party regardless of candidate'.

Variations in local voting behaviour

	% who say they vote for the ...			
	Party regardless	Party & candidate	Candidate regardless	Don't vote
Party identification				
Conservative	57	26	6	9
Labour	62	25	4	8
Liberal Democrat	42	42	6	10
Highest educational qualification				
Degree	43	40	6	10
No qualification	55	24	5	15

It seems that, so far as voters are concerned, the spread of party politics may not seem to be as harmful to the health of local democracy as previous survey evidence has led us to believe. However, voters are not unaware of the potential centralising nature of party politics. We found that those who were opposed to party politics were also more likely to want less control of local government by central government. It is possible that the spread of party politics may have been partly responsible for the drop in the number who think that what happens in local elections decides what happens locally. But, equally, it is just as possible that the spread of party politics has been crucial to the maintenance of the comprehensibility of local elections in the face of the growth of the number of voters which the average councillor represents.

The role of the councillor

As we indicated at the beginning of this chapter, the debate about the future of local government has inevitably raised questions about the *role* we should expect councillors to perform. Indeed, the reforms of local government introduced by Lady Thatcher's governments were so extensive as to force a fundamental reconsideration of the role of the councillor (Audit Commission, 1988). These changes brought about a shift from a direct involvement in decisions on provision to the more strategic 'arms-length' role implied by the concept of local authorities as enabling bodies which purchase services from the private sector rather than providing them directly (Ridley, 1988). The result was to sharpen the distinction between the representative and decision-making roles of the councillor.

The Major government's review of local government, launched in 1991, set out tentative proposals for a resolution of this tension in a consultation document. This outlined several options, among which was a 'cabinet' system based on a small group of councillors with the authority to run the council (Department of the Environment, 1991). The arguments for this proposal - which themselves harked back to the Maud inquiry of the mid-1960s - pointed to the sharp distinction between the representative and management roles of councillors (Rao, 1994b).

The government clearly favoured the concentration of management decisions in a handful of leading councillors. However, few councillors are willing to accept so stark a division of responsibility, or to trade one role for the other. Although councillors spend the majority of their time on management activities, most give first preference and greatest priority to dealing with individual problems and helping their constituents - therein, they say, lies much of the satisfaction of being a councillor (Maud, 1967b; Rao, 1994a; Young and Rao, 1994).

But what does the public expect? Surprisingly, nobody has asked them before, but in our survey we sought to establish what importance people think councillors *ought* to give to their different roles. We asked:

> *Which of the following do you think is the more important for a councillor to do: to take up problems and complaints people have about the council's services; or to help manage the council's services so that they are run as well as possible?*

The tension in councillors' minds is reflected in a lack of consensus amongst the public. Exactly half think managing services should be the more important activity - equally, as many as two-fifths favour the representative role of the councillor. Not surprisingly, local authority tenants - who provide much of the personal casework undertaken by councillors - are rather more likely than average to think councillors should concentrate on taking up problems. Those with at least *some* experience of higher education are most likely to favour the management role. But even amongst these groups there is anything but a consensus.

The proper role of councillors

	% saying it is more important for councillors to...	
	...take up problems	...manage services
Highest educational qualification		
Degree or other higher educational qualification	32	56
'O' level	38	52
CSE	46	44
Housing tenure		
Owner occupier	37	52
Local authority tenant	46	42
Other renting	43	43

There are marked parallels between how people believe councillors ought to spend their public time and the activity patterns and preferences of councillors themselves. Do these parallels extend beyond this to the councillors' loyalties, which may be owed variously to their ward, to their larger local authority area, or to the party on whose ticket they were elected? Or, indeed, do their own views take precedence over these interests?

It is conventional to distinguish between the 'trustee' and 'delegate' roles of councillors, this commonly being traced to Edmund Burke's 1783 address to the electors of Bristol (Eulau, Whalke, Buchanan and Ferguson, 1959; Eulau and Whalke, 1978). As trustees, councillors rely upon their own judgement in deciding what stance to take over local issues - while as delegates they suspend their own independent view in favour of the preferences of their constituents. Studies of the trustee role suggest a further distinction between 'moralistic' and 'rationalistic' orientations. In the first, the representative acts as a free agent, and may disregard the interests of those he or she represents. By contrast, rationalistic councillors act on their own judgement as to where the interests of their electors lie. But - in reality - choices are not so clear cut. Whether a rationalistic trustee or a delegate, councillors still have to choose between the concerns of their immediate ward and those of their larger local authority area. And they may well also have to accommodate the quite separate claims of party loyalty.

If these are the ways in which councillors themselves approach their representative roles, what do their electors expect of them? We asked respondents to say what they thought that the 'most important' influence on a councillor should be. The results are startling.

**% saying that it is most important for
councillors to take into account:**

His or her own views	1
The interests of the ward he or she represents	40
The interests of all the people in the council's area	52
His or her party's views	2

We see that the extreme view of the councillor as 'moralistic' trustee enjoys the support of just one per cent of our sample. Forty per cent thought it most mportant for a councillor to consider the interests of the whole council area he or she represents - and just over half thought the interests of the ward should predominate.

Those aged under 25 are far *more* likely to say that councillors should take into account the interests of the whole council area than people above this age. The most likely explanation for this is that, after the age of 24, people are more likely to have acquired property and a commitment to living in a particular area. As a result, they are likely to develop a much sharper appreciation of ward interests, for it is at this most local level that threats to amenity and property values tend to materialise. But the most important message from these data is that the traditional concepts of representative democracy - which focus on how far representatives know what their electors want, act on the basis of what they think they want, or pursue their own judgement - have little to do with the contemporary working of local government (Rao, 1994a). Instead, there is an overwhelming expectation that councillors should place local interests - either at ward level or across the local area - first. And there is also a clear indication that the public thinks there are limits to the role of party politics - only two per cent thought the party view should prevail.

But how far do people believe councillors are likely to conform with this expectation? We asked:

> *How much do you trust local councillors of **any** party to place the needs of their area above the interests of their own political party ... just about all of the time, most of the time, only some of the time or almost never?*

Less than one in three thought that councillors could be trusted to do so either 'all' or 'most of the time', although only 14 per cent thought they never could be trusted to do so. The majority appears to have a wary cynicism about their councillors, saying that they can be trusted 'only some of the time'. Still, as Curtice and Jowell report in their chapter, the public appears considerably more inclined to trust local councillors than they do their MPs.

The emphasis that the public places on the need for a councillor to look after local interests is reflected in the personal qualities it thinks most important for a local councillor to have. Just over seven in ten say that it

is important that councillors should have been brought up in the area they represent and a similar proportion say that they should have a knowledge of local matters. No other quality was mentioned by much more than four in ten. Further, the public also places relatively more importance on a local councillor having local connections than they do an MP. The ideal councillor is no carpet-bagger but a true local representative.

The other qualities we asked about were felt to be less important for councillors than for MPs, the sharpest contrast being on the need to be well-educated. It might be expected that having a good education would be thought to be of relevance if councillors are to be effective managers of local services. In fact, among those who emphasised the management role, the only quality more likely to be thought important among councillors than MPs was business experience, and even then only marginally.

The desirable qualities of councillors and MPs

% saying it is important for them to...	Councillors	MPs
... have been brought up in the area they represent	73	61
... have a knowledge of local matters	69	n/a
... be well-educated	41	58
... be independent-minded	40	52
... be loyal to the party they represent	30	43
... know what being poor means	29	38
... have business experience	28	35
... have Trade Union experience	11	14

n/a = not asked

How much importance the public attaches to local councillors being well-educated can be traced back to the Maud survey of 1965. Although there appears to have been some increase in the importance attached to this quality since we last asked the question in the first *British Social Attitudes* survey in 1983, the proportion thinking it is important is still well below the level found by the Maud survey. In contrast, the public has been constant in its wish that councillors should have local connections. Clearly this is one aspect of local government which the public very much wants to remain local.

Trends in important qualities in councillors

% saying it is important for councillors to...	1965	1983	1994
... have been brought up in the area they represent	77	76	73
... be well-educated	59	31	41

Source: 1965: Maud Committee Survey

Becoming a councillor: pathways and barriers

The potential councillor

So far we have concentrated upon the public as elector and ignored the fact that every elector over 21 is - in principle - also a potential councillor. Although past studies have thrown considerable light upon political recruitment, they have revealed that the process is by no means straightforward (Stanyer, 1977; Gordon, 1979). Schwartz's classical model, for example, states that no less than three sets of factors influence who eventually ends up seeking public office. These are, firstly, the personality traits, expectations and dispositions of the individuals themselves (together with the social characteristics associated with these); secondly, their degree of access to local social and community organisations which provide useful political experience and resources; and, thirdly, the processes of selection which secure an advantage to those with certain characteristics at the expense of others (Schwartz, 1969).

We can look at the role of some of these influences in our survey, although others could be examined only in a full-blown study dedicated to the ways in which people come to be local election candidates. We can assess how confident our respondents are of their potential to become councillors (dispositions), and how involved they are in the politics of their community (resources). Further, we can identify who has stood as a local election candidate or would consider doing so, and see whether or not they appear to be representative of the population at large. We can also review what are perceived to be the barriers to more people wanting to become councillors.

The confident elector

Schwartz's model of the recruitment process claims that personal characteristics or dispositions come first in the chain of factors that determine whether or not an individual is likely to stand for election. Confidence is clearly an important characteristic, one which the Maud Committee research identified as "a reflection of the individual's standing in the community and his or her power to influence local events". Such confidence does not appear to be in short supply. Over one in three agree that "I feel I could do as good a job as councillor as most other people" and almost two in five believe that "people like me can have a real influence on politics if they are prepared to get involved". On this reckoning there should be little difficulty in finding people willing to stand as councillors although, as many previous studies have discovered, political confidence is higher amongst the better educated and higher social classes than in the rest of the community.[5]

		Agree/ strongly agree	Neither agree nor disagre	Disagree/ strongly disagree
I could do as good a job	%	35	30	31
People like me have influence	%	38	32	27

The involved elector

Political confidence need not be accompanied by actual involvement in community affairs. In order to identify what the Maud Committee referred to as the 'community conscious elector', we asked our respondents whether they were members of one or more different kinds of local voluntary groups such as a residents' association, parent-teachers' association or local conservation group.

At first sight, the level of community involvement is not that dissimilar to the level of political confidence. Just over a quarter of our respondents said that they were a member of at least one local organisation. However, membership of an organisation does not necessarily imply active involvement. Indeed, by far the largest membership reported (by 13 per cent) was of a neighbourhood watch scheme. Such schemes, which encourage local residents to keep a watch on their area for any suspicious signs of crime, generally require relatively little active involvement by any of their members. Thereafter, the highest reported level of membership, apart from the seven per cent who said that they were members of a local organisation of a kind which we had not mentioned, was the four per cent who belonged to residents' or tenants' associations. Meanwhile, despite their prominence in local government, just three per cent were members of a political party.[6] Surprisingly, given the growth of environmental pressure groups in recent years, even fewer - two per cent - reported belonging to a local conservation or environmental group.

Further, as many previous studies have shown (see for example, Newton, 1974), political party membership and participation in local community organisations are disproportionately middle-class activities. For example, no less than 37 per cent of those in the salariat were members of at least one local community organisation, compared with just 16 per cent of those in the working class. Similarly, members are also more likely to be highly educated than non-members. True, the membership of some kinds of organisations such as residents and tenants' associations is less socially skewed than others, but it is clear that - like personality traits and dispositions - the resources which are important on the pathway to becoming a councillor are more available to some groups in society than to others.

Barriers to standing

Certainly those who have stood for election as a councillor - or have even considered doing so - are not only rare but also far from being socially representative of the population at large. In our sample, just one per cent had ever stood and only four per cent had ever even considered doing so. However, these figures are no lower than those established by the Maud Committee thirty years ago - when there were many more seats to be contested and thus many more opportunities for election (Horton, 1967).

We found men to be no less than twice as likely as women to have considered standing for election. Forty per cent of those who had actually stood for election were graduates, compared with ten per cent of the sample in general. All of them were owner occupiers and they were also most likely to have been residents of longer than average standing in their localities. Although based on small numbers, these results are well in line with recent research on councillors which demonstrates that they are still disproportionately male and well educated (Young and Rao, 1994).

Why do so few people apparently want to become councillors? It was not fruitful to ask those who had *not* considered standing for election why they had not done so; instead, we asked all our respondents why they thought *other people* generally did not do so.

The most commonly cited reason given by our respondents is simply that it just doesn't occur to people to think of standing as a councillor. This came well ahead of items which touch upon some of the factors often found in academic models of political recruitment - lack of time, skills and money - none of which was dramatically more likely to be cited than any other. But all of these factors clearly come ahead of an issue which has been frequently emphasised in recent discussions of both why so few people want to become councillors and why there is such a high level of councillor turnover. This is the belief that local government has lost too much power and - encouragingly for the health of local democracy - this reason comes at the very bottom of the rank-ordering provided by our respondents.[7]

Perceptions of why people do not stand for election as councillors

% saying a 'very common' reason why people are put off standing for election:

It just doesn't occur to them to think of standing	47
They don't feel they have enough time	38
They don't feel they have the skills to do the job	37
They think local government is influenced too much by party politics	32
They cannot afford it financially	32
They don't think enough people would support them	28
They think local government has too little power to change things	22

Equally, the deterrent effect of party politics which some have feared is not particularly conspicuous among the reasons for not standing offered by our respondents. Unsurprisingly, those who favour the non-party system are rather more likely to cite this as a reason for people not standing than those who favour the party system. But there is no doubt that political parties *do* act as gatekeepers on the path to becoming a councillor. No less than six in ten of the small number in our sample who *had* ever stood as councillors were currently members of a political party - compared with only one in eight of those who had considered standing but had not done so. If political parties are to continue to play such an important role in the recruitment of local councillors, then an expansion of their membership above the current level of just three per cent of the population would seem essential.

Overall, the most striking feature of the picture painted by our respondents as to why people do not stand for election as councillors is its similarity to that found by the Maud Committee in 1965. At that time, what loomed large in electors' minds were lack of personal confidence in their ability to do the job, lack of time and lack of knowledge about council work. Coupled with the fact that the proportion of people who have *never* considered standing as a councillor is exactly the same as it was in those days, we are forced to conclude that the problems of recruiting councillors are no greater - or less - than they were thirty years ago.

Conclusion

Local government has never been a particularly well-regarded institution and this continues to be the case. But there are now some signs that its cultural underpinnings may be crumbling as well. True, bare majorities of people still register positive assessments of the local democratic process - they believe that voting decides what happens locally and that who one votes for *can* make a difference. But on one crucial measure for which we have a thirty-year time trend, faith in local democracy has continued to slide. Three-quarters believed that voting decided local affairs in 1965; 60 per cent did so in 1985; now just 54 per cent do so.

To some degree, this finding might be attributed to the growing sophistication of the public or to changes in real circumstances. 'Local' decision making is indeed markedly more in thrall to central influence today than in the past. Yet, even allowing for this, our findings suggest that confidence in local democratic processes does not run deep. For example, our evidence on attitudes to councillors throws up some paradoxical conclusions. The predominant expectations are that councillors should be people with the strongest local connections (and this has remained rock-steady over 30 years), and that their over-riding concern should be the representation of local interests. That they are not widely *trusted* to do so betrays a degree of cynicism; that electors should then vote

the party ticket regardless of the qualities of their candidates appears perverse.

A similar paradox is to be found with regard to community involvement. Our respondents show high levels of confidence that they *can* influence affairs or do as good a job as a sitting councillor, yet few are actually involved in local community organisations; even fewer are willing to stand as a candidate for election to their local council, and scarcely any have experience of actually doing so. That as many as 93 per cent had not even *considered* seeking elective office is perhaps the most sobering comment offered by the findings of our survey.

Notes

1. It is possible that one of the reasons why support for local determination has not been fully restored is the change in question wording to reflect the title of the new source of local revenue. 'Rates' were familiar and unequivocally local; 'council tax' may on the other hand suggest something within the national government's fiscal portfolio.
2. The trend was first observed in the analysis of the 1985 survey and was confirmed in the PSI study of 1990 (Bloch and John, 1990). It runs counter to the expectation voiced at the time of the Maud survey. Noting that belief in local democracy was associated with high education, the Maud Committee assumed that support for local democracy would rise as educational levels rose. Three studies have now confirmed that the opposite is occurring.
3. There is something of a paradox here. Local election results show that party politics has largely eliminated uncontested elections, indicating that parties function as a more effective channel of recruitment to elective office. On the other hand, survey data show that party politics may discourage certain sorts of people from standing.
4. We have classified respondents according to the population density of the local authority in which they live. Those living in 'very urban' areas are those in the top quartile on this measure; those in 'fairly urban' areas are those in the second quartile, etc.
5. The value of these measures is attested by the fact that those who score highly on them exhibit a higher propensity to become involved in political action in general. It is also the case that those who are politically confident in this sense have high scores on the measures of Personal and Collective Assertiveness (Young, 1992).
6. This figure would seem to confirm that membership of political parties in Britain has continued its long-term decline. As recently as 1987 the British Election Study found that six per cent were members of a political party, well down on the 14 per cent who were members in 1964 (Curtice, 1995). Of course, our data were collected before the substantial rise in Labour Party membership which has ensued in the year following Tony Blair's election as leader of the Labour Party, although over the same period Conservative Party membership has reportedly continued to decline.
7. However, councillors and ex-councillors themselves have been more than ready to cite this as a barrier (Bloch, 1992).

References

Audit Commission (1988), *We Can't Go On Meeting Like This*, London: HMSO.

Bloch, A. (1992), *The Turnover of Local Councillors*, York: Joseph Rowntree Foundation.

Bloch, A. and John, P. (1990), *Attitudes to Local Government: a Survey of Electors*, York: Joseph Rowntree Foundation.

Buxton, R. (1973), *Local Government*, 2nd edition, Harmondsworth: Penguin.

Clements, R. V. (1969), *Local Notables and the City Council*, London: Macmillan.

Curtice, J. (1995), 'Political Sociology 1945-92', in Obelkevich, J. and Catterall, P. (eds.), *Understanding Post-War British Society*, London: Routledge.

Curtice, J., Payne, C. and Waller, R. (1983), 'The Alliance's first nationwide test: lessons of the 1982 English local elections', *Electoral Studies*, **3**, 3-22.

Department of the Environment (1991), *Consultation Paper on the Internal Management of Local Authorities in England*.

Eulau, H. and Whalke, J. C. (eds.) (1978), *The Politics of Representation: Continuities in Theory and Research*, Beverly Hills: Sage.

Eulau, H., Whalke J. C., Buchanan, W. and Ferguson L. C. (1959), 'The role of the representative: some empirical observations on the theory of Edmund Burke', *American Political Science Review*, **53(3)**, 742-56.

Goldsmith, M. (1992), *Options for the Future: Local Democracy Abroad*, Luton: LGMB.

Gordon, I. (1979), 'The recruitment of local politicians', *Policy and Politics*, **7(1)**, 1-37.

Hennock, E. P. (1973), *Fit and Proper Persons: Ideal and Reality in Nineteenth Century Urban Government*, London: Edward Arnold.

Horton, M. (1967), Committee of Inquiry into the Management of Local Government, *The Local Government Elector*, Vol. 3, London: HMSO.

Marsh, A. (1977), *Protest and Political Consciousness*, London: Sage.

Maud, J. (1967a), Committee on the Management of Local Government, Vol. 1, *Report of the Committee*, London: HMSO.

Maud, J. (1967b), Committee on the Management of Local Government, Vol. 2, *The Local Government Councillor*, London: HMSO.

Miller, W. (1986), 'Local electoral behaviour', in Committee of Inquiry into the Conduct of Local Authority Business, *Research Volume III: the Local Government Elector*, 105-172, London: HMSO.

Miller, W. (1988), *Irrelevant Elections? The Quality of Local Democracy in Britain*, Oxford: Clarendon.

Newton, K. (1974), 'Role orientations and their sources among elected representatives in English local politics', *Journal of Politics*, **36**, 615-636.

Newton, K. (1976), *Second City Politics: Democratic Processes and Decision-Making in Birmingham*, London: Oxford University Press.

Rao, N. (1994a), *The Making and Un-making of Local Self-Government*, Aldershot: Dartmouth.

Rao, N. (1994b), 'Continuity and change: responses to the pressures for institutional reform in Britain', in Borraz, O. *et al*, *Local Leadership and Decision-making: a Study of France, Germany, the United States and Britain*, 81-92, York: Joseph Rowntree Foundation.

Ridley, N. (1988), *The Local Right: Enabling Not Providing*, London: Centre for Policy Studies.

Sartori, G. (1968), 'Representational systems', in *International Encyclopedia of the Social Sciences*, 465-74, New York: Macmillan.

Schwartz, D. (1969), 'Towards a theory of political recruitment', *Western Political Quarterly*, **22**, 552-71.

Stanyer, J. (1977), 'Electors, candidates and councillors: some technical problems in the study of political recruitment processes in local government', *Policy and Politics*, **6(1)**, 71-92.

Young, K. (1994), 'Local government', in Kavanagh, D. and Seldon, A. (eds.), *The Major Effect*, 83-98, London: Macmillan.

Young, K. (1992), 'Class, race and opportunity', in Jowell, R., Brook, L., Prior, G. and Taylor, B. (eds.), *British Social Attitudes: the 10th Report*, Aldershot: Dartmouth.

Young, K. (1986a), 'Attitudes to local government', in Committee of Inquiry into the Conduct of Local Authority Business, *Research Volume III: the Local Government Elector*, 15-100, London: HMSO.

Young, K. (1986b), 'Party politics in local government: an historical perspective', in Committee of Inquiry into the Conduct of Local Authority Business, *Research Volume IV: Aspects of Local Democracy*, 83-105, London: HMSO.

Young, K. and Davies, M. (1990), *The Politics of Local Government Since Widdicombe*, York: Joseph Rowntree Foundation.

Young, K. and Rao, N. (1994), *Coming to Terms With Change: the Local Government Councillor in 1993*, York: Joseph Rowntree Foundation.

Acknowledgement

We are grateful to the Department of the Environment for the financial support that enabled us to ask the questions reported here.

6 The state of the Union: attitudes towards Europe

Geoffrey Evans [*]

In terms of politics, the summer of 1995 was an eventful one. Once again, the Conservative Party became embroiled in a leadership contest ostensibly over the question of Europe. John Major survived this particular trial, but the government divisions exposed are unlikely to disappear quietly. The debate about European integration is undoubtedly on the agenda of the practitioners of party politics. But what is its position in the hearts and minds of the public?

Although long an issue of major significance for politicians, the process of European integration has generally been seen as one in which British voters are acquiescent rather than directive. However, it is increasingly argued that, to succeed, further European integration is likely to require widespread public endorsement. This was thrown into sharp focus by events surrounding the ratification of the Maastricht Treaty - in particular, the failure of the Danes in a 1992 referendum to endorse the ratification of the Treaty and the extremely narrow pro-Maastricht result in the French referendum. Both events brought a specific issue - that of monetary union - to the fore.[1]

This chapter examines the public's beliefs about the desirability of closer British links with the rest of Europe. How much support for European integration exists in Britain? In particular, to what extent is the public willing to give the European Union the power to make cross-border policy decisions? A key issue here is identifying those sections of the public which contain the main pockets of support for - and opposition to - closer integration. Finally, we consider the ramifications of public opinion for

---

[*] Fellow in the Centre for European Studies, Nuffield College, Oxford

party politics, a question likely to be of growing significance as European integration proceeds.

Attitudes towards the European Union

How have attitudes towards Europe evolved over the years? It might be that familiarity has brought about an increasing acceptance of integration - or, conversely, that problems such as those associated with Maastricht have produced a reaction against Europe. Alternatively, public attitudes may have polarized as the implications of integration for different sections of the population have become clearer.

From 1983, when the *British Social Attitudes* survey series began, until 1991, we asked:

> *Do you think Britain should continue to be a member of the European Community or should it withdraw?* [2]

The initial impression is of a population increasingly accustomed to being part of the European Community.[3] The figures show a steady increase in acceptance of membership - by 1991 over three-quarters thought that Britain should remain a member, compared with just over a half in 1983.

Attitudes towards the European Community (EC)

	1983 %	1984 %	1985 %	1986 %	1987 %	1989 %	1990 %	1991 %
Britain's membership of the EC ...								
... should continue	53	48	56	61	63	68	76	77
... should withdraw	42	45	38	33	32	26	19	17
Don't know	5	6	6	6	6	6	5	6

For supporters of the European Union the picture appears rosy. But are Eurosceptics really so out of touch with public opinion? Superficially it might appear so, but attitudes are complex phenomena - they need to be carefully inspected before conclusions about public opinion can be drawn. Moreover, as the question was not asked after 1991, the impact of Maastricht cannot be assessed.

We can, however, look at responses to another, related, question:

> *On the whole, do you think that Britain's interests are better served by closer links with Western Europe, or closer links with America?*

Although this question does not focus specifically on views about the European Union, it raises an important contemporary issue. Rather than simply remaining in Europe, do people think that *closer* links with Europe would be beneficial?

This gives us quite a different picture. In particular, after the Maastricht Treaty in 1991, support for closer links with Europe dropped - with a corresponding rise in the proportion of people who think Britain is best served by avoiding *any* links with either Western Europe or America. So the late 1980s through to 1991 may have been the high-water mark of support for European integration. Since Maastricht, public opinion seems to have cooled.

Britain's interests and links with Western Europe and America

	1984 %	1985 %	1986 %	1987 %	1989 %	1990 %	1993 %	1994 %
Interests best served by ...								
... closer links with Europe	53	48	55	57	50	52	42	45
... closer links with America	21	18	18	18	18	18	25	21
Both equally	16	20	17	14	20	18	18	17
Neither	3	4	3	3	3	3	6	9
Don't know	7	11	7	8	10	9	11	8

The two questions we have considered so far have quite different implications for our understanding of contemporary attitudes towards Europe. This suggests that we require evidence from a wider range of survey questions and the issues they tap.

Public support for European integration

Do people currently want *closer* links with the rest of the European Union or, like some members of the Conservative Party, do they favour a little 'clear blue water' between Britain and its fellow member states?

In 1994, we asked three relevant questions in order to address the range of views held on the issue of British integration into the European Union (or, as it was then, the European Community).

Britain's relationship with the European Community

Britain's relationship with the EC ...	%
... should be closer	37
... should be less close	23
... is about right	34
Don't know	7

Britain should do all it can to ...	%
... unite fully with the EC	40
... protect its independence from the EC	53
Don't know	7

Britain's long-term policy should be to ...	%
... leave the EC	11
... stay in the EC and try to reduce EC powers	25
... leave things as they are	20
... stay in the EC and try to increase EC powers	28
... work for the formation of a single European government	8
Don't know	7

With our first question, over a third are in favour of 'closer links' with Europe. But there is also a substantial minority - over a fifth - who seek to distance the country from European Union influence. Our more strongly worded question - whether Britain should unite 'fully' with the European Union or protect its 'independence' - results in answers which are more clearly slanted towards the Eurosceptic view. On this measure, just over half oppose further integration. Finally, attitudes towards 'long-term' goals are finely balanced between the pro- and anti- integration stance, with around a third in favour of each and a fifth who think that things should not change. This question also shows that the desire to weaken European Union influence does not *necessarily* mean leaving the Union - just as a preference for closer involvement does not mean that a single European government is the ultimate goal.

So there seems to be a mixture of both support for integration and a desire to maintain some distance from Europe. On the first of our questions, supporters outweigh opponents by a small margin; on the second, the reverse is the case and on the third there is an even split. But, despite this, the answers to these questions are highly correlated. This means that, at an *individual* level, there are strong links between the answers given to each question.[4] Although the proportion of people adopting pro- or anti-integration positions differs, it is the *same* group of people who tend to be pro-integration or anti-integration.

In fact, based upon their answers to these three questions, 21 per cent of our respondents have a consistently 'pro-integrationist' view and 17 per cent an 'anti-integrationist' one. These two groups are particularly interesting

as they form the 'hard core' on each side of the debate about Europe. We shall return to them at a later point.

Different policy areas and support for integration

At this point we might conclude that people are evenly split on the question of Europe - there is no great demand to leave the Union, but also no desire for full immersion in a single super-state. However, support for the general idea of European integration may not necessarily be a good predictor of where people stand when it comes to the *practicalities* of economic and political union.[5] As it proceeds, integration will involve many debates over the extent of influence that the Union should have over member states' internal policies and practices. What happens to public attitudes when integration is specified in these more concrete terms?

Among the major issues to be addressed during the process of integration is that of a shared currency. European Monetary Union is probably the biggest step towards institutional integration under consideration in the foreseeable future. Do public attitudes towards this issue reflect the levels of support for integration we have found so far? To address this, we asked respondents to choose between three statements about the possible future of the pound in Europe. Their answers suggest that the task of obtaining popular support for a single European currency is not an enviable one.

The future of the pound in the EC

	%
Replace the pound by a single currency	17
Use both the pound and a new European currency in Britain	18
Keep the pound as the only currency for Britain	62

It seems that the pound is a symbol to which people are strongly attached. Very few want to lose it - or even give it shared status with a European currency unit. The refusal to endorse this latter option is especially interesting. Despite the fact that it allows people to 'have their cake and eat it', there remain few takers. There can be little doubt that, at present, Monetary Union is not at all popular with the electorate.

Yet Monetary Union is only one possible example of a merging of European policy programmes. Other areas will emerge as possible candidates for harmonisation; these include taxation, defence, immigration, pollution and employment policies. All are also likely to be contentious and areas of intense electoral competition. Given attitudes towards Monetary Union, will people be willing to forego control of these areas of national self-regulation?

We asked people who they thought should mostly make decisions about particular policy areas - the European Community, individual governments or both equally.

The EC and decision making in specific areas

| | | Who should mostly make decisions? | | |
		European Community	Individual governments	Both equally
Decisions about ...				
... taxes	%	4	77	13
... immigration	%	11	60	22
... defence	%	13	49	32
... rights of people at work	%	20	48	27
... controlling pollution	%	29	29	37

Public acceptance of European Union involvement in policy decision making fluctuates considerably according to the policy area under consideration. More than three-quarters oppose the European Union having any say in member states' taxation policies (and by implication in *British* taxation policy). Sixty per cent do not want Europe to have any say in immigration policy. One possible reason why immigration invites less opposition than taxation is the recognition that immigration is a problem shared by several member states. There is even less opposition to the European Union making decisions about defence or employment rights - only around half thought these areas should remain solely the domain of individual governments. But the only area where there is an even balance between those supporting individual state decision making and European decision making is that of pollution control. An awareness that pollution does not respect national boundaries may lie behind this relatively greater openness to supra-national regulation.

Clearly, although the general idea of European integration achieves a moderate level of endorsement, the actual intervention of the European Union in Britain's domestic and foreign policy decision making lies - at least for the present - a little beyond most people's perception of the role of the Union.

This is not to say that there is *no* relationship between general support for integration and attitudes towards European Union involvement in specific policy areas. Not surprisingly, people who support the general aim of integration are far more likely to support European-level decision making in all of the specific policy areas we asked about.[6] Nevertheless, even among the 21 per cent who are consistently pro-integration, only a minority actually endorses European Union influence on national policy formulation. Indeed, the highest proportion of this group to endorse European-level decision making did so with regard to pollution control - and even here only half supported the European option.

Support for EC decision making in specific areas

% saying decisions should be mostly made by the EC on	Pro-integration	Anti-integration
Taxes	9	1
Controlling pollution	48	16
Defence	24	4
Rights at work	40	6
Immigration	25	1
% in favour of European Monetary Union[7]	39	4

Who supports European integration?

What sorts of people are pro- or anti- European integration? Previous research has tended to stress either economic motivations for supporting the growth of the European Union (Gabel and Palmer, 1995; Eichenberg and Dalton, 1993) or growing cosmopolitanism in response to changing values (Inglehart, 1977, 1990; although cf. Janssen, 1991). These two types of explanation have quite different implications when it comes to looking at who supports integration. For instance, working-class respondents might be expected to support integration because of the benefits associated with the social chapter - but also might be expected to oppose it because of their more traditional and parochial social attitudes (Lipset, 1959). On this latter basis we would also expect the higher educated and most politically informed to be most supportive of integration (Inglehart, 1977).

Clearly, to unravel the complexities of these different explanations of attitude formation is beyond the scope of this chapter. But we can develop a picture of where the main pockets of support for, and opposition to, integration lie.

Political values and integration

Our first goal is to understand how attitudes towards European integration relate to the deep-rooted political values and ideologies of the British public. To answer this question we need to examine the two main axes of ideological conflict in British politics. The first of these is the traditional *left-right* division, reflecting beliefs about economic issues such as inequality, government intervention and the distribution of income and wealth. The second represents a division between those with 'authoritarian' values - that is, a belief in 'traditional' values and the importance of law and order - and those with 'libertarian' values - that is, the endorsement of freedom of expression and other cornerstones of civil libertarianism.

Left-right and libertarian-authoritarian values are quite independent of one another.[8] Whether an individual is 'left-wing' or 'right-wing' tells us little about whether he or she holds 'libertarian' or 'authoritarian' values. So how do these distinct sets of values relate to attitudes towards integration? Are attitudes towards Europe more closely linked to a person's position on the left-right axis? Or are libertarian-authoritarian values - often depicted as part of the 'new politics' agenda (Lipset, 1981) - more relevant?

To assess this, we asked all respondents a number of questions which have been carefully developed over time to measure these two dimensions of political belief.[9] When we look at the answers to these questions and attitudes towards European integration, we find that *both* left-right and libertarian-authoritarian values do matter. Generally speaking, those who take a pro-integration stance towards Europe tend to be more left-wing and more libertarian. Those who are anti-integration are more likely to be right-wing and to have authoritarian beliefs. Furthermore, on certain aspects of European integration, divisions between left and right are more important than divisions between libertarians and authoritarians - and *vice versa*.

The figure below shows this in detail. It focuses, first, on general pro- or anti-integration feelings (as measured by the three questions discussed earlier) and, secondly, on attitudes towards two important aspects of European integration - European Monetary Union and European Union decision making about the rights of people at work. It shows where these attitudes stand in relation to left-right and libertarian-authoritarian values. With regard to general attitudes towards integration - whether someone is for or against it - it is clear that an individual's viewpoint is linked to his or her libertarian-authoritarian values. The 'gap' between the views of people with more libertarian and more authoritarian values is greater than that between left and right. But left-right values *do* also matter. So being pro-integration is linked to both libertarianism and left-wing values, just as being anti-integration is linked to authoritarian values and right-wing views. However, when it comes to European Union control over employment rights, the key division is between left and right. With regard to European Monetary Union the difference between left and right is not nearly so marked as that between libertarians and authoritarians - with the former being much more likely than the latter to be in favour of monetary union.

Attitudes towards Europe: the importance of left-right and libertarian-authoritarian values

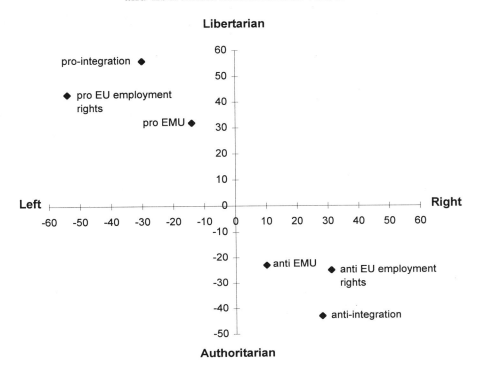

Our analysis also tells us that the views of the Eurosceptic wing of the Conservative Party strike a chord with people who, because of their left-right and libertarian-authoritarian values, are likely to be in agreement with them on other issues. Of course, whether there are *enough* of these voters to guarantee success in a general election is another question, but opposition to Europe appears to fit comfortably enough with the established political values of Conservative voters.

Social bases of support and opposition

What are the social bases of attitudes towards integration? Our findings here may have long-term implications. If, for instance, we find that levels of support for integration are higher than average among the young then, as new cohorts arrive on the electoral register, overall support for integration could increase. Similarly, if support is higher among those with further educational qualifications, we would expect overall support for integration to rise as does the proportion of people with such qualifications.

In many respects, the social characteristics of pro- and anti-integrationists are as might be expected. Thus, the young, graduates and the salariat (those in professional and managerial occupations) are more likely than average to be in favour of integration. For example, nearly half of those with degree-level qualifications are pro-integrationist - compared with less than a fifth of those without such qualifications.

Whether or not someone has an interest in politics also matters. But although those with high levels of interest are more likely than average to be pro-integrationist than those who are less interested, they are also more likely to be anti-integrationist. The key issue here seems to be one of *polarization* - those interested in politics are simply more likely to have a particular viewpoint, whether positive or negative, than those who are less interested. The responses of men and women follow a similar pattern, no doubt partly reflecting women's lower levels of expressed interest in politics.

The social bases of views about European integration

		Pro-integration	Anti-integration
All	%	21	17
Sex			
Men	%	25	23
Women	%	18	12
Age			
18-34	%	27	10
35-54	%	21	19
55 and over	%	14	22
Social class[10]			
Salariat	%	30	17
Self-employed	%	12	27
Working class	%	17	15
Highest qualification			
Degree or equivalent	%	47	9
Lower than degree	%	18	18
Political interest			
High	%	31	21
Low	%	12	13

These findings appear good news for pro-integrationists since many of the characteristics associated with a pro-integrationist outlook are, themselves,

becoming more widespread. For instance, the proportion of people with degree-level qualifications is growing - as are the numbers of people in salariat occupations. Most signs, then, point towards long-term increases in support for integration. But it does seem that higher levels of interest in politics will not necessarily increase support for European integration - they may merely result in a higher proportion of people having a clearer pro-integrationist or anti-integrationist outlook.

We have already seen that *general* support for integration does not necessarily translate into actual support when it comes to specific policy areas. We might also expect this to be the case in terms of the support for integration shown by different social groups. For instance, certain groups might take quite different positions depending upon the particular policy area under consideration. This will depend largely upon their perceptions as to how a particular policy will affect their interests. So policies such as the minimum wage legislation contained in the social chapter might appeal to working-class respondents who are the most likely of our groups to be low paid. In contrast, harmonisation of European Union pollution regulation might have greater general appeal for the more middle-class and highly-educated green lobby.

We did not find much evidence of this in our data. On the whole, when considering specific policy areas, social divisions tended to follow those obtained for the general aim of integration. The most noticeable difference concerns taxation. On this issue, the higher educated and the salariat (who were more likely than average to support integration in general) were actually slightly less pro-integration than average - numbering only around two or three per cent. This reflects the more-or-less universal rejection of European Union involvement in British taxation policy. We also found that when it comes to Economic Monetary Union, the social differences discussed above become more muted.

It should be remembered, of course, that many social characteristics are themselves related. For instance, the link between having a salariat occupation and being a supporter of integration may simply result from the fact that large numbers of university-educated respondents are in professional and managerial occupations - and that education is the key factor when it comes to someone's feelings about Europe. To test for this possibility, all the social characteristics described above were included in a multivariate regression analysis.[11] In many respects, the results of this analysis confirm the findings we have already discussed. Thus, both higher education *and* social class matter in terms of whether or not someone supports integration; taking education into account does *not* remove the differences we find between classes. Young people remain more supportive than old people, and women more so than men. However, the importance of political interest disappears - a consequence of the relationships between such interest and education, class, age and sex.

Why do people support or oppose integration?

As we have seen, we cannot view integration as simply tied either to the 'new politics' of liberalism *versus* authoritarianism or to more traditional economic divisions between left and right. Reasons for supporting integration are likely to involve beliefs about both economic costs and benefits *and* non-economic concerns - fears of loss of independence and sovereignty, for instance.

One obvious basis for attitudes towards European integration is the calculation of its potential economic and political effects. Is it in Britain's interests to assimilate? We asked:

> Do you think that closer links with the European Community would give Britain **more** influence in the world, **less** influence in the world, or would it make no difference?

We also asked:

> And would closer links with the European Community make Britain **stronger** economically, **weaker** economically, or would it make no difference?

Answers to these questions are mixed but are, on balance, reasonably positive. In both cases, around one in five choose the 'anti-integration' option - that closer links would give Britain 'less influence' or make her 'weaker economically'. Responses are also strongly linked with views about integration. People who believe 'closer links' will benefit Britain politically and economically are more likely than average to support integration.

Implications of closer links with the European Community

		Pro- integration	Anti- integration
Closer links will give Britain ...			
... more influence	%	44	2
... make no difference	%	13	17
... less influence	%	4	50
Closer links will make Britain ...			
... stronger economically	%	41	5
... make no difference	%	9	12
... weaker economically	%	3	53

These findings are perhaps not surprising. They may simply reflect an underlying pro-integration or anti-integration viewpoint - rather than being a considered appraisal of the actual benefits of integration for Britain.

Nonetheless, they are also justifications for beliefs concerning integration and - as such - cannot be dismissed lightly.

Opposition to European integration need not stem from worries about its effect on Britain's economic or political position. Some may have concerns about the *non-economic* consequences of integration. One such topic which surfaces intermittently in politics is immigration. To some, this is a problem which would be exacerbated by reduced passport controls between Britain and the rest of the European Union - or by giving the Union a role in deciding British immigration policy. To address this issue we look at responses to the following question:

> *Please say, for people from European Community countries, whether you think Britain should allow more settlement, less settlement, or about the same amount as now.*

A sizeable minority - 40 per cent - would like to see less European Union immigration. But by comparison, no less than 60 per cent think there should be less immigration from India and Pakistan. Nevertheless, our data show that there is a link between opposition to immigration and opposition to integration. Only 13 per cent of those who think there should be less immigration from Europe are consistently pro-integration - compared with 21 per cent of people as a whole - and over a quarter are anti-integration.[12]

Immigration from European Community states

Britain should allow ...		Pro-integration	Anti-integration
... more settlement	%	41	7
... about the same	%	25	12
... less settlement	%	13	27

Opposition to integration might also reflect a deep-seated mistrust of other member states. Fear of German domination, in particular, may play a part in ambivalence towards the European Union. Of course, a desire for the containment of German strength was a factor in the establishment of the European Economic Community in the first place. But this does not mean that those who are still concerned about the role of Germany should want even *closer* links.

This issue is tapped by a question we asked about the threat posed to 'world peace' by a number of countries. On this measure, concern about Germany is not widespread. Overall, only around a fifth (19 per cent) think Germany is a 'very serious' or 'quite serious' threat to world peace. This is comparable to the proportion who think that the United States of America is a threat to world peace - and is less than half the proportion who think the same of China. However, fear of Germany is indeed linked to an anti-European Union position[13] - and also to opposition to giving the

European Union a say in British defence policy. Of those who do *not* see
Germany as a serious threat to world peace, a third have a pro-integration
viewpoint. Only one in ten of this group is anti-integration.

Fears about Germany

		Pro- integration	Anti- integration
The threat of Germany is ...			
... very or quite serious	%	17	24
... not very serious	%	20	19
... no threat at all	%	34	10

A final possible motive for supporting or opposing European integration
relates to devolution. Scottish and Welsh separatism is arguably more
viable under the flag of a greater Europe than under a divided one. Indeed,
we found that a quarter of our Scottish respondents supported the
statement 'Scotland should become independent, separate from the UK, but
part of the European Community'.[14] This view about Scottish separation
was shared by only seven per cent of those from the English provinces and
12 per cent of those from London. In Wales, just eight per cent supported
the same principle for Wales.

Despite their greater support for the specific goal of devolution under an
European Union umbrella, the Scots are only slightly more pro-integration
on other issues than the provincial English - and are no more so than the
Welsh, for whom devolution is not so important an issue. In fact, it is the
cosmopolitanism of London that provides the strongest regional base for
integration.

Support for European integration throughout Britain

% who are pro-integration

Scotland	24
Wales	28
London	34
English provinces	18

European integration and partisanship

What role have political parties played in shaping attitudes towards Europe?
Or have they primarily tailored their programmes to match public
preferences? Many discussions of integration have emphasised the role of
party leadership in *influencing* public attitudes towards Europe (see
Flickinger, 1994). But parties' positions on this subject have shifted
considerably in recent years. Labour, for instance, moved from advocating
complete withdrawal from the European Community in 1983, to ardent

support by 1989 (George and Rosamund, 1992). During 1995 the Shadow Foreign Secretary even engaged in extensive pro-integration proselytising across the country. In contrast, the Conservatives - the main pro-European party of the 1970s - have become openly less Europhile. Given these changes in message, it is not surprising that divisions between party supporters over European integration are not as sharply drawn as they might be. Nonetheless, among Labour Party supporters there are over twice as many who favour integration - and half as many who oppose it - as there are among Conservative supporters. For Liberal Democrats the picture is mixed. Although a high proportion - a quarter - favours integration, a high proportion also opposes it.

Party support and attitudes towards European integration

Party supported		Pro-integration	Anti-integration
Conservative	%	15	23
Labour	%	33	12
Liberal Democrat	%	25	20
Not party supporter	%	18	17

Despite these differences - which largely remain even when different policy areas are considered - it does seem that it is politicians themselves who are most in dispute over Europe. This is clear when we compare our data with that from the British Candidate Survey carried out in 1992. This survey of Members of Parliament, parliamentary candidates and parliamentary applicants asked respondents the same question as we asked in 1994 - whether they thought 'Britain's interests are better served by closer links with Western Europe, or closer links with America'.

The differences between politicians and the public are stark. In 1992, the parties were clearly divided in their views on Europe. While Labour and Liberal candidates were almost unanimous in their support for closer links, support among Conservatives was weak. In fact, Labour and Liberal candidates were over three times more likely than Conservatives to say that they wanted closer links with Europe. By contrast, among the public in 1994 there is no evidence of such extreme polarization along party lines. True, both party supporters and party sympathisers are divided in their views.[15] But the differences between them are far less marked than they were among politicians in 1992.

Support for closer links with Europe:
politicians and public compared

	Politicians (1992) %	Party supporters (1994) %	Party sympathisers (1994) %
Conservative	23	48	43
Labour	82	52	51
Liberal Democrat	83	59	42

Source: 1992: The British Candidate Survey

The uncommitted voter

Among people who are *not* party supporters, support for closer links with
Western Europe is - at 36 per cent - lower than among those who do
support a party. This lack of support among party 'sympathisers' (who
only 'lean towards' a party) and uncommitted voters is also found when
looking at other aspects of European integration. But this does not mean
that they are strongly anti-European - merely that they are less likely to
have strong views on the subject.

Uncommitted voters are precisely the group who, in the run-up to the
next general election, will be of the greatest interest to party tacticians.
Will their votes be won or lost on the issue of Europe?

To address this issue, we now look at the people in our sample who do
not support a particular party. We asked this group whether they felt
closer to one party than another or, if they did not, who they would vote
for if there were a general election tomorrow. We then used logistic
regression - a statistical modelling technique - to see which sorts of attitudes
best predict the party allegiances of this group. Our analysis assumes that
people take a range of issues into account when choosing a party, rather
than obtaining their views from the party they support (Himmelweit *et al*,
1985). The lack of consistent party messages over time means that this is
not such an unrealistic assumption as it might have been in the 1970s. We
also assume that, if integration actually influences party allegiance, this issue
will have an effect even when other well-established attitudinal predictors
of allegiance are taken into account. In addition to attitudes towards
Europe, we considered three other sets of attitudes - the 'left-right' and
'libertarian-authoritarian' dimensions of political belief discussed earlier and
attitudes towards the environment, increasingly seen as bearing upon party
allegiance (Kitschelt, 1994).[16] All three of these sets of attitudes were
converted into scales for this purpose, and each respondent given a 'score'
on each scale depending upon their answers.[17]

In both our models - one predicting Conservative support and one
predicting Labour support - attitudes towards Europe do not emerge as

being very important.[18] Rather, it is the attitudes which underlie our 'left-right' value scale which are highly significant in both cases. The higher someone scores on this scale (where the highest score represents the most right-wing position) the more likely they are to support the Conservative Party and the less likely they are to support Labour. Once this is taken into account, 'libertarian-authoritarian' values are still important when predicting Conservative support - but not whether or not a person supports the Labour Party. Here a high score represents a more libertarian outlook - and this decreases the likelihood of Conservative support. Conversely, having a 'pro-environment' stance is linked to increased Labour support - but is not important when considering whether or not someone supports the Conservative Party.

Even when these sets of attitudes are taken into account, some attitudes towards Europe *are* significant in predicting party allegiance among uncommitted voters. Being in favour of European Union employment legislation is, for example, linked to a decreased likelihood of supporting the Conservative Party; more surprisingly, favouring Economic Monetary Union is linked to an increased likelihood of supporting the Conservatives. Overall, being in favour in European integration is linked to an increased likelihood of Labour Party support.

In general, our analyses suggest that - while Europe is not irrelevant - it is unlikely to be an *important* influence on party choice among non-committed voters.

Conclusions

After 20 years of membership in the European Community, integration continues to be an issue of major significance in British political life. It not only divides the leadership of the Conservative Party - and indeed politicians within all the main political parties - but also divides the public. Education, class, age and regional differences are all important here - but so too are both 'old' and 'new' political values. Although attitudes towards integration can be partially explained by beliefs about its economic benefits to Britain and Britain's influence on European affairs, they also reflect fears about immigration and suspicion of Germany - the major force in the European Union.

The finding that political interest - and presumably knowledge - is associated with slightly higher levels of support for integration is consistent with the more detailed findings of a recent deliberative poll (Curtice and Gray, 1995). Nevertheless, the main concomitant of political interest is *not* increased support for integration. Rather, increased interest results in increased *polarization* among the public.[19] Therefore, as European integration becomes a more and more dominant issue, we should expect people increasingly to take sides - and not simply to adopt a pro-European position. Further, levels of support for the *general* principle of closer European links are higher than support for either Monetary Union or for

increased European Union influence on British policy decision making. As these more specific issues arrive on the integration agenda, we might expect a noticeable fall in pro-integration sentiment. In fact, even on the most general level, consistent support for integration is very much the preserve of the liberal intelligentsia - or what might be called 'the chattering classes'.[20] It should not be forgotten that this group, though politically active and vocal, is small. Pro-European politicians - whether Labour, Liberal Democrat or Conservative - still have a great deal of work to do before the British public embraces the European cause with open arms.

If we turn to party political considerations, our analysis raises the question of whether the right-wing of the Conservative Party is proceeding down an electorally productive path. Are the populist instincts of the Europhobes accurate? In a sense, yes. As we have seen, opposition to integration - rather than support - is more characteristic of the ideology of Conservative supporters. Nevertheless, for most electors, integration is not an issue on which they have consistent views, oscillating as they do between a variety of positions and often choosing the 'status quo' option. This pattern is especially common among floating voters. Moreover, our analysis shows that they are far more likely to be swayed to the Conservative cause by issues other than European integration.

Consider also that *opposition* to integration is strongest among the self-employed - the traditional heartland of support for the right - whereas *support* is strongest among the middle classes, also the source of a substantial proportion of Conservative votes. An anti-European stance is unlikely to help the Conservatives regain support from the middle class. Although the self-employed and small businessmen are relatively Eurosceptic, they are already the strongest supporters of the Conservatives, and - even more crucially - there are rather few of them.

In the working classes, support for integration is somewhat lukewarm. It is possible that the Conservatives could try to pick up working-class support on an anti-European card - but this is unlikely to be successful. Most members of the working class do not clearly oppose integration - they cluster in the 'mixed' response categories. Further, as has been observed previously on numerous occasions, working-class voters are more concerned about economic issues than non-economic ones (Lipset, 1959; Heath and Evans, 1988). Finally, of course, in certain policy areas (such as taxation) they are as pro-European as the middle class.

What then for Labour? As usual, it is divided into its 'new left' - typically highly educated, liberal and pro-European - and its traditional left - typically not highly educated, nor liberal nor pro-European. But following the logic outlined above, a pro-European position *could* win them some votes from the middle classes without losing them support among the workers. For Labour, the self-employed are probably a lost cause and of little electoral consequence. A 'gentle' pro-European approach could probably work well enough.

These strategic speculations quite probably depend on Britain maintaining a positive political input to European affairs, while not conceding decision-

making rights over domestic issues. Whether or not this will be possible remains to be seen. Our findings suggest that - although politicians have so far led the way into Europe - direction from above is increasingly unlikely to be sufficient. A growing number of issues will emerge which cannot be hidden behind convenient Euro-bureaucracy (Franklin *et al*, 1994). Whether further European integration can continue without strong popular support is uncertain. But unless those favouring integration convert the public to their cause, it may have to proceed regardless.

Notes

1. For more discussion of the causes and consequences of these events with reference to public opinion, see Franklin *et al* (1994).
2. From 1983 until 1989 this question referred to 'the EEC - the Common Market'. The question was not fielded after the 1991 survey as it was felt that the issues it raised were no longer part of mainstream political debate.
3. This is consistent with previous examinations of 'over time' changes in attitudes towards the EEC using the Eurobarometer series (i.e. Flickinger, 1994).
4. The correlations between answers to the three questions are all above 0.50 which, given the small number of response categories available and the distributions of those responses, is an extremely high figure.
5. Studies in other related areas of research into public attitudes have found marked differences between distributions of attitudes towards abstract principles and their instantiation in the context of particular policies, and sometimes very weak links between positions taken on them (i.e. Converse, 1964; Ajzen and Fishbein, 1980; Sniderman *et al*, 1991).
6. The five policy questions were part of the self-completion questionnaire which was filled in after the face-to-face interview, whereas the other questions were asked in a battery in the main body of the questionnaire. Given that the links between answers to questions in surveys tend to weaken if they are asked at separate times, the strength of association between the two batteries is particularly impressive.
7. This comprises all those respondents who, when asked about the future of the pound, chose the response 'replace the pound by a single currency'.
8. The correlation between a person's position on the left-right axis and his or her position on the liberal-authoritarian axis is very low, measuring only 0.13.
9. Both the left-right and libertarian-authoritarian scales were constructed from the responses to six 'agree-disagree' questions with 5-point response scales (strongly agree/agree/neither agree nor disagree/disagree/strongly disagree).
     The items forming the left-right scale were as follows:
       Ordinary people get their fair share of the nation's wealth
       There is no need for strong trade unions to protect employee's working conditions
       Big business benefits owners at the expense of workers
       Government should redistribute income from the better-off to those who are less well-off
       Private enterprise is the best way to solve Britain's economic problems
       Management will always try to get the better of employees if it gets the chance.

Answers have been recoded so that a high score equals a free market, right-wing position.

The libertarian-authoritarian scale had the following items:

Young people today don't have enough respect for traditional British values
Censorship of films and magazines is necessary to uphold moral standards
People who break the law should be given stiffer sentences
Schools should teach children to obey authority
The law should be obeyed even if a particular law is wrong
For some crimes, the death penalty is the most appropriate sentence.

A high score equals a libertarian position.

Both scales have been tested for internal consistency and validity: the Cronbach's alpha for the left-right scale is a highly respectable .78; for the libertarian scale it is almost as high (.72). See Heath and Evans (1988); Heath, Evans and Martin (1994); Evans and Heath (1995); Evans, Heath and Lalljee (1996, forthcoming) for more detailed examination of left-right and libertarian-authoritarian values.

10. The social class categories referred to here are derived from the Goldthorpe schema which is explained in detail in Appendix I to this volume.

11. The dependent variable under consideration was whether or not the respondent was pro-integration. Similar findings were obtained from analyses of attitudes towards EMU and towards European Union involvement in different policy areas.

12. We should note, however, that in multivariate analyses (not shown here) in which beliefs about immigration from several countries were modelled, it was found that views on immigration from Eastern Europe, the West Indies or Asia were *not* related to attitudes towards integration. Only European Union immigration remained a significant predictor of integration. It would be unwise therefore to assume that opposition towards integration and to the role of the European Union in immigration policy, results from a more general ethnocentrism - it appears to be a concern focused only on the European Union itself.

13. As with immigration, when beliefs about German threats to peace were modelled along with beliefs about the threat posed by several other nations - including Russia, the USA, and Japan - only views on Germany were significantly related to beliefs about integration. Thus opposition to integration derives from the perceived threat of German aggression, rather than a more general unease about militarism. The sources of opposition are also rather specific in that they concern only fear of German threats to peace - appraisals of German 'influence in world affairs' are not significantly associated with attitudes towards integration.

14. We asked all respondents living in England or Scotland:

An issue in Scotland is the question of an elected Assembly - a special parliament for Scotland dealing with Scottish affairs. Which of these statements comes closest to your view?

Scotland should become independent, separate from the UK and the European Community

Scotland should become independent, separate from the UK, but part of the European Community

Scotland should remain part of the UK but with its own elected Assembly that has some taxation and spending powers

There should be no change from the present system

The same question was asked about Wales of·Welsh respondents only.

15. Party supporters are those who consider themselves supporters of a particular party. Party sympathisers are those who consider themselves closer to one party than to another. For further details, see Appendix I to this volume.

16. Attitudes towards environmental issues are measured by combining the answers to three 'agree-disagree' questions: 'The government should do more to protect the

environment, even if it leads to higher taxes'; 'The government should do more to protect the environment, even if it leads to lower profits and fewer jobs'; 'Ordinary people should do more to protect the environment, even if it means paying higher prices'. The internal consistency of the answers to these questions was high (Cronbach's alpha = 0.78). Answers are coded so that high scores on the scale indicate a pro-environmentalist position.

17. The 'left-right' attitude scale is coded so that the highest score is the most right-wing. In the 'libertarian-authoritarian' scale the highest score is the most libertarian, and in the environmental scale the highest score is the most pro-environmental issues.

18. The results of the logistic regression models are shown below. For a further discussion of this technique and its use when predicting dichotomous party choices, see Aldrich and Nelson (1984).

Attitudes and voting intention among non-committed voters

Logistic regression models

	Model 1 Conservative vote		Model 2 Labour vote	
	B coefficient	Standard error	B coefficient	Standard error
Left-right	.21	(.04) **	-.22	(.04) **
Libertarian-authoritarian	-.10	(.04) **	.03	(.03)
Environmental attitudes	-.11	(.06)	.11	(.05) *
Pro-integration	.06	(.11)	.27	(.10) *
Pro-EMU	.41	(.16) *	-.31	(.17)
Pro-EU on tax	-.29	(.29)	.25	(.22)
Pro-EU on pollution	-.11	(.17)	-.02	(.18)
Pro-EU on defence	-.04	(.19)	-.23	(.19)
Pro-EU on employment rights	-.42	(.20) *	.08	(.18)
Pro-EU on immigration	.03	(.20)	.29	(.18)
N =	472		482	

* = sig @ p < .05
** = sig @ p < .01

19. Also, as mentioned above, the already small impact of interest in politics effectively disappeared when the social influences on support were included in a multivariate analysis.

20. For example, among Labour and Liberal Democrat supporters with degrees, no fewer than 73 per cent gave consistent pro-European responses across all three questions on the general aim of integration.

References

Ajzen, I. and Fishbein, M. (1980), *Understanding Attitudes and Predicting Social Behaviour*, Englewood Cliffs N.J.: Prentice Hall.
Aldrich, J. and Nelson, F. (1984), *Linear, Probability, Logit and Probit Models*, Beverly Hills: Sage.

Converse, P. (1964), 'The structure of belief systems in mass publics', in Apter, D. (ed.), *Ideology and Discontent*, New York: Free Press.

Curtice, J. and Gray, R. (1995), 'Deliberative poll shows voters keen on Europe when fully informed', *New Statesman and Society*, 16th June.

Eichenberg, R. and Dalton, R. (1993), 'Europeans and the European Community: the dynamics of public support for European integration', *International Organization*, 47, 507-34.

Evans, G. and Heath, A. (1995), 'The measurement of left-right and libertarian-authoritarian values: comparing balanced and unbalanced scales', *Quality and Quantity*, 29, 191-206.

Evans, G., Heath, A., and Lalljee, M. (1996, forthcoming), 'Measuring left-right and libertarian-authoritarian values in the British electorate', *British Journal of Sociology*, 47.

Flickinger, R. (1994), 'British political parties and public attitudes towards the European Community: leading, following or getting out of the way?', in Broughton, D., Farrell, D., Denver, D. and Rallings, C. (eds.), *British Elections and Parties Yearbook 1994*, 197-214, London: Frank Cass.

Franklin, M., Marsh, M. and McLaren, L. (1994), 'Uncorking the bottle: popular opposition to European unification in the wake of Maastricht', *Journal of Common Market Studies*, 32, 455-72.

Gabel, M. and Palmer, H. (1995), 'Understanding variation in public support for European integration', *European Journal of Political Research*, 27, 3-19.

George, S. and Rosamund, B. (1992), 'The European Community', in Smith, M. and Spear, J. (eds.), *The Changing Labour Party*, London: Routledge.

Heath, A. and Evans, G. (1988), 'Working-class conservatives and middle-class socialists', in Jowell, R., Witherspoon, S. and Brook, L. (eds.), *British Social Attitudes: the 5th Report*, Aldershot: Gower.

Heath, A., Evans, G. and Martin, J. (1994), 'The measurement of core beliefs and values: the development of balanced socialist/laissez-faire and libertarian-authoritarian scales', *British Journal of Political Science*, 24, 115-32.

Himmelweit, H., Humphreys, P. and Jaeger, M. (1985), *How Voters Decide* (revised edition), Milton Keynes: Open University Press.

Inglehart, R. (1977), *The Silent Revolution*, Princeton: Princeton University Press.

Inglehart, R. (1990), *Culture Shift in Advanced Industrial Society*, Princeton: Princeton University Press.

Janssen, J. (1991), 'Postmaterialism, cognitive mobilization and public support for European integration', *British Journal of Political Science*, 21, 443-68.

Kitschelt, H. (1994), *The Transformation of European Social Democracy*, Cambridge: Cambridge University Press.

Lipset, S. (1959), 'Democracy and working-class authoritarianism', *American Sociological Review*, 24, 482-501.

Lipset, S. (1981), *Political Man* (2nd Edition), Garden City, N.Y.: Doubleday.

Norris, P. (1994), 'Labour Party factionalism and extremism', in Heath, A., Jowell, R. and Curtice, J. (eds.), *Labour's Last Chance? The 1992 Election and Beyond*, Aldershot: Dartmouth.

Sniderman, P., Tetlock, P. and Brody, R. (1991), *Reasoning and Choice: Explorations in Political Psychology*, Cambridge: Cambridge University Press.

7 The sceptical electorate

John Curtice and Roger Jowell *

Few independent commentators these days seem to dispute that the British public is losing whatever confidence it ever had in its politicians (King, 1993; Crewe, 1995). And, in the wake of a seemingly endless sequence of financial and sexual scandals involving both ministers and backbench MPs, even some politicians are claiming as much (Ashdown, 1994). The word 'sleaze' has entered Britain's everyday political vocabulary. As a result, the government has been more or less obliged to establish a permanent committee of 'the great and the good' to examine and improve rules governing conduct in public life (Nolan, 1995).

Recent opinion polls have corroborated this picture of public cynicism about the integrity of politicians. For instance, a Gallup poll in April 1995 found that more than one-half of British people now regard the honesty and ethical standards of MPs as 'low' or 'very low'. Ten years earlier, only around a third had taken this view (Gallup, 1995: 27). In 1994 another Gallup poll found that nearly two-thirds of the British public believed that "most MPs make a lot of money by using public office improperly" (Crewe, 1995).

Such figures may, of course, tell us little more than that the electorate reacts adversely to repeated reports of sexual and financial impropriety

* John Curtice is Senior Lecturer in Politics and Director of the Social Statistics Laboratory, University of Strathclyde. Roger Jowell is Director of SCPR and a Visiting Professor at the LSE. John Curtice is also Deputy Director and Roger Jowell Co-director of the ESRC Centre for Research into Elections and Social Trends (CREST), based at SCPR and Nuffield College Oxford.

among ministers and MPs. Any sense of public outrage that may now exist could easily abate as the stories that feed it diminish. After all, the public's memory is notoriously short. Long-term damage to Britain's democratic health is by no means inevitable. Rather, if the rules of conduct for politicians are now to be strengthened and independently scrutinised, there may be a long-term improvement in public confidence.

From the point of view of Britain's democratic health, it is more important in the long term that the electorate should not lose faith in its system of political institutions, of which politicians in the House of Commons are only one part. This is not just a matter of what people currently feel about particular British political institutions, but of whether their underlying attitudes towards politics have changed. Certainly in the United States commentators such as Lipset and Schneider (1983) and Galbraith (1992) have pointed to what seems to be a serious secular decline in the American public's belief, and its participation, in social, economic and political institutions. What evidence is there of this in Britain?

To answer this question we need some notion of what values and beliefs are vital to the health of a democracy. How can we tell the difference between what may be no more than greater scepticism and vigilance on the part of the electorate, and a real crisis of cynicism about, and disaffection with, the way in which democracy works? The most obvious way to address this question is through the theory of the 'civic culture'.

The civic culture

The present apparent crisis of confidence in British politics and politicians is in stark contrast to the mood of the 1950s and early 1960s. Despite similar crises such as the 'Profumo affair', Britain was then often held up as the very model of a healthy democracy - stable but open, effective but responsive. A particularly influential account of why this was so is contained in the work of two American political scientists. In their book, *The Civic Culture*, Almond and Verba (1963) reported that, of the five countries they studied, Britain had the most appropriate balance of two crucial attributes needed by a democracy.

The first was a sense of *political efficacy*[1], a belief among ordinary people that they have a fair chance of influencing aspects of public policy which they wish to change. The second was *political trust*, an underlying public confidence in the willingness of political leaders and the apparatus of government to act in the national interest.

In appropriate balance, these two attributes formed a *civic culture*. Too much of one relative to the other would threaten democracy. If political efficacy, for instance, were to outstrip political trust, people would tend to take power into their own hands and to make the country ungovernable. Conversely, if political trust were to outstrip political efficacy, people would be inclined to give too much power to government, making it

unaccountable. Moreover, in the absence of *both* political efficacy and political trust, there would be widespread public alienation and apathy.

Almond and Verba's path-breaking work, however, has also been criticised (see Kavanagh, 1972; Kavanagh, 1980; Topf, 1989). A particular criticism was that they had, in effect, drawn causal inferences from mere associations. Thus, although they had demonstrated that Britain, for instance, had a distinctive (and in their terms thriving) civic culture, they had then drawn the dubious conclusion that this attribute was responsible for Britain's strong and stable democratic history. Yet the causal chain may well have worked the other way around. Britain's political culture could be the result of its political system.

Nonetheless, the concepts of political efficacy and political trust are valuable tools and we shall employ them here to explore changes in the way that British people view their political world and the role they play in it.

The decline of the civic culture

Since the early 1960s, when Almond and Verba were writing, many a commentator has argued that, even if Britain once had an ideal political culture, those days were past. Particularly important was Marsh who suggested that "political trust is at a much lower ebb than would seem healthy from Almond and Verba's point of view" (Marsh, 1977: 232). He also drew a helpful distinction between two kinds of political efficacy. First there was *personal efficacy*, the confidence among citizens that they could participate in and influence politics by, say, writing a letter to a newspaper, contacting an MP, and so on. Britain's scores on this attribute were relatively high. Also important, however, was *system efficacy*, the confidence among citizens that the nation's political institutions and those who operate them are able to listen and respond to citizens' demands and grievances. According to Marsh's work, Britain's scores on this attribute were relatively low.

This combination of high personal efficacy and low system efficacy in Britain was, Marsh argued, potentially explosive. If people were simultaneously confident of their own ability to participate in and influence political change, yet lacked confidence in the ability of the political system to respond, they would become increasingly likely to resort to 'unconventional' forms of political behaviour, such as protests and demonstrations, which could potentially threaten the stability of the political system.

Marsh's pessimism, taken up by Beer (1982), may in part be explained by the period in which his work was produced - shortly after the student riots of 1968 in Europe in which young, middle-class, well-educated students who could expect to secure the leading positions in their society were instead rebelling against it. Doubts were also developing about the ability of governments to cope with the demands of a growing and increasingly active

pressure group community (King, 1976; Brittan, 1977), reaching their height in 1974 when the then Conservative government, enmeshed in a bitter dispute against striking miners, called a general election to decide 'who governs Britain?' - and lost.

In any event, the political science literature of the 1970s and early 1980s reminds us that concerns about declining political trust and efficacy in Britain are certainly not new and may well be episodic. We therefore need to look carefully at the level and nature of political trust and efficacy in our survey compared with previous measurements and assess whether any variations we find appear to be systematic changes or mere fluctuations in the national mood. Moreover, building on the theoretical framework of Almond and Verba, we must also examine to what extent a decline in political trust or efficacy actually seems to matter. According to their arguments, any significant change over time in the balance between political trust and political efficacy will be deleterious to the health of a democracy, leading people towards extremes of either protest or apathy. Indeed, Johnston (1993) has now added to this list of potential woes by arguing that low political trust also results in a lack of tolerance for the democratic rights of others, especially minorities. To the extent that our data allow, we shall search for evidence of these anticipated consequences.

Over the past few years, a variety of reforms to the British constitution have been advocated. Formed in 1988, the organisation Charter 88 has consistently promoted such changes as a bill of rights, separate parliaments for Scotland and Wales, reform of the House of Lords and the introduction of some form of proportional representation (Holme and Elliott, 1988). Many of these proposals have now been taken up by the opposition Labour Party.

Supporters of such measures claim that their own dissatisfaction with these fundamental aspects of Britain's system of government is shared by the public at large (see for example, Dunleavy and Weir, 1991; Weir, 1992; Dunleavy and Weir, 1995). Far from resorting to protest or apathy, they assert that the British public wants to *extend* its opportunities to participate in and influence political debates (see also Benn, 1970). We will therefore examine whether support for constitutional reform is linked to levels of political efficacy and political trust.

Key questions to be answered

In this chapter we try to answer four key questions in order to throw light on the extent of change in Britain's political culture over the years, and the consequences of any such changes.

First, how much trust does the British public place in its political institutions and has this changed over the years? We compare our findings with those of Almond and Verba, and also those of Marsh, in order to find out.

Secondly, since the implications of any change in the level of political trust depend on what has happened to the level of political efficacy (see also Parry *et al*, 1992), we must take account of that phenomenon too, again comparing it with the benchmarks provided by Almond and Verba and Marsh.

Thirdly, having considered the nature of Britain's changing political culture, we will identify the implications of these changes. For instance, if the civic culture has declined, has it brought about the anticipated drop in support for democratic norms, or for tolerance of minority rights? Are people, as predicted, more willing than they used to be to contemplate 'unconventional' forms of political participation? And to what extent do any of these changes seem to be integrally linked to changes in levels of political trust or efficacy?

Finally, allowing for the possibility of a less pessimistic interpretation of changes in political culture than that taken by Marsh or Beer, we examine our data to see whether support for constitutional reform is growing - and, if it is, to what extent and among whom. We will also examine how support for reform relates to levels of political trust and political efficacy.

We will finally take a short detour to examine one of the underpinning assumptions behind Almond and Verba's work - that the stability of society itself depends largely on the extent and balance of political trust and efficacy among its citizens. To do this we compare (*via* both the *British Social Attitudes* survey and its sister *Northern Ireland Social Attitudes* survey) Britain's political culture with that of Northern Ireland. For, if Almond and Verba's thesis about the relationship between political culture and democratic stability is correct, Northern Ireland's political culture - with its record of strife and the breakdown of its political institutions - should look very different from Britain's. We shall see.

Trends in trust and confidence

How much trust and confidence do the British have in their political institutions, and is there any evidence of a decline? There is little doubt that more British people nowadays than around twenty years ago believe that there is something wrong with the way the country's political institutions are working. Evidence for this comes from answers our respondents gave to a question that was first asked in a survey undertaken for the Kilbrandon Commission on the Constitution in the early 1970s, and at periodic intervals thereafter. The question reads:

Which of these statements best describes your opinion on the present system of governing Britain?

It works extremely well and could not be improved
It could be improved in small ways but it mainly works well
It could be improved quite a lot
It needs a great deal of improvement

As the table below shows, while in 1973 the public divided more or less evenly between broad satisfaction and dissatisfaction, now the ratio is more than two to one in favour of the critics.

Trends in evaluations of system of government

The system of governing Britain ...	1973 %	1977 %	1991 %	1994 %
... 'could not be improved' or 'could be improved in small ways'	48	34	33	29
... could be improved 'quite a lot' or 'a great deal'	49	62	63	69

Sources: 1973: Crowther-Hunt and Peacock, 1973; 1977: Opinion Research Centre Survey; 1991: MORI/Rowntree Trust State of the Nation Survey

On the other hand, the table above also shows that this is by no means a recent change. The major part of the decline seems to have taken place between 1973 and 1977. This may well be a consequence of the oil crisis and the miners' strike which had helped to bring down the Conservative government in February 1974, together with the subsequent economic and other difficulties of the 1974-79 Labour government (among which was a failed attempt to introduce devolution to Scotland and Wales). In any case, the rate of decline has been lower since then, implying that recent events seem to have had only a modest impact.[2]

Even so, our data hardly constitute a vote of public confidence in Britain's system of government. Moreover, criticism seems to be aimed mainly at government itself rather than being directed at all the major institutions in British society. This can be seen from the following table which looks at whether people believe a variety of other major institutions in both the public and the private sector are well-run.

% saying well-run

	1983	1987	1994
Universities	n/a	65	73
The police	72	66	67
Banks	85	91	63
BBC	67	69	62
Manufacturing	40	48	59
State schools	n/a	30	52
The civil service	40	46	48
Trade unions	27	24	48
The press	49	39	47
Local government	33	29	39
National Health Service	49	35	33

Note: In 1983 respondents were asked whether or not each institution was 'well-run' or 'not very well-run'. In 1987 and 1994 they were invited to choose from a four-point scale ranging from 'very well-run' to 'not at all well-run'. The figures in the table for those years are the proportion saying either 'very well-run' or 'well-run'.

n/a = not asked in that year

The table reveals no *general* trend since either 1983 or 1987. Rather, individual institutions seem to have changed their image, falling from or rising in grace in comparison with others. Thus, trade unions, local government and state schools, all formerly at or near the bottom of the league, have improved their image, while the banking system - doubtless in response to adverse press comment in recent years - has suffered a precipitate drop from its prior position where it was seen as almost above criticism.

So public criticism of Britain's political system is not, it seems, simply part of a general growth in dissatisfaction with the way the country is run. Even so, as long as the electorate still broadly trusts the *motivations* of those in office, believing them for the most part to be attempting (albeit vainly at times) to act in the best interest of the community as a whole, the decline in satisfaction is surely far from irreversible. Unfortunately, however, this does not appear to be the case, as the next table shows. The figures come from responses to a question first used in 1974, which we have replicated on a number of occasions. It asks:

> *How much do you trust British governments of **any** party to place the needs of the nation above the interests of their own political party? Just about always, most of the time, only some of the time or almost never?*

Note that the question asks about government as an institution, not about either the present government or particular politicians. The answers reveal not only that the public has been pretty sceptical (even cynical) about its

political system for at least twenty years, but that this scepticism has now reached new heights.[3] Only 24 per cent of the population now believe that British governments always or mostly place the national interest above their party interests, compared with 38 per cent who believed this only eight years ago.[4]

Trends in trust in government

Governments put needs of nation above interests of party ...	1974	1986	1991	1994
... 'just about always' or 'most of the time'	39	38	33	24
... 'only some of the time' or 'almost never'	57	57	63	73

Source: 1974: Political Action Study

The public's lack of trust in government is underlined by the answers to two further questions. Just 27 per cent trust (always or most of the time) top civil servants "to stand firm against a minister wanting to provide false information to parliament". Seven years ago the figure was 37 per cent.[5] And astonishingly few, just nine per cent, trust "politicians of any party to tell the truth when in a tight corner" (asked for the first time in this round).

Beyond central government things get a little brighter, albeit only marginally. Nearly a third trust "local councillors of any party to place the needs of their area above the interests of their party", the same as in 1987 (Jowell and Topf, 1988). And 47 per cent trust the police "not to bend the rules in trying to get a conviction", around five points down on 1987. We doubt whether in 1994 Almond and Verba would still find the British particularly notable for their degree of confidence in the probity of the police.

The low level of trust revealed by these questions is not shared by all groups alike. As the table below shows, Conservative identifiers tend in general to have more political trust than do Labour and Liberal Democrat identifiers. For instance, two in five Conservative identifiers - as opposed to only around one in five Labour and Liberal Democrat identifiers - trust a government of any party to put the needs of the nation above the interests of their party. While we tried to frame our question so that people were encouraged to think about governments in *general* rather than the current Conservative administration in particular, it still seems likely that people's responses were partially coloured by their partisanship. This may well explain why the substantial party divide diminishes sharply when it comes to people's attitudes towards local councillors.

Trust by party identification

% who say the following can be trusted 'just about always' or 'most of the time'	Party identification		
	Conser-vative	Labour	Liberal Democrat
Government of any party to place needs of nation above party interests	40	17	22
Politicians to tell the truth in a tight corner	15	5	6
Top civil servants to stand firm against a minister wanting to provide false information to parliament	34	21	34
Local councillors to place needs of area above interests of own political party	36	29	37
The police not to bend rules in trying to get a conviction	60	36	51

This partisan colouring of responses could have important implications for our interpretation of the decline in political trust. As their period of exclusion from power at Westminster has lengthened, could not Labour identifiers in particular just have become increasingly reluctant to trust the institutions of central government? If so, the decline in political trust would be largely confined to opposition identifiers and it could be regarded as a temporary phenomenon, likely to disappear (or even be reversed) if or when the Conservatives lose power.

But this is not the case. The proportions trusting government have fallen by virtually the same amount among all three sets of party identifiers. Thus, 54 per cent of Conservative identifiers trusted government in 1987 and 40 per cent do so now, a drop of 14 points. The equivalent figures for Labour and the Liberal Democrats are 14 and 15 points respectively.

So the decline in political trust in recent years is not simply a partisan response to continued Conservative rule at Westminster, but a clear growth of disaffection with the operation of central government and its institutions.[6]

Recently, there has been some suggestion that young people are particularly likely to have low levels of faith in the political system (Cannon, 1994). But our data provide little or no support for this view (see also the chapter by Park in this volume).

Trust by age

% who say the following can be trusted 'just about always' or 'most of the time'	18-24	25-44	45-64	65+
Government of any party to place needs of nation above party interests	21	24	25	26
Politicians to tell the truth in a tight corner	11	8	7	10
Top civil servants to stand firm against a minister wanting to provide false information to parliament	25	28	26	28
Local councillors to place needs of area above interests of own political party	31	31	32	31
The police not to bend rules in trying to get a conviction	39	50	45	49

With the notable exception of perceptions of the police, the views of younger people are more or less indistinguishable on these items from those of their elders. Moreover, this has been true since 1987. The decline in trust in government has occurred among all age groups, just as it has among those of all political persuasions.

A sense of efficacy

As we have noted, before we can establish the likely *consequences* of a decline in political trust, we need to examine levels of political efficacy. We also made a distinction between personal efficacy, the belief in one's own ability to articulate a demand for change, and system efficacy, the belief that the system can and will respond to such calls for change. As the next table shows, levels of both forms of efficacy appear to have fallen in recent years.

Trends in system efficacy

% who strongly agree	1974	1986	1987	1991	1994
Generally speaking, those we elect as MPs lose touch with people pretty quickly	19	16	16	16	25
Parties are only interested in people's votes, not in their opinions	19	19	15	16	25
It doesn't really matter which party is in power, in the end things go on much the same.	n/a	n/a	n/a	11	16

Source: 1974: Political Action Study. In that study respondents were given a
    four-point scale ranging from 'strongly agree' to 'strongly disagree'. In
    the subsequent *British Social Attitudes* studies, answers were given on a
    five-point scale with a mid-point labelled 'neither agree nor disagree'.
n/a = not asked

Levels of system efficacy in Britain, like levels of political trust, are
remarkably low. When we add those who 'agree' with each proposition to
those in the table above who 'strongly agree', we find that nearly three in
four people nowadays believe both that MPs are out of touch and that
political parties operate cynically as vote-collectors alone. Three in five
believe that, whichever party is in power, nothing much changes. On the
other hand, political efficacy according to these questions has never been
high. Even twenty years ago, Marsh found that two-thirds agreed with the
first two of the propositions listed above.[7] Despite this, there has been a
distinct rise in the last three years in the proportion of people who
'strongly agree' with these statements. In short, the British public appears
now to have less confidence in the ability of its political system to respond
to its wishes than has ever been recorded before.[8]

So much for *system* efficacy. What about trends in *personal* efficacy -
people's sense of their own ability to express what they want from the
political system? As the next table shows, it is clear that the sense of
efficacy which Almond and Verba argued helped to balance the British
public's level of political trust has also fallen away. True, personal efficacy,
like system efficacy and political trust, has never been very high. But the
proportion who 'strongly agree' with each of the following negative
propositions has reached new heights. Most notably, over one in four
people now believe strongly that they have 'no say' in what their
government does, twice as many as in 1974.

Trends in personal efficacy

% who strongly agree that	1974	1986	1987	1991	1994
People like me have no say in what the government does	14	23	20	16	28
Voting is the only way people like me can have any say about how the government runs things	15	n/a	n/a	12	19
Sometimes politics and government seem so complicated that a person like me cannot really understand what is going on	21	17	n/a	16	22

Source: 1974: Political Action Study. See also the note to the previous table.
n/a = not asked

Our data are certainly very different from Almond and Verba's. They found that as many as 40 per cent *disagreed* that they had 'no say' in government. Less than one in four do so now. Similarly, they found that as many as one in three said that government and politics were *not* too complicated to understand; now no more than one in five feel this way. There were already signs in Marsh's data that personal efficacy was in decline; now the evidence is unambiguous.[9]

Just as we found that trust in *local* government is rather higher than trust in central government, so is people's sense of political efficacy higher with respect to local government than with respect to central government (see also the chapter by Young and Rao in this volume). For instance, fewer than one-half of the sample believes that *councillors* "lose touch with people pretty quickly", as opposed to nearly three-quarters who take this view about MPs. Similarly, more people believe that voting in council elections makes a difference, and fewer people believe that local government is too complicated to understand. Efficacy, like trust, appears to be lowest when it comes to central government.

Not surprisingly, one attribute that has consistently been linked with efficacy is education. Indeed, Almond and Verba suggested that education provides the 'keys to participation' (Almond and Verba, 1963: 381); Marsh also found that graduates were more likely to engage in both conventional and unconventional political behaviour because of their strong sense of efficacy. (See also Heath and Topf, 1986; Heath and Topf, 1987; Kavanagh, 1980; Topf, 1989.)

This link is confirmed by our survey. In the next table each respondent has been categorised as having low, medium or high *personal* efficacy on the basis of their answers to all three of the questions which have traditionally been used to measure this concept.[10] A similar procedure was adopted in the case of *system* efficacy.

Fewer than one in six graduates has a low sense of personal efficacy compared with almost two-thirds of those whose highest qualification is a

CSE or less. Not surprisingly, the difference is a little less dramatic in respect of system efficacy, but it is still very large. Only a third of graduates have a low sense of system efficacy compared with 70 per cent of those whose highest qualification is a CSE or less.

Political efficacy by education

	Highest educational qualification			
	Degree	A level	O level	CSE or below
	%	%	%	%
Personal efficacy				
Low	16	46	66	65
Medium	52	41	28	33
High	32	14	6	2
System efficacy				
Low	32	52	59	70
Medium	46	31	31	25
High	22	13	10	4

Although expected, these results nonetheless leave us with something of a puzzle. After all, if education is associated with a greater sense of political efficacy, why has the latter not become more widespread over the last thirty years in tandem with the former? It would seem then that Britain's changing political culture cannot be explained by its changing social fabric. Rather, it appears to be a reaction to changes in the perceived operation of the political system itself. Thus, contrary to the view of Almond and Verba, the workings of the political system seem to have influenced Britain's political culture rather than the other way around.

Threats to democracy?

Propensity to protest

According to the literature, a decline in both political trust and political efficacy is likely to pose serious threats to the health of a nation's democracy. The predicted consequences are political apathy and alienation, leading to less participation in conventional politics (though possibly more participation in unconventional or protest politics, particularly by the highly educated)[11]. A further possible consequence is less tolerance of the rights of minorities.

However, our own results suggest that, for the most part, Britain's changing political culture has not (yet, at any rate) brought about any consistent increase in apathy, alienation or intolerance. Indeed, our data cast doubt on the very existence of any clear link between political trust, political efficacy and political participation.

Our first piece of evidence comes from a question which we have asked on a number of occasions since 1983 and which Almond and Verba also addressed, though in a different way.[12] We asked:

Suppose a law was being considered by parliament which you thought was really unjust and harmful. Which, if any, of the things on this card do you think you would do?

We then followed up by asking everyone whether they had actually *done* any of the things listed below.[13]

Trends in potential political action

% saying they would	1983	1984	1986	1989	1991	1994
Sign a petition	55	58	65	71	78	68
Contact their MP	46	56	52	55	49	58
Contact radio, TV or newspaper	14	18	15	14	14	22
Go on a protest or demonstration	8	9	11	14	14	17
Speak to an influential person	10	15	15	15	17	15
Contact a government department	7	9	12	12	11	14
Form a group of like-minded people	6	8	8	10	7	10
Raise the issue in an organisation they already belong to	9	8	10	11	9	7
None of these	13	8	10	8	6	7

Confirming what Almond and Verba found more than twenty years ago, our results show that only a small minority of the population claim that it would simply do *nothing* in response to what it saw as an unjust law. But there is no sign here of any reduction in the public's propensity to protest. On the contrary, over the last eleven years there has been a fairly general - though unsteady - movement in the opposite direction (see also Young, 1992). This can be seen more clearly from the following table which focuses on the total number of actions respondents say that they would undertake.

Trends in numbers of potential actions

% saying they would undertake	1983	1984	1986	1989	1991	1994
Three or more actions	14	20	25	30	29	33
One or two actions	72	71	65	61	64	58
No action	12	8	10	8	6	7

On average, people would now undertake more actions than before. While the very conventional acts of signing a petition and contacting an MP still

predominate, there has also been a steady increase in the proportion saying they would go on a protest or a demonstration, comfortably the most unconventional of the actions on our list. Meanwhile, the recent marked increase in those who would contact the media might simply reflect the growth in those media outlets, especially radio, which invite audience participation.

For the most part there is no clear relationship between a respondent's level of political trust and his or her propensity to engage in a particular form of political action - or in taking any action at all. Using a simple measure of political trust based on answers to the questions we outlined earlier,[14] we found that those with high and low political trust scores were almost identical in their propensities to take political action. So a fall in political trust does not seem to be responsible for the increased willingness of people to take action *in general*. On the other hand, as the next table shows, low political trust *is* positively associated with a willingness to take particular actions - namely, to go on a protest or demonstration and to contact the media. Conversely, low political trust is linked to a decreased willingness to contact an MP. This confirms, perhaps, that politicians are less likely to be perceived by the more disaffected as a route to getting an effective response. In any event, to the extent that there is any new danger to democracy in Britain, these data suggest that it would be more likely to come from protest than from alienation or apathy.

Willingness to act by political trust

	Level of political trust		
	High	Medium	Low
% saying they would			
Go on a protest or demonstration	12	17	23
Contact radio, TV or newspaper	19	23	24
Contact their MP	62	58	53

But we must be somewhat suspicious about the hypothetical nature of these questions. Responses to "what would you do if...?" questions may be good indicators of *attitudes* but they are notoriously bad predictors of *behaviour*. Better evidence might come from responses to questions asking what people have actually done. While, for instance, fewer than one in ten admitted that they would do nothing in response to an unjust law, the next table shows that more than half in our latest survey actually did nothing. Naturally, this may simply indicate that many have never come across a law they regarded as unjust. But we would nonetheless expect an increase in reported willingness to take action to be accompanied by a corresponding rise in the number of actions taken.

Until our most recent survey it seemed that this was the case. In particular, the proportion indicating they had taken none of the actions on our list fell from slightly over a half in 1986 to slightly over a third in 1991. But in 1994 the proportion has returned to over one-half. As a result, it is

by no means clear that people are actually more likely to participate in politics now than they were in the mid-1980s.[15]

Trends in numbers of actions taken

% saying they have undertaken	1986	1989	1991	1994
Three or more actions	5	7	8	8
One or two actions	38	43	53	38
No action	56	48	37	53

There is little sign either that people are tending to replace unconventional actions for conventional ones. For instance, the percentage who have been on a protest or demonstration has held steady at nine per cent on each of the last three occasions on which the question was asked.

However, reported involvement in unconventional political action is related to political trust, in just the same way as is willingness to become involved. Indeed, echoing the work of Parry et al (1992), we find that those with low political trust are marginally more likely to have engaged in some kind of political action, thereby contradicting the expectation that declining political trust results in lower activity overall.[16]

So how do we account for the growing recent gap between willingness to engage in political action and actually having done so? One possibility is the decline we have charted in personal efficacy. As Parry et al (1992) found, personal efficacy is far more strongly related to reported (and potential) action than is political trust. Our findings back this up. As many as 61 per cent of those with a low sense of personal efficacy had not undertaken any of the actions we asked about, compared with 48 per cent of those with a medium level of efficacy and only 29 per cent of those with a high level (see also Young, 1985).

Tolerance of other people's rights

So far we have focused on what people anticipate doing and what they have actually done. Equally important for the health of democracy, however, is their attitude towards the civil and political rights of others. In particular, we need to examine whether, as anticipated, the decline in political trust has brought in its wake a reduction in people's tolerance of others (particularly minorities, perhaps) to engage in politics and enjoy the full rights of citizenship.

Here, at first sight, there is more reason for concern. We asked respondents whether or not they would allow each of six different forms of protest activity. The first three (protest meetings, pamphlets and demonstrations) are ones which most political theorists would regard as essential freedoms within a liberal democracy. As the next table shows, however, the public's endorsement of these rights is less convincing than

most civil libertarians might wish. Unqualified support for even the least threatening of the activities listed - holding public meetings - is now down to 48 per cent, by far the lowest since we began asking this question in 1985. Unqualified support for the publication of pamphlets has also fallen to an all-time low, as has support for demonstrations.

Admissibility of protest

% saying following should definitely be allowed	1985	1986	1990	1994
Organising public meetings to protest against the government	59	55	62	48
Publishing pamphlets to protest against the government	55	43	53	41
Organising protest marches and demonstrations	36	30	39	30

According to these figures, support for political and civil rights has apparently declined. But over the same time period, we also asked about the admissibility of three more controversial, even illegal, forms of protest: organising a nationwide strike; occupying government buildings; and damaging government buildings. Since such small minorities would definitely allow any of these activities (ranging from 12 per cent to less than one-half a per cent), we show instead the percentages that would definitely *not* allow each activity.

Tolerance of undemocratic protest

% saying following should definitely *not* be allowed	1985	1986	1990	1994
Seriously damaging government buildings	91	91	91	83
Occupying a government office and stopping work there for several days	61	61	58	50
Organising a nationwide strike of all workers against the government	52	54	43	39

In contrast to the three *conventional* forms of protest, to which the public has become less sympathetic, people seem to be growing rather more tolerant of the three 'unconventional' forms of protest. However, it is by no means clear that these trends can be accounted for by the decline in political trust. While those with low levels of trust are a little less likely than others to oppose unconventional actions, they are no more likely to oppose conventional ones.

The increase in sympathy for illegal forms of political protest is reinforced by answers to another question we have included since 1983. It asks:

In general would you say that people should obey the law without exception, or are there exceptional occasions on which people should follow their consciences even if it means breaking the law?

After showing little sign of change for ten years, now for the first time there has been a sharp increase in those plumping for the superiority of conscience over law.[17]   Correspondingly, there has been a fall in the proportion saying that even an unfair law should always be obeyed (see also the chapter by Brook and Cape in this volume).   Moreover, attitudes towards this issue are clearly associated with political trust. Those with low trust are noticeably more likely than are those with high trust to opt for conscience over law (69 per cent and 47 per cent respectively).

Trends in attitudes towards the law

	1983	1984	1986	1989	1991	1994
	%	%	%	%	%	%
The law should always be obeyed	53	57	55	50	52	41
Follow conscience in exceptional circumstances	46	42	43	48	47	56

This question is, in essence, about the boundaries between the powers of the state and the rights of citizens. The decline in political trust appears to have encouraged a shift in favour of the rights of citizens. This is confirmed by responses to other questions too. Contrary to Johnston (1993), those with a low level of trust were noticeably more likely to come down in favour of civil liberties rather than state control of one kind or another.

Similarly, there is little evidence in our data that those with low trust are particularly intolerant of minorities and minority rights. We asked a series of questions about whether or not various social changes which have benefited different minorities had gone too far. In the event, as the next table shows, those with low political trust are *more* likely to believe that they had *not* gone far enough. On all four aspects of minority rights which we investigated - applying to gypsies, women, ethnic minorities and homosexuals - sympathy is inversely related to political trust.

Political trust and attitudes towards minorities

% saying 'not gone far enough'	Level of political trust		
	High	Medium	Low
Attempts to provide sites for gypsies and travellers to stay	40	44	51
Equal opportunities for women in Britain	31	42	50
Attempts to give equal opportunities to black people and Asians in Britain	32	41	42
Attempts to give equal opportunities to homosexuals - that is, gays and lesbians	13	18	27

There are other isolated examples where those with low political trust *are* marginally less liberal in their attitudes towards the rights of others, but they hardly give support to the view that a decline in political trust opens the door to authoritarianism in Britain. On the contrary, those with low political trust are slightly more likely than others to be at the more liberal end of our libertarian-authoritarian scale, as described in the chapter by Brook and Cape.

Electoral participation

Having looked thus far at various forms of political participation, we now come to the one in which most people actually engage - voting in a general election. This is, in any case, meant to be the principal mechanism through which an electorate can influence its government.

It would be extremely difficult to conclude from our data that the decline in political trust is threatening electoral participation. For instance, just nine per cent feel that 'it is not really worth voting' in a general election. True, this compares with only three per cent who, in 1992, gave this answer in the British Election Study (BES), but the BES is conducted immediately after a general election when there is almost certainly a higher level of enthusiasm for voting than is the case mid-term (and there is probably a higher propensity among voters than non-voters to participate in that survey than in ours).

In any event, there is no evidence that a low level of political trust discourages people from voting. Despite being less likely to *say* that it is everyone's duty to vote, those with low political trust are just as likely as those with high trust to report actually having voted both in the last general and local elections. They are also just as likely to report having a strong party identification and to claim an interest in politics. In short, the next table hardly suggests that those with low political trust are less integrated into the electoral process in general than are those with greater trust.

Political trust and indicators of electoral involvement

	Level of political trust		
	High	Medium	Low
Voted in 1992 general election	82	80	79
Voted in last local elections	49	51	49
Very/fairly strong party identification	43	43	42
'A great deal' or 'quite a lot' of interest in politics	32	30	37
Agree that 'it is everyone's duty to vote'	70	72	57

Implications for Britain's democratic health

The decline we have measured in levels of political trust and political efficacy in Britain does not seem to be having the deleterious consequences that several commentators feared it would. Certainly there is no evidence that the British are becoming more apathetic about, or alienated from, their democratic institutions. The signs of change we have uncovered are less dramatic, such as a somewhat greater tolerance over time of the unconventional and of the dictates of conscience over law. In general, the defences against the danger of authoritarianism have, on some counts, probably been strengthened rather than weakened. We therefore tend to agree with Parry *et al* when they say that "cynicism...can in its different way be 'healthy' for an active democracy" (1992: 188).

The demand for constitutional reform

The last of the four key questions we promised to address was whether the decline in political trust in Britain is leading to demands for democratic renewal in the form of constitutional reform. A prior question, however, is whether any evidence actually exists of a growing and consistent movement favouring constitutional reform.

The reforms being pressed for by groups such as Charter 88 include electoral reform, separate parliaments for Scotland and Wales, reform of the House of Lords and a bill of rights. Meanwhile there are also continuing debates about how best to bring peace to Northern Ireland, the best way forward for Britain in the European Union and, more recently, the appropriate role of the royal family.

We included questions in our survey that tried to tap attitudes to all these issues and, where possible, to chart changes. Only in respect of three of them is there currently a clear majority in favour of change - the House of Lords, a parliament for Scotland, and the future status of Northern Ireland.

Exactly one-half of people support reform of the House of Lords, as opposed to just over a third who want it to remain as it is. This is almost an exact reversal of the balance of opinion in 1983, when we first included this question in the survey. In contrast, attitudes towards the long-term future of Northern Ireland have barely altered since 1983. Indeed, the proportion - 58 per cent - who, in our most recent survey, say that the long-term policy for Northern Ireland should be reunification with the rest of Ireland is precisely the same as in 1983. However, our fieldwork in 1994 was completed just before the Irish Republican Army announced its ceasefire. The next fieldwork round in the survey series will tell us what impact, if any, this has had.

Questions concerning Scotland's political future have to reflect the fact that a number of possible options have been canvassed. In fact, we invited respondents to choose between the four outlined below. Scottish opinion polls consistently show that around one in five Scots is opposed to any change in Scotland's constitutional status. But, as the table shows, the British as a whole are only a little more resistant to change. Around one in three people oppose any reform at all. Among the remainder by far the most popular option is for Scotland to have its own devolved Assembly. There has been little recent change in the distribution of responses.

Attitudes towards Scottish devolution

	1992	1994
Scotland should become independent, separate from the UK and the European Community	4	5
Scotland should become independent, separate from the UK, but part of the European Community	9	10
Scotland should remain part of the UK, but with its own elected Assembly that has some taxation and spending powers	52	47
There should be no change from the present system	28	28

Source: 1992: British Election Study

As for the monarchy, we last included questions about it in 1983. The results showed such overwhelming support that we thought there was little point in including the questions again. In the intervening eleven years, however, there has certainly been a change in attitudes. To be sure, there is still fairly solid public resistance to constitutional change, with two-thirds wanting to retain a monarchy. But, whereas in 1983 around two in three people believed it was 'very important' to keep the monarchy, now fewer than one in three take this view. The public's longstanding passion for its royal family has distinctly cooled. While it is still regarded by the public as comfortably the safest constitutional option available, it is perhaps no longer seen as indispensable.

We did not feel we could ask respondents plainly as to whether or not they were in favour of a bill of rights for Britain, because many would not have known what we meant. Rather, we asked them about one of the key underlying principles of a bill of rights - whether the courts should have the right to overturn certain laws made by parliament, or whether parliament should have the final say. To the extent that people understood and appreciated the distinction, public opinion was almost evenly divided on the issue (43 per cent in favour of giving power to the courts, 39 per cent for parliament having the final say),[18] but, as expected, there were rather too many 'don't knows' for comfort. Moreover, we have no prior reading on this subject against which to compare our findings. All we can conclude, therefore, is that this is hardly a burning issue (yet), certainly as far as the public is concerned.

The same conclusion can be drawn about attitudes towards electoral reform. Here we asked two separate questions in different parts of the questionnaire. On the self-completion questionnaire we asked:

> How much do you agree or disagree with this statement: Britain should introduce proportional representation so that the number of **MPs** each party gets matches more closely the number of **votes** each party gets?

Faced with this simple proposition, as many as 49 per cent of the sample agreed, with only 18 per cent disagreeing. Moreover, according to this measure, opposition to proportional representation appears to have declined since the last general election, when as many as 27 per cent disagreed.[19]

On the face to face questionnaire, however, we asked a question which posed a pair of alternatives that attempted briefly to summarise the key arguments used by advocates on either side of the issue, as follows:

> Some people say that we should change the voting system to allow smaller political parties to get a fairer share of MPs. Others say that we should keep the voting system as it is, to produce more effective government. Which view comes closest to your own, that we should change the voting system or keep it as it is?

As on each previous occasion when we have posed the question in this way, the majority in favour of proportional representation consistently fades away. Now only one in three of the same respondents favours a change in the voting system, while a formidable 60 per cent favour the *status quo*. Moreover, as the next table shows, there is no sign here of any increase in support for electoral reform over the last decade. If anything, the reverse is true.

Trends in attitudes towards electoral reform

	1983	1986	1987	1987b	1990	1991	1992	1994
	%	%	%	%	%	%	%	%
Change voting system	39	32	30	36	34	37	33	34
Keep as it is	54	60	64	58	59	58	60	60

Sources: 1983, 1987b, 1992: British Election Studies

If the way in which an issue is posed to respondents makes so much difference to their answers, we can safely conclude that many people have no firm views one way or the other. Certainly, it seems that the public's response to this issue in any future referendum is likely to depend critically on the way in which the debate (and perhaps the question itself) is framed (see Curtice, 1993).

Given such a lack of consistency in attitudes towards the specific issue of electoral reform, it is no surprise to discover that supporters of one type of constitutional reform are not necessarily the same as those in favour of others, despite the fact that they are often presented as a package.

To demonstrate this more systematically, we undertook a factor analysis of all of the items concerning constitutional change considered so far (excluding that on Northern Ireland which, apart from its possible implications for the position of Scotland, is rarely linked to the reform agenda on the mainland). This revealed the existence in the public mind of no less than three separate dimensions to the reform issue. One is the issue of electoral reform itself; a second is attitudes towards the monarchy, the House of Lords and to a lesser extent devolution; and a third, quite separate, dimension is the question of a bill of rights.[20]

Still, the degree of support for one constitutional reform or another should not be understated. Indeed, on most issues there is either majority support for change or at least a trend in favour of reform. The two issues on which this is more doubtful are a bill of rights and electoral reform. We doubt whether the debate on a bill of rights has entered the public's consciousness sufficiently for public attitudes to be reliably measured. And as far as electoral reform is concerned, public attitudes are demonstrably inconsistent and not necessarily related to attitudes towards other items on the reform agenda.

Returning then to the primary question we posed: how far is overall support for constitutional reform, which is considerable, related to levels of political trust and political efficacy?

We would anticipate that support for reform should be highest among those with a low sense of political trust. This indeed proves to be the case. However, as the next table shows, this relationship applies to some items on the reform agenda more than it does to others.

Constitutional reform and political trust

% saying:	Level of political trust		
	High	Medium	Low
Independence or devolution for Scotland	56	64	69
Change needed to House of Lords	38	53	65
Courts should have power to overturn laws made by Parliament	33	43	61
Coalition government would be better for Britain	42	50	60
Should introduce proportional representation so smaller parties get fairer share of MPs	45	52	50
'Abolish' or 'not important to keep' monarchy	21	35	50
Should change voting system	25	36	45

We find a similar pattern when we look at the responses to these items by levels of system efficacy.

But there is also a clear association with party identification. As the table below shows, Conservative identifiers are always least keen on reform, while Labour and Liberal identifiers have somewhat different priorities.

Constitutional reform and party identification

% saying	Party identification		
	Conservative	Labour	Liberal Democrat
Independence or devolution for Scotland	58	64	66
Change needed to House of Lords	36	60	55
Courts should have power to overturn laws made by Parliament	32	54	38
Coalition government would be better for Britain	34	52	65
Should introduce proportional representation so smaller parties get fairer share of MPs	38	52	67
'Abolish' or 'not important to keep' monarchy	16	45	28
Should change voting system	23	39	49

However, when we compare some of these results with previous readings, it is clear that the increase in public support for constitutional reform cannot be accounted for by partisan politics alone. The change in support is by no means confined to one party's supporters rather than another's. For instance, a 17 point drop in the proportion of Labour identifiers who believe that the House of Lords should remain unchanged is more than matched by a drop of 20 points among Conservative identifiers. The

Conservative Party's opposition to constitutional reform seems to have had surprisingly little impact on its supporters.

Thus, the decline in political trust and political efficacy appears at last to have had one clear consequence in the shape of reinforcing support for constitutional reform. Far from becoming more alienated and disaffected, the public seems to have responded to its growing scepticism about politicians and the political system by becoming more willing to look afresh at the machinery of democracy in Britain. Whether this is good or bad news depends on one's attitude towards the merits of Britain's existing constitution. But it is clearly a far cry from the predictions of Marsh and of Almond and Verba.

Coda: a look across the Irish Sea

As we noted earlier, a distinctive feature of Almond and Verba's work is its attempt to explain political developments in a nation from an examination of the attitudes of its citizens. Thus, they attributed Britain's stability as a democracy to the balance between its citizens' levels of political trust and political efficacy respectively. In this chapter we have cast doubt on these relationships. We can, however, extend our analysis further by comparing the British data with those for Northern Ireland.

The accolade granted to Britain by Almond and Verba that it is a strikingly successful liberal democracy would never surely have been granted to Northern Ireland. From 1969 until late in 1994, Northern Ireland experienced continuous social and political strife, referred to in the province as 'the troubles'. Mainly as a result of these problems, the province lost its own devolved system of government in 1972 and failed in two subsequent attempts to restore it. In short, Northern Ireland has experienced chronic social and political instability for a full twenty-five years.

If Almond and Verba are correct, therefore, we should anticipate that the pattern of responses we obtain in Northern Ireland should be very different from those in Great Britain. In particular, there would surely be lower levels of political trust and system efficacy, coupled with a greater level of support for, and willingness to engage in, unconventional and undemocratic political action.

This is far from the case. Indeed, what is most striking is the *similarity* in the pattern of responses on either side of the Irish Sea. As the next table shows, the stark fact is that Northern Ireland's political culture looks, for the most part, remarkably like Britain's. Despite the sectarian controversies that for many years have surrounded the work of the Royal Ulster Constabulary, this similarity even extends to such areas as trust in the police.

Political trust in Britain and Northern Ireland

% who say the following can be trusted 'just about always' or 'most of the time'	Great Britain	Northern Ireland
Government of any party to place needs of nation above party interests	25	21
The police not to bend rules in trying to get a conviction	47	47
Local councillors to place needs of area above interests of their own political party	33	31
Top civil servants to stand firm against a minister wanting to provide false information	30	27
Politicians to tell the truth in a tight corner	10	9

A similar picture emerges when we examine system efficacy. True, people in Northern Ireland are considerably more likely to say that it does not matter which party is in power - probably a reflection of the fact that Northern Irish voters are unable to vote for parties who have any chance of forming the government at Westminster. But, on the two other principal measures of system efficacy shown in the next table, the differences are hardly dramatic. Indeed, in response to another question, people in Northern Ireland (34 per cent) are actually slightly *more* likely to think that government works well and needs little change than are those in Britain (29 per cent).

System efficacy in Britain and Northern Ireland

% who agree that	Great Britain	Northern Ireland
Generally speaking, those we elect as MPs lose touch with people pretty quickly	72	79
Parties are only interested in people's votes, not in their opinions	72	77
It doesn't really matter which party is in power, in the end things go on much the same	57	70

Even more important and surprising, perhaps, is the fact that people in Northern Ireland are largely indistinguishable from people in Britain in terms of their tolerance of both conventional and unconventional forms of protest. As before, the first of the two tables below refers to the percentage who would definitely *allow* each action, while the second refers to the percentage who would definitely *not* allow each action.

Attitudes to political protest in Britain and Northern Ireland

% saying following should definitely be allowed	Great Britain	Northern Ireland
Organising public meetings to protest against the government	48	42
Publishing pamphlets to protest against the government	41	41
Organising protest marches and demonstrations	30	32
% saying following should definitely *not* be allowed		
Seriously damaging government buildings	83	82
Occupying a government office and stopping work there for several days	50	46
Organising a nationwide strike of all workers against the government	39	39

It is thus not possible to attribute Northern Ireland's troubled political history to its political culture, at least as measured by the questions asked in this study and elsewhere. It is not even possible to distinguish between Britain's political culture and that in Northern Ireland. This being so, it is little wonder that the various changes in Britain's political culture that we have uncovered have had so little of the impact that Almond and Verba and Marsh anticipated.

Conclusion

British people have clearly become less trusting of their politicians and political institutions in the last two decades. They are also more sceptical about the ability of the system to respond to the demands of the citizenry. Yet it is far from clear whether these developments have been unhealthy for the nation's democracy.

There is, for instance, no evidence to suggest that the decline in political trust has brought about a corresponding decline in people's willingness to participate in the nation's political life. Instead, it may have helped increase tolerance of the unconventional and thereby reinforced, rather than endangered, minority rights. It also seems to have encouraged support for constitutional reform.

Thus, far from undermining the health of British democracy, a less trusting and more vigilant public might already be helping to bring about an improvement in Britain's democratic condition. It may, for instance, be encouraging more open debate than in the past about how best to reform those aspects of the British political system which, according to the citizens themselves, are no longer working very well. A healthy measure of public scepticism, it seems, may be no bad thing.

Notes

1.   Almond and Verba themselves used the term 'civic competence'. We prefer to use the term 'political efficacy' which has been more widely used since Marsh (1977).

2.   However we should note that a follow-up to the 1991 MORI/Rowntree Trust State of the Nation Survey conducted this year, using quota sampling, reported only 22 per cent who now think the present system satisfactory compared to 76 per cent who think it needs improvement. Similarly, the EU's Eurobarometer survey, using a slightly different question, has reported a drop in the last two years in the proportion of British who say they are 'satisfied' with the way democracy works in their country, dropping for the first time to below 50 per cent. In the mid-1970s the proportion satisfied was typically between 60 and 65 per cent.

3.   In evidence to the Nolan committee, Ivor Crewe - referring to attitudes towards politicians rather than the political system - reaches much the same conclusion. He says: "...there is no doubt that distrust and alienation has risen to a higher level than ever before. It was always fairly prevalent; it is now in many regards almost universal" (Crewe, 1995).

4.   Indeed when the question was asked as part of the 1987 British Election Study immediately after the general election in that year, as many as 43 per cent trusted governments to put the national interest first. This is some six points higher than the proportion in the *British Social Attitudes* survey of that year which was conducted before the general election campaign. This suggests that by far the most common form of political participation for most people, voting in a general election, may help (temporarily at least) to increase their level of political trust. If so, it suggests that the existence of stable democratic processes can indeed influence the political culture of a nation.

5.   The 1987 figure is taken from the 1987 British Election Study.

6.   The substantial difference in the propensity of Conservative and Labour identifiers to trust the police was also present in 1987 when 62 per cent of Conservative identifiers trusted them always or most of the time but only 41 per cent of Labour identifiers did so.

7.   Marsh's figures are not strictly comparable to our own because he used a four-point rather than a five-point scale. Between 10 and 14 per cent of our respondents said they neither agreed nor disagreed with these items in our survey. Marsh's methodology tends to push these respondents into agreement or disagreement, and would thus be expected to produce higher levels of agreement. Comparing the two sets of figures is therefore likely to underestimate the degree of change. This is why we concentrate in the table on those who strongly agree, a group less likely to be influenced by the implementation of a five-point rather than a four-point scale.

   The sensitivity of responses to the precise way in which they are administered is underlined by the fact that we included the statement, "It doesn't really matter which party is in power; in the end things go on much the same" in both our self-completion and face to face questionnaires (the latter being the results included in the table). Despite being answered by the same group of respondents, 48 per cent agreed with the proposition on the self-completion survey compared with 58 per cent when asked face to face.

8.   One other reason why this might be the case is that people now have less confidence than before in the ability of governments to be able to solve the problems with which they have to deal. But there is no evidence to support this

proposition. As the following table shows, the proportion who think the government can do 'very little' to achieve certain objectives is fully in line with the mood recorded at various times over the last eleven years.

Trends in government efficacy

% saying governments can do very little to ...	1983	1984	1986	1987	1994
Keep prices down	26	38	29	22	36
Reduce unemployment	35	46	40	27	34
Cut crime	30	n/a	n/a	28	32
Improve the general standard of living	22	30	30	n/a	28
Improve the health and social services	11	19	15	11	17

Sources: 1983 and 1987: British Election Study
n/a = not asked

9. Almond and Verba's respondents were asked simply whether they agreed or disagreed with each of these items, whereas ours were given a five-point scale. However, with regard to both items the balance of opinion has clearly moved in favour of agreement. Further, our wording of the latter item (which was identical with Marsh's) was slightly different from that of Almond and Verba. They used the proposition: "some people say that politics and government are so complicated that the average man cannot really understand what is going on".

10. Respondents who strongly agreed with an item were given a score of one for that item, those who simply agreed a score of two, etc. We then calculated the respondent's average score across all three items. Those with an average score of less than 2.5 were assigned to the low political efficacy category, those with a score of 3.5 or above to the high category, and the remainder to the medium category.

11. Unlike political efficacy, there is relatively little correlation between political trust and education. For example, while only one-fifth of those with a CSE (or less) trust the government to put the needs of the nation first, no more than a quarter of graduates do so either.

12. However, the question asked by Almond and Verba (and Marsh) was open-ended and so cannot be compared with our findings. For a useful summary of their results see Kavanagh, 1980: 150.

13. Note that in 1983 the question about what the respondent would do followed others (themselves somewhat different from the question reported here which was asked from 1986 onwards) about whether or not he or she had ever felt there had been an unjust law passed by parliament and, if so, what he or she had done about it. In addition, the question began "Suppose a law was being considered *now* by Parliament..." These differences in the context in which the 'would do' question was asked in 1983 and its wording should be borne in mind in interpreting the somewhat different pattern of responses in 1983 from 1984.

14. The measure was created by giving respondents a score of 1 for each item on which they said they trusted the organisation or group 'just about always' or 'most of the time', 2 if they said 'only some of the time' and 3 if they said 'almost never'. Respondents who said that they did 'not know' were also given a score of 1 for that item. This produced a scale with values ranging from 5 to 15. Those with a score of 8 or less were then classified as having high trust, those with a score of 9 to 11, medium trust, and those with a score of 12 or more, low trust.

15. We might also note here a fall in reported party membership from six per cent in 1987 to three per cent in our latest survey. For further details see the chapter by Young and Rao in this volume.

16. Our results are similar despite the fact that Parry *et al* (1992) used different instruments to measure what they termed 'political cynicism' and efficacy. They found that cynicism was 'associated with action, not inaction', but that it was also associated with taking unconventional action. In the case of the latter they found a particular propensity to take direct action among those with both low political trust and high personal efficacy. This interaction is also clearly present in our data. Only four per cent of those with low trust and low personal efficacy report having been on a demonstration compared with 28 per cent of those with low trust and high personal efficacy.

17. We should note that we administered the same item on the self-completion questionnaire as well as face to face. Encouragingly, the results were very similar, suggesting that the distribution of answers is robust irrespective of the mode in which the question is administered. The question was also asked on the self-completion questionnaire in 1985 and 1990 when it did *not* also appear on the face to face questionnaire (and so is not included in the table of trends). In both those years, which happened to correspond with the miners' strike and the rebellion against the poll tax respectively, similar proportions to the 1994 findings (58 per cent and 52 per cent respectively) supported following conscience above law. Given that the mode in which the question is asked apparently makes little difference, it seems likely that similar majorities would have been recorded in 1985 and 1990 if the question had been asked face to face. So this year's results may not be quite so unprecedented as they at first seem. Moreover, this suggests that the answers to this question may well be influenced at least as much by short-term political events as by any long-term decline in political trust.

18. Our finding is in stark contrast to that in the more recent MORI/State of the Nation poll which found that 79 per cent agreed that 'Britain needs a Bill of Rights to protect individual liberty' (Dunleavy and Weir, 1995). We suspect, however, that faced with such a proposition many respondents would not wish to pass up the prospect of additional rights. Our findings show far less support for one of the major implications of any bill of rights.

19. This figure comes from the 1992 British Election Study.

20. The principal factor loadings on each dimension (ignoring signs) were:
Factor 1: Agree PR fairer 0.81; Change electoral system 0.79; Coalition Government 0.58. (eigenvalue 2.00)
Factor 2: Monarchy 0.75; House of Lords 0.70; Scottish Parliament 0.53 (eigenvalue 1.23)
Factor 3: Courts have say 0.88 (eigenvalue 1.02).
All other loadings were less than 0.20. The solution accounted for 61 per cent of the variance.

References

Almond, G. and Verba, S. (1963), *The Civic Culture: Political Attitudes and Democracy in Five Nations*, Princeton, N.J.: Princeton University Press.

Ashdown, P. (1994), *Beyond Westminster: Finding Hope in Britain*, London: Simon and Schuster.

Beer, S. (1982), *Britain Against Itself: The Political Contradictions of Collectivism*, London: Faber and Faber.

Benn, A. (1970), *The New Politics: A Socialist Reconnaissance*, London: Fabian Society, Fabian Tract No. 402.

Brittan, S. (1977), *The Economic Consequences of Democracy*, London: Temple Smith.

Cannon, D. (1994), 'Generation X and the new work ethic', *The Seven Million Project Working Paper 1*, London: DEMOS.

Crewe, I. (1995), Oral evidence in Nolan (chmn.), 'Standards in public life: 1st report of the Committee on Standards in Public Life, Vol. II', *Transcripts of Evidence*, Cm. 2850-II, London: HMSO.

Crowther-Hunt, Lord and Peacock, A. (1973), 'Royal Commission on the Constitution 1969-73', *Memorandum of Dissent*, Vol. 2, London: HMSO.

Curtice, J. (1993), 'Popular support for electoral reform: the lessons of the 1992 election', *Scottish Affairs*, **4**, 23-32.

Dunleavy, P. and Weir, S. (1991), 'Ignore the people at your peril', *The Independent*, 25 April.

Dunleavy, P. and Weir, S. (1995), 'It's all over for the old constitution', *The Independent*, 30 May.

Galbraith, J. (1992), *The Culture of Contentment*, Harmondsworth: Penguin.

Gallup (1995), *Gallup Political and Economic Index*, **417**.

Heath, A. and Topf, R. (1986), 'Educational expansion and political change in Britain, 1964-1983', *European Journal of Political Research*, **14**, 543-67.

Heath, A. and Topf, R. (1987), 'Political culture', in Jowell, R., Witherspoon, S. and Brook, L. (eds.), *British Social Attitudes: the 5th Report*, Aldershot: Gower.

Holme, R. and Elliott, M. (eds.) (1988), *1688-1988 Time for a New Constitution*, London: Macmillan.

Johnston, M. (1993), 'Disengaging from democracy', in Jowell, R., Brook, L. and Dowds, L. with Ahrendt, D., *International Social Attitudes: the 10th BSA Report*, Aldershot: Dartmouth.

Jowell, R. and Topf, R. (1988), 'Trust in the Establishment', in Jowell, R., Witherspoon, S. and Brook, L. (eds.), *British Social Attitudes: the 5th Report*, Aldershot: Gower.

Kavanagh, D. (1972), *Political Culture*, London: Macmillan.

Kavanagh, D. (1980), 'Political culture in Great Britain: the decline of the political culture', in Almond, G. and Verba, S. (eds.), *The Civic Culture Revisited*, Newbury Park, Ca.: Sage.

King, A. (1976), 'The problem of overload', in King, A. (ed.), *Why is Britain Becoming Harder to Govern?* London: BBC.

King, A. (1993), 'Public pours scorn on pontificating politicians', *Daily Telegraph*, 13 September.

Lipset, S. M. and Schneider, W. (1983), *The Confidence Gap: Business, Labor and Government in the Public Mind*, New York: Free Press.

Marsh, A. (1977), *Protest and Political Consciousness*, Beverly Hills: Sage.

Nolan, Lord (chmn.) (1995), *Standards in Public Life: 1st Report of the Committee on Standards in Public Life*, Cm. 2850, London: HMSO.

Parry, G., Moyser, G. and Day, N. (1992), *Political Participation and Democracy in Britain*, Cambridge: Cambridge University Press.

Topf, R. (1989), 'Political change and political culture in Britain, 1959-87', in Gibbins, J. (ed.), *Contemporary Political Culture: Politics in a Postmodern Age*, London: Sage.

Weir, S. (1992), 'Waiting for change: public opinion and electoral reform', *Public Opinion Quarterly*, **48**, 197-221.

Young, K. (1985), 'Shades of opinion', in Jowell, R. and Witherspoon, S. (eds.), *British Social Attitudes: the 1985 Report*, Aldershot: Gower.

Young, K. (1992), 'Class, race and opportunity', in Jowell, R., Brook, L., Prior, G. and Taylor, B. (eds.), *British Social Attitudes: the 9th Report*, Aldershot: Dartmouth.

Acknowledgements

The authors wish to thank The Leverhulme Trust for funding to support the module of questions on trust in the political process. Many of these will be repeated in 1996. We also wish to thank Ann Mair of the Social Statistics Laboratory, University of Strathclyde, without whose computing support this chapter would never have been written.

8 Differences of degree: attitudes towards universities

Chris Rootes and Anthony Heath [*]

The expansion of higher education has been one of the most notable social changes of the post-war period. Nearly a third of all young people now enter full-time higher education, compared with seven per cent little more than thirty years ago (Halsey, 1992: 95). The numbers of mature and part-time students have risen even more rapidly. As a result, the total number of students has tripled over the last thirty years - from 429,000 in 1965 to 1.3 million in 1991 (Department for Education, 1993: 8). Since then, far from slackening, the pace of change has quickened yet again. Enrolments have increased and, with the abandonment of the binary higher education system in 1992, all former polytechnics and several colleges of education now have university status.

But is the British public happy with such growth and with the performance of the country's universities? Has there, perhaps, been an *over*expansion of higher education and, consequently, a decline in the public's confidence in universities? These are the questions this chapter sets out to answer.

Why might attitudes have changed?

The first wave of expansion in higher education took place in the 1960s. In part, it was a response to the demographic bubble produced by the post-

[*] Chris Rootes is Senior Lecturer in Sociology and Director of the Centre for the Study of Social and Political Movements at the University of Kent at Canterbury. Anthony Heath is Official Fellow in Sociology at Nuffield College, Oxford and Co-director of the Centre for Research into Elections and Social Trends (CREST).

war 'baby boom' - there were simply more young people to educate; consequently, higher education needed to expand simply to accommodate the same proportion of people as before. At the same time, most national governments had become convinced that investment in higher education would benefit the nation as a whole. Producing a more highly educated workforce would enhance economic performance and thus improve - or at least maintain - the nation's competitive position. In Britain, as elsewhere, manual work was declining and there was growing demand from business and industry for qualified manpower to fill the expanding numbers of managerial, professional and technical positions in salaried occupations (what we call the 'salariat'). Graduates, in particular, tended to be employers' preferred choice of recruit for these new vacancies - gaining substantial economic benefits from their investments in higher education as a result.

This was not all. Higher educational qualifications became increasingly regarded as necessary for admission to, and advancement in, salariat careers. Consequently, parents became more concerned to ensure that their children had access to higher education. Demand was particularly strong from parents who were themselves employed in the expanding professional and managerial occupations of the salariat, but who had been denied the opportunity of higher education in their own youth (Halsey, Heath and Ridge, 1980).

It is by no means obvious that the same pressures for expansion are present today. Far from growing, the number of 18-21 year olds has been falling in recent years. Press reports of graduate unemployment and of the allegedly declining rates of return on individuals' investments in higher education might suggest that there is now an *over*supply of graduates (Schofield, 1995).[1]   With the ballooning cost of student support, the government has partly replaced grants with loans and required universities, like other publicly-funded bodies, to make 'efficiency gains' which have significantly eroded the real level of spending per student. These changes have - in turn - led to well-publicised concern about student poverty and indebtedness, to a rise in the proportion of students who drop out of their courses, and to worries that expansion has reduced the quality of the education provided.

Parents too may have lost their enthusiasm for expansion. Those who are less affluent may have become more concerned about the cost of sending their children to university - and the reduced returns from doing so. More privileged families may have become worried that university expansion is weakening their competitive advantage. Indeed, as the growth of the salariat slows and its position consolidates, its members might be expected to become increasingly concerned to maintain their relatively privileged positions and to pass these on to their children (Goldthorpe, 1982). Consequently, they would seek to make it more difficult for those from other classes to gain access to salaried occupations. One means of doing this is to resort to 'credentialism' - restricting entry to certain positions to those with formal educational qualifications - while ensuring that the

number of people who acquire such qualifications is limited (Parkin, 1974, 1979; Collins, 1979).[2]

As graduate numbers swell, we might expect graduates themselves to take a particular interest in protecting the value of their educational investment. To be sure, they still have excellent chances of reaching the salariat (Heath, Mills and Roberts, 1992), but a degree no longer leads automatically to a rewarding position.[3] The proportion of the salariat with a university degree is rising rapidly. Even as recently as 1987, only 30 per cent of professionals and 12 per cent of managers in Britain were graduates (*Social Trends* 19, 1989). Just six years later the proportions had risen to 61 per cent of professionals and 19 per cent of managers, while a further 16 per cent of professionals and 19 per cent of managers had a higher educational qualification below degree level (*Social Trends* 25, 1995: 57). These figures clearly suggest that oversupply might be looming - and with it the erosion of graduates' relative market position - at a time when student numbers have just expanded rapidly once more.

We begin this chapter by reviewing briefly the evidence of public support for university expansion - and, in particular, the support shown by employers and graduates themselves. We then turn to a more detailed examination of what people expect from universities and of the public's satisfaction with their performance.

Attitudes to expansion

Has public support for expansion declined? Since the start of the *British Social Attitudes* survey series, we have regularly asked:

> *Do you feel that opportunities for young people in Britain to go on to higher education - to a university or college - should be increased or reduced, or are they at about the right level now?*

The results give little credence to the notion that support for expansion in higher education is flagging. Indeed, since 1985 those who think that opportunities should be increased have outnumbered those who are satisfied with the *status quo*. The proportion who think opportunities to go on to higher education should be increased 'a lot' rose from 22 per cent in 1983 to 32 per cent in 1990[4] and, despite the expansion of student numbers since then, that figure has not fallen at all over the last four years. True, since 1983 there has been some decline in the proportion saying that opportunities should be increased 'a little' - but overall the mood favouring expansion is still marginally stronger than it was a decade ago.

Attitudes towards the expansion of higher education

Opportunities for higher education should be ...	1983	1985	1987	1990	1993	1994
... increased a lot	22	25	29	32	32	32
... increased a little	22	24	24	20	17	17
... about right level now	49	43	42	43	46	46
... reduced a little or a lot	5	4	3	2	3	3

These are really rather remarkable results. Even if the public approves of the expansion which has occurred so far, over time we might expect the proportion in favour of *further* expansion to fall, as well as the proportion thinking that opportunities were 'about right' to rise as unsatisfied demand is increasingly met. If there were serious discontent with universities or their products, we might expect people to demand a reduction in provision. Instead, support for further expansion continues undiminished.

However, as we shall see later, many people are not well acquainted with what goes on in universities. They may well not be aware of the extent to which universities have grown. But what about those who *should* know how things have changed? What, for example, are the views of employers and managers who are, after all, the principal recruiters of those emerging from university? In fact, employers and managers in large establishments (those with 25 or more employees) tend to be even *more* favourable towards expansion than the public as a whole. It is they who are most likely to recruit graduates, and their enthusiasm for expansion is now greater than ever before. Those in smaller establishments are generally somewhat less keen.

Attitudes towards the expansion of higher education among employers and managers[5]

% saying opportunities for higher education should be 'increased a lot'	1983	1985	1987	1990	1993	1994
Employers and managers in large establishments	27	23	33	34	28	38
Employers and managers in small establishments	13	23	30	30	38	31
All other respondents	22	26	28	32	32	32

We shall look in more detail at employers' and managers' expectations of, and satisfaction with, higher education later. But this first overview gives no support to the idea that employers are becoming disillusioned with higher education or that they wish to reverse its expansion.

What of graduates themselves? As we have suggested, graduates might be unenthusiastic about a further expansion in higher education if they

thought that it would devalue the worth of their own educational investment. Once again, however, our data suggest this is not the case. In fact, the higher a person's educational qualifications, the *more* likely she or he is to think higher educational opportunities should be increased 'a lot'. In our latest survey, half the graduates took this view - compared with only just over a quarter of those with no qualifications above CSE level. Yet, back in 1985[6], respondents' educational experience made little difference to their views about university expansion. Since then, with the exception of a 'blip' in 1993[7], both graduates and those with higher education to below degree level have become more likely to say that opportunities for higher education should be 'increased a lot', while opinion among those with lesser qualifications has changed relatively little.

It is a matter of speculation why this should be so. One possibility is that graduates, many of whom are the first generation in their family to enjoy higher education and the advantages it confers, are increasingly convinced of its universal value. Conversely, the less well-qualified - confined more and more to declining manual and personal service occupations - may feel that higher education is of little benefit to them or their offspring.

**Attitudes towards the expansion of higher education,
by level of education**

% saying opportunities for higher education should be 'increased a lot'	1985	1987	1990	1993	1994
Highest qualification					
Higher education: degree level	29	39	49	35	49
Higher education: below degree level	23	31	34	38	35
A level or equivalent	35	38	32	35	36
O level or equivalent	25	31	35	31	27
CSE or below	24	24	26	30	28

Funding expansion

There is thus continuing support for increasing opportunities to attend university. But obviously any such expansion has to be funded. How high a priority does the public give to spending *more* government money on universities? Or do people think that those who attend universities should pay more towards the cost of their own education?

Despite a decade of lamentation and dire warnings about spending cuts by those who work in universities, higher education is *not* a high priority for extra spending as far as the public is concerned. Indeed, our latest survey found that university students came last out of five groups suggested as targets for extra government spending. Less than one in ten named them as a first priority and only a quarter chose them as either a first or second priority. This is nothing new. On only one of the six occasions that we

asked this question have university students *not* come last, and then only
by a whisker. Those who have caught the public's attention are nursery
and pre-school children, with the proportion choosing them as their top
priority doubling between 1993 and 1994. Both the government and the
opposition have recently put forward proposals for the expansion of pre-
school provision and in so doing appear clearly to have caught the public
mood. But nursery school children still play second fiddle to both children
with special needs and secondary school children. Each of these two groups
continues to be a priority for just under a third of respondents.

First priority for extra spending on education

	1983	1985	1987	1990	1993	1994
Less able children with special needs	32	34	29	29	34	28
Secondary school children	29	31	37	27	29	28
Nursery or pre-school children	10	10	8	16	11	21
Primary school children	16	13	15	15	16	11
Students at colleges or universities*	9	9	9	9	7	9

* Before 1993 this item read '..colleges, universities or polytechnics'

Perhaps those who *recruit* graduates place a greater emphasis on the need
for more funding for universities? The very opposite is true - just three per
cent of employers and managers in large enterprises said that extra spending
on college students was their top priority. True, employers and managers
in smaller organisations were a little more favourably disposed than the
public as a whole - with 13 per cent making university students their first
priority. But, in general, it seems that employers and managers are unlikely
to lobby hard for extra spending to match their relative enthusiasm for
expansion in higher education.

Graduates differ in this respect. They are more than twice as likely as
those with no qualifications above CSE level to name university students
as their first priority for extra spending, 16 per cent doing so. Students
again come top of their list when it comes to naming their second priority.
Graduates also differ strikingly from the rest of the population by giving
a very low ranking to spending on less able children with special needs.
Only seven per cent said this was their first priority, compared with no less
than 40 per cent of those with no qualifications above CSE level.[8] This is
not a one-off aberration. While graduates have not always ranked extra
spending on college students *ahead* of more expenditure on children with
special needs, they have consistently placed less emphasis on the latter than
have those with less exalted qualifications. This gap is now wider than
ever.

If there is not much enthusiasm for increased spending on university
students, despite considerable support for expansion, we might anticipate
that the public thinks students themselves (or their parents) should pay
more for their education. Government policy has already moved in this

direction. Student loans were introduced in 1990 as a means of partly funding students' maintenance costs, and the proportion of student support which they provide has increased considerably since then. But some have gone further by arguing that students should also contribute towards the costs of their *teaching*. Indeed, there appears to be some support for this move within universities themselves, mainly as a means of compensating for the decreased amount of government money they receive for each student admitted.

Yet there is little evidence that there would be public support for such a move. Only just over a quarter believe that students 'should pay something towards their own teaching fees', a figure that has changed little since 1993. Graduates themselves are even less keen on the idea - only 17 per cent favour it, compared with 32 per cent of those with no qualifications above CSE level.

Thus the message so far appears to be a mixed one - certainly as far as universities are concerned. While there is considerable public support for their expansion, it is far from clear quite how the public expects this to be funded.

Satisfaction with universities

In a climate characterised by increasing criticism of many national institutions, one might expect to find a measure of dissatisfaction with universities. Certainly, the government has felt it necessary to introduce a range of measures over the last ten years to monitor the quality of their teaching, research and internal administration. Meanwhile employers are regularly reported as complaining about the difficulty of recruiting graduates with the personal and intellectual skills they seek. True, such reports may be more sensationalist than systematic, but they might nevertheless have inflicted harm on the image of higher education.

This is far from the case. We asked respondents how well they thought universities were administered. No fewer than 73 per cent thought they were 'well-run' or 'very well-run'. This puts universities ahead of ten other institutions (including the police and banks) about which we asked the same question. Furthermore, people are more likely to think universities are well-run nowadays than they were when we asked the same question seven years ago (for further details, see the chapter by Curtice and Jowell in this volume).

Of course, it could still be the case that the public is dissatisfied with *specific* aspects of universities' performance. This ultimately depends upon what people expect universities to achieve. To address this issue we asked how important people think it is that universities aim to develop six particular qualities in their students. These qualities are shown in the next table. We then asked whether - in practice - these qualities *were* developed by universities.[9]

The results show that the public clearly has a very utilitarian view of university education. Over eight in ten think it either 'essential' or 'very important' that universities teach their students to 'speak and write clearly', acquire 'knowledge that equips people for life' and learn the 'skills and knowledge which will help them get a good job'. In contrast, only a bare majority think it 'essential' or 'very important' that universities develop one of the traditional objectives of a liberal 'civilising' education - a 'readiness to challenge other people's ideas'.

Importance of qualities that universities should develop in their students

Quality	Essential %	Very important %	Fairly important %	Not very/ not at all important %
An ability to speak and write clearly	48	39	10	1
Knowledge that equips people for life	38	43	14	2
Skills and knowledge which will help them get a good job	37	51	9	2
Self-confidence	31	46	18	1
How to live among people from different backgrounds	23	43	26	5
A readiness to challenge other people's ideas	14	38	36	8

How do those with experience of higher education rate these qualities? There is a difference here between graduates and those who have higher education qualifications below degree level. Graduates, for instance, display rather more enthusiasm than average for the 'civilising' mission of universities. Nearly a third (32 per cent) think it 'essential' that universities teach students how to live among people from different backgrounds, and over a quarter (27 per cent) think it 'essential' that they develop a readiness to challenge other people's ideas. In contrast, those who have higher educational qualifications *below* degree level (generally vocational and technical qualifications) are more enthusiastic about the utilitarian function of universities.[10] Well over half this group - 57 per cent - think it 'essential' that universities give students the ability to read and write clearly and over four in ten see it as 'essential' that they provide the knowledge necessary to equip them for life, and the skills which will help them get a good job.

Whether the public in general has always taken a predominantly utilitarian view of higher education or whether this is a new development we cannot say. Images of the lost world of the gentleman scholar, embellished by such sumptuous costume dramas as the televised version of

Brideshead Revisited, and titles such as *The Degradation of the Academic Dogma* (Nisbet, 1972) and *Decline of Donnish Dominion* (Halsey, 1992) suggest such utilitarianism is new, but it should not be forgotten that, even when their curricula were most biased toward 'humanistic' studies, the primary function of universities was regarded as education for the professions. Tension between the 'civilising' and utilitarian purposes of the university has arisen so often that Halsey is almost certainly right to suggest that the 'crisis' of the university is a misnomer and that it is, rather, "a chronic peril" (Halsey, 1992: 57).

If the public is quite clear about what it thinks universities should do, what does it think they actually *achieve*? In fact, a majority believes that universities do develop the qualities we asked about at least 'quite a lot'. However, in no case do more than two-thirds take this view. There is no clear distinction between the perceived successes of the universities in delivering the more civilising qualities and the more utilitarian ones.

Universities' performance in developing qualities in students

% saying quality developed 'very much' or 'quite a lot'

Self-confidence	65
A readiness to challenge other people's ideas	63
Skills and knowledge which will help them get a good job	63
An ability to speak and write clearly	62
How to live among people from different backgrounds	56
Knowledge that equips people for life in general	50

There is one important feature of these results which is not shown here. For each of the qualities we asked about, *at least* one person in ten was unable to give an answer. Furthermore, this is undoubtedly a conservative estimate of the degree of ignorance about the performance of universities. It suggests that - though they may be well regarded - for many their activities are shrouded in mystery. In contrast, when it came to saying how important it was that universities *should* develop a particular quality, only around two or three per cent felt unable to give an answer.

True, graduates themselves have little difficulty in assessing the success of universities. But this is hardly surprising. On only one of the six qualities did as many as four per cent say they could not give an answer. But among those with no qualifications or whose highest qualification was a CSE, between 15 and 24 per cent were unable to choose. Knowledge about what universities actually *do* is clearly socially skewed.

Still, among those who did answer the question, there is little evidence that, behind the general perception that universities are well-run, there lurks a concern about particular aspects of their performance. But there is a danger in taking these figures as adequate measures of satisfaction. Some of those who think that universities are successful in developing a particular quality might actually believe that they should not be attempting to do so.

Conversely, those who say that universities are *not* developing a particular quality in students can hardly be seen as dissatisfied if they do not think that this particular quality is important in the first place.

This difficulty can be overcome.[11] We classified people as being satisfied with the job universities are doing only if they met one of two conditions. The first was to say that it is 'essential' or 'very important' that students should develop a particular quality *and* also to say that universities are succeeding 'very much' or 'quite a lot' in this task. The second condition was to consider a quality no more than 'fairly important' and to believe that universities *are* developing it 'not very much' or 'not at all'.

This leaves us with two groups who can be considered dissatisfied. One consists of those people who believe it is 'essential' or 'very important' that universities should develop a particular quality - but who believe that universities develop that quality 'not very much' or 'not at all'. In short, this group believes that universities are doing *too little* for their students. The other group consists of those who say that the development of a particular quality is 'not very important' or 'not at all important', but think that universities develop it 'very much' or 'quite a lot'. People who are critical of the humanistic aspects of universities, feeling that they do too much to encourage their students to challenge and protest, might fall into this camp.

Even this strategy is not without its drawbacks.[12] In interpreting the figures that follow, we should bear in mind that they show satisfaction levels only among those who have an opinion - and that this group contains a disproportionate number who have done relatively well out of the existing educational system.

Satisfaction with universities' performance

Quality		Satisfied with development	Dissatisfied (develop too little)	Dissatisfied (develop too much)
Self-confidence	%	75	25	-
A readiness to challenge other people's ideas	%	73	23	4
Skills and knowledge which help them get a good job	%	72	28	-
An ability to speak and write clearly	%	71	29	-
How to live among people from different backgrounds	%	66	33	2
Knowledge that equips people for life in general	%	59	42	-

Our analysis does not uncover any widespread evidence of dissatisfaction. Clear majorities appear satisfied with respect to all six qualities. Indeed,

only on two - 'how to live among people from different backgrounds' and 'knowledge that equips people for life in general' - are fewer than two-thirds satisfied with universities' performance. There does not appear to be any clear distinction between the 'civilising' and utilitarian functions of higher education. The greatest source of dissatisfaction with universities seems to be the perception of a minority that they are 'ivory towers' which fail adequately to prepare their students for life in the 'real world'.

What most clearly does *not* give rise to dissatisfaction is the view that universities *over*develop particular qualities. As we might have guessed, it is the 'readiness to challenge other people's ideas' that is most often thought to be developed too much. But, even here, only a meagre four per cent take this view.

But who is satisfied?

How universal is this pattern? If *knowledge* of what universities achieve varies so much by educational level, perhaps satisfaction does also. And what about our two key groups - graduates and employers and managers? Is their support for university expansion matched by satisfaction with what the universities are actually achieving?

In fact, employers and managers seem to be *less* satisfied than the public with universities' performance in respect of the three qualities that in general appear most vocationally useful. This is especially true of employers and managers in large establishments who are 16 percentage points *less* likely to be satisfied with universities' success in providing their students with 'knowledge that equips people for life in general' than are those who are not employers or managers.[13]

Perhaps surprisingly, graduates also tend to be more critical of universities than the general public. Further, like employers and managers, the two qualities with whose development they are most dissatisfied are the 'ability to write and speak clearly' and 'knowledge that equips people for life in general'. In addition, concern with the vocational role of universities exists even among their past students. However, graduates do *not* share the 'ivory tower' image of the universities. For instance, as a group they are *least* likely to be dissatisfied with universities' success at enabling their students to live 'among people from different backgrounds'.

Satisfaction with universities' performance among employers and managers

% satisfied with development of the following qualities	Large employers and managers	Small employers and managers	Others
A readiness to challenge other people's ideas	74	76	72
Self-confidence	71	77	75
Skills and knowledge which will help them get a good job	63	66	72
How to live among people from different backgrounds	63	70	65
An ability to speak and write clearly	57	68	72
Knowledge that equips people for life in general	45	49	61

Satisfaction with universities' performance, by level of education

	Highest educational qualification				
% satisfied with development of the following qualities	Degree	Other HE qualification	A level	0 level	CSE or below
A readiness to challenge other people's ideas	74	71	69	77	74
How to live among people from different backgrounds	71	57	71	66	66
Self-confidence	69	74	75	72	77
Skills and knowledge which help them to get a good job	67	63	64	75	78
An ability to speak and write clearly	62	57	70	69	79
Knowledge that equips people for life in general	50	44	54	52	72

There is, of course, some overlap between those who are graduates and those who are employers and managers. Many graduates go into management and, as we noted earlier, many managers are now graduates. So perhaps we have just been looking in two different ways at groups which are not really distinct. But if this is the case, is it their experience

as employers and managers of recruiting graduates - or their own experience of higher education?

To answer this question we need to conduct a multivariate analysis in which we take *both* of these characteristics into account.[14] We conducted such an analysis to see which factor most influences the degree to which employers and managers are satisfied with universities' performance in giving students 'the knowledge that equips people for life in general'. The results show that it is education that really matters. In other words, once we take into account their levels of education, large employers and managers are not distinguishable from the rest of the public in their satisfaction with the performance of universities - even in respect of the very quality with which they appear most dissatisfied.

While graduates are less likely than average to be satisfied with universities' performance, it is those with experience of higher education to *below* degree level who are the most dissatisfied. Only with respect to one quality - universities' development of self-confidence among their students - does their level of satisfaction match the general average. They are particularly critical of universities' performance when it comes to more vocational qualities. Indeed, well under half are satisfied with universities' success in equipping people for life in general.

Why this should be so is less clear. Their experience of higher education will have been more explicitly vocational than that of most graduates - and this may colour their views as to what universities should achieve. Furthermore, most will have attended institutions other than universities and, as a result, may be less aware or appreciative than graduates of the more esoteric and less directly vocational role of universities. But, equally, theirs could be the informed opinion of a group largely confined to occupational positions subordinate to those of graduates - and who see at close quarters the shortcomings of recent graduate recruits. Given their strikingly low level of satisfaction with the extent to which universities teach students to live among people of different backgrounds, perhaps even their recognition of the self-confidence of graduates is double-edged. This recognition may well convey both an appreciation of confidence and resentment at what is perceived as overconfidence bordering on arrogance. Alternatively, their views may be sour grapes - a hypercritical estimation of universities, rooted in the frustrations and resentments of people who occupy ancillary positions in a world in which the best paid and most powerful jobs are increasingly reserved for graduates.

Conclusion

Despite the considerable growth in their number, graduates do not - as yet - show any desire to pull up the ladder of advancement behind them. Such commitment to the extension of educational opportunities might seem to contradict the claim that those who benefit from higher education will increasingly seek to exclude others who could potentially compete for

positions and advantage. But graduates' views may well be more self-interested than they may seem at first sight. In particular, they may be especially concerned with enhancing the educational opportunities available to their own offspring. Thus, they give a markedly higher priority than do non-graduates to additional spending on college students (and to nursery and secondary education as well). But they give a markedly lower priority to extra spending on the group into which their children are less likely to fall - less able children with special educational needs.

To single out graduates for accusations of self-interest would, however, be mistaken. It is, after all, people with *no* educational qualifications who give lowest priority to additional spending on college students - and it is they, too, who are the most heavily in favour of extra spending on less able children with special needs. Presumably the unqualified see little prospect that they or their offspring will benefit from additional spending on college students, and a much greater possibility that their children might benefit from increased provision for special needs.

Nevertheless, what could be interpreted as self-interest might be better and more systematically interpreted as a reflection of the social distribution of *knowledge*. Just as the unqualified are less likely to know what universities are doing, so graduates are relatively unlikely to have personal experience of the problems of educating less able children. So long as the social worlds of education remain so divided, continued disagreement about educational priorities seems inevitable.

All of this suggests that those who run Britain's universities cannot afford to be complacent. True, the universities clearly benefit from a favourable public image. They are thought to be well-run, the public is clearly satisfied with the way in which they educate their students, and there is demand for yet more places within them.

However, those who have experienced a university education tend to be more critical of their performance than the general public. And, despite the high standing of universities among the public, there are indications that their present excellence is taken for granted. This, at least, is one way of interpreting the low priority that university and college students are accorded in the competition for extra spending[15]. Furthermore, there is evidence of widespread ignorance among the less well educationally qualified about what it is that universities actually *do*. This, alongside the suspicion of a substantial minority that university education is faintly impractical and a little too remote from the rest of society, will not help to raise universities from the bottom of the public's list of spending priorities.

The challenge now confronting the universities is twofold. Clearly, they must better inform the public about the nature and purposes of university education. But they must also impress upon them, and the politicians who represent them, the necessity of providing the funds which are required to maintain high standards, let alone to deliver the further expansion which is so widely desired.

Notes

1. Press reports can exaggerate what is still a relatively uncommon problem. In fact, graduate unemployment tends to rise and fall with the economic cycle, and graduates remain less likely than non-graduates to experience unemployment. Nevertheless, the existence and persistence of even a modest level of graduate unemployment may be sufficient to excite public concern.

2. Goldthorpe argues that credentialism should be seen as the strategy of a class which is engaged in 'distributional conflict' over social power and advantage. At times of such conflict, members of privileged groups will appeal to 'meritocracy' as a means of legitimising their position "with the definition and criteria of merit being so conceived as to maximise its members' competitive advantages" (Goldthorpe, 1982: 180-181).

3. It is estimated that 40 per cent of British graduates find employment at lower levels than those for which they are qualified. A 1990 government report on *Highly Qualified People* estimated that "a degree was considered essential for only a third of the jobs to which employers had recently recruited new graduates" (Ainley, 1994: 16).

4. This difference is statistically significant at the one per cent level.

5. This table and all subsequent tables which look at specific sub-groups exclude from the base those who did not answer the particular question.

6. We did not ask our respondents their educational qualifications in 1983 and so cannot identify graduates on that survey.

7. The sudden decline in graduates' support for expansion may be just a statistical quirk, or it may be a reaction to the sudden spurt of expansion (about which graduates might be expected to be better informed and more worried) which commenced in 1990. Equally, the recovery in graduates' enthusiasm for expansion in 1994 might reflect the fiscally motivated freeze imposed upon university admissions.

8. The difference between graduates and the rest of the population on this item is statistically significant at the 0.1 per cent level.

9. One possible problem with these questions is that it is not clear *which* institutions respondents had in mind when they answered them. For instance, some may only have been thinking about the 'old' universities - while others may have considered both these and the 'new' universities created after the abolition of the binary divide. If this does make a difference to people's answers *and* if such differences vary systematically between different social groups, then some of the apparent variations between social groups could reflect their different *understanding* of the question, rather than differences in their views on education.

10 Although we should note that, unlike those reported in respect of graduates, the figures reported here for those with higher education below degree level are not quite significantly different from those for the rest of the population.

11. We might simply have subtracted scores on the 'what qualities do universities develop' items from those on the corresponding 'what qualities should universities develop' items. This would assume that someone who says it is 'essential' that universities should develop a quality in their students is broadly satisfied if he or she says that universities actually do develop that quality 'very much', but is dissatisfied in varying degrees if she or he believes that universities only develop that quality 'quite a lot', 'not very much' or 'hardly at all'. This, however, would be a crude measure because we should merely be comparing rankings on each of two four-point scales when there is no clear equivalence between the categories on the 'should' dimension and those on the 'actually do' dimension. Equally, it is not clear that the scales are linear. On the 'do' measure the difference between 'quite

a lot' and 'not very much' seems rather bigger than that between, say, 'very much' and 'quite a lot'. For these reasons, we concluded that computing a simple difference measure would give a more misleading picture than the one we have in the end adopted.

12. Notably, in terms of any particular quality, we have had to exclude from our measure of satisfaction the relatively large number of people who could not say how successful the universities are, together with the much smaller number who were unable to say what they should do.

13. This difference is statistically significant at the 0.1 per cent level.

14. We carried out a logistic regression in which the dependent variable was satisfaction with universities' provision of 'knowledge that equips people for life in general'. The explanatory variables used were highest educational qualification (5 categories) and class (3 categories). The parameter estimates and their standard errors were as follows:

Class:	large employers and managers	0.47	(0.27)
	small employers and managers	0.47	(0.25)
	other respondents	0.00	
Highest education:	Degree	0.86	(0.25)
	Other higher education	1.08	(0.22)
	'A' level or equivalent	0.67	(0.21)
	'O' level or equivalent	0.76	(0.20)
	CSE or equivalent and below	0.00	
Constant		0.03	(0.12)
Model improvement		43.6	
df		6	
Number		835	

The parameter estimates for employers and managers are not significantly different from zero (they are less than twice their standard errors). However, all the education parameters *are* significantly different from zero, meaning that people with qualifications above CSE level are significantly different in their satisfaction with universities from those with qualifications at or below CSE level.

15. As a means of tapping the public's attitude towards additional funding for the strictly educational activities of universities, this question is not ideal. It is possible, for instance, that some respondents interpreted it as implying that there should be additional grant aid for students' *living expenses* rather than additional funding for higher education itself.

References

Ainley, P. (1994), *Degrees of Difference: Higher Education in the 1990s*, London: Lawrence and Wishart.

Collins, R. (1979), *The Credential Society*, New York: Academic Press.

Department for Education (1993), *Education Statistics for the UK*, London: HMSO.

Goldthorpe, J. (1982), 'On the service class, its formation and future', in Giddens, A. and Mackenzie, G. (eds.), *Social Class and the Division of Labour*, Cambridge: Cambridge University Press.

Halsey, A.H. (1992), *Decline of Donnish Dominion: the British Academic Professions in the Twentieth Century*, Oxford: Clarendon Press.

Halsey, A.H., Heath, A. and Ridge, J. (1980), *Origins and Destinations*, Oxford: Clarendon Press.

Heath, A., Mills, C. and Roberts, J. (1992), 'Towards meritocracy: recent evidence on an old problem', in Crouch, C. and Heath, A. (eds.), *Social Research and Social Reform*, Oxford: Clarendon Press.

Nisbet, R. (1972), *The Degradation of the Academic Dogma*, London: Heinemann.

Parkin, F. (1974), 'Strategies of social closure in class formation', in Parkin, F. (ed.), *The Social Analysis of Class Structure*, London: Tavistock.

Parkin, F. (1979), *Marxism and Class Theory: a Bourgeois Critique*, London: Tavistock.

Schofield, P. (1995), 'Limited degree of market value', *The Independent on Sunday*, 16 July, B15.

Social Trends **19** (1989), London: HMSO.

Social Trends **25** (1995), London: HMSO.

Acknowledgement

We are grateful to the Department for Education for the funding that enables us to continue asking questions on education.

9 Libertarianism in retreat?

Lindsay Brook and Ed Cape [*]

Four years ago, when we reported some of the findings from our 1990 'civil liberties' questions (Brook and Cape, 1991), we regretted the fact that we had not asked many of them at a much earlier date. We were concerned that public sensitivity to such issues might have been stimulated by a whole series of recent *causes célèbres* - the Tisdall and Ponting trials, the *Spycatcher* saga, the ban on union membership at GCHQ, the Zircon affair, and the outcry against Clause 28 - the effect of all of which might soon fade.

Moreover, the 1980s had seen a raft of new legislative measures designed to restore what was considered to be the proper balance between the rights of the individual citizen and the best interests of the majority. Although opposition parties and civil liberties lobbyists had contested these fiercely, arguing that the balance was rapidly being tilted too much in favour of the employer, the police and the state, they did so in the context of a rising crime rate, a number of inner city and prison riots, as well as episodic clashes between police and protesters at Greenham Common, the Yorkshire pit-heads, Wapping, Trafalgar Square and elsewhere. Against this background, we wondered whether the public might have been rather more sympathetic or more indifferent than usual to the changing legislative climate. As we argued then, "many libertarian concerns...are about protections for minorities of one sort or another; for the bulk of the population these issues are therefore somewhat abstract and hypothetical.

[*] Lindsay Brook is a Research Director at SCPR and a Co-director of the *British Social Attitudes* survey series. Ed Cape is Principal Lecturer, Faculty of Law, University of the West of England.

Those who are not directly affected may believe that the checks and balances are acceptable, and that 'ordinary people' are able to get on with their day-to-day lives with no discernible infringement by the state upon their rights as citizens; some encroachment on minority rights is therefore acceptable if it leads to a more stable society" (Brook and Cape, 1991: 182-83).

Now, however, we wonder whether the 1990 survey did, after all, take place in such an unusual context. Our 1994 survey was also preceded by a flurry of legislation in response to growing concern (fed eagerly by the mass media) about crime and public disorder. Not only were there three Criminal Justice Acts passed (in 1991, 1993 and 1994), but also the Bail (Amendment) Act of 1993, the Drug Trafficking Act and the Police and Magistrates' Courts Act (both passed in 1994). All impinge to a greater or lesser degree on civil libertarian issues.

What is notable, however, is the mounting controversy that these measures have attracted. Especially contentious was the 1994 Criminal Justice and Public Order Act, justified by the Home Secretary to the 1993 Conservative Party conference as a means of righting the balance in the criminal justice system which for the last 30 years had "been tilted too far in favour of the criminal and against the protection of the public".

Although the Act did not receive royal assent until just after our fieldwork period, many of its provisions - such as the setting up of a national DNA database, increasing police powers to crack down on 'rave' goers and travellers, tightening bail conditions and sentencing policy - had been widely and hotly debated for months beforehand. Indeed, some of them had also been very publicly pilloried in the House of Lords[1] and the mass media.

It was in the same period that the Royal Commission on Criminal Justice - set up following the release of the Birmingham Six - issued its report (Royal Commission on Criminal Justice, 1993). Welcomed in the main by government and the police, it was greeted by many other interested groups as something of a disappointment. They felt that the commission's report had been too preoccupied with resources and had failed to establish any clear set of principles for the criminal justice system (see, for example, Ashworth, 1993; McConville and Bridges, 1994). The Legal Action Group summed up the views of many when it said that the Commission had "conspicuously failed to address the issue which led to its creation: the causes of miscarriages of justice" (Legal Action Group, 1993: 3).

According to McConville and Bridges (1994), the serious political divide that now exists on these sorts of issues is of fairly recent origin. Until 1991, they argue, there had been a broad political consensus on 'law and order' issues and a decade of liberal advances in, for instance, the treatment of young offenders. They believe that the consensus broke down, not so much in response to the discovery of various miscarriages of justice, but more as a result of moves towards 'populist anti-reformism'.

With crime rising, we might well expect growing support for more punitive measures to get 'tough on crime'. On the other hand, the spate

of recent examples of miscarriages of justice - such as the Birmingham Six, the Tottenham Three, Stefan Kizsko, and Judith Ward - might well have swayed people against tilting the balance in favour of the police and eroding the rights of defendants. In this chapter we try to gauge the general direction in which popular opinion has been moving and the factors that may underpin civil libertarian or authoritarian values. Our conclusion after examining the evidence in *the 8th Report* was that committed civil libertarians had cause to be somewhat despondent. As we shall show, this is even more true four years later, though not on all issues. We divide our evidence below into two broad sections: attitudes to crime and punishment, and attitudes to the rights of political, social and ethnic minorities.

Crime and punishment

Protecting the innocent

One of the cornerstones of the British legal system is that the accused is 'innocent until proved guilty'. The committed civil libertarian, while recognising that this might inevitably lead to the acquittal of some guilty defendants, would nonetheless regard it as an acceptable and necessary risk.[2] Around three in five respondents agree. However, as the table below shows, the proportion of the public who thinks it is worse to risk convicting an innocent person than to risk acquitting a guilty one is smaller now than it has been for nine years. Correspondingly, there has been a small rise in the proportion who think it worse to risk letting the guilty go free. Moreover, as the last row shows, public ambivalence on this issue has increased quite markedly.

All systems of justice make mistakes, but which do you think is worse...

	1985	1990	1994
	%	%	%
... to convict an innocent person	67	62	58
or, to let a guilty person go free?	20	19	24
Can't choose	12	19	18

So, while the libertarian may be reassured by the overall level of public support for protecting the innocent, there are certainly signs that this cornerstone is beginning to crumble somewhat.

Reintroduction of capital punishment

Since 1983 when our series began, and indeed well before that, a substantial majority of the public has favoured the death penalty for murder. Despite this support, increasing majorities of MPs regularly vote against the

reintroduction of the death penalty. In *the 8th Report*, however, we noted some softening of public attitudes in the period from 1985 to 1990. Had public support for the death penalty begun to wane? It does not appear so. True, the trend did not reverse itself between 1990 and 1994, but nor did it strengthen. Indeed, there has been no change at all to speak of. A solid three in five people remain in favour of reintroducing capital punishment for all murders.

	1983	1985	1990	1994
% in favour of capital punishment for:				
Murder in the course of a terrorist act	74	77	70	70
Murder of a police officer*	70	71	67	67
Other murders	63	66	61	59

* In 1983 and 1985, 'murder of a policeman'.

We speculated in *the 8th Report* that, with a whole series of recent miscarriages of justice in cases involving murder, support for capital punishment would surely be dented. It seems that we were wrong. It seems that public support for the death penalty is already at an irreducible minimum.

Identifying and catching wrongdoers

One of the most striking shifts of opinion uncovered in this round of the survey concerns the powers the public would cede to the police in their efforts to identify and catch wrongdoers. In 1990 we asked about the acceptability of video surveillance in public places. Then, as now, virtually no one objected to the use of cameras at a football ground to detect trouble-makers; but many were rather more wary about their use elsewhere. In 1994 their installation on roads or in housing estates is seen to be much less objectionable.

	% saying 'definitely'	
	1990	1994
Video cameras should be allowed ...		
... on roads to detect speeding drivers	55	74
... on housing estates to detect vandals	53	70

What explanations could there be for such a big shift in opinion over just four years? Part of the answer, we suspect, is that video surveillance has become a common feature of everyday life, with more and more people realising it is here to stay. Ninety-five per cent of local authorities in Britain have established, or are considering establishing, CCTV surveillance on their housing estates, despite an absence of research evidence as to its effectiveness (see Liberty, 1995). Video cameras are also more and more

common on main roads and highways and may increasingly be regarded as a good way of catching 'anti-social' motorists. Another part of the explanation for the increasing public acceptability of video surveillance may be the number of celebrated instances in which the presence of a camera has demonstrably been vital in identifying suspects, such as in the film of the abduction of James Bulger.

In 1985 and 1994 we asked two parallel sets of questions about police surveillance, detention and interception of telephone calls and mail. One set was about a suspect 'without a long criminal record'; the other, designed to test respondents' civil libertarian credentials to the limit, was about a suspect 'with a long criminal record'. Both questions were fielded again in the latest round. What powers would the public give to the police in the case of a man with no 'form'?

*Suppose the police get an anonymous tip that a man **without** a criminal record is planning to break into a warehouse. Do you think that the police should be allowed, without a court order...*

	% saying 'definitely' or 'probably'	
	1985	1994
... to keep the man under surveillance	72	79
... to detain the man overnight for questioning	33	37
... to tap his telephone	14	21
... to open his mail	8	14

While there has been little change in the proportions who would 'definitely' allow each of the four measures, there has been an increase in the proportions who think that even the most controversial and intrusive measure should 'probably' be allowed. A recent report by the Audit Commission (1993) urged the police to 'target the criminal, not just the crime', and this advice appears to command increasing public support. Almost four in five now support surveillance of suspects, even on the basis of the thinnest possible evidence (an anonymous tip). The civil libertarian may take some comfort from the fact that a large majority of the population appears to have an enduring distaste for granting police the independent power to tap telephones and intercept private mail. But, as the figures above show, a growing minority now takes the opposite view.

Moreover, such libertarian values as exist in respect of someone without a criminal record tend to evaporate in respect of someone with one. When the anonymous tip-off concerns a man *with* a criminal record, there is a steep increase in the proportion prepared to sacrifice his rights in favour of potential crime prevention. Thus, as the next table shows, almost half of the public would give the police the right to tap his telephone and over a third to open his mail. In both cases, support for increased police powers

over an individual's right to privacy has increased substantially in the last four years, after remaining stable between 1985 and 1990.

*Suppose the police get an anonymous tip that a man **with** a long criminal record is planning to break into a warehouse. Do you think that the police should be allowed, without a court order...*

	% saying 'definitely' or 'probably'		
	1985	1990	1994
... to keep the man under surveillance	90	90	95
... to detain the man overnight for questioning	64	63	67
... to tap his telephone	37	38	46
... to open his mail	23	24	36

The increasingly clear distinction that respondents make between a suspect with no 'form' and one with a string of convictions to his name suggests that the targeting of people with a criminal record is increasingly regarded as legitimate, even to the extent of depriving them of certain basic protections that other people are entitled to enjoy.

These are not the only ways in which growing numbers of the public believe that police powers are unnecessarily restricted at present. True, the majority go along with the police themselves in not wanting officers routinely to carry guns[3], but the minority who take the opposite view has nonetheless doubled since 1990 (from 14 to 28 per cent). Surely, then, there will be still less public opposition to other measures now in experimental use by the police, such as extendable batons and CS gas?

The introduction of identity cards

Usually advocated specifically in the context of reducing crime, identity cards (voluntary or mandatory) are now very much back on the political agenda, their introduction for football supporters having been the subject of hot debate in 1989. Now, to the dismay of libertarians on the left and the right, a government Green Paper in favour of identity cards has been published (Home Office, 1995). Most specific objections to identity cards relate to their possible misuse. Indeed, even the Data Protection Registrar has joined in the debate, voicing her concern over the possible erosion of privacy that could be involved (*The Guardian*, 22 June 1995). The main opposition parties have yet to form a view on the Green Paper.

When we first asked about the issue in 1990, we found that public opinion was fairly evenly divided, with 37 per cent in favour and 40 per cent against compulsory identity cards. Now, however, the balance of public opinion is two to one in favour (53 per cent as against 26 per cent),

a dramatic shift over such a short period. The large proportion of those who are undecided (about one in five) is unchanged.

However, we wonder whether this shift we have uncovered is not partly artefactual. We mistakenly inserted a new question in 1994 *before* the general one about identity cards, and we feel that it might well have influenced answers to the general question. To test reaction to the notion that identity cards should be introduced specifically for benefit recipients, we asked whether "people claiming state benefits should have to carry an identity card to help prevent fraud". Nearly 70 per cent of the public endorsed this idea, suggesting a greater distaste for benefit fraud than for compulsory identity cards. That being so, we suspect that the large increase we recorded in support of universal identity cards might well have been due to their (newly implied) association with curbing benefit fraud. We shall repeat the questions next year to test this supposition.

Trying suspects and sentencing wrongdoers

We turn now to public perceptions of the role of the courts. We included two questions about the rights of defendants. The first concerned the admissibility of an uncorroborated confession that is later retracted, and the second the courts' appropriate response to an accused person's exercise of the 'right to silence' under police questioning.

In 1990, 74 per cent of respondents thought that a retracted confession should *not* on its own be enough to convict someone. This robust public support for a defendant's rights is now only slightly less in evidence (at 69 per cent) than it was in 1990. This view was represented by many of those giving evidence to the Royal Commission on Criminal Justice. In the event, however, the Commission's Report recommended only that trial judges should be obliged to warn juries of the dangers of 'confession evidence'; even this proposal was not then taken up in the new legislation.

As if to emphasise its distance from public opinion, the Royal Commission strongly recommended that a suspect's 'right to silence' be retained, but again its advice was overturned by the 1994 Criminal Justice and Public Order Act (which abolished it).[4] In tune with the government on this issue, public support for a defendant's right to remain silent under questioning fell sharply from the already fairly low level of 42 per cent in 1990 to 31 per cent now. This may be yet another example of public opinion moving in the same direction as legislative provisions. So, although members of the public still favour retaining several important safeguards against the perversion of justice, they are becoming increasingly impatient with what they see, perhaps, as little more than a ruse on the part of certain defendants to escape conviction.[5]

Another aspect of the judicial system for which we have trend data is the sentencing policy of courts. Respondents were invited to agree or disagree with each of the two statements in the table below.

			Agree strongly/ agree	Neither agree nor disagree	Disagree/ disagree strongly
Too many criminals are let	1990	%	79	15	6
off lightly by the courts	1994	%	86	9	4
The prisons contain too many					
people who ought to be given	1990	%	48	27	23
a lighter punishment	1994	%	28	31	40

We noted four years ago that only a minority of people had much confidence in the custodial sentencing practices of courts, and this remains true of the first item. Indeed the vote of no confidence in the courts has risen from 79 per cent to an overwhelming 86 per cent. But just as people are much more likely to criticise the courts for being too lenient towards serious offenders, they are also much *less* likely now to criticise them for being too strict on the petty criminal.

Evidence is mounting, then, that the more hawkish stance towards crime, taken by both government and opposition of late, is in tune with public sentiment. It could be that where politicians lead popular opinion is likely to follow or, perhaps, the other way around.

Prisons

Given that a growing proportion of people feel that the courts are too lenient on serious criminals, how do they feel about the treatment of prisoners once they have been 'sent down'? We asked whether, 'as long as there is no threat to security', prisoners should be allowed to enjoy a number of 'privileges'. These included having as many books as they want, earning a little money, arranging for visits to their homes, and having conjugal visits to prison.

Almost everybody (around 90 per cent) supports the right of prisoners to have free access to books, and a large majority (around 70 per cent) believes that they should be allowed to earn a little money in prison. But home and conjugal visits were seen as less appropriate. In both cases, only around a quarter thought they should be allowed.

The government has recently announced a national framework for 'incentives' (such as earnings schemes) and 'earned' privileges (such as more visitors). These modest changes are likely, on our evidence, to meet with public approval. At the same time, regulations have been introduced under which the number of prisoners temporarily released is likely to fall sharply (NACRO, 1995). This move, too, will probably be much in tune with popular sentiment.

Minority rights

We have found then that the British public has become somewhat more punitive and less libertarian in its attitudes towards crime and punishment since our last measure in 1990. But what of society's attitudes towards its political and ethnic minorities? Its civil libertarian credentials should, to a large extent, be judged by its treatment of such potential 'outgroups'.

Rights to political protest

There can be few more fundamental rights in a democracy than to engage in orderly political protest (see also the chapter by Curtice and Jowell in this volume). In 1990 we found impressive majorities in favour of people's rights to engage in *peaceful* protest against 'a government action they strongly oppose'. Moreover, support for these forms of protest had strengthened over the five years since these questions were first asked in 1985. The most recent figures, however, provide evidence of a sharp retreat during the last five years. The next table shows the proportions who said at each round that these rights should 'definitely' exist (for that is where the retreat lies). There have been remarkable falls in the figures in each row of the table. Indeed, none of these three rights of protest, which many would argue are critical features of any democracy, now attracts the wholehearted support of a majority of the British public (though all three do attract comfortable majorities who would 'definitely' *or* 'probably' allow them). From a libertarian viewpoint, therefore, these findings are hardly reassuring.

	1985	1990	1994
% saying that the following should definitely be allowed			
Public protest meetings	59	62	48
Protest pamphlets	55	53	41
Marches and demonstrations	36	39	30

The claims of conscience

Since the mid-1980s, the *British Social Attitudes* survey has asked questions about the primacy of the law over individual conscience. Responses differ somewhat according to the way in which the question is framed. Among the items is the following question:

In general, would you say that people should obey the law without exception, or are there exceptional occasions on which people should follow their consciences, even if it means breaking the law?

	1985	1990	1994
	%	%	%
Obey the law without exception	37	41	36
Follow conscience on occasions	58	52	57
Can't choose/not answered	5	7	7

In 1990, there appeared to be an increase in the proportion of the population who thought that the law should never be breached, with only a bare majority taking the view that conscience should prevail on occasions. Now it appears that this was merely a temporary blip, public opinion returning to exactly where it was in 1985.

Our second question reveals an even more stable - but lower - proportion in favour of following one's conscience.

The law should be obeyed, even if a particular law is wrong

	1990	1994
	%	%
Agree	46	40
Neither agree nor disagree	25	29
Disagree	29	30

The difference between the responses stems largely from the fact that the second question offers respondents a 'neutral' mid-point. Many of those who at the earlier question came down on the side of 'following conscience' would have chosen a midpoint had it been available. Even so, the responses to both questions paint much the same picture - that of a decline since 1990 in the proportion of people who support the primacy of the law over individual conscience. Here at last, then, is some evidence of movement away from, rather than towards, the tough end of the tender-tough continuum.

Do the poor get the blame?

Jordan (1989) and others have argued that a 'good society' is built upon the foundations of contributions from *all* its citizens. An important element is how the better-off in a society treat the less well-off. As Taylor-Gooby shows in his chapter, evidence exists of an increase in the public's concern about this relationship. In the first place, there has been a steady rise over the years - from 55 per cent in 1986 to 71 per cent in 1994 - in the proportion who perceive 'quite a lot' of poverty in Britain. Further, people

are more likely now than they were in the mid-1980s to believe that poverty comes about through factors beyond the control of those who suffer from it.

But a recognition that poverty exists and a sympathy for people in need are only two facets of the picture. There is also evidence of a widespread feeling that the cards are increasingly stacked against the poor. In particular, if a poor person were to get into trouble with the law, popular opinion is that he or she would get a worse deal than a rich person in the same circumstances. We asked:

*Suppose two people - one rich and one poor - each appeared in court charged with a crime that they did **not** commit. What do you think their chances are of being found **guilty**?*

	1990	1994
	%	%
The rich person is more likely to be found guilty	2	2
Both have the same chance	38	30
The poor person is more likely to be found guilty	56	66

This perception of the growing inequity of the legal system against poor people is held among all social groups, irrespective of gender, age, class and political allegiance. Neither the recent Criminal Justice Acts nor the 1994 Police and Magistrates' Court Act are likely, it seems, to increase public confidence in this aspect of the legal system at any rate. Little wonder then that around two in five people also agree with the proposition that 'once people are made local magistrates[6], they lose touch with ordinary people pretty quickly'.

The perceived inequity of the courts may be just one of the many reasons why almost half of those questioned in 1994 are also dissatisfied with current legal aid rules. While only one in ten people believe that providing financial help towards the cost of going to court has 'gone too far', as many as one-half believe it has 'not gone far enough'.

Ethnic minorities

The 9th Report recorded optimistic signals about the future of race relations in Britain (Young, 1992). There has since been further progress in the shape of a sharp drop, for instance, in the proportion of white people who would object to having a 'West Indian' or an 'Asian' boss. It was therefore counterintuitive when we found that the proportion of people attributing similar egalitarian sentiments to others had scarcely changed since 1990; nor had the proportion of the population (around one-half) who believe that the legal system is evenhanded between black and white defendants (see also Hood, 1992). Even more counterintuitive, perhaps, was the steep rise (from 21 per cent to 40 per cent) in the proportion who assert that racism in

Britain is likely to get still more widespread over the next few years. On reflection, however, we might have expected these responses as society actually becomes less racist in its attitudes and behaviour. We might then anticipate rather more public awareness of and sensitivity towards racism in Britain than had existed beforehand, and this may be no bad thing.

On an even more positive note for egalitarians, the principle of an anti-discrimination law now captures the support of between two-thirds and three-quarters of the population, even though only around one in four people want the existing law to be implemented 'more strictly'. There is also only minority support (36 per cent) for bringing in a 'special law against racial violence'.[7]

Both Conservative and Labour governments since the 1960s have favoured tough controls on immigration to Britain. In recent years Britain has also been among the least willing of the developed nations to admit large numbers of refugees - a practice, according to Amnesty International (1995), that breaches international human rights standards as well as the government's own guidelines. Certainly, since the introduction of the Asylum and Immigration Appeals Act in 1993, rejected asylum claims have leapt from 14 per cent of all claims in the first half of 1993 to 74 per cent in the first quarter of 1994, and the number of successful appeals has fallen (Foley, 1995).

How much public support do these government policies generally command? We have regularly asked respondents whether Britain should allow more, less or about the same level of immigration by people from various Commonwealth countries and from the European Union. These questions are always accompanied by another asking whether Britain should be stricter or less strict in allowing the close relatives of those already here to join them. In 1990 we added Britain's treatment of political refugees to the list of concerns covered. Then in 1994 we added two further groups to the list of potential immigrants - people from China and Hong Kong and people from Eastern Europe.

As the next table shows, the public seems largely in sympathy with the government's general stance on these issues.

	1983	1986	1990	1994
% in favour of *less* settlement of				
...Indians and Pakistanis	71	68	62	60
...West Indians	67	64	58	54
...People from China and Hong Kong	n/a	n/a	n/a	52
...People from Eastern Europe	n/a	n/a	n/a	48
...People from EU countries	44	46	41	40
...Australians and New Zealanders	28	34	31	30
% in favour of				
...Stricter controls on the families of immigrants	57	58	56	53
...Restrictions on political refugees	n/a	n/a	48	44

n/a = not asked

Colour first and culture second continue to influence responses, overriding the claims of longstanding New Commonwealth ties and even, apparently, of people's close family links. Thus settlers from Australasia, Western Europe and Eastern Europe would all, in principle, get a warmer welcome from the British public than would settlers from the Indian subcontinent, the Caribbean or Hong Kong. Moreover, although there has been a clear softening of attitudes towards Asian and West Indian settlers over the last eleven years, this has coincided with a period of very low settlement by these groups. These two processes may, of course, be linked. The somewhat more liberal attitude we have registered towards immigration over the years may largely be the consequence of the steady reduction in the number of immigrants from these countries. In effect, then, the public may simply be endorsing a process that has shifted in their preferred direction.

Is the balance being tilted too far?

As we noted earlier, a nation's civil libertarian credentials are often thought to depend partly on the way it treats its most vulnerable members. We selected three particular minority groups - homosexuals, ethnic minorities, and gypsies and travellers - asking in each case whether attempts to give them equal opportunities (or, in the case of gypsies, appropriate sites) had gone too far or not far enough. In fact we gave respondents a five-point scale from 'much too far' to 'not nearly far enough', but in the next table we compress their replies into a three-point one.

		Gone too far	About right	Not gone far enough
Attempts to give equal opportunities to homosexuals	%	46	32	18
Attempts to give equal opportunities to black people and Asians in Britain	%	24	33	39
Providing sites for gypsies and travellers to stay	%	20	30	44

There still seems to be a good deal of public sympathy for 'righting wrongs' on behalf of ethnic minorities and, to a greater extent still, gypsies and travellers. In each case only a small minority is in favour of reversing change; in the case of gypsies and travellers, the balance of public opinion is more than two to one in favour of doing more for them than of doing less. Gay men and lesbians, however, evoke much less sympathy. Not only do nearly one-half of the public believe that things have 'gone too far' in giving them equal opportunities, but fewer than one person in five favours doing any more to reduce discrimination against them. This is not, it seems, a reflection of disapproval on the grounds of sexual morality, on which attitudes have become rather less censorious over the years (see Ahrendt and Young, 1994). It could of course be that most people are sceptical that discrimination against gay men and lesbians exists in the first place. But according to recent evidence from Snape *et al* (1995), they would be wrong to make this assumption.

So Britain does not emerge with flying colours from an examination of its attitudes towards its minorities. Nor does it appear that things have changed much over the years. On the other hand, the responses do not suggest that we are witnessing a comfortable majority retreating into the citadel and closing the gates behind them. Rather, the results seem to reflect much more familiar British prejudices and vulnerabilities.

The shift towards toughness

There is consistent evidence that Britain has become less libertarian during the 1990s, especially in respect of public attitudes towards crime and punishment. Moreover, this change has extended to all sections of society. Although, as in 1990, educational attainment, age and party affiliation are all linked to general attitudes towards these issues, when we look at *changes* in attitudes over the four years, we can find no single subgroup among the dozen or so examined, which has been conspicuously swimming against the tide.

Why should this be so? Given that the most noticeable changes have been in attitudes towards crime and punishment, we expected that the most likely place to look for the eye of the storm would be among those who had experienced crime. But we were wrong. We found virtually no association between ever having been threatened or burgled and the

tendency to want tougher measures against crime and criminals. Any notion of a beleaguered citizenry cannot, it seems, be sustained.

However, as Dowds and Ahrendt find in their chapter, there is something of a link between *fear* of crime and authoritarian attitudes. For instance, among those who say that being a victim of crime is 'a big worry', around 60 per cent feel that 'too many criminals are let off lightly by the courts'. In contrast, among those who say that they never worry about being a victim of crime, only 40 per cent take this view. But even this link proves to be rather unstable. When we examine attitudes towards other specific measures against crime, such as limiting the right to silence, the association largely disappears.

The major factor behind the fragility of public support for libertarian solutions to many of these issues may be found in the strength or otherwise of people's underlying values. Since 1987, the *British Social Attitudes* surveys have included a set of items which aim to measure where respondents stand on two underlying value dimensions - left-right and libertarian-authoritarian (Heath *et al*, 1986). The left-right dimension consists of five agree-disagree items which are essentially about egalitarianism and the extent to which governments ought to intervene in the economy to promote greater equality.[8] The liberal-authoritarian dimension consists of six agree-disagree items which capture the extent to which people in general opt for individual freedoms as against social order and conformity.[9]

Though hardly surprising, we are nonetheless relieved to report that a person's position on our libertarian-authoritarian scale is indeed strongly associated with the direction of his or her responses to the items we have been examining in this chapter. We could not be certain that this would be so, since people's responses to general principles do not necessarily correspond very closely to their responses to specific solutions. As always, however, the picture is complicated by an intervening factor, though not quite the one we might have anticipated.

We know, of course, that both libertarians and authoritarians can be found in all political parties. Nonetheless, because the parties themselves have become so publicly divided on many of the issues examined, we expected people's party loyalties to be a much more significant and consistent influence on their patterns of response than they turned out to be. Instead, the intervening factor that appears to matter most is a person's position on the left-right dimension. In short, the more a person tends to be *both* left-wing and libertarian, as measured by our two scales, the more consistent is their libertarianism in respect of a wide range of the more specific issues discussed in this chapter.

As only one example of this (many others tell the same story), we range our respondents in the next table according to their positions on the two scales of underlying values. Then, for each combination of positions, we show the proportion who oppose the death penalty for 'other' murders (that is, other than the murder of a police officer or murder as part of a terrorist act).

% Opposed to the death penalty for murder[10]

	Position on left-right scale		
Position on libertarian-authoritarian scale	Left	Centre	Right
Libertarian	59	46	44
Mixed	9	6	8
Authoritarian	2	2	1

In the first place, opposition to the death penalty is almost wholly confined to the top row of the table, that is to those who are the most libertarian in their underlying values. Those with mixed views (in the second row) are much closer to those whose underlying values are authoritarian, whose answers appear in the third row. However, even among those classified as libertarian, it is only among those who are also classified as left-wing where we find majority opposition to the death penalty. Yet, as the first *column* of the table demonstrates, being left-wing *per se* does almost nothing to encourage opposition to the death penalty among those whose underlying values are either mixed or authoritarian

So it appears that a robust and consistent libertarian response to the sorts of questions we have been discussing in this chapter tends to be found only among the fairly small group of people with this particular *combination* of left-wing and libertarian values. That being so, it is no wonder that periodic drifts or shifts should occur - in one direction or another - in the attitudes of the rest of the population (the great majority) towards many of these complex issues.

Conclusions

Civil libertarian sentiment in Britain has a fragile base. Four years ago, we described the British public as 'fainthearted libertarians', and our latest data give no grounds for questioning this judgement. This is not to imply, however, that on all issues public support for restrictive and punitive measures is either high or growing. That is not the case. But from the viewpoint of the libertarian, there are few crumbs of comfort in the latest figures.

Counterintuitively, perhaps, the public's increasing reluctance to embrace libertarian values does not appear to be linked to experience of crime. Nor is this reluctance associated much with fear of crime. Rather, it has more to do with the cluster of values that seem to be required to maintain a consistent libertarian position. In the current political climate, in which 'pocket-book' issues predominate, there is probably little fertile ground in which libertarian causes are likely to take root and flourish. Real party political differences exist on some issues, such as in attitudes to the poor or the limits of mass protest, but there are libertarians and authoritarians in all parties.

On the other hand, since education is associated with libertarian values and since Britain is becoming a better-educated nation, there is some prospect of the gradual substitution of more authoritarian values by more libertarian ones. But, in the short term, it appears that any party which nailed its colours too publicly to a libertarian mast would stand to lose rather than gain public support.

Notes

1. For instance, there was Lord Wigoder's withering attack during the Bill's second reading: "If I look at the history of the Bill from the time of its inception, I confess that I begin to think of the Home Secretary as a sort of 'Coco Pops' Home Secretary. I visualise him eating his breakfast cereal every morning surrounded by the tabloid newspapers, and almost every morning what he thinks is a bright idea flashes across his mind. Lo and behold, by lunchtime the same day he has tabled an amendment to the Criminal Justice Bill, without any reflection, discussion, consultation or research. That is not a very satisfactory way of proceeding." (Hansard, 1994).
2. For instance the Report of the Royal Commission, in recommending the retention of the 'right of silence', stated that "the possibility of an increase in the conviction of the guilty is outweighed by the risk that the extra pressure on suspects to talk in the police station, and the adverse inferences invited if they do not, may result in more convictions of the innocent" (The Royal Commission on Criminal Justice, 1993: 54).
3. In April 1995, by a majority of 79 to 21 per cent, Police Federation members rejected the proposal that they should routinely carry guns.
4. The 'right to silence' is commonly referred to as having been abolished although, strictly speaking, the legislative changes concern the consequences of failing to answer questions put by police officers.
5. The Home Secretary, at the 1993 Conservative Party conference, took this view when he told his audience that "the so-called right to silence is ruthlessly exploited by terrorists". Opponents of the abolition of the right to silence argue that there are also many valid reasons for refusing to give evidence in court or answer police questions.
6. In Scotland, 'sheriffs'.
7. The Home Office estimates that there are between 130,000 and 140,000 incidents of racial attack and harassment each year. Between 1979 and 1995 there were 70 prosecutions for incitement to racial hatred (Foley, 1995: 299).
8. The scale is formed from the answers respondents gave when asked for the extent of their agreement or disagreement with the following five items:

   Government should redistribute income from the better-off to those who are less well-off
   Big business benefits owners at the expense of workers
   Ordinary working people do not get their fair share of the nation's wealth
   There is one law for the rich and one for the poor
   Management will always try to get the better of employees if it gets the chance

   Answers are recorded on a five-point scale ranging from 'agree strongly' (scored 1) to 'disagree strongly' (scored 5). A respondent's scale score is thus simply the sum of his or her scores on these five items, with a range of between 5 and 25. In the table, those classified as left-wing have a score of 10 or less, and those

classified as right-wing a score of 14 or more. These cut-offs produce groups of roughly equal size.

9.   The scale is formed from answers showing the extent of agreement or disagreement with the following six items:

> *Young people today don't have enough respect for traditional British values*
> *People who break the law should be given stiffer sentences*
> *For some crimes, the death penalty is the most appropriate sentence*
> *Schools should teach children to obey authority*
> *The law should be obeyed, even if a particular law is wrong*
> *Censorship of films and magazines is necessary to uphold moral standards*

The scale is formed in the same way as the left-right scale, except that the range of scores is from 6 to 30. In the table, those classified as libertarian have a score of 15 or more, while those classified as authoritarian have a score of 11 or less.

10. We asked respondents:

> *Are you in favour of or against the death penalty for*
> *a) murder in the course of a terrorist act*
> *b) murder of a police officer*
> *c) other murders?*

The percentages in the table relate to responses to c) as explained in the text.

References

Able, R. (1994), *Speech and Respect*, London: Sweet and Maxwell.

Ahrendt, D. and Young, K. (1994), 'Authoritarianism updated', in Jowell, R., Curtice, J., Brook, L. and Ahrendt, D., *British Social Attitudes: the 11th Report*, Aldershot: Dartmouth.

Amnesty International (1995), *Prisoners Without a Voice: Asylum-seekers Detained in the UK*.

Ashworth, A. (1993), 'Plea, venue and discontinuance', *Criminal Law Review*, **830**.

Audit Commission (1993), *Helping with Enquiries: Tackling Crime Efficiently*, London: HMSO.

Brook, L. and Cape, E. (1991), 'Civil liberties', in Jowell, R., Brook, L. and Taylor, B., *British Social Attitudes: the 8th Report*, Aldershot: Dartmouth.

Card, R. and Ward, R. (1994), *The Criminal Justice and Public Order Act 1994*, London: Jordans.

Foley, C. (1995), *Human Rights, Human Wrongs: the Alternative Report to the United Nations Human Rights Committee*, London: Rivers Oram Press.

Gibson, B., Cavadino, P., Rutherford, A., Ashworth, A. and Harding, J. (1994), *Criminal Justice in Transition*, Winchester: Waterside.

Hansard (1994), House of Lords, Criminal Justice and Public Order Bill, 2nd reading, col. 395.

Heath, A., Jowell, R., Curtice, J. and Witherspoon, S. (1986), *End of Award Report to the ESRC: Methodological Aspects of Attitude Research*, London: SCPR.

Home Office (1995), *Identity Cards - A Consultation Document*, London: HMSO.

Hood, R. (1992), *Race and Sentencing*, Oxford: Clarendon Press.

Jordan, B. (1989), *The Common Good: Citizenship, Morality and Self-interest*, Oxford: Basil Blackwell.

Legal Action Group (August, 1993), *Legal Action*.

Liberty (1995), *Agenda*, **14**.

McConville, M. and Bridges, L. (1994), *Criminal Justice in Crisis*, Aldershot: Edward Elgar.

NACRO (1995), *Criminal Justice Digest*, **84**.

Royal Commission on Criminal Justice (1993), *Report*, Cm 2263, London: HMSO.

Snape, D., Thomson, K. and Chetwynd, M. (1995), *Discrimination Against Gay Men and Lesbians*, London: SCPR.

Young, K. (1992), 'Race, class and opportunity', in Jowell, R., Brook, L., Prior, G. and Taylor, B., *British Social Attitudes: the 9th Report*, Aldershot: Dartmouth.

Acknowledgements

The authors thank The Nuffield Foundation for funding to support modules of questions on civil liberties in the 1990 and 1994 *British Social Attitudes* questionnaires. We are also grateful to the ESRC for funding under its Crime and Social Order Programme (Award No. L210 252 010), which enabled SCPR to field questions on fear of crime, some of which are used in the analyses in this chapter.

Appendix I
Technical details of the survey

British Social Attitudes

1994 marked the first time that three versions of the questionnaire were fielded instead of two. This change meant that a wider range of topic areas could be covered, each 'module' of questions being asked either of the full sample (now increased from around 3,000 to around 3,500 respondents) or of a random two-thirds or one-third of the sample. The structure of the questionnaire (versions A, B and C) is shown at the beginning of Appendix III.

Also for the first time in 1994, in collaboration with Barnardos, a *Young People's Social Attitudes* survey was fielded among 12-19 year olds resident in the households of adult respondents. Further details are given below.

Sample design

The *British Social Attitudes* survey is designed to yield a representative sample of adults aged 18 or over. The sampling frame for the 1994 survey, as for its predecessor in 1993, was the Postcode Address File (PAF), a list of addresses (or postal delivery points) compiled by the Post Office.

Until 1991 all *British Social Attitudes* samples were drawn from the Electoral Register (ER). However, following concern that this sampling frame might be deficient in its coverage of certain population sub-groups,

a 'splicing' experiment was conducted in 1991.[*]   Its purpose was to
investigate whether a switch to PAF would disrupt the time-series - for
instance, by lowering response rates or affecting the distribution of
responses to particular questions. In the event, it was concluded that the
change from ER to PAF was unlikely to affect time trends in any
noticeable way, and that no adjustment factors were necessary.   Since
significant differences in efficiency exist between PAF and ER and because
we considered it untenable to continue to use a frame that is known to be
biased, we decided to adopt PAF as the sampling frame for future *British
Social Attitudes* surveys. For further details of the 1991 PAF/ER 'splicing'
experiment, see Lynn and Taylor (1993).

For practical reasons, the sample is confined to those living in private
households. People living in institutions (though not in private households
at such institutions) are excluded, as are households whose addresses were
not on the Postcode Address File.

The sampling method involved a multi-stage design, with three separate
stages of selection.

Selection of sectors

At the first stage, postcode sectors were selected systematically from a list
of all postal sectors in Great Britain. Before selection, any sectors with
fewer than 500 addresses were identified and grouped together with an
adjacent sector; in Scotland all sectors north of the Caledonian Canal were
deleted (because of the prohibitive costs of interviewing there). Sectors
were then stratified on the basis of:

-   Registrar General's Standard Region

-   Population density (persons per hectare) with variable banding
    used according to region, in order to create three equal-sized strata
    per region

-   Ranking by percentage of homes that were owner-occupied, from
    the 1991 Census figures.

Two hundred postcode sectors were selected, with probability proportional
to the number of addresses in each sector.

---

[*]   We are grateful to the Market Research Development Fund for contributing towards
the costs of this experiment.

Selection of addresses

Thirty addresses were selected in each of the 200 sectors. The sample was therefore 200 x 30 = 6,000 addresses, selected by starting from a random point on the list of addresses for each sector, and choosing each address at a fixed interval. The fixed interval was calculated for each sector in order to generate the correct number of addresses.

The Multiple-Output Indicator (MOI) available through PAF was used when selecting addresses. MOI shows the number of accommodation spaces sharing one address. Thus, if the MOI indicates more than one accommodation space at a given address, the chances of the given address being selected from the list of addresses would increase so that it matched the total number of accommodation spaces. As would be expected, the vast majority (99.2 per cent) of MOIs had a value of one. The remainder, which ranged between two and eight, were incorporated into the weighting procedures (described on the next page).

Selection of individuals

Interviewers called at each address selected from PAF and listed all those eligible for inclusion in the sample - that is, all persons currently aged 18 or over and resident at the selected address. The interviewer then selected one respondent by a random selection procedure (using a Kish grid). Where there were two or more households or 'dwelling units' at the selected address, interviewers first had to select one household or dwelling unit using a Kish grid; they then followed the same procedure to select a person for interview.

Questionnaire versions

Each address in each sector (sampling point) was allocated to either the A, B or C third of the sample. The first address in the sampling point was allocated the A version, the second the B version, the third the C version and so on. Each version was thus assigned to 2,000 addresses.

Computer-Assisted Personal Interviewing

In 1993 it was decided to mount a split-sample experiment designed to test the applicability of Computer-Assisted Personal Interviewing (CAPI) to the *British Social Attitudes* survey series. CAPI has been used increasingly over the past decade as an alternative to traditional interviewing techniques (or PAPI). As the name implies, CAPI involves the use of lap-top computers during interview, with interviewers entering responses directly into the computer. One of the advantages of CAPI is that it significantly reduces

both the amount of time spent on data processing and the number of coding and editing errors. Over a longer period, there could also be significant cost savings. There was however a concern that a different interviewing technique might alter the distribution of responses and so affect the year-on-year consistency of *British Social Attitudes* data.

Following the experiment, it was decided to change over to CAPI completely in 1994 (the self-completion questionnaire of course still being administered in the conventional way). The results of the experiment are discussed in Chapter 10 of *the 11th Report* (Lynn and Purdon, 1994).

Weighting

Data were weighted to take account of the fact that not all the units covered in the survey had the same probability of selection. The weighting reflected the relative selection probabilities of the individual at the three main stages of selection: address, household and individual.

First, because addresses were selected using the Multiple Output Indicator (MOI), weights had to be applied to compensate for the greater probability of an address with an MOI of more than one being selected, compared to an address with an MOI of one. Secondly, data were weighted to compensate for the fact that dwelling units at an address which contained a large number of dwelling units were less likely to be selected for inclusion in the survey than ones which did not share an address. The reason we use this procedure is that in most cases these two stages will cancel each other out, resulting in more efficient weights. Thirdly, data were weighted to compensate for the lower selection probabilities of adults living in large households compared with those living in small households.

The distribution of weights used is shown below:

Weight	No.	%	Scaled weight
0.25	9	0.2	0.1317
0.33	2	0.1	0.1756
0.38	1	0.0	0.1975
0.50	8	0.2	0.2634
0.75	2	0.1	0.3950
1.00	1099	31.7	0.5267
1.50	3	0.1	0.7901
1.67	1	0.0	0.8778
2.00	1816	52.3	1.0534
3.00	366	10.6	1.5801
3.33	1	0.0	1.7557
4.00	121	3.5	2.1068
5.00	22	0.6	2.6335
6.00	8	0.2	3.1602
7.00	1	0.0	3.6869
8.00	4	0.1	4.2136
10.00	1	0.0	5.2670
12.00	4	0.1	6.3204

All weights fell within a range between 0.25 and 12. The average weight applied was 1.9. The weighted sample was scaled down to make the number of weighted productive cases exactly equal to the number of unweighted productive cases (n = 3,469).

All the figures presented in this Report are based on weighted data.

Fieldwork

Interviewing was mainly carried out during May, June and July 1994, with a small number of interviews taking place until October.

Fieldwork was conducted by interviewers drawn from SCPR's regular panel. All interviewers attended a one-day briefing conference to familiarise them with the selection procedures and questionnaires.

The average interview length was 61 minutes for version A of the questionnaire, 60 minutes for version B and 55 minutes for version C. The final response achieved is shown below:

	No.	%
Addresses issued	6,000	
Vacant, derelict and other out of scope	680	
In scope	5,320	100.0
Interview achieved	3,469	65.2
Interview not achieved	1,851	34.8
Refused [1]	1,454	27.3
Non-contacted [2]	218	4.1
Other non-response	179	3.4

[1] 'Refusals' comprise refusals before selection of an individual at the address, refusals to the office, refusal by the selected person, 'proxy' refusals (on behalf of the selected respondent) and broken appointments after which the selected person could not be recontacted.

[2] 'Non-contacts' comprise households where no one was contacted and those where the selected person could not be contacted (never found at home, known to be away on business, on holiday, in hospital, and so on).

Both the A and C versions of the questionnaire achieved a response rate of 65.5 per cent; for the B version it was 64.7 per cent.

As in earlier rounds of the series, respondents were asked to fill in a self-completion questionnaire which, whenever possible, was collected by the interviewer. Otherwise, the respondent was asked to post it to SCPR. If necessary, up to three postal reminders were sent to obtain the self-completion supplement.

A total of 540 respondents (16 per cent of those interviewed) did not return their self-completion questionnaire. Version A of the self-completion

questionnaire was returned by 85 per cent of respondents to the face-to-face interview, version B by 84 per cent and version C also by 84 per cent. As in previous rounds, we judged that it was not necessary to apply additional weights to correct for non-response.

Advance letter

On the 1991 BSA survey, an experiment had been conducted which showed that sending advance letters to sampled addresses *before* fieldwork begins has very little impact on response rates. However, interviewers do find that an advance letter helps them to introduce the survey on the doorstep, and a majority of respondents have said that they preferred some advance notice. For these reasons, letters describing the purpose of the survey and the coverage of the questionnaire were again posted to sampled addresses approximately one week before the start of fieldwork on the 1994 survey.

Analysis variables

A number of standard analyses have been used in the tables that appear in this report. The analysis groups requiring further definition are set out below. For further details, see Brook, Park and Thomson (1995, forthcoming).

Region

The Registrar General's 10 Standard Regions have been used, except that we have distinguished between Greater London and the remainder of the South-East. Sometimes these have been grouped into what we have termed 'compressed region': 'Northern' includes the North, North-West, Yorkshire and Humberside. East Anglia is included in the 'South', as is the South-West.

Standard Occupational Classification

Respondents are classified according to their own occupation, not that of the 'head of household'. Their spouses or partners are similarly classified. The main social class variables used in the analyses in this report are the Registrar General's Social Class and Socio-economic Group (SEG).

Since 1991, the OPCS *Standard Occupational Classification* (SOC) has been used for the occupation coding of the BSA survey.* SOC has an hierarchical structure, consisting of 371 Unit Groups which can be aggregated into 77 Minor Groups, 22 Sub-major Groups and 9 Major Groups.

Registrar General's Social Class

Each respondent's Social Class is based on his or her current or last occupation. Thus, all respondents in paid work at the time of the interview, waiting to take up a paid job already offered, retired, seeking work, or looking after the home, have their occupation (present, past or future, as appropriate) classified into Occupational Unit Groups according to SOC. The combination of occupational classification with employment status generates the following six Social Classes:

I	Professional, etc. occupations	
II	Managerial and technical occupations	'Non-manual'
III (Non-manual)	Skilled occupations	
III (Manual)	Skilled occupations	
IV	Partly skilled occupations	'Manual'
V	Unskilled occupations	

They are usually collapsed into four groups: I & II, III Non-manual, III Manual, and IV & V.

The remaining respondents are grouped as 'never had a job' or 'not classifiable', but are not shown in the tables. For some analyses, it may be more appropriate to classify respondents according to their *current* social class, which takes into account only their present economic position. In this case, in addition to the six social classes listed above, the remaining respondents not currently in paid work fall into one of the following categories: 'not classifiable', 'retired', 'looking after the home', 'unemployed' or 'others not in paid occupations'.

---

* Before 1991, occupational coding was carried out according to the OPCS *Classification of Occupations 1980* (CO80). However, analysts can be confident that the change to SOC does not affect year-on-year comparability of social class variables in the *British Social Attitudes* survey. For further details see Appendix I in Jowell *et al* (1992).

Socio-economic Group

As with Social Class, each respondent's Socio-economic Group (SEG) is based on his or her current or last occupation. SEG aims to bring together people with jobs of similar social and economic status, and is derived from a combination of employment status and occupation. The full SEG classification identifies 18 categories, but these are usually condensed into six groups:

- Professionals, employers and managers
- Intermediate non-manual workers
- Junior non-manual workers
- Skilled manual workers
- Semi-skilled manual workers
- Unskilled manual workers

As with Social Class, the remaining respondents are grouped as 'never had a job' or 'not classifiable', but are not shown in the tables.

Goldthorpe schema

The Goldthorpe schema classifies occupations by their 'general comparability', considering such factors as sources and levels of income, economic security, promotion prospects, and level of job autonomy and authority. The Goldthorpe schema was derived from the SOC unit groups combined with employment status. Two versions of the schema are coded: the full schema has 11 categories; the 'compressed schema' combines these into the five classes shown below.

- Salariat (professional and managerial)
- Routine non-manual workers (office and sales)
- Petty bourgeoisie (the self-employed, including farmers, with and without employees)
- Manual foremen and supervisors
- Working class (skilled, semi-skilled and unskilled manual workers, personal service and agricultural workers)

There is a residual category comprising those who have never had a job or who gave insufficient information for classification purposes.

Industry

All respondents whose occupation could be coded were allocated a Standard Industrial Classification (SIC, 1980). Two-digit class codes were applied. As with Social Class, SIC may be generated on the basis of the respondent's current occupation only, or on his or her most recently-classifiable occupation.

Party identification

Respondents can be classified as identifying with a particular political party, or party grouping, on one of three counts: if they consider themselves supporters of that party, as closer to it than to others, or as more likely to support it in the event of a general election (responses are derived from Qs. 23-26). The three groups are generally described respectively as *partisans*, *sympathisers* and *residual identifiers*. In combination, the three groups are referred to in both text and tables as 'identifiers'.

Other analysis variables

These are taken directly from the questionnaire and to that extent are self-explanatory. The principal ones used in the in-text tables are:

Sex (Q.16)

Age (Q.784)

Household income (Q.880)

Economic position (Q.81)

Religion (Qs.753, 761)

Highest educational qualification obtained (Qs.798-801)

Marital status (Q.781)

Benefits received (Qs.863-864)

Sampling errors

No sample precisely reflects the characteristics of the population it represents because of both sampling and non-sampling errors. If a sample were designed as a random sample (if every adult had an equal and independent chance of inclusion in the sample) then we could calculate the sampling error of any percentage, *p*, using the formula:

$$s.e. \ (p) \ = \ \sqrt{\frac{p(100-p)}{n}}$$

where *n* is the number of respondents on which the percentage is based. Once the sampling error had been calculated, it would be a straightforward exercise to calculate a confidence interval for the true population

percentage. For example, a 95 per cent confidence interval would be given by the formula:

$$p \pm 1.96 \times s.e.(p)$$

Clearly, for a simple random sample (srs), the sampling error depends only on the values of p and n. However, simple random sampling is almost never used in practice because of its inefficiency in terms of time and cost.

As noted above, the *British Social Attitudes* sample, like that drawn for most large-scale surveys, was clustered according to a stratified multi-stage design into 200 postcode sectors (or combinations of sectors). With a complex design like this, the sampling error of a percentage giving a particular response is not simply a function of the number of respondents in the sample and the size of the percentage; it also depends on how that percentage response is spread within and between sample points. The complex design may be assessed relative to simple random sampling by calculating a range of design factors (DEFTs) associated with it, where

$$\text{DEFT} = \sqrt{\frac{\text{Variance of estimator with complex design, sample size n}}{\text{Variance of estimator with srs design, sample size n}}}$$

and represents the multiplying factor to be applied to the simple random sampling error to produce its complex equivalent. A design factor of one means that the complex sample has achieved the same precision as a simple random sample of the same size. A design factor greater than one means the complex sample is less precise than its simple random sample equivalent. If the DEFT for a particular characteristic is known, a 95 per cent confidence interval for a percentage may be calculated using the formula:

$$p \pm 1.96 \times complex\ sampling\ error\ (p)$$

$$= p \pm 1.96 \times \text{DEFT} \times \sqrt{\frac{p(100-p)}{n}}$$

Calculations of sampling errors and design effects were made using the World Fertility Survey 'Clusters' programme.

The following table gives examples of the confidence intervals and DEFTs calculated for a range of different questions, some fielded on all three versions of the questionnaire and some on one only; some asked on the interview questionnaire and some on the self-completion supplement. It shows that most of the questions asked of all sample members have a confidence interval of around plus or minus two to three per cent of the survey proportion. This means that we can be 95 per cent certain that the true population proportion is within two to three per cent (in either direction) of the proportion we report. The confidence intervals calculated

for questions asked of only half the sample tend to be greater than those calculated for questions asked of the entire sample.

It should be noted that the design effects for certain variables (notably those most associated with the area a person lives in) are greater than those for other variables. This is particularly the case for party identification and housing tenure. For instance, Labour identifiers and local authority tenants tend to be concentrated in certain areas; consequently the design effects calculated for these variables in a clustered sample are greater than the design effects calculated for variables less strongly associated with area, such as attitudinal variables.

		% (p)	Complex standard error of p (%)	95 per cent confidence interval	DEFT
Classification variables					
DV*	**Party identification**				
	Conservative	28.9	1.1	26.7 - 31.1	1.43
	Liberal Democrat	14.4	0.8	12.8 - 16.0	1.34
	Labour	40.6	1.2	38.2 - 43.0	1.43
DV*	**Housing tenure**				
	Owns	70.2	1.2	67.8 - 72.6	1.53
	Rents from local authority	17.1	1.0	15.2 - 19.1	1.52
	Rents privately	11.4	0.7	9.9 - 12.9	1.37
DV*	**Religion**				
	No religion	38.5	1.0	36.5 - 40.5	1.21
	Church of England	33.1	0.9	31.3 - 35.0	1.17
	Catholic	9.5	0.6	8.3 - 10.7	1.23
Q.795	**Age of completing continuous full-time education**				
	16 or under	65.1	1.2	62.6 - 67.5	1.51
	17 or 18	16.5	0.8	14.9 - 18.1	1.27
	19 or over	14.6	0.9	12.8 - 16.4	1.48

* DV = Derived variable

Attitudinal variables		% (p)	Complex standard error of p (%)	95 per cent confidence interval	DEFT
Q.43	Benefits for the unemployed are ...				
	... too low	53.2	1.1	51.1 - 55.4	1.27
	... too high	24.0	0.9	22.3 - 25.7	1.18
A.277	Attempts to give equal opportunities to homo-sexuals have ...				
	... gone much too far	18.5	1.2	16.1 - 20.9	1.05
	... gone too far	27.1	1.4	24.3 - 29.8	1.03
	... about right	31.6	1.6	28.4 - 34.8	1.16
	... not gone far enough	15.0	1.2	12.6 - 17.5	1.17
	... not gone nearly far enough	3.0	0.5	1.9 - 4.0	1.03
B.431	Britain should do all it can to ...				
	... unite fully with the EC	40.3	1.4	37.6 - 43.1	0.97
	... protect its independence from the EC	52.6	1.5	49.5 - 55.6	1.04
C.634	In a year from now, respon-dent expects unemployment to have gone up a lot	20.3	1.4	17.5 - 23.1	1.81
A2.36a	Death penalty for murder in course of a terrorist act ...				
	... in favour	70.2	1.8	66.5 - 73.9	1.25
	... against	26.3	1.7	22.8 - 29.7	1.22
B2.20c	Nuclear power stations create ...				
	... very serious risks for the future	44.5	1.9	40.8 - 48.2	1.17
	... quite serious risks	31.4	1.8	27.8 - 35.1	1.23
	... only slight risks	17.3	1.1	15.2 - 19.5	0.89
	... hardly any risks	4.7	0.7	3.3 - 6.0	1.02
C2.45a	Law should allow abortion if the woman decides ... not to have the child				
	... yes	54.4	1.8	50.7 - 58.0	1.15
	... no	41.6	1.8	38.0 - 45.2	1.15

These calculations are based on the total sample from the 1994 survey (3,469 respondents); on A version respondents (1,137 for the main questionnaire and 970 for the self-completion); on B version respondents (1,165 and 975 respectively); or on C version respondents (1,167 and 984 respectively). As the examples above show, sampling errors for proportions based only on respondents to just one of the three versions of the

questionnaire, or on subgroups within the sample, are somewhat larger than they would have been had the questions been asked of everyone.

Young People's Social Attitudes

In 1994, for the first time in the *British Social Attitudes* survey series, we fielded a parallel survey of young people aged between 12 and 19. This survey, the *Young People's Social Attitudes* survey, was conceived and designed in collaboration with Barnardos' Policy and Development Unit. Barnardos also provided the funding.

Sample design

All young people aged between 12 and 19 who lived in the same household as an adult *British Social Attitudes* respondent were eligible for interview. The principles governing the sample design of the adult survey have been described earlier in this Appendix. Eighteen and nineteen year olds who were administered the adult questionnaire as part of the main sample were *not* eligible for the survey among 12-19 year olds.

The questionnaire

Unlike the main BSA survey, there was only one version of the questionnaire administered to 12-19 year olds. In contrast to the main survey, the interview was carried out using traditional paper and pen methods, rather than CAPI. Approximately half the questions in the *Young People's Social Attitudes* questionnaire were also asked (using exactly the same wording) on one, two or all three versions of the *British Social Attitudes* survey. For these questions, then, the responses of young people can be compared both to those of *all* adults in the sample, and also to those of the adult respondent living in their household. The remaining questions were unique to the *Young People's Social Attitudes* survey and covered issues of special relevance to young people.

Topics covered in the *Young People's Social Attitudes* survey were as follows:

'Age of consent' questions
Judgements of right and wrong
Education, school life and sex education
Fear and experience of crime
Crime and punishment
Gender roles and family life
Race prejudice and discrimination
Political knowledge, political interest and party identity
Important factors in 'doing well in life'
Life ambitions and aspirations

A number of demographic and other classificatory questions were also included (such as age, sex, religion, current activity and educational experience and expectations). Other background variables (such as those used to derive socio-economic grade) had been included in the adult questionnaire and so were not fielded again in the *Young People's Social Attitudes* questionnaire.

For a copy of the young people's questionnaire, with the percentage distribution of responses added, see Roberts and Sachdev (1996, forthcoming).

Weighting

As with the adult data, the *Young People's Social Attitudes* data were weighted to take account of the relative selection probabilities of the adult respondent at the two main stages of selection: address and household. In this respect the young people's data were weighted in the same way as the adult data. However, the young people's data did not need to be weighted further to take account of the differential selection probabilities of the adult respondent: since all 12-19 year olds within the household were eligible for interview, there was no need to calculate equivalent weights to reflect teenagers' selection probability.

Once the young people's survey weights had been calculated, they were scaled to make the number of weighted productive cases exactly equal to the number of unweighted productive cases (n = 580).

Fieldwork

Interviews were carried out by the same interviewers who worked on the adult *British Social Attitudes* survey. After the interview with the adult in the household, the interviewer established the number of eligible young

people living as household members and, where appropriate, asked permission to interview them. In most cases the interviewer had to return to the household on at least one occasion.

The final response achieved is shown below:

	No.	%
In scope	735	100
Interview achieved	580	79
Interview not achieved	155	21
Refused	116	16
Non-contact	17	2
Other non-response	22	3

The average interview length was 31 minutes.

Northern Ireland Social Attitudes (NISA)

In 1994, for the fifth year, the *British Social Attitudes* survey was extended to include Northern Ireland, supported as in 1993 by funding from all the Northern Ireland Departments. This time, however, not one but two versions of the questionnaire were fielded to accommodate a greater number of questions; the target sample size also increased from around 900 to around 1,400 respondents. As in previous years, the questionnaire consisted of 'core' questions (asked of *all* respondents in both Britain and Northern Ireland), some (but not all) of the other modules fielded on the mainland, and a special module mainly concerned with community relations in Northern Ireland. For most topic areas, therefore, users of the data have the opportunity to compare the attitudes of respondents in Northern Ireland to those of respondents in Britain.

British Social Attitudes researchers at SCPR and at the Policy Planning and Research Unit (PPRU) in Belfast, which carried out the sampling and fieldwork, met beforehand to plan the survey timetable and documentation and to design the questionnaire modules. As with previous NISA surveys, final responsibility for the questionnaire rested with SCPR.

The results of the NISA surveys are presented and discussed in a series of annual books, edited by researchers at the Centre for Social Research, The Queen's University of Belfast. The volume reporting on the results of the 1994 NISA survey will appear in mid 1996 (see Breen *et al*, 1996, forthcoming). For further information about the technical details of the 1994 *Northern Ireland Social Attitudes* survey, see Sweeney and McClelland in the Appendices to Breen *et al* (*ibid.*)

International Social Survey Programme (ISSP)

The ISSP is run by a group of research organisations, each of which undertakes to field annually an agreed module of questions on a chosen topic area. Since 1985, an ISSP module has been included in one of the *British Social Attitudes* self-completion questionnaires. Each module is chosen for repetition at intervals to allow comparisons both between countries (currently standing at 22) and over time. In 1994, the chosen subject was 'Women and Changing Gender Roles', a part-replication of the module first fielded on BSA in 1989. The 1994 ISSP module comprises Qs.2.01-2.21 of the C version of the self-completion questionnaire.

For further details see Brook, Park and Thomson (1995, forthcoming).

References

Breen, R., Devine, P. and Robinson, G. (eds.) (1996, forthcoming), *Social Attitudes in Northern Ireland: the 5th Report*, Belfast: Appletree Press.

Brook, L., Park, A. and Thomson, K. (1995, forthcoming), *British Social Attitudes 1994 Survey: Technical Report*, London: SCPR.

Jowell, R., Brook, L., Prior, G. and Taylor, B. (eds.) (1992), Appendix I, in *British Social Attitudes: the 9th Report*, Aldershot: Dartmouth.

Lynn, P. and Purdon, S. (1994), 'Time-series and lap-tops: the change to computer-assisted interviewing' in Jowell, R., Curtice, J., Brook, L. and Ahrendt, D. (eds.), *British Social Attitudes: the 11th Report*, Aldershot: Dartmouth.

Lynn, P. and Taylor, B. (1993), 'On the bias and variance of samples of individuals: a comparison of the Electoral Registers and Postcode Address File as sampling frames', *Working Paper No. 27*, London: CREST at SCPR.

Roberts, H. and Sachdev, D. (eds.) (1996, forthcoming), *Young People's Social Attitudes*.

Appendix II
Notes on the tabulations

1. Figures in the tables are from the 1994 survey unless otherwise indicated.
2. Tables are percentaged as indicated.
3. In tables, '*' indicates less than 0.5 per cent but greater than zero, and '-' indicates zero.
4. When findings based on the responses of fewer than 50 respondents are reported in the text, reference is made to the small base size. Any percentages based on fewer than 50 respondents (unweighted) are bracketed in the tables.
5. Percentages equal to or greater than 0.5 have been rounded up in all tables (eg. 0.5 per cent = one per cent, 36.5 per cent = 37 per cent).
6. In many tables the proportions of respondents answering 'don't know' or not giving an answer are omitted. This, together with the effects of rounding and weighting, means that percentages will not always add to 100 per cent.
7. The self-completion questionnaire was not completed by all respondents to the main questionnaire (see Appendix I). Percentage responses to the self-completion questionnaire are based on all those who completed it.

Appendix III
The questionnaires

As explained in Appendix I, three different versions of the adults' questionnaire (A, B and C) were administered, each with its own self-completion supplement. The diagram that follows shows the structure of the questionnaires and the topics covered (not all of which are reported on in this volume).

The three interview questionnaires reproduced on the following pages are derived from the Blaise program in which they were written. For ease of reference, each item has been allocated a question number. Gaps in the numbering system indicate items that are essential components of the Blaise program but which are not themselves questions, and so have been omitted. In addition, on all six questionnaires we have removed the keying codes and inserted instead the percentage distribution of answers to each question. We have also included the SPSS variable name, bracketed and in italics, beside each question. Above the questions we have included routeing instructions. A routeing instruction should be considered as staying in force until the next routeing instruction. Percentages for the core questions are based on the total weighted sample, while those for questions in versions A, B or C are based on the appropriate weighted subsamples. We reproduce first version A of the interview questionnaire in full; then those parts of version B and version C that differ. The three versions of the self-completion questionnaire follow.

The percentage distributions do not necessarily add up to 100 because of weighting and rounding, or for one or more of the following reasons:

(i)   Some sub-questions are filtered - that is, they are asked of only a proportion of respondents. In these cases the percentages add up (approximately) to the proportions who were asked them. Where,

however, a *series* of questions is filtered, we have indicated the weighted base at the beginning of that series (for example, all employees), and throughout have derived percentages from that base.

(ii)   If fewer than 50 respondents (unweighted) are asked a question, frequencies (the *number* of people giving each response) are shown, rather than percentages.

(iii)   At a few questions, respondents were invited to give more than one answer and so percentages may add to well over 100 per cent. These are clearly marked by interviewer instructions on the questionnaires.

As reported in Appendix I, the *British Social Attitudes* self-completion questionnaire was not completed by 16 per cent of respondents who were successfully interviewed. To allow for comparisons over time, the answers in the supplement have been repercentaged on the base of those respondents who returned it (for version A: 986 weighted; for version B: 971 weighted; and for version C: 1,000 weighted). This means that the figures are comparable with those given in all earlier reports in this series except in *the 1984 Report*, where the percentages in Appendix III need to be recalculated if comparisons are to be made.

Structure of the questionnaires

CAPI questionnaire plan

A	B	C
	1. Newspaper readership Party identification/politics	
	2. Public spending, welfare benefits and health care	
	3. Economic activity, the labour market, gender issues at the workplace and childcare	
4. Civil liberties	4. Europe/international relations	4. Economic prospects
5. Race		5. Charitable giving
6. Local government		6. Poverty/single parents
7. Political trust	7. Countryside/environment	7. Gender (short)
8. Europe (short)	8. Transport	8. Education
	9. Fear of crime	
	10. Short housing 11. Religion and ethnic origin 12. Classification	

Self-completion questionnaire plan

A	B	C
1. Civil liberties	1. Europe/international relations	1. ISSP Women and family
	2. Health care	
	3. Childcare	
4. Local government		4. Gender
5. Immigration, sentencing and prisons		5. Single parents
6. 'Predictions'	6. Countryside/environment	6. Charitable giving
7. Political trust	7. Transport	7. Education
8. Issues of conscience - 1		8. Issues of conscience - 2
	9. Fear of crime	
	10. Welfare state and other attitude scales	

VERSION A   INTERVIEW QUESTIONNAIRE

INTRODUCTION

ASK ALL

Q1   [Serial]
      Serial
      Range: 60001 ... 69997   n=3469

Q5   [Version]

%	
32.9	A
32.9	B
34.2	C

Q9   [First] **(NOT ON DATA FILE)**
      INTERVIEWER: FOR YOUR INFORMATION... you are in the
      Questionnaire for

      Serial number: (serial number)

      - TO RETURN TO THE MENU, PRESS <Esc>
      - TO GO DIRECTLY TO 'ADMIN', PRESS <Ctrl + Enter>
      - OTHERWISE TO CONTINUE WITH INTERVIEW PRESS '1' AND
      <Enter>.

Q10   [In:Num]
      Please type in your interviewer number

Q15   [StrtTime] **(ENTERED AUTOMATICALLY BY SYSTEM CLOCK)**
      Start Time

NEWSPAPER READERSHIP/ PARTY IDENTIFICATION/ POLITICS   n=3469

ASK ALL

Q16   [RSex]
      INTERVIEWER CHECK : PLEASE CODE SEX OF RESPONDENT

%	
46.6	Male
53.4	Female
-	(Don't Know)
-	(Refusal/NA)

Q17   [ReadPap]
      Do you normally read any daily **morning** newspaper at least 3
      times a week?

%	
61.4	Yes
38.6	No
-	(Don't Know)
0.0	(Refusal/NA)

Q18   **IF 'Yes' AT [ReadPap]**
      [WhPaper]
      Which one do you normally read?
      IF MORE THAN ONE ASK: Which one do you read **most**
      frequently?
      CODE ONE ONLY

%	
5.5	(Scottish) Daily Express
8.5	Daily Mail
13.3	Daily Mirror/Record
11.5	Daily Star
14.6	The Sun
2.2	Today
4.2	Daily Telegraph
0.2	Financial Times
2.5	The Guardian
1.7	The Independent
2.2	The Times
0.1	Morning Star
3.8	Other Irish/Northern Irish/Scottish regional or local **daily** morning paper (WRITE IN)
0.7	Other (WRITE IN)
-	(Don't Know)
0.0	(Refusal/NA)

ASK ALL

Q23   [SupParty]
      Generally speaking, do you think of yourself as a
      supporter of any one political party?

%	
47.3	Yes
52.4	No
0.2	(Don't Know)
0.1	(Refusal/NA)

2

n= 2282

Q33 [Politics]
How much interest do you generally have in what is going on in politics ... READ OUT ...
%
9.4   ...a great deal,
22.7 quite a lot,
35.2 some,
24.8 not very much,
7.8   or, none at all?
0.1   (Don't Know)
-     (Refusal/NA)

n=3469

Q24 IF 'No' AT [SupParty]
[ClosePty]
Do you think of yourself as a little closer to one political party than to the others?
%
25.8 Yes
26.5 No
0.1   (Don't Know)
0.3   (Refusal/NA)

Q26 IF 'Yes' AT [SupParty] OR 'Yes'/'No' AT [ClosePty]
[PartyId1]
IF 'Yes' AT [SupParty] OR AT [ClosePty] : Which one?
IF 'No' AT [ClosePty] : If there were a general election tomorrow, which political party do you think you would be most likely to support?
%
28.8 Conservative
40.4 Labour
14.3 Liberal Democrats
1.7   Scottish Nationalist
0.3   Plaid Cymru
0.4   Other party
1.1   Other answer
8.1   None
1.1   Green Party
2.4   (Don't Know)
0.4   (Refusal/NA)

Q31 IF ANY PARTY AT [PartyFW]
[IdStrng]
Would you call yourself very strong (name of party) fairly strong, or not very strong?
%
9.6   Very strong (name of party)
32.8 Fairly strong
44.6 Not very strong
0.1   (Don't Know)
4.0   (Refusal/NA)

n= 2282

Q32 VERSIONS A AND B: ASK ALL
CARD
[VoteResn]
Which of the four statements on this card comes closest to the way you vote in a general election?
%
53.0 I vote for a party regardless of the candidate
25.7 I vote for a party only if I approve of the candidate
5.6   I vote for a candidate regardless of his or her party
15.0 I do not generally vote at all
0.6   (Don't Know)
0.1   (Refusal/NA)

3

PUBLIC SPENDING, WELFARE BENEFITS AND HEALTH CARE   [n=1187]

VERSION C: ASK ALL

Q37 [Spend1]
CARD
Here are some items of government spending. Which of them, if any, would be your highest priority for extra spending? Please read through the whole list before deciding.
ENTER ONE CODE ONLY FOR HIGHEST PRIORITY

Q38 [Spend2]
And which next?
ENTER ONE CODE ONLY FOR NEXT HIGHEST

	[Spend1]	[Spend2]
	%	%
Education	30.4	30.0
Defence	1.6	2.5
Health	44.0	28.2
Housing	5.5	12.7
Public transport	1.0	2.4
Roads	1.4	2.1
Police and prisons	5.2	7.7
Social security benefits	4.7	6.5
Help for industry	5.1	6.4
Overseas aid	0.5	0.8
(None of these)	0.6	0.4
(Don't Know)	0.1	0.3
(Refusal/NA)	-	-

Q39 [SocBen1]
CARD
Thinking now only of the government's spending on social benefits like those on the card. Which, if any, of these would be your highest priority for extra spending?
ENTER ONE CODE ONLY FOR HIGHEST PRIORITY

Q40 [SocBen2]
And which next?
ENTER ONE CODE ONLY FOR NEXT HIGHEST

	[SocBen1]	[SocBen2]
	%	%
Retirement pensions	41.1	23.0
Child benefits	16.6	17.3
Benefits for the unemployed	12.3	14.2
Benefits for disabled people	23.7	33.3
Benefits for single parents	4.9	9.3
(None of these)	1.2	2.4
(Don't Know)	0.1	0.6
(Refusal/NA)	-	-

5

[n=3469]

ASK ALL
Q41 [FalseClm]
I will read two statements. For each one please say whether you agree or disagree.
Large numbers of people these days falsely claim benefits.
IF AGREE OR DISAGREE: Strongly or slightly?

Q42 [FailClm]
(And do you agree or disagree that...)
Large numbers of people who are eligible for benefits these days fail to claim them.
IF AGREE OR DISAGREE: Strongly or slightly?

	[FalseClm]	[FailClm]
	%	%
Agree strongly	46.1	44.5
Agree slightly	25.8	35.1
Disagree slightly	13.1	10.9
Disagree strongly	10.0	4.0
(Don't Know)	4.9	5.4
(Refusal/NA)	0.1	0.0

Q43 [Dole]
Opinions differ about the level of benefits for unemployed people.
Which of these two statements comes closest to your own view ... READ OUT ...

%
53.2 ...benefits for unemployed people are too low and cause hardship,
24.0 or, benefits for unemployed people are too high and discourage them from finding jobs,
13.8 (Neither)
0.0 (Both - some hardship but because wages are so low, no incentive)
0.2 (About right - in between the two)
5.2 Other answer (WRITE IN)
3.5 (Don't Know)
0.0 (Refusal/NA)

Q46 [TaxSpend]
CARD
Suppose the government had to choose between the three options on this card. Which do you think it should choose?

%
3.8 Reduce taxes and spend less on health, education and social benefits
33.1 Keep taxes and spending on these services at the same level as now
58.3 Increase taxes and spend more on health, education and social benefits
3.5 None
1.3 (Don't Know)
- (Refusal/NA)

6

n=3469

Q47 *[NHSSat]*
CARD
All in all, how satisfied or dissatisfied would you say you are with the way in which the National Health Service runs nowadays?
Choose a phrase from this card.

Q48 *[GPSat]*
CARD AGAIN
From your own experience, or from what you have heard, please say how satisfied or dissatisfied you are with the way in which each of these parts of the National Health Service runs nowadays.
First, local doctors or GPs?

Q49 *[DentSat]*
CARD AGAIN
(And how satisfied or dissatisfied are you with the NHS as regards...)
National Health Service dentists?

Q50 *[InPatSat]*
CARD AGAIN
(And how satisfied or dissatisfied are you with the NHS as regards...)
Being in hospital as an in-patient?

Q51 *[OutPaSat]*
CARD AGAIN
(And how satisfied or dissatisfied are you with the NHS as regards...)
Attending hospital as an out-patient?

	[NhsSat]	*[GPSat]*	*[DentSat]*	*[InPatSat]*	*[OutPaSat]*
	%	%	%	%	%
Very satisfied	9.7	34.8	18.8	22.8	14.8
Quite satisfied	34.1	44.7	38.1	35.6	41.5
Neither satisfied nor dissatisfied	17.2	8.9	17.0	17.0	17.5
Quite dissatisfied	22.1	7.6	13.4	11.7	15.1
Very dissatisfied	16.2	3.3	8.1	4.6	6.1
(Don't Know)	0.6	0.8	4.6	8.4	5.0
(Refusal/NA)	-	-	-	0.0	-

Q52 *[PrivMed]*
Are you covered by a private health insurance scheme, that is an insurance scheme that allows you to get private medical **treatment**?
% **ADD IF NECESSARY:** For example, BUPA or PPP.
15.4 Yes
84.4 No
0.2 (Don't Know)
\- (Refusal/NA)

n=3469

IF Yes AT [PrivMed]
Q53 *[PrivPaid]*
Does your employer (or your partner's employer) pay the majority of the cost of membership of this scheme?
%
8.2 Yes
7.1 No
0.1 (Don't Know)
0.2 (Refusal/NA)

ASK ALL
Q54 *[NHSLimit]*
It has been suggested that the National Health Service should be available **only to those with lower incomes**. This would mean that contributions and taxes could be lower and most people would then take out medical insurance or pay for health care.
% Do you support or oppose this idea?
20.3 Support
77.6 Oppose
2.0 (Don't Know)
\- (Refusal/NA)

Q55 *[InPat1]*
CARD
Now, suppose you had to go into a local NHS hospital for observation and maybe an operation. From what you know or have heard, please say whether you think the hospital doctors would tell you all you feel you need to know?

Q56 *[InPat2]*
CARD AGAIN
(And please say whether you think ...)
...the hospital doctors would take seriously any views you may have on the sorts of treatment available?

Q57 *[InPat3]*
CARD AGAIN
(And please say whether you think ...)
...the operation would take place on the day it was booked for?

Q58 *[InPat4]*
CARD AGAIN
(And please say whether you think ...)
...you would be allowed home only when you were really well enough to leave?

	[InPat1]	*[InPat2]*	*[InPat3]*	*[InPat4]*
	%	%	%	%
Definitely would	20.3	11.5	10.0	16.2
Probably would	49.1	46.5	49.3	37.9
Probably would not	23.7	30.8	28.2	32.4
Definitely would not	5.3	7.2	8.0	11.2
(Don't Know)	1.6	4.1	4.5	2.3
(Refusal/NA)	0.0	-	0.0	0.0

n=3469

Q59 [InPat5]
CARD AGAIN
(And please say whether you think ...)
...the nurses would take seriously any complaints you may have?

Q60 [InPat6]
CARD AGAIN
(And please say whether you think ...)
...the hospital doctors would take seriously any complaints you may have?

Q61 [InPat7]
CARD AGAIN
(And please say whether you think ...)
...there would be a particular nurse responsible for dealing with any problems you may have?

	[InPat5]	[InPat6]	[InPat7]
	%	%	%
Definitely would	24.8	18.8	14.6
Probably would	56.1	55.6	34.3
Probably would not	14.4	19.5	33.8
Definitely would not	2.5	3.6	7.5
(Don't Know)	2.3	2.4	9.7
(Refusal/NA)	0.0	-	0.0

Q62 [OutPat1]
CARD AGAIN
Now suppose you had a back problem and your GP referred you to a hospital out-patients' department.
From what you know or have heard, please say whether you think...
...you would get an appointment within three months?

Q63 [OutPat2]
CARD AGAIN
(And please say whether you think ...)
...when you arrived, the doctor would see you within half an hour of your appointment time?

Q64 [OutPat3]
CARD AGAIN
(And please say whether you think ...)
...if you wanted to complain about the treatment you received, you would be able to without any fuss or bother?

9

n=3469

Q65 [WhchHosp]
CARD AGAIN
Now suppose you needed to go into hospital for an operation. Do you think you would have a say about which hospital you went to?

	[OutPat1]	[OutPat2]	[OutPat3]	[WhchHosp]
	%	%	%	%
Definitely would	12.8	7.0	12.7	6.1
Probably would	33.3	27.7	41.5	19.2
Probably would not	33.1	39.5	31.2	45.3
Definitely would not	15.3	22.8	9.6	24.7
(Don't Know)	5.4	3.1	5.1	4.5
(Refusal/NA)	-	-	0.0	0.1

Q66 [GPChange]
Suppose you wanted to change your GP and go to a different practice, how difficult or easy do you think this would be to arrange? Would it be ... **READ OUT** ...

	%
...very difficult,	5.3
fairly difficult,	19.6
not very difficult,	38.3
or, not at all difficult?	30.5
(Don't Know)	6.2
(Refusal/NA)	0.0

Q67 [WryHlth]
CARD
I am going to read out things that some people worry about. For each one please say how worried you are about it these days.
First, your health?

Q68 [WryFam]
CARD AGAIN
(Please say how worried you are these days about ...)
...family problems?

Q69 [WryCrime]
CARD AGAIN
(Please say how worried you are these days about ...)
...crime?

	[WryHlth]	[WryFam]	[WryCrime]
	%	%	%
Very worried	5.6	7.8	49.2
Fairly worried	22.7	23.0	38.0
Not very worried	48.5	39.0	9.9
Not at all worried	23.2	29.9	2.9
(Don't Know)	0.0	0.1	0.0
(Refusal/NA)	0.0	0.1	-

10

ECONOMIC ACTIVITY, THE LABOUR MARKET, GENDER ISSUES AT THE WORKPLACE AND CHILDCARE

n=3469

Q81 ASK ALL (Figures refer to first answer on the list)
[REconAct]
CARD
Which of these descriptions applies to what you were doing last week, that is, in the seven days ending last Sunday?
CODE ALL THAT APPLY
PROBE: Any others?
Multicoded (Maximum of 10 codes)
Respondent's economic activity.

%	
3.9	In full-time education (not paid for by employer, including on vacation)
0.4	On government training/employment programme (eg. Employment Training, Youth Training, etc)
52.2	In paid work (or away temporarily) for at least 10 hours in week
0.6	Waiting to take up paid work already accepted
5.4	Unemployed and registered at a benefit office
0.5	Unemployed, not registered, but actively looking for a job
0.5	Unemployed, wanting a job (of at least 10 hrs per week) but not actively looking for a job
4.6	Permanently sick or disabled
17.1	Wholly retired from work
13.2	Looking after the home
1.5	(Doing something else) (WRITE IN)
0.0	Respondent Refused

n=1813

Q82 ASK ALL IN PAID WORK OR AWAY TEMPORARILY (IF 'In paid work' AT [REconAct])
[REmploye]
In your (main) job are you ... READ OUT ...

%	
85.6	... an employee,
14.3	or, self-employed?
0.1	(Don't Know)
-	(Refusal/NA)

n=1552

Q83 ASK ALL EMPLOYEES (IF 'employee'/DK AT [REmploye])
[EmploydT]
For how long have you been continuously employed by your present employer?
ENTER NUMBER. THEN SPECIFY MONTHS OR YEARS
Range: 1 ... 60
Median: 60 months
(Don't know)
(Refusal/NA)

Q85 [ESrJbTim]
In your present job, are you working ... READ OUT ....
RESPONDENT'S OWN DEFINITION

%	
77.1	... full-time,
22.9	or, part-time?
-	(Don't Know)
-	(Refusal/NA)

12

---

n=3469

Q70 [WryMoney]
CARD AGAIN
(Please say how worried you are these days about ...)
... money or bills?

Q71 [WryWorld]
CARD AGAIN
(Please say how worried you are these days about ...)
... things happening around the world?

	[WryMoney]	[WryWorld]
	%	%
Very worried	15.3	30.8
Fairly worried	28.5	46.2
Not very worried	38.8	18.4
Not at all worried	17.3	4.6
(Don't Know)	0.0	0.0
(Refusal/NA)	0.1	-

Q72 [BigWorry]
CARD
Which of the things on this card would you say is your biggest worry?
CODE ONE ONLY

%	
13.1	My health
14.0	Family problems
33.3	Crime
22.6	Money or bills
12.8	Things happening around the world
1.4	(All equally)
2.7	(None of these)
0.0	(Don't Know)
0.0	(Refusal/NA)

11

n=1552

Q86 [E2DbHours]
How many hours a week do you normally work in
your (main) job?
IF RESPONDENT CANNOT ANSWER, ASK ABOUT LAST WEEK.
ROUND TO NEAREST HOUR.
CODE 95 FOR 95+
Range: 10 .. 95
Median: 38 hours
0.1 (Don't Know)
0.1 (Refusal/NA)

Q87 [E2DbHrCat]
HOURS WORKED - CATEGORISED
%
7.2 10-15 hours a week
10.1 16-23 hours a week
4.8 24-29 hours a week
77.7 30 or more hours a week
0.1 (Don't Know)
0.1 (Refusal/NA)

Q88 [WageNow]
How would you describe the wages or salary you are paid for
the job you do - on the low side, reasonable, or on the
high side?
IF LOW: Very low or a bit low?
%
10.6 Very low
24.5 A bit low
55.6 Reasonable
8.9 On the high side
0.2 Other answer (WRITE IN)
0.1 (Don't Know)
0.1 (Refusal/NA)

Q91 [PayGap]
CARD
Thinking of the **highest** and the **lowest** paid people at your
place of work, how would you describe the **gap** between their
pay, as far as you know?
Please choose a phrase from this card.
%
21.8 Much too big a gap
30.2 Too big
38.8 About right
2.4 Too small
0.5 Much too small a gap
6.7 (Don't Know)
0.1 (Refusal/NA)

Q92 [WageXpct]
If you stay in this job, would you expect your wages or
salary over the coming year to **READ OUT** ...
%
13.5 ... rise by **more** than the cost of living,
36.8 rise by the **same** as the cost of living,
28.6 rise by **less** than the cost of living,
19.2 or, not to rise at all?
1.2 (Will not stay in job)
0.6 (Don't Know)
0.1 (Refusal/NA)

13

---

n=1552

Q93 IF 'Not rise at all' AT [WageXpct]
[WageDrop]
Would you expect your wages or salary to stay the same, or
in fact to go down?
%
17.8 Stay the same
1.4 Go down
0.0 (Don't Know)
0.7 (Refusal/NA)

Q94 **ASK ALL EMPLOYEES** (IF 'Employee'/DK AT [REmployee])
[NumEmp]
Over the coming year do you expect your workplace to be ...
READ OUT ...
%
19.5 ... increasing its number of employees,
27.0 reducing its number of employees,
51.3 or, will the number of employees stay about the same?
0.6 Other answer (WRITE IN)
1.5 (Don't Know)
0.1 (Refusal/NA)

Q97 [LeaveJob]
Thinking now about your own job. How likely or unlikely is
it that you will leave this employer over the next year for
any reason?
Is it ... READ OUT ...
%
13.2 ... very likely,
13.1 quite likely,
30.8 not very likely,
41.5 or, not at all likely?
1.3 (Don't Know)
     (Refusal/NA)

Q98 IF 'very likely' OR 'quite likely' AT [LeaveJob]
CARD
Why do you think you will leave? Please choose a phrase
from this card or tell me what other reason there is.
CODE ALL THAT APPLY
Multicoded (Maximum of 9 codes)
Firm will close down [WhyGo1]
I will be declared redundant [WhyGo2]
I will reach normal retirement age [WhyGo3]
My contract of employment will expire [WhyGo4]
I will take early retirement [WhyGo5]
I will decide to leave and work for another employer [WhyGo6]
I will decide to leave and work for myself, as
   self-employed [WhyGo7]
I will leave to look after home/children/relative [WhyGo8]
Other answer (WRITE IN) [WhyGo9]
(Don't know)
(Refusal/NA)

	[WhyGo1]	[WhyGo2]	[WhyGo3]	[WhyGo4]	[WhyGo5]
	%	%	%	%	%
Yes	1.1	4.7	1.3	1.6	1.0
No	25.2	21.7	25.1	24.7	25.4
(Don't Know)	1.3	1.3	1.3	1.3	1.3
(Refusal/NA)	-	-	-	-	-

	[WhyGo6]	[WhyGo7]	[WhyGo8]	[WhyGo9]	[WhyGo10]

14

n=1552

```
              [WhyGo6]  [WhyGo7]  [WhyGo10]  [WhyGo7]  [WhyGo8]
                 %         %          %         %         %
Yes            12.6                  1.7       1.9       3.0
No             13.7      24.6       24.5      23.4
(Don't Know)    1.3       1.3        1.3
(Refusal/NA)     -         -
```

ASK ALL EMPLOYEES (IF 'employee'/DK AT [REmployee])

Q110 [EUnemp]
During the last five years - that is since March 1989 - have you been unemployed and seeking work for any period?
```
   %
21.2  Yes
78.6  No
 0.1  (Don't Know)
 0.1  (Refusal/NA)
```

IF 'Yes' AT [EUnemp]

Q111 [EUnempT]
For how many months in total during the last five years?
ENTER NUMBER OF MONTHS
Range: 0 ... 60
Median: 6 months
```
0.1  (Don't know)
0.4  (Refusal/NA)
```

ASK ALL EMPLOYEES (IF 'employee'/DK AT [REmployee])

Q112 [WpUnions]
At your place of work are there unions, staff associations, or groups of unions recognised by the management for negotiating pay and conditions of employment?
IF YES, PROBE FOR UNION OR IF 'BOTH', CODE 1 STAFF ASSOCIATION
```
   %
49.4  Yes : trade union(s)
 4.9  Yes : staff association
43.8  No, none
  -   (Don't Know)
 1.8  (Refusal/NA)
```

IF 'Yes' AT [WpUnions]

Q113 [WpUnionW]
On the whole, do you think (these unions do their/this staff association does its) job well or not?
```
   %
30.0  Yes
20.8  No
 3.5  (Don't Know)
 1.8  (Refusal/NA)
```

n=1552

Q114 [TUShould]
CARD
Listed on the card are a number of things trade unions or staff associations can do. Which, if any, do you think is the most important thing they should try to do at your workplace?
UNIONS OR STAFF ASSOCIATIONS SHOULD TRY TO:
```
   %
11.1  Improve working conditions
 8.1  Improve pay
20.0  Protect existing jobs
 3.0  Have more say over how work is done day-to-day
 7.4  Have more say over management's long-term plans
 0.8  Work for equal opportunities for women
 0.4  Work for equal opportunities for ethnic minorities
 2.2  Reduce pay differences at the workplace
 1.0  (NONE OF THESE)
 0.4  (Don't Know)
 1.8  (Refusal/NA)
```

ASK ALL EMPLOYEES (IF 'Employee'/DK AT [REmployee])

Q115 [IndRel]
In general how would you describe relations between management and other employees at your workplace
... READ OUT ...
```
   %
28.5  ... very good,
46.9  ... quite good,
16.8  not very good,
 7.2  or, not at all good?
 0.5  (Don't Know)
 0.1  (Refusal/NA)
```

Q116 [WorkRun]
And in general, would you say your workplace was
... READ OUT ...
```
   %
22.2  ... very well managed,
54.2  quite well managed,
23.2  or, not well managed?
 0.4  (Refusal/NA)
```

Q117 [ELookJob]
Suppose you lost your job for one reason or another - would you start looking for another job, would you wait for several months or longer before you started looking, or would you decide not to look for another job?
```
   %
87.2  Start looking
 6.0  Wait several months or longer
 6.5  Decide not to look
 0.3  (Don't Know)
  -   (Refusal/NA)
```

n=1552

Q118   IF 'Start looking' AT [ElookJob]
[EFindJob]
How long do you think it would take you to find an acceptable replacement job?
IF 'NEVER' PLEASE CODE 96
ENTER NUMBER. THEN SPECIFY MONTHS OR YEARS
Range: 1 .. 96
Median: 3 months
(Don't know)
(Refusal/NA)

10.9
0.4

Q120   ASK ALL EMPLOYEES (IF 'employee'/DK AT [REmployee])
[ESelfEm]
For any period during the last five years, have you worked as a self-employed person as your main job?
Yes
No
(Don't know)
(Refusal/NA)

5.3
94.5
0.2
-

Q121   IF 'Yes' AT [ESelfEm]
[ESelfEmT]
In total, for how many months during the last five years have you been self-employed?
Range: 1 .. 60
Median: 12 months
(Don't know)
(Refusal/NA)

Q122   IF 'No' AT [ESelfEm]
[ESelfSer]
How seriously in the last five years have you considered working as a self-employed person... ... READ OUT ...
... very seriously,
quite seriously,
not very seriously,
or, not at all seriously?
(Don't Know)
(Refusal/NA)

3.4
9.3
13.6
68.2
5.3
0.2

Q123   ASK ALL EMPLOYEES (IF 'Employee'/DK AT [REmployee])
[EmpEarn]
Now for some more general questions about your work. For some people their job is simply something they do in order to earn a living. For others it means much more than that. On balance, is your present job ... READ OUT ...
... just a means of earning a living,
or, does it mean much more to you than that?
(Don't Know)
(Refusal/NA)

37.7
61.9
0.4
-

17

n=1552

Q124   IF 'just a means of earning a living' AT [EmpEarn]
[EmpLiv]
Is that because ... READ OUT ...
.. there are no better jobs around here,
you don't have the right skills to get a better job,
or, because you would feel the same about any job you had?
(Don't Know)
(Refusal/NA)

13.1
10.3
12.5
1.6
0.5

Q125   ALL EMPLOYEES (IF 'Employee'/DK AT [REmployee])
[EPrefJob]
If without having to work, you had what you would regard as a reasonable living income, do you think you would still prefer to have a paid job or wouldn't you bother?
Still prefer paid job
Wouldn't bother
Other answer (WRITE IN)
(Don't Know)
(Refusal/NA)

68.6
29.3
1.8
0.3
-

Q128   [PrefHour]
Thinking about the number of hours you work each week including regular overtime, would you prefer a job where you worked . READ OUT ...
... more hours per week,
fewer hours per week,
or, are you happy with the number of hours you work at present?
(Don't Know)
(Refusal/NA)

5.4
35.0
59.4
0.2
-

Q129   IF 'more hours per week' AT [PrefHour]
[MoreHour]
Is the reason why you don't work more hours because ...
READ OUT ...
... your employer can't offer you more hours,
or, your personal circumstances don't allow it?
(Both)
Other answer (WRITE IN)
(Don't Know)
(Refusal/NA)

4.3
0.7
0.2
0.1
-
0.2

Q132   IF 'fewer hours per week' AT [PrefHour]
[FewHour]
In which of these ways would you like your working hours to be shortened READ OUT ...
... shorter hours each day,
or, fewer days each week?
Other answer (WRITE IN)
(Don't Know)
(Refusal/NA)

11.0
22.5
1.4
0.1
0.2

18

n=1552

Q135 [EarnHour]
Would you still like to work fewer hours, if it meant earning less money as a result?
%
9.8 Yes
23.3 No
1.9 It depends
0.2 (Don't Know)
- (Refusal/NA)

ASK ALL EMPLOYEES (IF 'Employee'/DK AT [REmployee])

Q136 [EWrkHrd]
CARD
Which of these statements best describes your feelings about your job?
%
In my job :
9.4 I only work as hard as I have to
43.9 I work hard, but not so that it interferes with the rest of my life
46.5 I make a point of doing the best I can, even if it sometimes does interfere with the rest of my life
0.1 (Don't Know)
0.1 (Refusal/NA)

Q137 [EWrkArrA]
CARD
Please use this card to say whether any of the following arrangements are available to you, at your workplace ...
... Part-time working, allowing you to work less than the full working day?

Q138 [EWrkArrB]
CARD AGAIN
(Is this available to you at your workplace?)
... flexible hours, so that you can adjust your own daily working hours?

Q139 [EWrkArrC]
CARD AGAIN
(Is this available to you at your workplace?)
... job-sharing schemes, where part-timers share one full-time job?

	[EWrkArrA]	[EWrkArrB]	[EWrkArrC]
	%	%	%
Not available - and I would not use it if it were	37.5	21.1	52.6
Not available - but I would use it if it were	12.0	43.0	20.7
Available - but I do not use it	27.6	8.5	20.2
Available - and I do use it	21.6	26.8	3.6
(Don't Know)	1.3	0.6	2.9
(Refusal/NA)	-	-	-

n=1552

Q140 [EWrkArrD]
CARD AGAIN
(Is this available to you at your workplace?)
... working from home at least some of the time?

Q141 [EWrkArrE]
CARD AGAIN
(Is this available to you at your workplace?)
... term-time contracts, allowing parents special time off during school holidays?

Q142 [EWrkArrF]
CARD AGAIN
(Is this available to you at your workplace?)
... nurseries provided by your employer for the young children of employees?

	[EWrkArrD]	[EWrkArrE]	[EWrkArrF]
	%	%	%
Not available - and I would not use it if it were	50.0	52.2	62.9
Not available - but I would use it if it were	32.6	28.6	27.7
Available - but I do not use it	4.2	8.5	7.6
Available - and I do use it	12.3	5.6	0.3
(Don't Know)	0.8	4.9	1.5
(Refusal/NA)	0.1	0.2	0.1

Q143 [EWrkArrG]
CARD AGAIN
(Is this available to you at your workplace?)
... arrangements by your employer for the care of children during school holidays?

Q144 [EWrkArrH]
CARD AGAIN
(Is this available to you at your workplace?)
... childcare allowances towards the cost of child care?

ASK ALL FEMALE EMPLOYEES (IF 'Employee'/DK AT [REmployee] AND 'Female' AT [RSex])   n=775

Q145 [EWrkArrI]
CARD AGAIN
(Is this available to you at your workplace?)
... career breaks, that is keeping women's jobs open for a few years so that mothers can return to work after caring for young children?

	[EWrkArrG]	[EWrkArrH]	[EWrkArrI]
	%	%	%
Not available - and I would not use it if it were	61.6	54.5	35.0
Not available - but I would use it if it were	30.3	38.5	29.3
Available - but I do not use it	4.3	3.2	21.2
Available - and I do use it	0.8	0.3	5.0
(Don't Know)	2.7	4.3	9.6
(Refusal/NA)	0.2	0.1	-

Q146 ASK ALL MALE EMPLOYEES (IF 'Employee'/DK AT [REmploye] AND 'Male' AT [RSex])
[EWrkArrJ]
CARD AGAIN
(Is this available to you at your workplace?)
... paternity leave, allowing fathers extra leave, when their children are born? [n=778]

Q147 ASK ALL EMPLOYEES (IF 'Employee'/DK AT [REmploye])
[EWrkArrL]
CARD AGAIN
(Is this available to you at your workplace?)
... time off, either paid or unpaid, to care for sick children? [n=1552]

	[EWrkArrJ] %	[EWrkArrL] %
Not available - and I would not use it if it were	28.1	20.3
Not available - but I would use it if it were	32.2	26.2
Available - but I do not use it	20.7	28.7
Available - and I do use it	12.3	16.0
(Don't Know)	6.4	8.8
(Refusal/NA)	0.2	0.1

Q148 [EWrkArrK]
(Is this available to you at your workplace?)
Any other arrangement to help people combine jobs and childcare?
(PLEASE WRITE IN)
IF 'NONE', PRESS <enter>.

2.5   Use other
..5   (Don't Know)

Q149 ASK ALL MALE EMPLOYEES (IF 'Employee'/DK AT [REmploye] AND 'Male' AT [RSex]) [n=778]
[EWSmeWrk]
Where you work, are there any women doing the same sort of work as you?
%
48.9   Yes
50.3   No
0.1   (Work alone)
0.7   (No-one else doing the same job)
-   (Don't Know)
-   (Refusal/NA)

Q150 [EMSexWrk]
Do you think of your work as ... READ OUT ...
%
32.8   mainly men's work,
0.7   mainly women's work,
66.0   or, work that either men or women do?
0.4   Other answer (WRITE IN)
-   (Don't Know)
-   (Refusal/NA)

21

Q153 IF 'mainly men's work'/'Other'/DK/Refusal AT [EMSexWrk] [n=778]
[EMWomCld]
Do you think that women could do the same sort of work as you?
%
21.2   Yes
12.1   No
-   (Don't Know)
-   (Refusal/NA)

Q154 IF 'Yes'/DK AT [EMWomCld]
[EMWomCld]
Do you think that women would be willing to do the same sort of work as you?
%
14.2   Yes
6.8   No
0.1   (Don't Know)
-   (Refusal/NA)

Q155 ASK ALL FEMALE EMPLOYEES (IF 'employee'/DK AT [REmploye] AND 'Female' AT [RSex]) [n=775]
[EWSmeWrk]
Where you work, are there any men doing the same sort of work as you?
%
62.5   Yes
36.7   No
0.4   (Work alone)
0.4   (No-one else doing the same job)
-   (Don't Know)
-   (Refusal/NA)

Q156 [EWSexWrk]
Do you think if your work as ... READ OUT ...
%
19.8   mainly women's work,
1.8   mainly men's work,
78.2   or, work that either men or women do?
0.1   Other answer (WRITE IN)
-   (Don't Know)
-   (Refusal/NA)

Q159 IF 'mainly women's work'/Other/DK/Refusal AT [EWSexWrk]
[EWMenCld]
Do you think that men could do the same sort of work as you?
%
16.5   Yes
3.4   No
-   (Don't Know)
-   (Refusal/NA)

Q160 IF 'Yes'/DK AT [EWMenCld]
[EWMenCld]
Do you think that men would be willing to do the same sort of work as you?
%
6.5   Yes
9.7   No
0.3   (Don't Know)
-   (Refusal/NA)

22

n=259

Q161   **ASK ALL SELF-EMPLOYED (IF 'self-employed' AT [REmploye])**
[SerJbTim]
In your present job, are you working ... **READ OUT** ...
%
80.2   ... full-time,
17.8   or, part-time?
2.0   (Don't Know)
-   (Refusal/NA)

Q162   [SJbHours]
How many hours a week do you normally work in your (main) job?
IF RESPONDENT CANNOT ANSWER, ASK ABOUT LAST WEEK.
ROUND TO NEAREST HOUR
CODE 95 FOR 95+
Range: 10 ... 95
Median: 50 hours
1.8   (Don't know)
2.0   (Refusal/NA)

Q163   [SJbHrCat] (CALCULATED BY PROGRAM)
SELF-EMPLOYED HOURS WORKED - CATEGORISED
%
5.4   10-15 hours a week
2.8   16-23 hours a week
4.5   24-29 hours a week
83.5   30 or more hours a week
1.8   (Don't Know)
2.0   (Refusal/NA)

Q164   [SUnemp]
During the last five years - that is since March 1989 - have you been unemployed and seeking work for any period?
%
19.4   Yes
78.9   No
1.6   (Don't Know)
-   (Refusal/NA)

Q165   **IF 'Yes' AT [SUnemp]**
[SUnempT]
For how many months in total during the last five years (have you been unemployed) ?
ENTER NUMBER OF MONTHS
Range: 0 ... 60
Median: 6 months
0.2   (Don't know)
2.0   (Refusal/NA)

Q166   **ASK ALL SELF-EMPLOYED (IF 'self-employed' AT [REmploye])**
[SEmplee]
Have you, for any period in the last five years, worked as an employee as your main job rather than as self-employed?
%
31.3   Yes
67.0   No
1.6   (Don't Know)
-   (Refusal/NA)

23

n=259

Q167   **IF 'Yes' AT [SEmplee]**
[SEmpleeT]
In total for how many months during the last five years have you been an employee?
ENTER NUMBER OF MONTHS
Range: 1 ... 60
Median: 24 months
0.2   (Don't know)
1.6   (Refusal/NA)

Q168   **IF 'No'/DK/Refusal AT [SEmplee]**
[SEmplSer]
How seriously in the last five years have you considered getting a job as an employee ... **READ OUT** ...
%
4.3   ... very seriously,
7.1   quite seriously,
9.7   not very seriously,
45.9   or, not at all seriously?
1.6   (Don't Know)
-   (Refusal/NA)

Q169   **ASK ALL SELF-EMPLOYED (IF 'self-employed' AT [REmploye])**
[BusiOK]
Compared with a year ago, would you say your business is doing ... **READ OUT** ...
%
10.2   ... very well,
20.9   quite well,
42.2   about the same,
15.4   not very well,
4.3   or, not at all well?
5.1   (Business not in existence then)
2.0   (Don't Know)
-   (Refusal/NA)

Q170   [BusiFut]
And over the coming year, do you think your business will do ... **READ OUT** ...
%
35.9   ... better,
46.6   about the same,
12.4   or, worse than this year?
0.4   Other answer (WRITE IN)
2.6   (Don't Know)
2.0   (Refusal/NA)

Q173   [SPartnrs]
In your work or business, do you have any partners or other self-employed colleagues?
NOTE: DOES NOT INCLUDE EMPLOYEES
%
51.2   Yes, has partner(s)
47.2   No
-   (Don't Know)
1.6   (Refusal/NA)

24

Left column (page 25)

n=259

Q174 [SNumEmp]
And in your work or business, do you have any employees, or not?
NOTE: FAMILY MEMBERS MAY BE EMPLOYEES ONLY IF THEY RECEIVE A REGULAR WAGE OR SALARY

	%
Yes, has employee(s)	34.7
No	63.3
(Don't Know)	-
(Refusal/NA)	2.0

Q175 [SEmpEarn]
Now for some more general questions about your work.
For some people their job is simply something they do in order to earn a living. For others it means much more than that. On balance, is your present job ... **READ OUT** ...
... just a means of earning a living,
or, does it mean much more to you than that?

	%
	22.9
	74.7
(Don't Know)	0.4
(Refusal/NA)	2.0

IF 'just a means of earning a living' AT [SEmpEarn]

Q176 [SEmpLiv]
Is that because ... **READ OUT** ...
... there are no better jobs around here,
you don't have the right skills to get a better job,
or, because you would feel the same about any job you had?

	%
	8.1
	2.8
	9.5
(Don't Know)	2.4
(Refusal/NA)	2.4

ASK ALL SELF-EMPLOYED (IF 'self-employed' AT [REmploye])

Q177 [SPrefJob]
If without having to work, you had what you would regard as a reasonable living income do you think you would still prefer to have a paid job or wouldn't you bother?

	%
Still prefer paid job	67.5
Wouldn't bother	25.6
Other answer (**WRITE IN**)	4.9
(Don't Know)	-
(Refusal/NA)	2.0

Q180 [SWkHrd]
CARD
Which of these statements best describes your feelings about your job?

	%
In my job?	
I only work as hard as I have to	9.4
I work hard, but not so that it interferes with the rest of my life	22.8
I make a point of doing the best I can, even if it sometimes does interfere with the rest of my life	65.8
(Don't Know)	-
(Refusal/NA)	2.0

25

Right column (page 26)

ASK ALL NOT IN PAID WORK (IF NOT 'in paid work' AT [REconAct])

Q181 [NPWork10]
In the seven days ending last Sunday, did you have any paid work of less than 10 hours a week?

	%
Yes	7.1
No	92.9
(Don't Know)	-
(Refusal/NA)	-

n=1657

ASK ALL LOOKING AFTER HOME (IF 'looking after the home' AT [REconAct])

Q182 [EverJob]
Have you, during the **last five years**, ever had a full- or part-time job of 10 hours or more a week?

	%
Yes	35.2
No	64.4
(Don't Know)	-
(Refusal/NA)	0.3

IF 'No' AT [EverJob]

Q183 [FtJobSer]
How seriously in the past five years have you considered getting a full-time job
PROMPT, IF NECESSARY: Full-time is 30 or more hours a week
... READ OUT ...

IF 'not very seriously'/'not at all seriously' AT [FtJobSer]

Q184 [PtJobSer]
How seriously, in the past five years, have you considered getting a part-time job ... READ OUT ...

	[FtJobSer]	[PtJobSer]
	%	%
... very seriously,	2.9	1.1
quite seriously,	4.8	6.2
not very seriously,	7.9	11.0
or, not at all seriously?	48.9	38.2
(Don't Know)	-	0.2
(Refusal/NA)	0.3	0.3

n=459

ASK ALL IN PAID WORK (INCLUDING RESPONDENTS LOOKING AFTER THE HOME WHO HAVE HAD PAID WORK OF LESS THAN 10 HOURS IN LAST WEEK) (IF 'in paid work' AT [REconAct] PLUS THOSE 'looking after home' AT [REconAct] AND 'Yes' AT [NPWork10])

Q185 [WChdLT5]
Can I just check, do you have any children under five living at home?

	%
Yes	15.2
No	84.8
(Don't Know)	-
(Refusal/NA)	-

n=1869

26

Q186   IF 'No' AT [WChdLT5]
        [WChdS12]
        Do you have any children over five but under twelve living
        at home?

n=1869

%
Yes   14.3
No   70.5
(Don't Know)   -
(Refusal/NA)   -

Q187   ASK ALL WHO ARE WORKING AND HAVE CHILDREN UNDER 12
        (IF 'Yes' AT [WChdLT5] OR AT [WChdS12])
        CARD
        Which of the following best describes the way you arrange
        for your children to be looked after while you are at work?
        Any others? CODE ALL THAT APPLY
        Multicoded (Maximum of 12 codes)

n=552

%
I work only while they are at school   [WChArr01]   12.1
They look after themselves until I get home   [WChArr02]   2.7
I work from home   [WChArr03]   7.5
A mother's help or nanny looks after them at home [WChArr04] 5.4
They go to a workplace nursery   [WChArr05]   0.7
They go to a day nursery   [WChArr06]   6.2
They go to a child-minder   [WChArr07]   12.4
A relative looks after them   [WChArr08]   26.3
A friend or neighbour looks after them   [WChArr09]   7.4
My husband / wife / partner looks after them [WChArr10]   54.3
(None of these) [WChArr11]   0.9
Other answer (WRITE IN)   [WChArr00]   1.2
(Don't know)   -
(Refusal/NA)   -

Q190   IF 'day nursery' AT [WChArrPW]
        [WNrsry]
        Is that day nursery a private nursery, or does it receive
        funds from the local council?

%
Private nursery only   3.9
Council-funded nursery only   2.0
(Both - use both kinds)   0.3
(Don't Know)   -
(Refusal/NA)   -

Q191   ASK ALL WHO ARE WORKING AND HAVE CHILDREN UNDER 12
        (IF 'Yes' AT [WChdLT5] OR AT [WChdS12])
        [WChdCon]
        How convenient are the arrangements you now have for looking
        after your children? Are they ... READ OUT ...

%
very convenient,   63.2
fairly convenient,   30.0
not very convenient,   4.7
or, not at all convenient?   1.8
(Don't Know)   0.3
(Refusal/NA)   -

27

Q192   [WChdSat]
        And how satisfied overall are you with these
        arrangements? Are you ... READ OUT ...

n=552

%
... very satisfied,   64.4
fairly satisfied,   27.6
not very satisfied,   6.3
or, not at all satisfied?   1.2
(Don't Know)   0.5
(Refusal/NA)   -

Q193   [WChdPr1]
        CARD
        Suppose you could choose from any of the types of childcare
        on the card. Which would be your first choice for childcare
        while you are at work?
        Please read the whole list before deciding.
        ENTER ONE CODE ONLY FOR FIRST CHOICE

Q196   [WChdPr2]
        CARD
        ... and which would be your second choice?
        ENTER ONE CODE ONLY FOR SECOND CHOICE

	[WChdPr1]	[WChdPr2]
	%	%
I would work only while they are at school	18.6	9.6
They would look after themselves until I got home	0.4	0.9
I would work from home	5.6	6.0
A mother's help or nanny would look after them at home	4.9	6.5
They would go to a workplace nursery	6.3	6.8
They would go to a council-funded day nursery	5.9	5.2
They would go to a private day nursery	2.6	6.4
They would go to a child-minder	3.4	5.9
A relative would look after them	13.5	27.9
A friend or neighbour would look after them	2.0	8.4
My husband/wife/partner would look after them	35.7	14.5
(None of these)	0.2	1.3
Other answer (WRITE IN)	0.7	0.3
(Don't Know)	0.3	0.5
(Refusal/NA)	-	-

Q199   [WPrfWrk]
        And if you did have the childcare arrangement of your
        choice, would you prefer to ... READ OUT ...

%
... work more hours than now,   16.6
work fewer hours than now,   19.3
or, are you happy with the hours you work at present?   63.2
(Don't Know)   0.9
(Refusal/NA)   -

28

Q200   [n=552]
IF WOULD PREFER TO WORK MORE HOURS AND CURRENTLY NOT FULL-TIME (IF 'work more hours' AT [WPrfWrk] AND LESS THAN 30 HOURS AT [EdbHrCat] OR AT [SdbHrCat] PLUS THOSE 'looking after home' AT [REconAct] AND 'Yes' AT [NPWork101])
[WPrfFull]
Do you think you might work full-time then, or not?
%
8.1   Yes, might work full-time
3.9   No, would not
-    (Don't Know)
0.2   (Refusal/NA)

Q201
ASK ALL WHO ARE WORKING AND HAVE CHILDREN UNDER 12 (IF 'Yes' AT [WChdLT5] OR AT [WChd5121])
[WScFull]
When all your children have gone to secondary school, which do you think you are most likely to do ... READ OUT ...
%
72.4   ... work full-time,
24.8   work part-time,
1.3   or, not have a paid job at all?
1.4   (Don't Know)
-    (Refusal/NA)

Q202   [n=1813]
ASK ALL IN PAID WORK (OR AWAY TEMPORARILY) (IF 'in paid work' AT [REconAct])
[ESOldRsp]
Some people have responsibilities for looking after a disabled, sick, or elderly friend or relative. Is there anyone like this who depends on you to provide some regular care for them?
%
9.0   Yes
90.6   No
0.1   (Don't Know)
0.3   (Refusal/NA)

Q203
IF 'Yes' AT [ESOldRsp]
[ESOldCAfH]
Does this responsibility ... READ OUT ...
%
1.1   ... prevent you from working longer hours in your job,
7.9   ... or, does it make no difference to your working hours?
0.1   (Don't Know)
0.3   (Refusal/NA)

Q204   [n=402]
ASK ALL LOOKING AFTER THE HOME WITH NO PAID WORK (IF 'looking after the home' AT [REconAct] AND 'No' AT [NPWork101])
[HChdLT5]
Can I just check, do you have any children under five living at home?
%
27.5   Yes
72.1   No
0.4   (Refusal/NA)

29

Q205
IF 'No' AT [HChdLT5]
[HChd5121]
Do you have any children over five but under twelve living at home?
%
14.4   Yes
57.7   No
-    (Don't Know)
0.4   (Refusal/NA)

Q206   [n=170]
ASK ALL WHO ARE LOOKING AFTER THE HOME WITH NO PAID WORK AND HAVE CHILDREN UNDER 12 (IF 'Yes' AT [HChdLT5] OR AT [HChd5121])
CARD
Do you regularly use any of these childcare arrangements for your child or children during the day?
Multicoded (Maximum of 8 codes)
%
3.4   A mother's help or nanny looks after them at home   [HChArr04]
10.2   They go to a day-nursery   [HChArr06]
0.3   They go to a child-minder   [HChArr07]
10.2   A relative looks after them   [HChArr08]
5.0   A friend or neighbour looks after them   [HChArr09]
12.4   My husband / wife / partner looks after them   [HChArr10]
1.7   Other answer (WRITE IN)   [HChArrF11]
64.8   None of these   [HChArr00]
-    (Don't know)
0.9   (Refusal/NA)

Q209
IF 'day nursery' AT [HChArr06]
[HNursery]
Is that day nursery a private nursery, or does it receive funds from the local council?
%
2.5   Private nursery only
6.8   Council-funded nursery only
0.3   (Both - use both kinds)
0.6   (Don't know)
0.9   (Refusal/NA)

Q210   [n=402]
ASK ALL WHO ARE LOOKING AFTER THE HOME WITH NO PAID JOB AND HAVE CHILDREN UNDER 12 AND USING CHILD CARE REGULARLY (IF 'nanny' OR 'day-nursery' OR 'child-minder' OR 'relative' OR 'friend or neighbour' OR 'husband/wife/partner' OR 'other' AT [HChArr04-001])
[HChdCon]
How convenient are the arrangements you now have for looking after your children? Are they ... READ OUT ...
%
22.8   ... very convenient,
8.4   fairly convenient,
3.1   not very convenient,
-    or, not at all convenient?
-    (Don't Know)
0.9   (Refusal/NA)

30

Q211 [HChdSat]
And how satisfied overall are you with these arrangements?
Are you ... **READ OUT** ...

%
20.9 ... very satisfied,
10.9 fairly satisfied,
2.5 not very satisfied,
- or, not at all satisfied?
- (Don't Know)
0.9 (Refusal/NA)

**ASK ALL WHO ARE LOOKING AFTER THE HOME WITH PAID NO JOB
AND HAVE CHILDREN UNDER 12 (IF 'Yes' AT [HChdLT5] OR
AT [HChd5121])**
Q212 [HChdPr1]
CARD
Suppose you decided to take a job outside the home, and you
could choose from any of the types of childcare on the card.
Which would be your first choice for child-care while you
were at work?
Please read through the whole list before deciding.
ENTER ONE CODE ONLY FOR FIRST CHOICE

Q215 [HChdPr2]
CARD
... and which would be your second choice?
ENTER ONE CODE ONLY FOR SECOND CHOICE

	[HChdPr1]	[HChdPr2]
	%	%
I would work only while they are at school	45.3	13.5
They would look after themselves until I got home	-	-
I would work from home	4.3	10.4
A mother's help or nanny would look after them at home	4.5	3.1
They would go to a workplace nursery	3.7	2.5
They would go to a council-funded day nursery	4.0	6.8
They would go to a private day nursery	4.7	2.8
They would go to a child-minder	1.6	5.6
A relative would look after them	14.9	23.4
A friend or neighbour would look after them	4.0	10.2
My husband/wife/partner would look after them	8.7	14.3
NONE OF THESE (WRITE IN)	3.4	6.5
(Don't Know)	-	-
(Refusal/NA)	0.9	0.9

Q218 [HWChoic]
And if you did have the childcare arrangement of your
choice, would you prefer to.... **READ OUT** ...

%
54.1 ... work part-time
24.2 work full-time
18.6 or, would you choose not to work outside the home?
0.6 (Either full-time or part-time)
1.6 (Don't Know)
0.9 (Refusal/NA)

Q219 [HScFull]
When all your children have gone to secondary school, which
do you think you are most likely to do ... **READ OUT** ...

%
42.6 ... work full-time
41.7 work part-time
13.2 or, not have a paid job at all?
1.6 (Don't Know)
0.9 (Refusal/NA)

Q220 [HOldRspl]
Some people have responsibilities for looking after a
disabled, sick, or elderly friend or relative. Is there
anyone like this who depends on you to provide some regular
care for them?

%
13.6 Yes
85.4 No
- (Don't Know)
0.9 (Refusal/NA)

IF 'Yes' AT [HOldResp]
Q221 [HOldAfH1]
Does this responsibility ... **READ OUT** ...

%
5.9 ... prevent you from getting a paid job,
7.1 or, would you not want a paid job anyway?
0.6 (Don't Know)
0.9 (Refusal/NA)

**ASK ALL WHO ARE LOOKING AFTER THE HOME WITH NO PAID JOB
AND HAVE CHILDREN UNDER 12 (IF 'Yes' AT [HChdLT5] OR
AT [HChd5121])**
Q222 [ParNWrk1]
CARD
I am going to read out some reasons parents of young
children give for not working, or not working many hours.
Please use this card to say how important each of these
reasons is for you **personally**.
...I enjoy spending time with my children more than
working.

Q223 [ParNWrk2]
CARD
...It's better for the children if I am home to look after
them.
(How important is this reason for you personally?)

Q224 [ParNWrk3]
CARD
... It would cost too much to find suitable childcare.
(How important is this reason for you personally?)

Q225 [ParNWrk4]
CARD
...I cannot find the kind of childcare I would like.
(How important is this reason for you personally?)

n=221

Q231 [CurUnemP]
How long has this present period of unemployment and seeking work lasted so far?
ENTER NUMBER THEN SPECIFY MONTHS OR YEARS
Range: 1 .. 60
Median: 12 months
- (Don't know)
0.5 (Refusal/NA)

Q233 [JobQual]
How confident are you that you will find a job to match your qualifications ... READ OUT ...

	%
... very confident,	9.8
quite confident,	26.7
not very confident,	32.4
or, not at all confident?	30.7
(Don't Know)	-
(Refusal/NA)	0.5

Q234 [UFindJob]
Although it may be difficult to judge, how long from now do you think it will be before you find an acceptable job?
ENTER NUMBER THEN SPECIFY MONTHS OR YEARS
CODE 96 FOR NEVER
Range: 1 .. 96
Median: 3 months
10.5 Never
30.5 (Don't Know)
0.5 (Refusal/NA)

IF 3 MONTHS OR MORE, NEVER OR DK AT [UFindJob]

Q236 [URetrain]
How willing do you think you would be in these circumstances to retrain for a different job ... READ OUT ...

Q237 [UJobMove]
How willing would you be to move to a different area to find an acceptable job ... READ OUT ...

Q238 [UBadJob]
And how willing do you think you would be in these circumstances to take what you now consider to be an unacceptable job ... READ OUT ...

	[URetrain]	[UJobMove]	[UBadJob]
	%	%	%
... very willing,	34.8	13.4	6.2
quite willing,	24.0	16.2	25.0
or, not very willing?	16.7	45.7	44.3
(Don't Know)	0.5	1.2	1.0
(Refusal/NA)	0.5	0.5	0.5

34

---

n=170

	[ParNWrk1]	[ParNWrk2]	[ParNWrk3]	[ParNWrk4]
	%			
Very important	67.1	69.8	43.7	30.7
Fairly important	24.8	25.3	23.9	17.2
Not very important	2.5	2.5	7.3	9.3
Not at all important	2.5	-	6.8	3.4
Does not apply to me	2.5	1.6	16.7	37.2
(Don't Know)	-	-	0.6	1.2
(Refusal/NA)	0.9	0.9	0.9	0.9

Q226 [ParNWrk5]
CARD
... My life would be too difficult if I had to combine childcare and paid work.
(How important is this reason for you personally?)

Q227 [ParNWrk6]
CARD
... My partner would not want me to work.
(How important is this reason for you personally?)

Q228 [ParNWrk7]
CARD
... I cannot find the kind of work I want with suitable hours.
(How important is this reason for you personally?)

Q229 [ParNWrk8]
CARD
... I cannot find the kind of work I want near my home.
(How important is this reason for you personally?)

	[ParNWrk5]	[ParNWrk6]	[ParNWrk7]	[ParNWrk8]
	%			
Very important	29.3	10.1	34.6	29.9
Fairly important	28.5	15.2	18.9	19.4
Not very important	14.0	16.4	7.4	12.7
Not at all important	8.1	14.0	7.4	6.5
Does not apply to me	19.2	43.4	30.4	30.5
(Don't Know)	-	-	0.3	-
(Refusal/NA)	0.9	0.9	0.9	0.9

n=221

ASK ALL UNEMPLOYED (IF 'unemployed and registered at a benefit office'/'unemployed, not registered but actively looking for a job'/'unemployed wanting a job but not actively looking for a job AT [REconAct])

Q230 [UUnempT]
In total how many months in the last five years - that is, since March 1989 - have you been unemployed and seeking work?
Range: 1 .. 60
Median: 16 months
2.1 (Don't know)
0.5 (Refusal/NA)

33

ASK ALL UNEMPLOYED (IF 'unemployed and registered at a benefit office'/ 'unemployed, not registered but actively looking for a job'/ 'unemployedwanting a job but not actively looking for a job AT [REconAct]) n=221

Q239 [ConMove]
Have you ever actually considered moving to a different area - an area other than the one you live in now - to try to find work?
%
Yes   39.6
No   60.0
(Don't Know)   -
(Refusal/NA)   0.5

Q240 [UJobChnc]
Do you think that there is a real chance nowadays that you will get a job in this area, or is there no real chance nowadays?
Real chance   44.5
No real chance   48.4
(Don't Know)   6.7
(Refusal/NA)   0.5

Q241 [FPtWork]
Would you prefer full- or part-time work, if you had the choice?
%
Full-time   76.1
Part-time   21.0
Not looking for work   1.9
(Don't Know)   0.5
(Refusal/NA)   0.5

Q242 IF 'Part-time' AT [FPtWork]
[PartTime]
About how many hours per week would you like to work?
PROBE FOR BEST ESTIMATE
Range: 1 ... 30
Median: 20 hours
(Don't know)   0.2
(Refusal/NA)   1.0

Q243 ASK ALL UNEMPLOYED (IF 'unemployed and registered at a benefit office'/ 'unemployed, not registered but actively looking for a job'/ 'unemployed wanting a job but not actively looking for a job AT [REconAct])
[UnemEarn]
For some people work is simply something they do in order to earn a living. For others it means much more than that. In general, do you think of work as ... READ OUT ...
%
... just a means of earning a living,   37.6
or, does it mean much more to you than that? 61.2
(Don't Know)   -
(Refusal/NA)   0.5

Q244 IF 'just a means of earning a living' AT [UnemEarn] n=221
[Unempliv]
Is that because ... READ OUT ...
%
... there are no good jobs around here,   12.1
you don't have the right skills to get a good job, 8.8
or, because you would feel the same about any job you had? 15.9
(Don't Know)   0.7
(Refusal/NA)   1.2

n=593

Q245 ASK ALL WHOLLY RETIRED (IF 'wholly retired' AT [REconAct])
[RemplPen]
Do you receive a pension from any past employer?
%
Yes   53.5
No   46.4
(Don't Know)   -
(Refusal/NA)   0.1

Q246 [MsCheck]
May I just check, are you ... READ OUT ...
%
... married,   62.6
or, not married?   37.3
(Don't Know)   -
(Refusal/NA)   0.1

Q247 IF 'married' AT [MsCheck]
[SEmplPen]
Does your (husband/wife) receive a pension from any past employer?
%
Yes   21.2
No   41.3
(Don't Know)   0.1
(Refusal/NA)   0.1

Q248 ASK ALL WHOLLY RETIRED (IF 'wholly retired' AT [REconAct])
[PrPenGet]
And do you receive a pension from any private arrangements you have made in the past, that is apart from the state pension or one arranged through an employer?
%
Yes   9.1
No   90.6
(Don't Know)   -
(Refusal/NA)   0.3

Q249 IF 'married' AT [MsCheck]
[SPrPnGet]
And does your (husband/wife) receive a pension from any private arrangements (he/she) has made in the past, that is apart from the state pension or one arranged through an employer?
%
Yes   3.5
No   58.8
(Don't Know)   0.2
(Refusal/NA)   0.3

n=593

Q250   ASK ALL WHOLLY RETIRED (IF 'wholly retired' AT [REconAct]
[RetAge]
MEN: (Can I just check) are you over sixty-five?
WOMEN: (Can I just check) are you over sixty?

%
Yes   89.0
No   10.9
(Don't Know)   -
(Refusal/NA)   0.1

Q251   IF 'Yes' AT [RetAge]
[RPension]
On the whole would you say the present state pension is on the low side, reasonable, or on the high side?
IF 'ON THE LOW SIDE': Very low or a bit low?

%
Very low   36.2
A bit low   28.8
Reasonable   22.5
On the high side   0.4
(Don't Know)   1.1
(Refusal/NA)   0.1

Q252   [RPenInYr]
Do you expect your state pension in a year's time to purchase more than it does now, less, or about the same?

%
More   4.2
Less   59.3
About the same   24.0
(Don't Know)   1.5
(Refusal/NA)   0.1

Q253   ASK ALL WHOLLY RETIRED (IF 'wholly retired' AT [REconAct])
[RetirAg2]
At what age did you retire from work?
NEVER WORKED, CODE: 00
Range: 0 ... 80
Median: 60
(Never worked)
(Don't know)
(Refusal)

2.8
0.6
0.3

Q254   ASK ALL ON GOVERNMENT PROGRAMME OR WAITING TO TAKE UP WORK (IF 'on government training scheme' OR 'waiting to take up paid work' AT [REconAct])
[WgUnemp]
During the last five years - that is since March 1989 - have you been unemployed and seeking work for any period?

Numbers:
Yes   29
No   6
(Don't Know)   -
(Refusal/NA)   -

n=36

37

---

n=36

Q255   [WgEarn]
For some people work is simply something they do in order to earn a living. For others it means much more than that. In general, do you think of work as
... READ OUT ...
... just a means of earning a living,
or, does it mean much more to you than that?
(Don't Know)
(Refusal/NA)

Numbers:
11
24
1
-

Q256   IF 'just a means to earning a living' AT [WgEarn]
[WgLiv]
Is that because ... READ OUT ...
... there are no good jobs around here,
you don't have the right skills to get a good job,
or - because you would feel the same about any job you had?
(Don't Know)
(Refusal/NA)

Numbers:
7
2
2
-
1

n=135

Q257   ASK ALL IN FULL-TIME EDUCATION (IF 'in full-time education' AT [REconAct])
[EdUnemp]
During the last five years - that is since March 1989 - have you been unemployed and seeking work for any period?

%
Yes   26.8
No   73.2
(Don't Know)   -
(Refusal/NA)   -

38

CIVIL LIBERTIES (VERSION A)

VERSION A: ASK ALL   n=1140

Q263   [PaprDef]
Suppose a newspaper got hold of confidential government
defence plans and wanted to publish them ... READ OUT ...
%
24.9   Should the newspaper be allowed to publish the plans,
69.9   or, should the government have the power to prevent
5.2   publication?
0.0   (Don't Know)
       (Refusal/NA)

Q264   [LeakDef]
CARD
Suppose the government wanted to find out the name of the
person who had leaked these confidential defence plans.
Should the paper have the legal right to keep the person's
name secret, or not?
%
29.1   Definitely should have the legal right to keep name secret
16.3   Probably should
16.4   Probably should not
35.8   Definitely should not have the legal right
4.4   (Don't Know)
-      (Refusal/NA)

Q265   [PaprEcon]
Now suppose a newspaper got hold of confidential government
economic plans ... READ OUT ...
%
54.7   Should the newspaper be allowed to publish the plans,
40.4   or, should the government have the power to prevent
5.0   publication?
-      (Don't Know)
       (Refusal/NA)

Q266   [LeakEcon]
CARD AGAIN
Suppose the government wanted to find out the name of the
person who had leaked these confidential economic plans.
Should the paper have the legal right to keep the person's
name secret, or not?
%
32.7   Definitely should have the legal right to keep name secret
16.9   Probably should
17.3   Probably should not
28.6   Definitely should not have the legal right
4.6   (Don't Know)
-      (Refusal/NA)

Q267   [VCRoads]
CARD
Some people say that there ought to be video cameras in
public places to detect criminals. Others say this cuts down
on everyone's privacy. Do you think video cameras should or
should not be allowed in the following places?
...on roads to detect speeding drivers?

Q268   [VCFootbl]
CARD AGAIN
(Should or should not video cameras be allowed...)
...at football grounds to detect troublemakers?

Q269   [VCVandal]
CARD AGAIN
(Should or should not video cameras be allowed...)
...on housing estates to detect vandals?

	[VCRoads]	[VCFootbl]	[VCVandal]
	%	%	%
Definitely be allowed	74.0	89.4	70.2
Probably be allowed	18.3	8.6	19.9
Probably not be allowed	3.9	0.9	6.9
Definitely not be allowed	3.3	0.8	2.3
(Don't Know)	0.5	0.3	0.7
(Refusal/NA)	-	-	-

Q270   [RaceGlty]
Suppose two people - one white, one black - each appear in
court, charged with a crime they did not commit.
What do you think their chances are of being found guilty?
%   ... READ OUT ...
3.6   ... the white person is more likely to be found guilty,
48.7   they have the same chance,
43.5   or, the black person is more likely to be found guilty?
4.2   (Don't Know)
-      (Refusal/NA)

Q271   [RichGlty]
Now suppose another two people from different backgrounds -
one rich, one poor - each appear in court charged with a
crime they did not commit. What do you think their chances
are of being found guilty?
%   ... READ OUT ...
1.7   ... the rich person is more likely to be found guilty,
29.6   they have the same chance,
65.7   or, the poor person is more likely to be found guilty?
3.0   (Don't Know)
-      (Refusal/NA)

Q272   [IrisGlty]
Now suppose another two people - one British and one Irish -
each appear in court charged with a burglary they did not
commit. What do you think their chances are of being found
guilty?
%   ... READ OUT ...
1.9   ... the British person is more likely to be found guilty,
65.9   they have the same chance,
26.7   or, the Irish person is more likely to be found guilty?
5.3   (Don't Know)
0.1   (Refusal/NA)

n=1140

Q273 [JuryTry]
Which of these three statements comes closest to how you feel about trial by jury ... **READ OUT** ...

%

55.8 ... all accused people should always have the right to trial by jury

35.2 or, only a person accused of a serious offence should always have the right to trial by jury,

3.5 or, no accused person should always have the right to trial by jury

5.1 (Don't Know)

0.3 (Refusal/NA)

Q274 [ChOppWom]
CARD
Now I want to ask about some changes that have been happening in Britain over the years. For each one, please tell me whether you think it has gone too far, or not gone far enough.
How about attempts to give equal opportunities to women in Britain?

Q275 [ChOppMin]
CARD AGAIN
Attempts to give equal opportunities to black people and Asians in Britain?
(Has it gone too far, or not far enough?)

Q276 [ChNudSex]
CARD AGAIN
The right to show nudity and sex in films and magazines?
(Has it gone too far, or not far enough?)

Q277 [ChOppHom]
CARD AGAIN
Attempts to give equal opportunities to homosexuals - that is, gays and lesbians?
(Has it gone too far, or not far enough?)

	[ChOppWom]	[ChOppMin]	[ChNudSex]	[ChOppHom]
	%	%	%	%
Gone much too far	3.0	4.5	26.7	18.5
Gone too far	11.5	20.0	38.9	27.1
About right	43.6	33.2	27.3	31.6
Not gone far enough	35.6	33.9	4.8	15.0
Not gone nearly far enough	4.3	4.7	0.8	3.0
(Don't Know)	2.1	3.5	1.5	4.9
(Refusal/NA)	-	0.2	-	-

Q278 [ChGypTrv]
CARD AGAIN
Providing sites for gypsies and travellers to stay?
(Has it gone too far, or not far enough?)

Q279 [ChRgtDem]
CARD AGAIN
The right of people to go on protest marches and demonstrations?
(Has it gone too far, or not far enough?)

41

n=1140

Q280 [ChLwStrk]
Laws to make it difficult for people to go on strike?
(Has it gone too far, or not far enough?)

Q281 [ChLegAid]
Giving Legal Aid - that is, financial help with the cost of going to court?
(Has it gone too far, or not far enough?)

	[ChGypTrv]	[ChRgtDem]	[ChLwStrk]	[ChLegAid]
	%	%	%	%
Gone much too far	6.3	2.7	7.4	1.1
Gone too far	14.2	18.2	28.3	7.9
About right	29.5	62.0	44.9	31.0
Not gone far enough	38.9	11.5	11.8	41.6
Not gone nearly far enough	4.8	2.2	0.9	7.7
(Don't Know)	6.4	3.2	6.7	10.7
(Refusal/NA)	-	0.1	-	-

42

RACE (VERSIONS A AND B)

ASK ALL

Q284 [RaceOrig]
(Figures include the identical question asked at Q770 on Version C)
CARD ...
To which of these groups do you consider you belong?

	%
BLACK: of African or Caribbean or other origin	2.0
ASIAN: of Indian origin	1.8
ASIAN: of Pakistani origin	0.5
ASIAN: of Bangladeshi origin	0.1
ASIAN: of Chinese origin	0.3
ASIAN: of other origin (WRITE IN)	0.2
WHITE: of British origin	87.4
WHITE: of Irish origin	2.9
WHITE: of other origin (WRITE IN)	3.6
MIXED ORIGIN (WRITE IN)	0.9
(Don't Know)	0.1
(Refusal/NA)	0.2

n=3469

VERSIONS A AND B: ASK ALL

Q291 [PrejAs]
Now I would like to ask you some questions about racial prejudice in Britain. Thinking of Asians - that is, people whose families were originally from India, Pakistan or Bangladesh - who now live in Britain. Do you think there is a lot of prejudice against them in Britain nowadays, a little, or hardly any?

Q292 [PrejBlk]
And black people - that is people whose families were originally from the West Indies or Africa - who now live in Britain. Do you think there is a lot of prejudice against them in Britain nowadays, a little, or hardly any?

	[PrejAs]	[PrejBlk]
	%	%
A lot	58.8	46.8
A little	34.1	43.6
Hardly any	5.0	7.8
(Don't Know)	1.9	1.7
(Refusal/NA)	0.1	0.1

Q293 [PrejNow]
Do you think there is generally more racial prejudice in Britain now than there was 5 years ago, less, or about the same amount?

	%
More now	34.4
Less now	21.7
About the same	41.6
Other answer (WRITE IN)	0.1
(Don't Know)	2.2
(Refusal/NA)	0.0

n=2282

Q296 [PrejFut]
Do you think there will be more, less or about the same amount of racial prejudice in Britain in 5 years' time compared with now?

	%
More in 5 years	39.4
Less	20.2
About the same	34.8
Other answer (WRITE IN)	1.5
(Don't Know)	4.1
(Refusal/NA)	0.0

Q299 [SRPrej]
How would you describe yourself
... READ OUT ...

	%
... as very prejudiced against people of other races,	2.1
a little prejudiced,	33.9
or, not prejudiced at all?	62.9
Other answer (WRITE IN)	0.7
(Don't Know)	0.2
(Refusal/NA)	0.2

Q302 [AsJob]
On the whole, do you think people of Asian origin in Britain are not given jobs these days because of their race ... READ OUT ...

	%
... a lot,	20.2
a little,	41.7
or, hardly at all?	32.1
(Don't Know)	6.0
(Refusal/NA)	0.0

Q303 [WIJob]
On the whole, do you think people of West Indian origin in Britain are not given jobs these days because of their race ... READ OUT ...

	%
... a lot,	23.4
a little,	42.2
or, hardly at all?	28.3
(Don't Know)	6.0
(Refusal/NA)	0.0

Q304 [RaceLaw]
There is a law in Britain against racial discrimination, that is against giving unfair preference to a particular race in housing, jobs and so on. Do you generally support or oppose the idea of a law for this purpose?

	%
Support	73.2
Oppose	22.1
(Don't Know)	4.7
(Refusal/NA)	0.1

n=2282

n=2282

Q305 **IF 'Support' AT [RaceLaw]**
[RaceLstr]
Do you think that the present law against racial
discrimination should be ... **READ OUT** ....

%
27.5 ... used more strictly,
5.0 used less strictly,
37.0 or, is it about right? **PROBE IF NECESSARY**
3.7 (Don't Know)
4.8 (Refusal/NA)

Q306 **VERSIONS A AND B: ASK ALL**
[RaceViLw]
Some people say there should be a special law against
attacks on people because of their race. Others say these
attacks should be treated by the law like any other attacks.
Do you think there should be a special law against racial
violence or not?
PROBE: Definitely or probably should/should not?

%
20.1 Definitely should
15.6 Probably should
25.6 Probably should not
36.1 Definitely should not
2.5 (Don't Know)
0.0 (Refusal/NA)

n=1058

Q307 **VERSION A: IF 'White' AT [RaceOrig]**
[OBossAs]
Do you think most white people in Britain would mind or not
mind if a suitably qualified person of **Asian** origin were
appointed as their boss? **IF 'Would mind': A lot or a little?**

%
21.8 Mind a lot
33.8 Mind a little
39.5 Not mind
1.2 Other answer (WRITE IN)
3.4 (Don't Know)
0.3 (Refusal/NA)

Q310 **[SBossAe]**
And would you personally? Would you mind or not mind?
IF 'Would mind': A lot or a little?

%
6.3 Mind a lot
8.3 Mind a little
83.3 Not mind
1.0 Other answer (WRITE IN)
0.6 (Don't Know)
0.3 (Refusal/NA)

Q313 **[OMarAs]**
Do you think that **most** white people in Britain would mind or
not mind if one of their close relatives were to marry a
person of **Asian** origin? IF 'WOULD MIND': A lot or a little?

%
34.5 Mind a lot
37.2 Mind a little
22.3 Not mind
1.8 Other answer (WRITE IN)
3.9 (Don't Know)
0.3 (Refusal/NA)

45

Q316 **[SMarAs]**
And you personally? Would you mind or not mind?
IF 'Would mind': A lot or a little?

%
16.4 Mind a lot
20.4 Mind a little
59.8 Not mind
1.6 Other answer (WRITE IN)
1.5 (Don't Know)
0.3 (Refusal/NA)

n=1092

Q319 **VERSION B: IF 'White' AT [RaceOrig]**
[OBossWI]
Do you think that **most** white people in Britain would mind or not
mind if a suitably qualified person of **black or West Indian**
origin were appointed as their boss? **IF 'Would mind': A lot**
or a little?

%
17.9 Mind a lot
32.9 Mind a little
43.4 Not mind
1.6 Other answer (WRITE IN)
3.6 (Don't Know)
0.5 (Refusal/NA)

Q322 **[SBossWI]**
And would you personally? Would you mind or not mind?
IF 'Would mind': A lot or a little?

%
4.3 Mind a lot
8.2 Mind a little
85.1 Not mind
0.7 Other answer (WRITE IN)
1.0 (Don't Know)
0.6 (Refusal/NA)

Q325 **[OMarWI]**
Do you think that **most** white people in Britain would mind or
not mind if one of their close relatives were to marry a
person of **black or West Indian** origin? IF 'WOULD MIND': A
lot or a little?

%
32.9 Mind a lot
40.1 Mind a little
21.0 Not mind
0.9 Other answer (WRITE IN)
4.3 (Don't Know)
0.7 (Refusal/NA)

Q328 **[SMarWI]**
And you personally? Would you mind or not mind?
IF 'Would mind': A lot or a little?

%
16.4 Mind a lot
20.8 Mind a little
59.1 Not mind
1.8 Other answer (WRITE IN)
1.3 (Don't Know)
0.6 (Refusal/NA)

46

LOCAL GOVERNMENT (VERSION A AND B)

n=2282

VERSIONS A AND B: ASK ALL

Q333 [CntlCncl]
Do you think that local councils ought to be controlled by central government more, less or about the same amount as now?

%	
15.4	More
38.8	Less
40.2	About the same
5.6	(Don't Know)
0.0	(Refusal/NA)

Q334 [Rates]
Do you think the level of the council tax should be up to the local council to decide, or should central government have the final say?

%	
65.6	Local council
28.9	Central government
5.4	(Don't Know)
0.0	(Refusal/NA)

Q335 [CTaxVal]
CARD
And thinking about the level of the council tax in your area, do you think it gives good value or poor value for money?
Please choose a phrase from this card.

%	
3.1	Very good value for money
33.0	Good value
28.5	Neither good value nor poor value
26.2	Poor value
4.9	Very poor value for money
4.2	(Don't Know)
0.0	(Refusal/NA)

Q336 [DCBCName]
Do you happen to know the name of your city, district or (borough/burgh) council?

%	
81.1	Yes
18.3	No/Don't know
0.6	(Don't Know)
0.3	(Refusal/NA)

Q337 IF 'Yes' AT [DCBCName]
[NameDCBC]
What is its name?
ENTER NAME
Open Question (Maximum of 40 characters)

47

---

n=2282

VERSIONS A AND B: ASK ALL

Q339 [PrtyDCBC]
Do you happen to know which party or parties controls your local district or (borough/burgh) council at present?
IF YES: Which party or parties?
IF TWO OR MORE PARTIES, WRITE IN PARTIES UNDER 'SHARED CONTROL'

%	
23.1	No
18.7	Yes: Conservative
40.5	Yes: Labour
9.0	Yes: Liberal Democrats
0.7	Yes: Scottish Nationalist
0.0	Yes: Plaid Cymru
0.6	Yes: Independents
0.1	Other single party (WRITE IN)
4.7	Shared control (WRITE IN)
2.5	(Don't Know)
0.1	(Refusal/NA)

Q345 [CCInArea]
To the best of your knowledge, is there a (county/regional) council in your area?

%	
60.5	Yes
25.0	No
14.5	(Don't Know)
0.0	(Refusal/NA)

Q346 IF 'Yes' AT [CCInArea]
[CCName]
Do you happen to know the name of your (county/regional) council?

%	
49.7	Yes
9.9	No
0.9	(Don't Know)
14.5	(Refusal/NA)

Q347 IF 'Yes' AT [CCName]
[NameCC]
What is its name?
ENTER NAME
Open Question (Maximum of 40 characters)

48

n=2282

Q349 IF 'Yes' AT [CClnArea]
[PartyCC]
Do you happen to know which party or parties controls your
(county/regional) council at present?
IF YES: Which party or parties?
IF TWO OR MORE PARTIES, WRITE IN PARTIES UNDER 'SHARED CONTROL'

%
24.4 No
10.5 Yes: Conservative
17.0 Yes: Labour
3.2 Yes: Liberal Democrats
0.1 Yes: Scottish Nationalist
     Yes: Plaid Cymru
0.3 Yes: Independents
0.0 Other single party (WRITE IN)
1.7 Shared control (WRITE IN)
3.1 (Don't Know)
14.5 (Refusal/NA)

Q355 VERSIONS A AND B: ASK ALL
[LGMoney]
The two main sources of local government money are the
council tax and the grant from central government. Do you
think that in total your local council(s) get more money
from the council tax, or more from central government, or
about the same amount for each?
IF 'MORE FROM COUNCIL TAX' OR 'MORE FROM CENTRAL GOVERNMENT':
A lot more or a little more?

%
10.3 A lot more from the council tax
14.8 A little more from the council tax
25.6 About the same amount from each
9.6 A little more from central government
7.6 A lot more from central government
32.1 (Don't Know)
0.0 (Refusal/NA)

Q356 CARD
Are you currently a member of any of these?
IF YES: Which ones?   PROBE: Any others?   Until 'NO'
CODE ALL MENTIONED
Multicoded (Maximum of 9 codes)
%
74.1 (No, none of these)
4.4 Yes: Tenants'/residents' association [MemResid]
3.0 Yes: Parent-teachers association [MemPTA]
1.2 Yes: Board of school governors/School Board [MemSclGv]
3.0 Yes: A political party [MemPlPty]
0.6 Yes: Parish or town council [MemParCl]
0.5 Yes: Neighbourhood council/forum [MemNghCl]
12.8 Yes: Neighbourhood Watch Scheme [MemNghWt]
2.0 Yes: Local conservation or environmental group [MemEnvir]
6.7 Yes: Other local community or voluntary
         group (WRITE IN) [MemComVl]

-    (Don't know)
0.3 (Refusal/NA)

---

n=2282

Q360 [CnclMeet]
Have you attended a local council meeting or a public
meeting on a local issue, in the last twelve months?
DO NOT COUNT MEETINGS ATTENDED AS A COUNCILLOR OR AS
A COUNCIL OFFICIAL
%
9.6 Yes
90.1 No
0.2 (Don't Know)
0.0 (Refusal/NA)

Q361 IF 'Yes' AT [CnclMeet]
[WhyAtten]
Thinking about the last local meeting you attended, was
about some issue that affected you particularly, or was it
about a general issue affecting your area?
%
2.6 About an issue affecting me particularly
6.3 About a general issue affecting my area
0.7 (Both equally)
-   (Can't remember)
0.0 (Don't Know)
0.3 (Refusal/NA)

Q362 VERSIONS A AND B: ASK ALL
[VtMay94]
Did people in your neighbourhood have the chance to vote in
local elections this May?
%
66.9 Yes
29.0 No
4.1 (Don't Know)
0.0 (Refusal/NA)

Q363 IF 'No' AT [VtMay94]
[VtMay93]
And did people in your neighbourhood have the chance to vote
in local elections in May last year?
%
17.0 Yes
6.6 No
5.3 (Don't Know)
4.2 (Refusal/NA)

Q364 IF CHANCE TO VOTE AT LOCAL ELECTIONS IN 1994 OR 1993
(IF 'Yes' AT [VtMay94] OR AT [VtMay93])
[LocVoted]
A lot of people don't manage to vote in the local elections.
How about you? Did you manage to vote in the last local
elections in your area?
%
48.2 Yes
32.9 No
0.4 Too young to vote
2.1 Not eligible/Not on register
0.1 (Don't Know)
0.2 (Refusal/NA)

n=2282

Left column (page 51)

Q365   **IF VOTED IN LAST LOCAL ELECTIONS (IF 'Yes' AT [LocVoted])**
[LocPtyvt]
Which party did you vote for, or perhaps you voted for an independent candidate?

%
12.2   Conservative
20.0   Labour
10.8   Liberal Democrats
1.3   Scottish Nationalist
-      Plaid Cymru
1.3   Independent
0.2   Green
0.3   Other party (WRITE IN)
0.1   More than one (WRITE IN)
0.5   (Don't Know)
1.5   (Refusal/NA)

Q372   **IF DIDN'T VOTE IN LAST LOCAL ELECTIONS (IF 'No'/DK/Refusal AT [LocVoted])**
[LocPtyIf]
Which party would you have voted for, if you had voted?

%
8.0   Conservative
12.7   Labour
6.3   Liberal Democrats
0.5   Scottish Nationalist
0.1   Plaid Cymru
0.7   Independent
1.3   Green
0.1   Other party (WRITE IN)
4.9   More than one (WRITE IN)
0.9   (Refusal/NA)

Q379   **VERSIONS A AND B: ASK ALL**
CARD
Now thinking of MPs, which of the personal qualities on this card would you say are important for an MP to have? You may choose more than one, or none, or suggest others.
CODE ALL THAT APPLY
Multicoded (Maximum of 9 codes)

%
54.5   To be well educated   [MPEd]
40.9   To know what being poor means   [MPPoor]
30.2   To have business experience   [MPBus]
13.4   To have trade union experience   [MPUnion]
59.8   To have been brought up in the area he or she represents   [MPLocal]
42.2   To be loyal to the Party he or she represents   [MPLoyal]
47.6   To be independent minded   [MPInd]
13.4   None of these qualities   [MPNone]
0.6   Other important qualities   [MPOthi]
0.2   (Don't know)
1.3   (Refusal/NA)

---

n=2282

Right column (page 52)

Q382   **VERSIONS A AND B: ASK ALL**
CARD
And which of these qualities would you say are important for a local councillor to have?
Multicoded (Maximum of 10 codes)

%
40.3   To be well educated   [ClrEd]
29.7   To know what being poor means   [ClrPoor]
27.2   To have business experience   [ClrBus]
11.1   To have trade union experience   [ClrUnion]
71.9   To have been brought up in the area he or she represents   [ClrLocal]
30.4   To be loyal to the Party he or she represents   [ClrLoyal]
39.5   To be independent minded   [ClrInd]
68.2   To have a knowledge of local matters   [ClrKnLoc]
0.2   None of these qualities   [ClrNone]
8.7   Other important qualities   [ClrOthi]
0.2   (Don't know)
1.2   (Refusal/NA)

Q385   [StandCnd]
Have you ever considered standing for election as a (county/regional), district, city or (borough/burgh) councillor?
IF YES: Have you ever actually stood, or not?

%
0.9   Yes, and stood
3.8   Yes, but have not stood
93.0   No, have not considered
2.2   (No, disqualified from standing because of job)
0.1   (Don't Know)
0.0   (Refusal/NA)

Q386   [AreaTime]
How long have you lived in your present area
... READ OUT ...
... less than a year,
or, one year or more?
(Don't Know)
(Refusal/NA)

Q387   **IF 'One year or more' AT [AreaTime]**
[Nghbrhd]
How many years?
PROBE FOR BEST ESTIMATE
Median: 16 years
-      (Don't know)
0.1   (Refusal/NA)

Q388   **VERSIONS A AND B: ASK ALL**
[LiveWork]
Is the place where you work (from) in the same local government district or (borough/burgh) as the place where you live?

%
46.3   Yes
46.4   No
6.5   (Don't Know)
0.8   (Refusal/NA)

POLITICAL TRUST (VERSION A)

n=1140

Q395 VERSION A: ASK ALL
[GovtWork]
CARD
Which of these statements best describes your opinion on the present system of governing Britain?
%
1.8 Works extremely well and could not be improved
27.4 Could be improved in small ways but mainly works well
40.7 Could be improved quite a lot
28.0 Needs a great deal of improvement
1.8 (Don't Know)
0.3 (Refusal/NA)

Q396 *[Lords]*
Do you think that the House of Lords should remain as it is or is some change needed?
36.2 Remain as is
49.9 Change needed
13.9 (Don't Know)
- (Refusal/NA)

IF WANTING CHANGE IN THE HOUSE OF LORDS (IF 'Change needed' AT [Lords])
Q397 *[LordsHow]*
%
Do you think the House of Lords should be ... READ OUT ...
11.5 ... replaced by a different body,
10.3 abolished and replaced by nothing,
26.4 or, should there be some other kind of change?
1.7 (Don't Know)
13.9 (Refusal/NA)

Q398 VERSION A: ASK ALL
[Monarchy]
How about the monarchy or the royal family in Britain?
How important or unimportant do you think it is for Britain to continue to have a monarchy ... READ OUT ...
32.1 ... very important,
33.6 quite important,
18.0 not very important,
5.4 not at all important,
9.5 or, do you think the monarchy should be abolished?
1.1 (Don't Know)
0.3 (Refusal/NA)

54

---

n=2282

Q389 *[Voted92]*
Talking to people, we have found that a lot of people don't manage to vote. How about you? Did you manage to vote in the last general election in April 1992?
%
79.6 Yes, voted
16.0 No
2.2 Too young to to vote
1.8 Not eligible/not on register
0.3 (Don't Know)
0.0 (Refusal/NA)

IF VOTED IN 1992 (IF 'Yes' AT [Voted92])
Q390 *[Party92]*
Can you remember which party did you vote for in the 1992 general election?
DO NOT PROMPT. RECORD EXACT ANSWER GIVEN
32.3 Conservative
29.3 Labour
12.5 Liberal Democrats
1.0 Scottish Nationalist
0.3 Plaid Cymru
0.6 Green
0.5 Other party (WRITE IN)
1.4 (Don't Know)
1.8 (Refusal/NA)

53

Q399 **CARD** [n=1140]
Suppose a law was being considered by Parliament which you thought was really unjust and harmful. Which, if any, of the things on this card do you think you would do? Any others? **CODE ALL THAT APPLY**
Multicoded (Maximum of 8 codes)

Q400 **CARD**
And have you ever done any of the things on this card about a government action which you thought was unjust and harmful? Which ones? Any others? **CODE ALL THAT APPLY**
Multicoded (Maximum of 8 codes)

	Q399 %	Q400 %
Contact my MP [DoMP] [DoneMP]	57.5	14.0
Speak to an influential person [DoSpk] [DoneSpk]	14.3	3.3
Contact a government department [DoGov] [DoneGov]	14.1	3.3
Contact radio, TV or newspaper [DoTV] [DoneTV]	21.2	4.7
Sign a petition [DoSign] [DoneSign]	66.7	38.6
Raise the issue in an organisation I already belong to [DoRais] [DoneRais]	7.3	3.7
Go on a protest or demonstration [DoProt] [DoneProt]	16.4	8.9
Form a group of like-minded people [DoGrp] [DoneGrp]	10.2	2.5
(No, none of these) [DoNone] [Done None]	7.3	53.1
(Don't know)	-	0.4
(Refusal/NA)	1.6	0.1

Q401 [BreakLaw]
Are there any circumstances in which you might break a law to which you were very strongly opposed?
%
Yes 29.5
No 66.0
(Don't Know) 4.4
(Refusal/NA) 0.1

Q402 [Coalitn]
Which do you think is generally better for Britain ... **READ OUT** ...
%
... to have a government formed by one political party, 44.6
or, for two or more parties to get together to form a government? 49.3
(Don't Know) 6.1
(Refusal/NA) -

Q403 [VoteSyst]
Some people say that we should change the voting system to allow smaller political parties to get a fairer share of MPs. Others say that we should keep the voting system as it is, to produce more effective government. Which view comes closest to your own ... **READ OUT** ...
IF ASKED, REFERS TO 'PROPORTIONAL REPRESENTATION'
%
... that we should change the voting system, 34.4
or, keep it as it is? 60.2
(Don't Know) 5.4
(Refusal/NA) -

55

Q404 **ASK IN SCOTLAND AND ENGLAND** [n=1079]
[ScotParl]
An issue in Scotland is the question of an elected Assembly - a special parliament for Scotland dealing with Scottish affairs. Which of these statements comes closest to your view?
%
Scotland should become independent, separate from the UK and the European Community 5.1
Scotland should become independent, separate from the UK, but part of the European Community 9.5
Scotland should remain part of the UK but with its own elected Assembly that has some taxation and spending powers 47.3
There should be no change from the present system 28.4
Other answer (WRITE IN) 1.3
(Don't Know) 8.2
(Refusal/NA) 0.1

Q407 **ASK IN WALES** [n=62]
[WelshParl]
An issue in Wales is the question of an elected Assembly - a special parliament for Wales dealing with Welsh affairs. Which of these statements comes closest to your view?
%
Wales should become independent, separate from the UK and the European Community 4.3
Wales should become independent, separate from the UK but part of the European Community 7.7
Wales should remain part of the UK, but with its own elected Assembly that has some taxation and spending powers 48.7
There should be no change from the present system 38.5
Other answer (WRITE IN) 0.9
(Don't Know) -
(Refusal/NA) -

Q410 **VERSION A: ASK ALL** [n=1140]
[ObeyLaw]
In general would you say that people should obey the law without exception, or are there exceptional occasions on which people should follow their consciences even if it means breaking the law?
%
Obey law without exception 41.3
Follow conscience on occasions 56.1
(Don't Know) 2.5
(Refusal/NA) 0.1

Q411 [GovNoSay]
CARD
Please choose a phrase from this card to say how much you agree or disagree with the following statements.
People like me have no say in what the government does.

Q412 [LoseTch]
CARD
Generally speaking, those we elect as MPs lose touch with people pretty quickly

56

n-1140

Q413 [VoteIntr]
CARD
Parties are only interested in people's votes, not in their opinions

Q414 [VoteOnly]
CARD
Voting is the only way people like me can have any say about how the government runs things

	[GovNoSay]	[LoseTch]	[VoteIntr]	[VoteOnly]
	%	%	%	%
Agree strongly	27.7	25.0	25.4	19.1
Agree	36.7	47.2	46.8	53.4
Neither agree nor disagree	11.7	11.9	10.2	8.2
Disagree	19.8	12.8	15.7	16.4
Disagree strongly	3.2	1.4	0.6	1.5
(Don't Know)	1.0	1.8	1.2	1.4
(Refusal/NA)	0.0	-	-	-

Q415 [GovComp]
CARD
Sometimes politics and government seem so complicated that a person like me cannot really understand what is going on

Q416 [PtyNMat]
CARD
It doesn't really matter which party is in power, in the end things go on much the same

Q417 [InfPolit]
CARD
I think I am better informed than most people about politics and government

	[GovComp]	[PtyNMat]	[InfPolit]
	%	%	%
Agree strongly	21.7	15.6	2.1
Agree	48.1	41.5	17.1
Neither agree nor disagree	10.2	7.6	28.1
Disagree	16.1	27.9	43.8
Disagree strongly	3.4	6.2	8.2
(Don't Know)	0.6	1.1	0.6
(Refusal/NA)	-	-	-

Q418 [GovTrust]
CARD
How much do you trust British governments of any party to place the needs of the nation above the interests of their own political party?

Q419 [ClrTrust]
CARD
And how much do you trust local councillors of any party to place the needs of their area above the interests of their own political party?

57

n-1140

Q420 [PapTrust]
CARD
How much do you trust British journalists on national newspapers to pursue the truth above getting a good story?

	[GovTrust]	[ClrTrust]	[PapTrust]
	%	%	%
Just about always	2.6	3.1	2.2
Most of the time	21.6	28.1	12.9
Only some of the time	52.6	51.0	42.2
Almost never	20.6	14.2	40.7
(Don't Know)	2.3	3.6	1.9
(Refusal/NA)	0.3	-	-

Q421 [PolTrust]
CARD
And how much do you trust British police not to bend the rules in trying to get a conviction?

Q422 [CSTrust]
CARD
And how much do you trust top civil servants to stand firm against a minister who wants to provide false information to parliament?

Q423 [MPsTrust]
CARD
How much do you trust politicians of any party in Britain to tell the truth when they are in a tight corner?

	[PolTrust]	[CSTrust]	[MPsTrust]
	%	%	%
Just about always	6.4	3.0	0.9
Most of the time	40.5	24.3	8.2
Only some of the time	38.3	43.1	39.6
Almost never	12.1	18.0	48.7
(Don't Know)	2.7	11.6	2.6
(Refusal/NA)	0.0	-	-

58

EUROPE/INTERNATIONAL RELATIONS (VERSION A AND B)

n=1142

Q427 **VERSION B: ASK ALL**
[ECGBCls]
Now a few questions about Britain's relationships with other countries.
As a member state, would you say that Britain's relationship with the European Community should be ... **READ OUT** ...

%
36.5 ... closer,
22.5 less close,
33.6 or, is it about right?
7.2 (Don't Know)
0.1 (Refusal/NA)

Q428 [ECLnkInf]
Do you think that closer links with the European Community would give Britain ... **READ OUT** ...

%
32.1 ... more influence in the world,
16.5 less influence in the world,
45.7 or, would it make no difference?
5.6 (Don't Know)
0.1 (Refusal/NA)

Q429 [ECLnkStr]
And would closer links with the European Community make Britain ... **READ OUT** ...

%
40.2 ... stronger economically,
20.0 weaker economically,
29.3 or, would it make no difference?
10.3 (Don't Know)
0.1 (Refusal/NA)

Q430 [Nation]
On the whole, do you think Britain's interests are better served by ... **READ OUT** ...

%
45.2 ... closer links with Western Europe,
20.8 or, closer links with America?
17.2 (Both equally)
9.1 (Neither)
7.6 (Don't Know)
0.1 (Refusal/NA)

Q431 [UniteEC]
Which of these comes closer to your views ... **READ OUT** ...
40.3 ...Britain should do all it can to unite fully with the European Community,
52.6 or, Britain should do all it can to protect its independence from the European Community?
7.0 (Don't Know)
0.1 (Refusal/NA)

Q432 [ECPolicy]
CARD
Do you think Britain's long-term policy should be ...
READ OUT
CODE ONE ONLY

%
11.1 ... to leave the European Community,
25.3 to stay in the EC and try to reduce its powers,
20.4 to leave things as they are,
27.8 to stay in the EC and try to increase the EC's powers,
8.4 or, to work for the formation of a single European government?
6.7 (Don't Know)
0.2 (Refusal/NA)

Q433 [EcuView]
CARD
And here are three statements about the future of the pound in the European Community.
Which one comes closest to your view?
CODE ONE ONLY

%
16.9 Replace the pound by a single currency
17.7 Use both the pound and a new European currency in Britain
61.5 Keep the pound as the only currency for Britain
3.9 (Don't Know)
- (Refusal/NA)

n=2262

Q434 **VERSION A AND B: ASK ALL**
[ECVotRes]
CARD
Which of the four statements on this card comes closest to the way you would vote in an European election?

%
41.3 I would vote for a party regardless of the candidate
26.1 I would vote for a party only if I approved of the candidate
7.3 I would vote for a candidate regardless of his or her party
23.1 I would generally not vote
2.2 (Don't Know)
0.0 (Refusal/NA)

n=1142

Q435 **VERSION B: ASK ALL**
[USANuke]
Do you think that the siting of American nuclear missiles in Britain would make Britain a safer or less safe place to live?

Q436 [OwnNuke]
And do you think that having its own independent nuclear missiles makes Britain a safer or less safe place to live?

	[USANuke]	[OwnNuke]
	%	%
Safer	20.7	45.4
Less safe	59.6	37.0
(No difference)	14.4	12.1
(Don't Know)	5.1	5.5
(Refusal/NA)	0.1	0.0

n=1142

Q437 [UKNucPO2]
CARD
Which of these statements comes closest to your own opinion on Britain's nuclear defence policy?
CODE ONE ONLY
%
23.3 Britain should get rid of its nuclear weapons
58.3 Britain should keep its nuclear weapons until others get rid of theirs
14.7 Britain should always have nuclear weapons
1.4 (None of these)
2.3 (Don't Know)
- (Refusal/NA)

Q438 [NucWar1]
How likely do you think it is that there will be a nuclear war between Russia and the West within the next 15 years? Is it ... READ OUT ...

Q439 [NtNucWar]
And what about a war not involving nuclear weapons? How likely is it that there will be such a war between Russia and the West within the next 15 years?
Is it ... READ OUT ...

	[NucWar1]	[NtNucWar]
	%	%
... very likely,	1.7	2.5
quite likely,	7.3	11.3
not very likely,	44.9	48.9
or, not at all likely?	41.9	32.1
(Don't Know)	4.2	5.2
(Refusal/NA)	0.0	-

Q440 [NIreland]
Do you think the long-term policy for Northern Ireland should be for it ... READ OUT ...
%
24.1 ... to remain part of the United Kingdom,
59.4 or, to reunify with the rest of Ireland?
2.2 Other (WRITE IN)
8.7 (Don't Know)
- (Refusal/NA)

Q443 [DecFutNI]
And who do you think should have the right to decide what the long-term future of Northern Ireland should be? Should it be ...
%
27.3 ... the people in Northern Ireland on their own,
51.5 or, the people of Ireland, both north and south,
16.1 or, the people both in Northern Ireland and in Britain?
1.7 Other answer (WRITE IN)
0.4 (Don't Know)
2.9 (Refusal/NA)

61

n=1142

Q446 [TroopOut]
Some people think that government policy towards Northern Ireland should include a complete withdrawal of British troops.
Would you personally support or oppose such a policy?
IF 'SUPPORT' OR 'OPPOSE', PROBE: Strongly or a little?
%
35.6 Support strongly
20.6 Support a little
20.8 Oppose a little
15.3 Oppose strongly
1.6 Other (WRITE IN)
5.6 (Don't Know)
- (Refusal/NA)

62

FEAR OF CRIME

n=3469

ASK ALL
[Victim]
Q713 Now, some questions about crime. Do you ever worry about the possibility that you, or anyone else who lives with you, might be the victim of crime?

	%
Yes	82.4
No	17.3
(Don't Know)	0.3
(Refusal/NA)	0.1

IF 'Yes' AT [Victim]
[VmWorry]
Q714 Is this ... READ OUT ...

	%
... a big worry	30.8
a bit of a worry	37.7
or, an occasional doubt?	13.8
(Don't Know)	0.0
(Refusal/NA)	0.3

ASK ALL
[WorCrime]
Q715 Because of worries about crime some people change their everyday life, for example, where they go or what they do. Other people don't change their lives at all. Do worries about crime affect your everyday life?

	%
Yes	28.7
No	69.0
(No worries about crime)	2.1
(Don't Know)	0.2
(Refusal/NA)	0.1

CARD
Q716 Here are some things that some people can do to avoid crime. Which of any of these do you do?
INTERVIEWER INSTRUCTION: THE CRIME MAY HAVE HAPPENED MORE THAN ONCE OR TOGETHER WITH ANOTHER CRIME
CODE ALL THAT APPLY
Multicoded (Maximum of 8 codes)

	%
I am careful to lock up my/our home (and/or car) [AvoidCr1]	94.4
I don't go out alone [AvoidCr2]	10.7
I don't go out at all [AvoidCr3]	0.6
I avoid going out at certain times [AvoidCr4]	30.0
I avoid going to certain places [AvoidCr5]	39.8
I avoid public transport [AvoidCr6]	4.9
I carry a personal alarm or a weapon [AvoidCr7]	4.9
I make sure other people in the family take precautions [AvoidCr8]	41.9
None [AvoidCr0]	1.9
Other answer (WRITE IN) [AvoidCr9]	5.4
(Don't know)	-
(Refusal/NA)	0.2

n=3469

ASK ALL
[MoveCrim]
Q719 Have you ever moved house because you or your family were worried about crime?

	%
Yes	4.1
No	95.7
(Don't Know)	0.1
(Refusal/NA)	0.1

IF 'No' AT [MoveCrim]
[MoveCri1]
Q720 And have you ever thought you would like to move house because you or your family were worried about crime?

	%
Yes	9.0
No	86.7
(Don't Know)	0.0
(Refusal/NA)	0.2

ASK ALL
[VicAttac]
Q721 And now some questions about crimes that may have happened to you.
THE CRIME MAY HAVE HAPPENED MORE THAN ONCE OR ON THE SAME OCCASION
Have you **yourself** ever been physically attacked?

[VicThrea]
Q722 (Have you **yourself** ever ....)
... been threatened?

[VicHmBur]
Q723 (Have you **yourself** ever ....)
... had your home burgled?

	[VicAttac]	[VicThrea]	[VicHmBur]
	%	%	%
Yes	17.6	27.0	26.5
No	82.3	72.9	73.4
(Don't Know)	0.1	0.1	0.0
(Refusal/NA)	0.1	0.1	0.1

[VictmCar]
Q724 (Have you **yourself** ever ....)
... had a car belonging to you or another family member stolen, or had things stolen from a car?

	%
Yes	56.7
No	39.4
No car/Never had a car	3.8
(Don't Know)	0.0
(Refusal/NA)	0.1

n=3469

Q725 [VicVandl]
(Have you yourself ever ...)
... had your home or a car damaged by vandals?

Q726 [VicOther]
(Have you yourself ever ...)
... had something else stolen?

	[VicVandl]	[VicOther]
	%	%
Yes	44.7	34.9
No	55.2	65.0
(Don't Know)	0.0	0.1
(Refusal/NA)	0.1	0.1

Q727 IF VICTIM OF CRIME (IF 'Yes' AT [VicAttac], [VicHmBur], [VicVandl], [VictmCar], OR [VicOther])
[VicAware]
Do you think that as a result of any of these experiences you are now more aware of crime, or has it made no difference?
%
More aware 59.6
No difference 22.0
(Don't Know) -
(Refusal/NA) 0.1

Q728 IF 'more aware' AT [VicAware]
[VictFear]
And has it actually made you more afraid of crime?
%
Yes 27.8
No 31.7
(Don't Know) 0.0
(Refusal/NA) 0.1

ASK ALL
Q729 [KnowVitm]
And do you know personally anyone else who has experienced any of these crimes?
%
Yes 86.6
No 13.3
(Don't Know) 0.1
(Refusal/NA) 0.1

Q730 IF 'Yes' AT [KnowVitm]
[KnowAwar]
Has knowing about someone else's experience of crime made you more aware of crime or has it made no difference?
%
More aware 64.2
No difference 22.3
(Don't Know) 0.0
(Refusal/NA) 0.2

Owing to a programming error [VicThrea] was omitted from this list.

Q731 IF 'More aware' AT [KnowVitm]
[KnowFear]
And has it actually made you more afraid of crime?
%
Yes 31.1
No 33.1
(Don't Know) 0.0
(Refusal/NA) 0.2

ASK ALL
Q732 [CrimNpTV]
Thinking about reports of crimes in newspapers or or on radio or on television. Do you think there are more reports nowadays than ten years ago, or fewer, or about the same number?
%
A lot more 60.6
More 29.5
About the same 7.6
Fewer 1.0
A lot fewer -
(Don't Know) 1.1
(Refusal/NA) 0.1

Q733 IF 'A lot more' OR 'More' AT [CrmNpTV]
[NpTVFear]
And do you think this has actually made you more afraid of crime?
%
Yes 45.7
No 44.3
(Don't Know) 0.1
(Refusal/NA) 1.2

ASK ALL
Q734 [SafeDark]
How safe do you feel walking alone in this area after dark
READ OUT...
%
... very safe 22.2
fairly safe 40.0
a bit unsafe 23.2
or very unsafe? 13.2
(Don't Know) 1.3
(Refusal/NA) 0.1

Q735 [Graffiti]
CARD
Please use this card to say how common or uncommon each of the following things is in your area.
Graffiti on walls or buildings?

Q736 [TeenOnSt]
CARD
(How common or uncommon is this in your area?)
Teenagers hanging around on the streets?

Q737 [Drunks]
CARD
(How common or uncommon is this in your area?)
Drunks or tramps on the streets?

n=3469

Q738 [Vandals]
CARD
(How common or uncommon is this in your area?)
Vandalism and deliberate damage to property?

Q739 [RaceTens]
CARD
(How common or uncommon is this in your area?)
Insults or attacks to do with someone's race or colour?

Q740 [Burglary]
CARD
(How common or uncommon is this in your area?)
Homes broken into?

Q741 [VehTheft]
CARD
(How common or uncommon is this in your area?)
Cars broken into or stolen?

Q742 [Attacks]
CARD
(How common or uncommon is this in your area?)
People attacked in the streets?

	[Graffiti]	[TeenOnSt]	[Drunks]	[Vandals]
	%	%	%	%
Very common	10.6	28.2	6.6	13.9
Fairly common	20.0	35.7	13.8	29.5
Not very common	49.6	26.5	45.0	43.4
Not at all common	19.4	9.0	34.0	12.2
(Don't Know)	0.4	0.6	0.5	0.9
(Refusal/NA)	0.1	0.1	0.1	0.1

	[RaceTens]	[Burglary]	[VehTheft]	[Attacks]
	%	%	%	%
Very common	2.9	18.4	24.8	2.3
Fairly common	7.8	41.8	39.3	8.6
Not very common	43.8	32.1	28.9	51.0
Not at all common	43.0	6.0	4.7	36.6
(Don't Know)	2.3	1.7	2.2	1.4
(Refusal/NA)	0.1	0.1	0.1	0.1

HOUSING (SHORT)

n=3469

Q747 [HomeType]
ASK ALL
Now a few questions on housing.
INTERVIEWER CODE FROM OBSERVATION AND CHECK WITH RESPONDENT
Would I be right in describing this accommodation as a...
READ OUT ONE YOU THINK APPLIES

%	
21.8	... detached house or bungalow,
34.5	... semi-detached house or bungalow,
28.2	... terraced house,
11.6	... self-contained, purpose-built flat/maisonette,
	(inc. in tenement block),
2.6	... self-contained converted flat/maisonette,
0.4	... room(s), not self-contained.
0.8	Other answer (WRITE IN)
0.0	(Don't Know)
0.1	(Refusal/NA)

Q750 [HomeEst]
May I just check, is your home part of a housing estate?
NOTE: MAY BE PUBLIC OR PRIVATE, BUT IT IS THE RESPONDENT'S VIEW WE WANT

%	
42.2	Yes, part of estate
57.6	No
0.1	(Don't Know)
0.1	(Refusal/NA)

Q751 [Tenure1]
Does your household own or rent this accommodation?
PROBE IF NECESSARY
IF OWNS: Outright or on a mortgage?
IF RENTS: From whom?

%	
25.3	OWNS: Own (leasehold/freehold) outright
44.9	OWNS: Buying (leasehold/freehold) on mortgage
16.8	RENTS: Local authority
0.4	RENTS: New Town Development Corporation
3.1	RENTS: Housing Association
1.4	RENTS: Property company
0.4	RENTS: Employer
1.3	RENTS: Other organisation
0.5	RENTS: Relative
4.6	RENTS: Other individual
0.2	Housing Trust
0.7	Rent free, squatting, etc
0.5	(Don't Know)
0.1	(Refusal/NA)

RELIGION AND ETHNIC ORIGIN [n=3469]

Q753 [Religion]
Do you regard yourself as belonging to any particular religion?

%
IF YES: Which?
CODE ONE ONLY - DO NOT PROMPT

%	
38.5	No religion
4.8	Christian - no denomination
9.5	Roman Catholic
33.1	Church of England/Anglican
1.2	Baptist
2.7	Methodist
3.9	Presbyterian/Church of Scotland
0.1	Free Presbyterian
0.0	Brethren
0.7	United Reform Church (URC)/Congregational
0.9	Other Protestant
0.8	Other Christian
0.7	Hindu
0.2	Jewish
1.3	Islam/Muslim
0.5	Sikh
0.1	Buddhist
0.6	Other non-Christian
0.1	(Don't Know)
0.1	(Refusal/NA)

Q761 ALL WHO DID NOT REFUSE AT [Religion]
[FamRelig]
In what religion, if any, were you brought up?
PROBE IF NECESSARY: What was your family's religion?
CODE ONE ONLY - DO NOT PROMPT

%	
8.2	No religion
4.6	Christian - no denomination
13.2	Roman Catholic
53.4	Church of England/Anglican
1.9	Baptist
5.4	Methodist
5.8	Presbyterian/Church of Scotland
0.1	Free Presbyterian
0.1	Brethren
0.8	United Reform Church (URC)/Congregational
1.0	Other Protestant
0.9	Other Christian
0.5	Hindu
0.5	Jewish
1.5	Islam/Muslim
0.5	Sikh
0.2	Buddhist
0.4	Other non-Christian
0.2	(Don't Know)
0.2	(Refusal/NA)

69

ALL GIVING A RELIGION AT [Religion] OR AT [FamRelig]
(IF 'Christian' THROUGH TO 'Other non-Christian' AT [Religion] OR AT [FamRelig])
Q769 [ChAttend]
Apart from such special occasions as weddings, funerals and baptisms, how often nowadays do you attend services or meetings connected with your religion?
PROBE IF NECESSARY

%	
12.0	Once a week or more
2.5	Less often but at least once in two weeks
6.2	Less often but at least once a month
9.5	Less often but at least twice a year
5.1	Less often but at least once a year
5.2	Less often
50.5	Never or practically never
0.4	Varies too much to say
0.4	(Don't Know)
-	(Refusal/NA)

VERSION C: ASK ALL
Q770 [RaceOrig] (see Q284)
CARD
To which of these groups do you consider you belong?
CODE ONE ONLY

BLACK: of African or Caribbean or other origin
ASIAN: of Indian origin
ASIAN: of Pakistani origin
ASIAN: of Bangladeshi origin
ASIAN: of Chinese origin
ASIAN: of other origin (WRITE IN)
WHITE: of British origin
WHITE: of Irish origin
WHITE: of other origin (WRITE IN)
MIXED ORIGIN (WRITE IN)
(Don't Know)
(Refusal/NA)

70

CLASSIFICATION

n=3469

ASK ALL

Q781 [MarStat]
Can I just check whether at present you are ... **READ OUT** ...
CODE FIRST TO APPLY

%
60.0 ...married,
5.9   living as married,
7.8   separated or divorced aftermarrying,
7.9   widowed,
18.2 or not married?
0.0   (Don't Know)
0.1   (Refusal/NA)

Q782 [Househld]
Finally, a few questions about you and your household.
Including yourself, how many people live here regularly as
members of this household ?
**CHECK INTERVIEWER MANUAL FOR DEFINITION OF HOUSEHOLD IF
NECESSARY.**

14.4 Just myself
34.8 Two people
19.0 Three people
20.8 Four people
7.5   Five people
2.6   Six people
0.4   Seven people
0.2   Eight people
-     Nine people
0.1   Ten people
0.1   Eleven people
-     (Don't Know)
0.1   (Refusal/NA)

HOUSEHOLD GRID: QUESTIONS ARE ASKED ONCE FOR EACH HOUSEHOLD MEMBER

EVERY PERSON IN THE GRID
(NOT ON DATA FILE)

Q784 [Name]
FIRST PERSON IN GRID: Please type in the name of respondent
SECOND AND SUBSEQUENT PERSONS IN GRID: Please type in the
name of person number (number)
SECOND AND SUBSEQUENT PERSON IN THE GRID

[P2Sex - P11Sex]
PLEASE CODE SEX OF (Name)
Male
Female
(Don't Know)
(Refusal/NA)

71

EVERY PERSON IN THE GRID

n=3469

[RAge] [P2Age P11Age] (MEDIAN REFERS TO [RAge])
FIRST PERSON IN GRID: Now I'd like to ask you a few details
about each person in your household.
Starting with yourself, what was your **age** last birthday?
PLEASE ENTER AGE OF (Name)
**SECOND AND SUBSEQUENT PERSONS IN GRID: PLEASE ENTER AGE OF
(Name)**
Median: 44 years
0.3   (Refusal/NA)

SECOND AND SUBSEQUENT PERSONS IN GRID
[P2Rel - P11Rel]
PLEASE ENTER RELATIONSHIP OF (Name) TO RESPONDENT
Partner/Spouse/Cohabitee
Son/daughter (inc step/adopted)
Parent/ parent-in-law
Other relative
Other non-relative
(Don't Know)
(Refusal/NA)

PERSONS AGED 16 AND OVER
[RResp] [P2Resp - P11Resp] (FIGURES REFER TO [RResp])
(Are you/Is he/she) legally responsible for the
accommodation?
(INCLUDE JOINT/SHARED RESPONSIBILITY)
%
84.1 Yes
15.8 No
-     (Don't Know)
0.1   (Refusal/NA)

END OF HOUSEHOLD GRID

ASK ALL

Q785 [OthChild]
Apart from people you have just mentioned who live in your
household, have you any (other) children, including
stepchildren, who grew up in your household?
'CHILDREN' MEANS THOSE THEN AGED UNDER 18, AND INCLUDES
THOSE NO LONGER LIVING
%
32.8 Yes
67.1 No
0.1   (Don't Know)
-     (Refusal/NA)

Q786 [RPrivEd]
Have you ever attended a fee-paying, private primary or
secondary school in the United Kingdom?
NOTE: PRIVATE' INCLUDES INDEPENDENT / PUBLIC SCHOOLS [not
'DIRECT GRANT', as these were/are not 'fee-paying'] BUT
EXCLUDES NURSERY SCHOOLS, VOLUNTARY-AIDED SCHOOLS AND 'OPTED
OUT' GRANT-MAINTAINED SCHOOLS
%
11.4 Yes
88.4 No
0.0   (Don't Know)
0.1   (Refusal/NA)

72

n=3469

Q787
IF MARRIED OR LIVING AS MARRIED (IF 'married' OR 'living as married' AT [MarStat])
[SPrivEd]
Has your (wife/husband/partner) ever attended a fee-paying, private primary or secondary school in the United Kingdom?
NOTE: 'PRIVATE' INCLUDES INDEPENDENT / PUBLIC SCHOOLS [not 'DIRECT GRANT', as these were/are not 'fee-paying'] BUT EXCLUDES NURSERY SCHOOLS, VOLUNTARY-AIDED SCHOOLS AND 'OPTED OUT' GRANT-MAINTAINED SCHOOLS

%
Yes 6.6
No 59.1
(Don't Know) 0.3
(Refusal/NA) -

Q788
IF RESPONDENT HAS CHILDREN AGED FIVE OR OVER (AS GIVEN IN HOUSEHOLD GRID) OR ANSWERED 'Yes' AT [ChldChk]
[ChPrvEd]
And (have any of your children / has your child) ever attended a fee-paying private primary or secondary school in United Kingdom?
NOTE: 'PRIVATE' INCLUDES INDEPENDENT / PUBLIC SCHOOLS [not 'DIRECT GRANT', as these were/are not 'fee-paying'] BUT EXCLUDES NURSERY SCHOOLS, VOLUNTARY-AIDED SCHOOLS AND 'OPTED OUT' GRANT-MAINTAINED SCHOOLS

%
Yes 7.1
No 50.9
(Don't Know) 0.1
(Refusal/NA) 0.0

ASK ALL
Q789
[DutyResp]
Who is the person mainly responsible for general domestic duties in this household?

%
Respondent mainly 48.8
Someone else mainly 29.3
Duties shared equally 21.8
(Don't Know) 0.1
(Refusal/NA) 0.1

Q790
IF 'someone else' OR 'duties shared' AT [DutyResp]
PLEASE SPECIFY THIS PERSONS/THESE PEOPLES RELATIONSHIP TO RESPONDENT
Multicoded (Maximum of 6 codes)

%
Wife/female partner of respondent [DutyWife] 29.4
Mother/mother-in-law of respondent [DutyMum] 8.1
Husband/male partner of respondent [DutyHusb] 6.9
Other female in household [DutyFem] 4.2
Other male in household [DutyMale] 3.4
Other answer [DutyOthr] 2.5
(Don't Know) -
(Refusal/NA) 0.0

73

n=3469

Q792
IF RESPONDENT HAS CHILDREN AGED 17 OR UNDER (AS GIVEN IN HOUSEHOLD GRID)
[ChldResp]
Who is the person mainly responsible for the general care of the child(ren) here?

%
Respondent mainly 15.6
Someone else mainly 8.0
Care shared equally 7.4
(Don't Know) -
(Refusal/NA) -

Q793
IF 'someone else' OR 'care shared equally' AT [ChldResp]
[OthClB]
PLEASE SPECIFY THIS PERSONS/THESE PEOPLES RELATIONSHIP TO RESPONDENT

%
Wife/female partner of respondent [ChldWife] 11.8
Mother/mother-in-law of respondent [ChldMum] 0.5
Husband/male partner of respondent [ChldHusb] 2.9
Other female in household [ChldFem] 0.3
Other male in household [ChldMale]
Other answer [ChldOthr] 0.3
(Don't Know) -
(Refusal/NA) -

ASK ALL
Q795
[TEA]
How old were you when you completed your continuous full-time education?
PROBE IF NECESSARY

%
15 or under 38.8
16 26.3
17 8.5
18 8.0
19 or over 14.6
Still at school 0.7
Still at college or university 2.6
Other answer (WRITE IN) 0.4
(Don't Know) 0.1
(Refusal/NA) 0.2

ASK ALL
Q798
[SchQual]
CARD
Have you passed any of the examinations on this card?

%
Yes 54.6
No 45.1
(Don't Know) 0.2
(Refusal/NA) 0.1

74

n=3469

Q799   IF 'Yes' AT [SchQual]
%   Which ones? PROBE: Any others?
       CODE ALL THAT APPLY
       Multicoded (Maximum of 16 codes)
17.4   CSE Grades 2-5   [EdQual1]
       GCSE Grades D-G

44.7   CSE-Grade 1   [EdQual2]
       GCE 'O'level
       GCSE - Grades A-C
       School certificate
       Scottish (SCE) Ordinary
       Scottish School-leaving Certificate lower grade
       SUPE Ordinary
       Northern Ireland Junior Certificate

18.9   GCE 'A'level/'S'level   [EdQual3]
       Higher school certificate
       Matriculation
       Scottish SCE/SLC/SUPE at Higher grade
       Northern Ireland Senior Certificate

1.7   Overseas school leaving exam or certificate   [EdQual4]

-      (Don't know)
0.4   (Refusal/NA)

       ASK ALL
Q800   [PSchQual]
       CARD
%   And have you passed any of the exams or got any of the
       qualifications on this card?
47.1   Yes
52.2   No
0.1   (Don't Know)
0.2   (Refusal/NA)

n=3469

Q801   IF 'Yes' AT [PSchQual]
%   Which ones? PROBE: Any others?
       CODE ALL THAT APPLY
       Multicoded (Maximum of 12 codes)
5.1   Recognised trade apprenticeship completed   [EdQual5]
9.8   RSA/other clerical, commercial qualification   [EdQual6]
9.1   City & Guilds Certificate - Craft/intermediate/
       Ordinary/Part I   [EdQual7]
4.6   City & Guilds Certificate - Advanced/Final/
       Part II or Part III   [EdQual8]
1.9   City & Guilds Certificate - Full technological   [EdQual9]
5.8   BEC/TEC General/Ordinary National Certificate (ONC) or
       Diploma (OND)   [EdQual10]
3.9   BEC/TEC Higher/Higher National Certificate (HNC) or
       Diploma (HND)   [EdQual11]
4.1   Teacher training qualification   [EdQual12]
2.8   Nursing qualification   [EdQual13]
5.6   Other technical or business qualification/
       certificate   [EdQual14]
10.2   University or CNAA degree or diploma   [EdQual15]
7.2   Other recognised academic or vocational qualification
       (WRITE IN)   [EdQual16]
-      (Don't know)
0.3   (Refusal/NA)

       IF NOT 'in paid work' OR 'waiting to take up paid work' AT
       [REconAct]
Q805   [JobChk]   (Q81)
%   Have you ever had a job?
44.5   Yes
2.6   No, never
       (Don't Know)
0.0   (Refusal/NA)

n=3378

ASK ALL WHO HAVE EVER WORKED (IF 'in paid work' OR 'waiting
to take up paid work' AT [REconAct]) OR 'Yes' AT [JobChk]
[RTitle] (NOT ON DATA FILE)

IF IN PAID WORK (IF 'in paid work' AT [REconAct]): Now I
want to ask you about your present job.
What is your job?
PROBE IF NECESSARY: What is the name or title of the job?

II' WAITING TO TAKE UP PAID WORK (IF 'waiting to take up paid
work' AT [REconAct]): Now I want to ask you about your
future job.
What is your job?
PROBE IF NECESSARY: What is the name or title of the job?

IF NOT IN PAID WORK (OR WAITING TO TAKE UP PAID WORK) BUT
EVER HAD JOB IN THE PAST (IF 'Yes' AT [JobChk]): Now I want
to ask you about your last job.
What was your job?
PROBE IF NECESSARY: What was the name or title of the job?
Q806   Open Question (Maximum of 50 characters)

Q807 [RTypeWk] (NOT ON DATA FILE)
What kind of work (do/will/did) you do most of the time?
IF RELEVANT: What materials/machinery (do/will/did) you use?
Open Question (Maximum of 50 characters)

Q808 [RTrain] (NOT ON DATA FILE)
What training or qualifications (are/were) needed for that job?
Open Question (Maximum of 50 characters)

Q809 [RSuper] [RMany]
(Do/Will/Did) you directly supervise or (are you/will you be/were you) directly responsible for the work of any other people?

	%
Yes	37.1
No	62.5
(Don't know)	0.2
(Refusal)	0.2

Median (of those supervising any): 5

Q811 [RSupman]
Can I just check, (are you/will you be/were you) ...
READ OUT ...

	%
...a manager,	16.8
a foreman or supervisor,	13.0
or not?	70.0
(Don't Know)	0.0
(Refusal/NA)	0.2

Q812 [REmployee]
Can I just check, (are you/will you be/were you) ...
READ OUT ...

	%
... an employee,	88.6
or, self-employed?	11.2
(Don't Know)	0.1
(Refusal/NA)	0.1

IF EMPLOYEE IN THE PAST OR PRESENT (IF 'employee' OR DK AT [REmployee])

Q813 [Premises]
(Is/Was) where you (work/will work/worked) your employer's only premises, or (are/were) there other premises elsewhere?

	%
Employer's only premises	26.8
Employer has other premises elsewhere	61.3
(Don't Know)	0.5
(Refusal/NA)	0.2

ASK ALL WHO HAVE EVER WORKED (IF 'paid work' OR 'waiting to take up paid work' AT [REconAct] OR 'Yes' AT [JobChk])

Q814 [REmpMake] (NOT ON DATA FILE)
What (does/did) your employer/you make or do at the place where you usually (work/will work/worked) (from)?
Open Question (Maximum of 50 characters)

77

Q815 [REmpWork]
Including yourself, how many people (are/were) employed at the place where you usually (work/will work/worked) (from)?
IF SELF-EMPLOYED: (do/will/did) you have any employees?
IF YES: PROBE FOR CORRECT PRECODE

n=3378

	%
None	4.3
Under 10	20.1
10-24	15.6
25-99	22.6
100-499	21.5
500 or more	14.3
(Don't Know)	1.3
(Refusal/NA)	0.3

Q816 [RPartFul]
(Is/Was) the job ... READ OUT ...

	%
...full-time (30+ HOURS)	76.7
or, part-time (10-29 HOURS)?	23.0
(Don't Know)	0.1
(Refusal/NA)	0.2

ASK ALL

Q831 [UnionSA]
(May I just check) are you now a member of a trade union or staff association?
CODE FIRST TO APPLY

	%
Yes, trade union	22.1
Yes, staff association	4.2
No	73.4
(Don't Know)	0.2
(Refusal/NA)	0.1

IF 'No' AT [UnionSA]

Q832 [TUSABver]
Have you ever been a member of a trade union or staff association?
CODE FIRST TO APPLY

	%
Yes, trade union	24.7
Yes, staff association	2.7
No	46.0
(Don't Know)	0.0
(Refusal/NA)	0.3

n=3469

78

n=2289

IF MARRIED OR LIVING AS MARRIED (IF 'married' OR 'living as married' AT [MarStat])

Q833 [SEconAct] (Figures refer to first answer on the list)
Which of these descriptions applied to what your (husband/wife/partner) was doing last week, that is the seven days ending last Sunday?
PROBE: Any others?
CODE ALL THAT APPLY
(Figures refer to first answer on the list)
Multicoded (Maximum of 11 codes)

%
0.4   In full-time education (not paid for by employer, including on vacation)
0.1   On government training/employment programme (eg. Employment Training, Youth Training, etc)
61.0   In paid work (or away temporarily) for at least 10 hours in week
0.4   Waiting to take up paid work already accepted
3.4   Unemployed and registered at a benefit office
0.3   Unemployed, not registered, but actively looking for a job
0.3   Unemployed, wanting a job (of at least 10 hrs a week), but not actively looking for a job
3.8   Permanently sick or disabled
14.5   Wholly retired from work
14.3   Looking after the home
0.2   (Doing something else) (WRITE IN)
-   (Don't Know)
  (Refusal/NA)

IF SPOUSE/PARTNER IS NOT IN WORK (IF 'in full-time education', 'on government training scheme', 'unemployed', 'permanently sick', 'wholly retired', 'looking after home', 'doing something else'AT [SEconAct])

Q837 [SLastJob]
How long ago did your (husband/wife/partner) last have a paid job (other than the government programme you mentioned) of at least 10 hours a week?

%
4.3   Within past 12 months
10.4   Over 1, up to 5 years ago
8.2   Over 5, up to 10 years ago
8.0   Over 10, up to 20 years ago
4.5   Over 20 years ago
2.4   Never had a paid job of 10+ hours a week
0.2   (Don't Know)
0.2   (Refusal/NA)

79

---

n=2234

ASK ALL WHOSE SPOUSE/PARTNER HAS EVER WORKED (IF 'in paid work'/'waiting to take up paid work' AT [SEconAct] OR 'Within past 12 months'/ 'Over 1, up to 5 years go'/ 'Over 5, up to 10 years ago'/ 'Over 10, up to 20 years ago'/ 'Over 20 years ago' AT [SLastJob] (NOT ON DATA FILE)

Q838 IF SPOUSE/PARTNER IN PAID WORK (IF 'paid work' AT [SEconAct]): Now I want to ask you about your (husband's/wife's/partner's) present job.
What is (his/her) job?
PROBE IF NECESSARY: What is the name or title of that job?

IF SPOUSE/PARTNER IS WAITING TO TAKE UP PAID WORK (IF 'waiting to take up paid work' AT [SEconAct]): Now I want to ask you about your (husband's/wife's/partner's) future job.
What is (his/her) job?
PROBE IF NECESSARY: What is the name or title of that job?

IF SPOUSE/PARTNER IS NOT IN PAID WORK (OR WAITING TO TAKE UP PAID WORK) BUT HAS EVER WORKED IN THE PAST: Now I want to ask you about your (husband's/wife's/partner's) past job.
What was (his/her) job?
PROBE IF NECESSARY: What was the name or title of that job?
Open Question (Maximum of 50 characters)
[STitle] (NOT ON DATA FILE)

Q833 [STypeWk] (NOT ON DATA FILE)
What kind of work (does/will/did) (he/she) do most of the time?
IF RELEVANT: What materials/machinery (does/will/did) (he/she) use?
Open Question (Maximum of 50 characters)

Q840 [STrain] (NOT ON DATA FILE)
What training or qualifications (are/were) needed for that job?
Open Question (Maximum of 50 characters)

Q841 [SSuper]
(Does/Will/Did) (he/she) directly supervise or (is/will/was) (he/she) (be) directly responsible for the work of any other people?
IF YES: How many?
%
34.2   Yes
61.1   No
3.6   (Don't know)
1.1   (Refusal)
Median (of those supervising any): 6

Q843 ASK ALL WHOSE SPOUSE/PARTNER HAS EVER WORKED
[SSupMan]
Can I just check, (is/will/was) (he/she) (be) ...
READ OUT ...
%
20.3   ...a manager,
11.0   a foreman or supervisor,
67.7   or not?
0.4   (Don't Know)
0.6   (Refusal/NA)

80

n=2234

Q844 [SEmployee]
% (Is/Will/Was) (he/she) (be) ... **READ OUT** ...
86.0 ... an employee
13.2 or, self-employed?
0.1 (Don't Know)
0.6 (Refusal/NA)

Q845 [SEmpMake] **(NOT ON DATA FILE)**
What (does/will/was) the employer (**IF SELF-EMPLOYED:**
(he/she)) make or do at the place where (he/she) usually
(works/will work/worked)?
IF SELF-EMPLOYED: (does/will/did) (he/she) have any
Open Question (Maximum of 50 characters)

Q846 [SEmpWork]
Including (himself/herself), roughly how many people
(are/were) employed at the place where (he/she) usually
(works/will work/worked) (from)?
IF SELF-EMPLOYED: (does/will/did) (he/she) have any
employees?
IF YES: PROBE FOR CORRECT PRECODE
% None
4.4 Under 10
19.8 10-24
14.1 25-99
19.6 100-499
21.2 500 or more
14.4 (Don't Know)
5.9 (Refusal/NA)
0.7

Q847 [SPartFull]
% (Is/Was) the job ... **READ OUT** ...
79.3 ... full-time (30+ HOURS)
19.9 or, part-time (10-29 HOURS)?
0.2 (Don't Know)
0.6 (Refusal/NA)

n=3469

ASK ALL
Q862 [CarOwn]
(May I just check) Do you, or does anyone else in your
household, own or have the regular use of a car or a van?
%
76.3 Yes
23.5 No
0.0 (Don't Know)
0.2 (Refusal/NA)

---

n=3469

Q863 [AnyBNew]
CARD
% Do you (or does your husband/wife/partner) receive any of
the **state** benefits on this card at present?
29.7 Yes
69.7 No
0.1 (Don't Know)
0.5 (Refusal/NA)

Q864 **IF 'Yes' AT [AnyBNew]**
[BenftFW]
Which ones?
Any others?
% **CODE ALL THAT APPLY**
Multicoded (Maximum of 12 codes)
2.5 Unemployment benefit [BenftN1]
11.7 Income support [BenftN2]
2.3 One-parent benefit [BenftN3]
2.1 Family credit [BenftN4]
9.4 Housing benefit (rent-rebate) [BenftN5]
0.9 Statutory sick pay/sickness benefit [BenftN6]
5.9 Invalidity benefit [BenftN7]
2.8 Disability living allowance [BenftN8]
2.7 Widow's pension [BenftN10]
8.9 Council tax rebate [BenftN11]
1.6 Attendance allowance [BenftN13]
0.6 Severe disablement allowance [BenftN14]
0.6 Other state benefit(s) (**PLEASE SAY WHAT**) [BenftN12]
0.1 (Don't know)
0.6 (Refusal/NA)

ASK ALL
Q879 [Disab]
Do you have any long-standing health problems or
disabilities which limit what you can do at work, at home or
in your leisure time?
**INTERVIEWER: 'LONG-STANDING' MEANS HAVE HAD PROBLEM FOR 3
YEARS OR MORE OR EXPECT PROBLEM TO LAST FOR 3 YEARS OR MORE**
%
21.4 Yes
78.4 No
0.1 (Don't Know)
0.2 (Refusal/NA)

Q880 [HHIncome]
CARD
Which of the letters on this card represents the total
income of your household from all sources **before tax**?
Please just tell me the letter.
NOTE: INCLUDES INCOME FROM BENEFITS, SAVINGS, ETC.

n=1812

Q881 IF IN PAID WORK (IF 'in paid work' AT REconAct] - Q81)
[REarn]
Which of the letters on this card represents your own gross or total earnings, before deduction of income tax and national insurance?

		[HHIncome]	[REarn]
Q	Less than £3999	7.1	9.7
T	£4000 - £5999	9.5	8.0
O	£6000 - £7999	7.6	9.3
K	£8000 - £9999	4.9	8.9
L	£10000 - £11999	6.4	10.8
B	£12000 - £14999	7.5	12.2
Z	£15000 - £17999	6.5	9.7
M	£18000 - £19999	4.8	5.2
F	£20000 - £22999	5.7	6.2
J	£23000 - £25999	5.1	4.3
D	£26000 - £28999	3.7	3.1
H	£29000 - £31999	3.2	1.0
C	£32000 - £34999	2.5	1.3
G	£35000 - £37999	2.2	1.0
P	£38000 - £40999	2.4	0.5
N	£41000 or more	6.1	2.5
	(Don't Know)	9.6	1.7
	(Refusal/NA)	5.2	4.6

ASK ALL
Q882 [OwnShare]
Do you (or does your husband/wife/partner) own any shares quoted on the Stock Exchange, including unit trusts?
%
25.8 Yes
73.1 No
0.3   (Don't Know)
0.8   (Refusal/NA)

n=3469

Q883 [Phone]
Is there a telephone in (your part of) this accommodation?
91.5 Yes
8.3   No
-     (Don't Know)
0.2   (Refusal/NA)

Q884 IF 'Yes' AT [Teleph]
[TelNum]
Some of my interviews are checked.
May I take your 'phone number for that purpose?
ADD IF NECESSARY:
Your 'phone number will not be passed to anyone outside SCPR.
IF NUMBER GIVEN, WRITE ON THE ARF - DO NOT KEY IT IN !
%
83.2 Number given
8.3   Number refused
-     (Don't Know)
0.2   (Refusal/NA)

---

n=3469

ASK ALL
Q885 [Comeback]
In a year's time we may be doing a similar survey and we may wish to include you again. Would this be all right?
%
88.2 Yes
11.1 No
0.5   (Don't Know)
0.1   (Refusal/NA)

Q886 [SCxplain] (NOT ON DATA FILE)
INTERVIEWER: THANK RESPONDENT FOR HIS OR HER HELP AND EXPLAIN ABOUT THE SELF-COMPLETION QUESTIONNAIRE.
PLEASE MAKE SURE YOU GIVE THE RESPONDENT VERSION (A/B/C)
THEN TELL US WHETHER IT IS TO BE ...
... filled in immediately after interview in your presence,
or, left behind to be filled in later,
or, if the respondent refused.

Q888 [Duration]
THIS INTERVIEW WAS STARTED AT (Start time) AND IT IS NOW (End time)
PLEASE ENTER LENGTH OF INTERVIEW IN MINUTES
(IF YOU HAVE HAD TO STOP AN INTERVIEW AND START AGAIN, JUST ENTER TIME SPENT INTERVIEWING)
Range: 1 ... 150
Median:
Version A: 60 minutes
Version B: 59 minutes
Version C: 53 minutes

Q889 [DateInt]
PLEASE TYPE IN DATE OF INTERVIEW

Q890 [AnyTeen] (NOT ON DATA FILE)
IF ANY TEENAGERS OTHER THAN RESPONDENT IN HOUSEHOLD
INTERVIEWER: FROM THE HOUSEHOLD GRID, THE FOLLOWING PEOPLE HAVE BEEN CODED AS AGED 12-19:
(RESPONDENT NOT INCLUDED)
Person number (Number)   (Name)
TRANSFER THIS INFORMATION TO YOUR ARF AND PLEASE ADMINISTER THE YOUNG PERSONS' QUESTIONNAIRE TO EACH OF THESE.
IF NO TEENAGERS (OTHER THAN RESPONDENT) IN HOUSEHOLD:
INTERVIEWER: FROM THE HOUSEHOLD GRID, THE FOLLOWING PEOPLE HAVE BEEN CODED AS AGED 12-19:
(RESPONDENT NOT INCLUDED)

VERSION B

COUNTRYSIDE/ENVIRONMENT (VERSION B) [n=1142]

VERSION B: ASK ALL

Q589 Now a few questions about the countryside.
What, if anything, do you think spoils or threatens the countryside in Britain these days?
What else? And what else? PROBE UNTIL 'NO'.
RECORD WORD FOR WORD.
CONTINUE IN A NOTE (ctrl + f4), IF NECESSARY
Open Question (Maximum of 100 characters)

%		
33.3	Litter/rubbish	[SpoLitr]
14.3	Residential buildings	[SpoResdt]
22.4	Other building	[SpoBldg]
35.0	Roads/motorways	[SpoRoads]
3.7	Traffic pollution	[SpoTrfPl]
9.1	Other traffic	[SpoTrOth]
7.8	Industrial growth	[SpoIndGr]
5.4	Industrial pollution	[SpoIndPl]
6.5	Other industrial	[SpoIndOt]
4.8	Agricultural/farm pollution	[SpoFrmPl]
4.2	Other agricultural/farming	[SpoFrmOt]
22.9	Other pollution	[SpoPolut]
9.5	Abuse of land	[SpoAbLnd]
8.6	Lack of care	[SpoNCare]
5.2	Tourism/leisure	[SpoLeisr]
3.0	Travellers	[SpoTrav1]
5.5	Other	[SpoOcher]
2.0	Nothing spoils or threatens the countryside	[SpoNo]
0.5	Unclassifiable	
4.4	(Don't know)	
-	(Refusal/NA)	

Q592 [CThreat1]
CARD
Which, if any, of the things on this card do you think is the **greatest threat** to the countryside?
If you think none of them is a threat, or something not on the card please say so.
CODE ONE ONLY
INTERVIEWER: DO NOT TRY TO CHANGE THE ANSWER AT PREVIOUS QUESTION ('Spoils')

VERSION B: ASK ALL WHO GAVE AN ANSWER AT [CThreat1] [n=1142]

Q595 [CThreat2]
And which do you think is the next greatest threat (to the countryside)?
CODE ONE ONLY

	[CThreat1]	[CThreat2]
	%	%
Motorways and road building	26.4	16.8
Industrial pollution	24.3	21.8
Removal by farmers of traditional landscapes, such as hedgerows, woodlands	6.0	8.3
Too many people visiting the countryside	1.0	1.5
Rubbish-tipping and litter	14.3	17.2
Urban growth and housing development	14.8	14.0
Use of chemicals and pesticides in farming	10.7	16.1
(None of these)	0.7	1.4
Other answer (WRITE IN)	1.7	2.2
(Don't Know)	0.2	0.6
(Refusal/NA)	0.0	0.0

VERSION B: ASK ALL

Q598 [Crowded1]
CARD
Beauty spots and other popular places in the countryside often get crowded. Suppose one of these was visited so much that enjoying its peace and quiet was being spoiled.
Using this card, are you in favour of or against..
..cutting down or closing car parks near the site?

Q599 [Crowded2]
(To limit the number of visitors, are you in favour of or against ...) ...stopping anyone at all from visiting it at particular times each year?

Q600 [Crowded3]
(To limit the number of visitors, are you in favour of or against ...) ...making visitors pay and using the the extra money to help protect it?

	[Crowded1]	[Crowded2]	[Crowded3]
	%	%	%
Strongly in favour	11.4	7.1	16.7
In favour	31.4	36.3	52.5
Neither in favour nor against	21.6	14.7	7.1
Against	25.8	33.0	17.7
Strongly against	8.8	8.5	5.6
(Don't Know)	1.0	0.3	0.4
(Refusal/NA)	0.0	0.0	0.0

Q601 [Crowded4]
(To limit the number of visitors, are you in favour of or against ...) ...issuing free permits in advance so people will have to plan their visits?

N=1142

Q602   [Crowded5]
(To limit the number of visitors, are you in favour of or against ...) ...cutting down on advertising and promoting it?

Q603   [Crowded6]
(To limit the number of visitors, are you in favour of or against ...) ...advertising and promoting other popular places in the countryside instead?

	[Crowded4]	[Crowded5]	[Crowded6]
	%	%	%
Strongly in favour	6.2	6.9	6.3
In favour	35.6	38.1	48.8
Neither in favour nor against	14.5	23.0	23.5
Against	35.7	27.6	18.0
Strongly against	7.5	3.2	2.0
(Don't know)	0.5	1.1	1.4
(Refusal/NA)	0.0	0.0	0.0

Q604   [ConDevt]
Suppose you heard that a housing development was being planned in a part of the countryside you knew and liked.
Would you be concerned by this, or not?
%
82.2   Yes, concerned
16.6   No
1.1   (Don't Know)
0.0   (Refusal/NA)

Q605   IF 'Yes' AT [ConDevt]
CARD
Would you personally be likely to do any of these things about it? Any others?
CODE ALL THAT APPLY
%
Multicoded (Maximum of 8 codes)
8.0   (No, would take no action) [DevtDo1]
32.5   Contact MP or councillor [DevtDo2]
14.8   Contact a government or planning department [DevtDo3]
7.6   Contact radio, TV or a newspaper [DevtDo4]
67.7   Sign a petition [DevtDo5]
7.0   Join a conservation group [DevtDo6]
18.5   Give money to a campaign [DevtDo7]
10.0   Volunteer to work for a campaign [DevtDo8]
11.8   Go on a protest march or demonstration [DevtDo9]
-   (Don't know)
-   (Refusal/NA)

Q606   [ConFlwr]
Now suppose you heard that a site where wildflowers grew was going to be ploughed for farmland.
Would you be concerned by this, or not?
%
54.7   Yes, concerned
43.7   No
1.5   (Don't Know)
0.1   (Refusal/NA)

87

Q607   IF 'Yes' AT [ConFlwr]
[FlwrDo]
CARD AGAIN
Would you personally be likely to do any of these things about it? Any others?
CODE ALL THAT APPLY
%
Multicoded (Maximum of 8 codes)
7.4   (No, would take no action) [FlwrDo1]
17.0   Contact an MP or councillor [FlwrDo2]
8.2   Contact a government or planning department [FlwrDo3]
5.4   Contact radio, TV or a newspaper [FlwrDo4]
39.4   Sign a petition [FlwrDo5]
6.8   Join a conservation group [FlwrDo6]
9.3   Give money to a campaign [FlwrDo7]
6.4   Volunteer to work for a campaign [FlwrDo8]
6.1   Go on a protest march or demonstration [FlwrDo9]
-   (Don't know)
0.0   (Refusal/NA)

Q608   VERSION B: ASK ALL
[CtryDone]
Have you ever done any of the things on the card to help protect the countryside?
%
47.9   Yes
51.8   No
0.2   (Don't Know)
0.0   (Refusal/NA)

Qb.09   IF 'Yes' AT [CtryDone]
[DoneCtry]
CARD
Which have you ever done to help protect the countryside? Any others?
CODE ALL THAT APPLY
%
Multicoded (Maximum of 8 codes)
7.9   Contacted an MP or councillor [CtryDon1]
7.0   Contacted a government or planning department [CtryDon2]
2.4   Contacted radio, TV or a newspaper [CtryDon3]
41.2   Signed a petition [CtryDon4]
4.8   Joined a conservation group [CtryDon5]
14.5   Given money to a campaign [CtryDon6]
3.5   Volunteered to work for a campaign [CtryDon7]
3.0   Gone on a protest march or demonstration [CtryDon8]
-   (Don't know)
0.1   (Refusal/NA)

88

TRANSPORT (VERSION B)

N=1142

VERSION B: ASK ALL

Q612 [TrfPrb6]
CARD
Now thinking about traffic and transport problems, how serious a problem is congestion on motorways?

Q613 [TrfPrb7]
CARD AGAIN
(And how serious a problem for you is ...)
... increased traffic on country roads and lanes?

Q614 [TrfPrb8]
CARD AGAIN
(And how serious a problem for you is ...)
... traffic congestion at popular places in the countryside?

	[TrfPrb6] %	[TrfPrb7] %	[TrfPrb8] %
A very serious problem	44.0	18.0	18.1
A serious problem	40.4	37.7	40.4
Not a very serious problem	10.2	32.9	29.5
Not a problem at all	1.4	9.3	8.7
(Don't Know)	4.0	2.1	3.3
(Refusal/NA)	0.0	0.0	0.0

Q615 [TrfPrb9]
CARD AGAIN
(And how serious a problem for you is ...)
... traffic congestion in towns and cities?

Q616 [TrfPrb10]
CARD AGAIN
(And how serious a problem for you is ...)
... exhaust fumes from traffic in towns and cities

Q617 [TrfPrb11]
CARD AGAIN
(And how serious a problem for you is ...) ... noise from traffic in towns and cities

	[TrfPrb9] %	[TrfPrb10] %	[TrfPrb11] %
A very serious problem	43.8	50.2	26.8
A serious problem	39.6	36.2	38.1
Not a very serious problem	11.2	8.8	27.0
Not a problem at all	4.9	4.1	7.3
(Don't Know)	0.6	0.6	0.7
(Refusal/NA)	0.0	0.0	0.0

n=1142

Q618 [TransCar]
May I just check; do you, or does anyone else in your household, own or have the regular use of a car or a van?
IF YES, PROBE FOR WHETHER RESPONDENT, OR OTHER PERSON(S), OR BOTH

	%
Yes, respondent	37.2
Yes, other	14.5
Yes, both	25.0
No	23.2
(Don't Know)	-
(Refusal/NA)	0.0

IF 'Yes' AT [TransCar]

Q619 [NumbCars]
How many vehicles in all?

	%
One	42.3
Two	26.0
Three	6.0
Four	1.7
Five or more	0.9
(Don't Know)	-
(Refusal/NA)	0.0

IF ONE OR MORE VEHICLES AT [NumbCars]

Q620 [CompCar]
Is this vehicle (Are any of these vehicles...) provided by an employer or run as a business expense?

	%
No, none	35.9
Yes, one (of them)	16.5
Yes, two (of them)	3.8
Yes, three or more (of them)	0.4
(Don't Know)	0.1
(Refusal/NA)	0.0

VERSION B: ASK ALL

Q621 [Drive]
(May I just check) do you drive a car at all these days?

	%
Yes	64.5
No	35.5
(Don't Know)	-
(Refusal/NA)	0.0

IF 'Yes' AT [Drive]

Q622 [Travel1]
CARD
How often nowadays do you usually ...
... travel by car as a driver?

VERSION B: ASK ALL

Q623 [Travel2]
CARD AGAIN
(And how often do you usually ...)
... travel by car as a passenger?

VERSION C

ECONOMIC PROSPECTS (VERSION C)

n=1187

Q633 **VERSION C: ASK ALL**
[Prices]
Now I would like to ask you about two economic problems - inflation and unemployment.
First, inflation: in a year from now, do you expect prices generally to have gone up, to have stayed the same, or to have gone down?
IF GONE UP OR GONE DOWN: By a lot or a little?

Q634 [Unemp]
Second, **unemployment:**
in a year from now, do you expect unemployment to have gone up, to have stayed the same, or to have gone down?
IF GONE UP OR GONE DOWN: By a lot or a little?

	[Prices]	[Unemp]
	%	%
To have gone up by a lot	28.3	20.3
To have gone up by a little	54.3	26.3
To have stayed the same	14.3	30.8
To have gone down by a little	2.1	20.1
To have gone down by a lot	0.4	1.8
(Don't Know)	0.6	0.8
(Refusal/NA)	-	-

Q635 [UnempInf]
If the government **had** to choose between keeping down inflation or keeping down unemployment, to which do you think it should give highest priority?

	%
Keeping down inflation	26.4
Keeping down unemployment	68.7
Other answer (WRITE IN)	0.9
(Don't Know)	1.7
(Refusal/NA)	0.1

Q638 [Concern]
Which do you think is of the most concern to you and your **family** ... READ OUT ....

	%
... inflation,	51.3
or, unemployment?	45.0
Other answer (WRITE IN)	0.7
(Don't Know)	0.8
(Refusal/NA)	0.1

---

n=1142

Q624 [Travel3]
CARD AGAIN
(And how often do you usually ....)
... travel by local bus?

Q625 [Travel4]
CARD AGAIN
(And how often do you usually ....)
... travel by train?

	[Travel1]	[Travel2]	[Travel3]	[Travel4]
	%	%	%	%
Every day or nearly every day	42.9	7.7	8.4	2.1
2-5 days a week	14.4	25.1	13.5	2.8
Once a week	4.1	24.6	8.4	3.0
Less often but at least once a month	1.3	15.9	6.4	7.5
Less often than that	1.2	13.4	13.7	34.5
Never nowadays	0.6	13.2	49.6	50.1
(Don't Know)	-	-	-	-
(Refusal/NA)	0.0	0.0	0.0	0.0

Q626 [Travel6]
CARD AGAIN
(And how often do you usually ...)
... travel by bicycle?

Q627 [Travel7]
CARD AGAIN
(And how often do you usually ...)
... walk for over half an hour to or from work, the shops or for any other purpose?

Q628 [Travel8]
CARD AGAIN
(And how often do you usually ...)
... walk for over half an hour just for **exercise or pleasure?**

	[Travel6]	[Travel7]	[Travel8]
	%	%	%
Every day or nearly every day	3.9	26.3	15.2
2-5 days a week	2.9	23.4	17.4
Once a week	3.6	13.9	17.1
Less often but at least once a month	4.0	6.6	11.5
Less often than that	6.5	6.6	10.0
Never nowadays	78.9	23.2	28.8
(Don't Know)	0.1	-	-
(Refusal/NA)	0.0	0.0	0.0

n=1187

Q641 [Industry]
Looking ahead over the next year, do you think Britain's general industrial performance will improve, stay much the same, or decline?
IF IMPROVE OR DECLINE: By a lot or a little?
%
2.8 Improve a lot
22.1 Improve a little
49.0 Stay much the same
18.2 Decline a little
4.7 Decline a lot
3.1 (Don't Know)
0.1 (Refusal/NA)

Q642 [IncomGap]
Thinking of income levels generally in Britain today, would you say that the gap between those with high incomes and those with low incomes is ... READ OUT ...
%
84.7 ... too large,
11.0 about right,
1.7 or, too small?
2.4 (Don't Know)
0.1 (Refusal/NA)

Q643 [TaxHi]
CARD
Generally, how would you describe levels of taxation?
Firstly, for those with high incomes?
Please choose a phrase from this card.

Q644 [TaxMid]
CARD AGAIN
Next for those with middle incomes?
Please choose a phrase from this card.

Q645 [TaxLow]
CARD AGAIN
Next for those with low incomes?
Please choose a phrase from this card.

	[TaxHi]	[TaxMid]	[TaxLow]
	%	%	%
Much too high	3.6	2.3	24.6
Too high	7.9	21.7	50.0
About right	29.7	65.2	20.6
Too low	44.2	7.9	2.0
Much too low	11.4	0.2	0.9
(Don't Know)	3.3	2.6	1.8
(Refusal/NA)	0.1	0.1	0.1

Q646 [SRInc]
Among which group would you place yourself ... READ OUT ...
%
3.5 ... high income,
48.6 middle income,
46.6 or, low income?
1.1 (Don't Know)
0.3 (Refusal/NA)

93

n=1187

Q647 [HIncDiff]
CARD
Which of the phrases on this card would you say comes closest to your feelings about your household's income these days?
%
29.3 Living comfortably on present income
48.5 Coping on present income
15.5 Finding it difficult on present income
6.3 Finding it very difficult on present income
0.3 Other answer (WRITE IN)
0.0 (Don't Know)
0.1 (Refusal/NA)

Q650 [HIncPast]
Looking back over the last year or so, would you say your household's income has ... READ OUT ...
%
48.4 ... fallen behind prices,
43.5 kept up with prices,
7.3 or, gone up by more than prices?
0.7 (Don't Know)
0.1 (Refusal/NA)

Q651 [HIncXpct]
And looking forward to the year ahead, do you expect your household's income will ... READ OUT ...
%
45.6 ... fall behind prices,
42.3 keep up with prices,
9.9 or, go up by more than prices?
2.2 (Don't Know)
0.1 (Refusal/NA)

94

CHARITABLE GIVING (VERSION C)

VERSION C: ASK ALL   n=1187

Q654 [Lottr1]
CARD
Money raised by the National Lottery will be spent on many kinds of causes. Please use this card to say what you think about spending extra money on helping homeless people in Britain

Q655 [Lottr2]
CARD
(And extra money raised by the National Lottery...)
... helping disabled people in Britain?

Q656 [Lottr3]
CARD
And what about money from the National Lottery being spent on helping starving people in poor countries?

Q657 [Lottr4]
CARD
(And extra money raised by the National Lottery...)
... helping ex-prisoners to find homes and jobs?

	[Lottr1] %	[Lottr2] %	[Lottr3] %	[Lottr4] %
An excellent way to spend it	24.0	31.8	9.2	3.5
A very good way	30.8	41.1	16.3	9.8
Quite a good way	31.4	23.7	28.8	40.6
Not a very good way	8.8	1.7	28.8	28.6
Should not be spent on this at all	3.6	1.2	16.1	15.6
(Don't Know)	1.3	0.2	0.6	1.9
(Refusal/NA)	0.1	0.1	0.1	0.1

Q658 [Lottr5]
CARD
(And extra money raised by the National Lottery...)
... helping to restore historic buildings in Britain?

Q659 [Lottr6]
CARD
And what about it being spent on supporting art galleries, theatres and orchestras in Britain?

Q660 [Lottr7]
CARD
(And extra money raised by the National Lottery...)
... helping to protect the environment?

Q661 [Lottr8]
CARD
(And extra money raised by the National Lottery...)
... providing sports facilities in Britain?

n=1187

	[Lottr5] %	[Lottr6] %	[Lottr7] %	[Lottr8] %
An excellent way to spend it	3.2	2.4	14.8	7.2
A very good way	10.5	9.6	37.5	26.0
Quite a good way	37.0	33.3	40.5	44.2
Not a very good way	34.9	35.4	4.0	16.7
Should not be spent on this at all	13.6	18.2	2.4	5.1
(Don't Know)	0.8	0.9	0.8	0.6
(Refusal/NA)	0.1	0.1	0.1	0.1

Q662 [Lottr9]
CARD
And National Lottery money spent on helping to prevent cruelty to animals in Britain?

Q663 [Lottr10]
CARD
(And extra money raised by the National Lottery...)
... helping to protect children in need in Britain?

Q664 [Lottr11]
CARD
And National Lottery money spent on medical research in Britain?

	[Lottr9] %	[Lottr10] %	[Lottr11] %
An excellent way to spend it	10.7	35.2	32.1
A very good way	23.9	43.3	38.3
Quite a good way	42.3	16.6	21.7
Not a very good way	16.5	3.0	3.9
Should not be spent on this at all	5.9	1.5	3.4
(Don't Know)	0.5	0.3	0.4
(Refusal/NA)	0.1	0.1	0.1

POVERTY/SINGLE PARENTS (VERSION C)   n=1187

Q666 VERSION C: ASK ALL
[UBlPoor]
Now some questions about welfare benefits.
Think of a 25-year-old unemployed woman living alone. Her only income comes from state benefits. Would you say that she ... READ OUT ...

%
1.2   ... has more than enough to live on,
21.3 has enough to live on,
54.3 is hard up,
15.7 or, is really poor?
7.5   (Don't Know)
0.0   (Refusal/NA)

Q667 [MumPoor]
What about an unemployed single mother with a young child. Their only income comes from state benefits. Would you say they ... READ OUT ...

%
2.7   ... have more than enough to live on,
17.7 have enough to live on,
49.1 are hard up,
24.2 or, are really poor?
6.2   (Don't Know)
0.1   (Refusal/NA)

Q668 [UBlOm45]
Now thinking again of that 25-year-old unemployed woman living alone. After rent, her income is £45 a week. Would you say that she ... READ OUT ...

%
1.8   ... has more than enough to live on,
25.4 has enough to live on,
55.0 is hard up,
16.1 or, is really poor?
1.5   (Don't Know)
0.1   (Refusal/NA)

Q669 [MumOm77]
And thinking again about that unemployed single mother with a young child. After rent, their income is £77 a week. Would you say they ... READ OUT ...

%
5.2   ... have more than enough to live on,
31.6 have enough to live on,
49.3 are hard up,
12.3 or, are really poor?
1.3   (Don't Know)
0.2   (Refusal/NA)

Q670 [MtUnmar1]
Imagine an unmarried couple who split up. They have a child at primary school who remains with the mother. Do you think that the father should always be made to make maintenance payments to support the child?

%
83.2 Yes
14.3 No
2.4   (Don't Know)
0.2   (Refusal/NA)

n=1187

Q671 [MtUnmar2]
If he does make maintenance payments for the child, should the amount depend on his income, or not?

%
87.5 Yes
11.6 No
0.8   (Don't Know)
0.1   (Refusal/NA)

Q672 [MtUnmar3]
Do you think the amount of maintenance should depend on the mother's income, or not?

%
75.1 Yes
23.1 No
1.7   (Don't Know)
0.1   (Refusal/NA)

Q673 [MtUnmar4]
Suppose the mother now marries someone else. Should the child's natural father go on paying maintenance for the child, should he stop, or should it depend on the step-father's income?

%
37.4 Continue
15.1 Stop
45.5 Depends
1.9   (Don't Know)
0.1   (Refusal/NA)

Q674 [WorseOff]
CARD
Please look at this card and say, as far as money is concerned, what you think happens when a marriage breaks up.

%
14.3 The woman nearly always comes off worse than the man
21.5 The woman usually comes off worse
23.8 The woman and the man usually come off about the same
21.0 The man usually comes off worse
5.9   The man nearly always comes off worse than the woman
9.6   (Varies/depends)
0.3   Other answer (WRITE IN)
3.3   (Don't Know)
0.2   (Refusal/NA)

Q677 [MuchPov]
Some people say there is very little real poverty in Britain today. Others say there is quite a lot. Which comes closest to your view ... READ OUT ...

%
27.7 ... that there is very little real poverty in Britain,
70.7 or, that there is quite a lot?
1.6   (Don't Know)
0.1   (Refusal/NA)

Q678 [PastPov]   n=1187
Over the last ten years, do you think that poverty in
Britain has been increasing, decreasing or staying at
about the same level?
%
67.5   Increasing
6.1   Decreasing
24.2   Staying at same level
2.0   (Don't Know)
0.1   (Refusal/NA)

Q679 [FuturPov]
And over the next ten years, do you think that poverty in
Britain will ... READ OUT ...
%
54.4   ... increase,
10.2   decrease,
31.5   or, stay at about the same level?
3.7   (Don't Know)
0.1   (Refusal/NA)

Q680 [Poverty1]
Would you say someone in Britain was or was not in poverty
if ...
... they had enough to buy the things they really
needed, but not enough to buy the things most people
take for granted?

Q681 [Poverty2]
(Would you say someone in Britain was or was not in poverty
if ...)
... they had enough to eat and live, but not enough to buy
other things they needed?

Q682 [Poverty3]
(Would you say someone in Britain was or was not in poverty
if ...)
... they had not got enough to eat and live without getting
into debt?

	[Poverty1]	[Poverty2]	[Poverty3]
	%	%	%
Was in poverty	28.4	60.2	90.1
Was not	69.7	38.3	8.6
(Don't Know)	1.8	1.4	1.2
(Refusal/NA)	0.1	0.1	0.1

Q683 [WhyNeed]
CARD
Why do you think there are people who live in need? Of the
four views on this card, which one comes closest to your
own? CODE ONE ONLY
%
15.4   Because they have been unlucky
14.6   Because of laziness or lack of willpower
29.5   Because of injustice in our society
33.0   It's an inevitable part of modern life
1.4   (None of these)
4.5   Other answer (WRITE IN)
1.6   (Don't Know)
0.1   (Refusal/NA)

Q686 [FeelPoor]   n=1187
How often do you and your household feel poor nowadays ...
READ OUT ....
%
41.1   ... never,
41.3   every now and then,
11.1   often,
6.1   or, almost all the time?
0.2   (Don't Know)
0.2   (Refusal/NA)

GENDER (SHORT) (VERSION C)   n=1187

VERSION C: ASK ALL

[Divorce]

Q687 Do you think that divorce in (Britain/Scotland) should be
... **READ OUT** ...

%
11.9 ... easier to obtain than it is now,
32.6 more difficult,
51.5 or, should things remain as they are?
3.7 (Don't Know)
0.3 (Refusal/NA)

[SexLaw]

Q688 There is a law in Britain against sex discrimination, that is against giving unfair preference to men - or to women - in employment, pay and so on. Do you generally support or oppose the idea of a law for this purpose?

%
81.6 Support
15.6 Oppose
2.7 (Don't Know)
0.1 (Refusal/NA)

IF 'Support' AT [SexLaw]

[StrctSex]

Q689 Do you think that the present law against sex discrimination should be ... **READ OUT** ...
PROBE IF NECESSARY: From what you know or have heard

%
34.2 ... used more strictly,
4.4 used less strictly,
40.4 or, is it about right?
2.5 (Don't Know)
2.8 (Refusal/NA)

101

EDUCATION (VERSION C)

VERSION C: ASK ALL

[PSOpp]

Q691 And now a few questions about education.
Thinking about the opportunities that children under 5 have to go to nursery schools or other pre-schooling, should these opportunities be increased, or reduced, or are they at about the right level now?
IF INCREASED OR REDUCED: A lot or a little?

%
47.6 Increased a lot
20.4 Increased a little
27.2 About right
0.6 Reduced a little
0.5 Reduced a lot
3.4 (Don't Know)
0.3 (Refusal/NA)

[PSAdv1]

Q692 Would you say that children who have some sort of pre-schooling do better in their later school work, do worse, or in the end does it make little difference ?

%
72.9 Do better
0.2 Do worse
18.9 Makes little difference
5.0 (Varies/depends on the person)
2.7 (Don't Know)
0.3 (Refusal/NA)

[PSBeha]

Q693 And what about their behaviour at school? Would you say children who have some sort of pre-schooling are better behaved in their later school life, less well behaved, or in the end does it make little difference ?

%
50.2 Better behaved
1.8 Less well behaved
37.9 Makes little difference
6.0 (Varies/depends on the person)
3.9 (Don't Know)
0.3 (Refusal/NA)

[PubRes]

Q694 It is now compulsory for state secondary schools to publish their exam results. How useful do you think this information is for parents of present or future pupils? is it ... **READ OUT** ...

102

n=1187

Q695   [PSTestl]
And how useful do you think it would be for parents if schools for seven to eleven year olds published their test results? Would it be...

	[PubRes]	[PSTestl]
	%	%
... very useful,	33.5	23.9
quite useful,	43.9	38.1
or, not really useful?	19.7	34.9
(Don't Know)	2.6	2.8
(Refusal/NA)	0.3	0.3

Q696   [ParInf1]
And how helpful do you think it would be for parents to have information on each of these things for state secondary schools in their area?
... truancy records?

Q697   [ParInf2]
(And how helpful do you think it would be for parents to have information on ...) ... class sizes?

Q698   [ParInf10]
(And how helpful do you think it would be for parents to have information on ...) ... the number of hours in class each day?

Q699   [ParInf7]
(And now helpful do you think it would be for parents to have information on ...) ... the number of school-leavers going to university?

Q700   [ParInf11]
(And now helpful do you think it would be for parents to have information on ...) ... the number of school-leavers managing to get a job?

	[ParInf1]	[ParInf2]	[ParInf10]	[ParInf7]	[ParInf11]
	%	%	%	%	%
Very helpful	49.1	49.8	33.7	35.9	44.3
Fairly helpful	33.0	37.4	42.8	40.3	34.6
Not very helpful	11.7	9.6	19.0	20.0	17.1
Should not be made available	3.6	0.6	1.8	1.1	1.5
(Don't Know)	2.4	2.3	2.5	2.4	2.3
(Refusal/NA)	0.3	0.3	0.3	0.3	0.3

103

---

n=1187

Q701   [PSayTeac]
CARD
Please choose a phrase from this card to show how much say parents should have in what is taught in schools?

Q702   [PSayDisc]
CARD AGAIN
And how much say should parents have in the kinds of punishment that are used in schools? Please choose an answer from this card.

	[PSayTeac]	[PSayDisc]
	%	%
All of the say	7.5	13.0
Some	79.5	66.1
Not very much	9.3	13.6
No say at all	2.7	6.4
(Don't Know)	0.8	0.8
(Refusal/NA)	0.3	0.3

Q703   [SchSelec]
CARD
Which of the following statements comes closest to your views about what kind of secondary school children should go to?

	%
Children should go to a different kind of secondary school, according to how well they do at primary school	49.1
All children should go to the same kind of secondary school, no matter how well or badly they do at primary school	47.7
(Don't Know)	2.9
(Refusal/NA)	0.3

Q704   [HEdOpp]
Do you feel that opportunities for young people in Britain to go on to higher education - to a university or college - should be increased or reduced, or are they at about the right level now?
IF INCREASED OR REDUCED: : A lot or a little?

	%
Increased a lot	31.8
Increased a little	17.1
About right	45.8
Reduced a little	1.5
Reduced a lot	0.5
(Don't Know)	3.1
(Refusal/NA)	0.3

Q705   [HEFees]
At present, British university students get their teaching fees paid by their Local Authorities.
Do you think that students should ... READ OUT ...
... pay something towards their own teaching fees,
or, should Local Authorities continue to pay the whole amount?

	%
	26.6
	68.9
(Don't Know)	4.3
(Refusal/NA)	0.3

104

n=1187

Q706 [EdSpend1]
CARD
Which of the groups on this card, if any, would be your highest priority for **extra** government spending on education?

ONE CODE ONLY FOR HIGHEST PRIORITY

Q707 [EdSpend2]
And which is your next highest priority?
ONE CODE ONLY FOR NEXT HIGHEST

	[EdSpend1] %	[EdSpend2] %
Nursery or pre-school children	20.9	14.4
Primary school children	10.7	20.2
Secondary school children	27.6	20.0
Less able children with special needs	28.1	25.8
Students at colleges or universities	9.1	15.7
(None of these)	1.3	1.6
(Don't Know)	1.9	2.0
(Refusal/NA)	0.3	0.3

Q708 [Future16]
Suppose you were advising a 16 year old about their future.
Would you say they should ... **READ OUT** ...

%
46.9 ... stay on in full-time education to get their 'A' levels,
21.1 or, study full-time to get other sorts of qualifications,
9.4   or, leave full-time education and get work experience in a job?
21.0 (Varies/depends on the person)
1.3   (Don't Know)
0.3   (Refusal/NA)

A

SCPR
SOCIAL & COMMUNITY PLANNING RESEARCH

Head Office: 35 NORTHAMPTON SQUARE,
LONDON EC1V 0AX
Tel: 0171-250 1866 Fax: 0171-250 1524

Field and DP Office: 100 KINGS ROAD,
BRENTWOOD, ESSEX CM14 4LX
Tel: 01277 200600 Fax: 01277 214117

P.1345/GB

Spring 1994

BRITISH SOCIAL ATTITUDES 1994
MAIN SAMPLE
SELF-COMPLETION QUESTIONNAIRE

OFFICE USE ONLY

6-8	Cluster number
9-13	Spare
14-15	Card no. [2][0]
16-18	Spare
27-31	Batch no.
32-34	Spare

INTERVIEWER TO ENTER

1-5	[6]	Serial number
19-22	[0]	Sampling point
23-26		Interviewer number

To the selected respondent:

Thank you very much for agreeing to take part in this important study - the tenth in this annual series. The study consists of this self-completion questionnaire, and the interview you have already completed. The results of the survey are published in a book each autumn; some of the questions are also being asked in twenty-one other countries, as part of an international survey.

Completing the questionnaire:

The questions inside cover a wide range of subjects, but each one can be answered simply by placing a tick (✓) or a number in one or more of the boxes. No special knowledge is required: we are confident that everyone will be able to take part, not just those with strong views or particular viewpoints. The questionnaire should not take very long to complete, and we hope you will find it interesting and enjoyable. Only you should fill it in, and not anyone else at your address. The answers you give will be treated as confidential and anonymous.

Returning the questionnaire:

Your interviewer will arrange with you the most convenient way of returning the questionnaire. If the interviewer has arranged to call back for it, please fill it in and keep it safely until then. If not, please complete it and post it back in the pre-paid, addressed envelope, AS SOON AS YOU POSSIBLY CAN.

THANK YOU AGAIN FOR YOUR HELP.

Social and Community Planning Research is an independent social research institute registered as a charitable trust. Its projects are funded by government departments, local authorities, universities and foundations to provide information on social issues in Britain. The British Social Attitudes survey series is funded mainly by one of the Sainsbury Family Charitable Trusts, with contributions also from other grant-giving bodies and government departments. Please contact us if you would like further information.

n = 986

A2.01 [SCOBEYLW]
In general, would you say that people should obey the law without exception, or are there exceptional occasions on which people should follow their consciences, even if it means breaking the law?

PLEASE TICK ONE BOX

	%	(NA)
Obey the law without exception	36.2	
Follow conscience on occasions	57.1	
Can't choose	4.1	
(NA)	2.5	

A2.02 There are some people whose views are considered extreme by the majority.
First, consider people who support organisations that want to change policy by planting bombs. Do you think such people should be allowed to ...

PLEASE TICK ONE BOX ON EACH LINE

		Definitely	Probably	Probably not	Definitely not	Can't choose	(NA)
[REVTEAS1] a.	... teach 15 year olds in schools?	% 1.3	2.6	8.8	85.0	1.6	0.7
[REVINTTV] b.	... give interviews on television to put their case?	% 7.6	20.6	15.9	51.9	1.7	2.2
[REYCAND] c.	... stand as candidates in elections?	% 5.6	9.3	11.1	68.2	2.7	3.1

A2.03 Second, consider people who believe that whites are racially superior to all other races. Do you think such people should be allowed to ...

PLEASE TICK ONE BOX ON EACH LINE

		Definitely	Probably	Probably not	Definitely not	Can't choose	(NA)
[PRJTEASC] a.	... teach 15 year olds in schools?	% 2.8	5.3	17.5	70.3	2.8	1.3
[PRJINTTV] b.	... give interviews on television to put their case?	% 7.0	21.4	20.8	45.2	2.2	3.3
[PRJCAND] c.	... stand as candidates in elections?	% 7.8	14.8	16.2	55.2	2.6	3.5

A2.04 [JUSTICE]
All systems of justice make mistakes, but which do you think is worse ...

PLEASE TICK ONE BOX

	%
... to convict an innocent person,	57.5
OR to let a guilty person go free?	24.0
Can't choose	18.3
(NA)	0.2

2

n = 986

A2.05 Suppose the police get an anonymous tip that a man with a long criminal record is planning to break into a warehouse. Do you think the police should be allowed, without a Court Order ...

PLEASE TICK ONE BOX ON EACH LINE

		Definitely	Probably	Probably not	Definitely not	Can't choose	(NA)
[CRIMIN1] a.	...to keep the man under surveillance?	% 72.8	21.8	2.0	1.7	0.6	1.2
[CRIMIN2] b.	...to tap his telephone?	% 20.7	25.5	24.3	22.5	2.0	5.0
[CRIMIN3] c.	...to open his mail?	% 13.7	19.8	25.5	33.8	2.2	5.0
[CRIMIN4] d.	...to detain the man overnight for questioning?	% 34.1	33.2	15.1	13.0	1.2	3.5

A2.06 Now, suppose the tip is about a man without a criminal record. Do you think the police should be allowed, without a Court Order ...

PLEASE TICK ONE BOX ON EACH LINE

		Definitely	Probably	Probably not	Definitely not	Can't choose	(NA)
[NONCRIM1] a.	...to keep the man under surveillance?	% 44.5	34.7	10.4	8.5	1.1	0.9
[NONCRIM2] b.	...to tap his telephone?	% 5.9	15.0	28.7	43.8	2.1	4.4
[NONCRIM3] c.	...to open his mail?	% 4.1	10.1	25.7	53.6	2.0	4.6
[NONCRIM4] d.	...to detain the man overnight for questioning?	% 12.2	24.9	25.8	31.4	1.7	4.0

A2.07 [VIDEODEM]
Which of these two statements comes closer to your own view?

PLEASE TICK ONE BOX

	%
The police should have a right to take video films of people at protests or demonstrations	67.5
OR People should have a right not to be videoed at protests or demonstrations without their consent	25.5
Can't choose	6.7
(NA)	0.3

A2.08 [BANBLASF]
Some books or films offend people who have strong religious beliefs. Should books and films that attack religions be prohibited by law or should they be allowed?

PLEASE TICK ONE BOX ONLY

	%
Definitely should be prohibited	10.2
Probably should be prohibited	17.2
Probably should be allowed	39.5
Definitely should be allowed	24.1
Can't choose	8.8
(NA)	0.2

4

A2.12 Please tick one box for each statement below to show how much you agree or disagree with it.

PLEASE TICK ONE BOX ON EACH LINE

n = 986

	Agree strongly	Agree	Neither agree nor disagree	Disagree	Disagree strongly	(NA)
[PCGUNS] a. On-duty police officers should always carry guns	% 7.9	19.7	28.4	30.3	14.0	1.5
[LITESENT] b. Too many convicted criminals are let off lightly by the courts	% 50.0	36.1	9.2	3.4	0.6	0.7
[CONFESSN] c. A confession made during police questioning and later withdrawn should not on its own be enough to convict someone	% 14.1	55.4	19.6	8.4	1.3	1.1
[BENIDCRD] d. People claiming state benefits should have to carry an identity card to help prevent fraud	% 35.8	35.5	13.3	10.6	3.4	1.4
IF YOU LIVE IN ENGLAND OR WALES: [MAGISTRT] n = 897 e. Once people are made local magistrates they lose touch with ordinary people pretty quickly	% 7.9	31.2	39.9	17.8	1.5	1.6
IF YOU LIVE IN SCOTLAND: [SHERIFF] n = 89 f. Once people are made sheriffs, they lose touch with ordinary people pretty quickly	% 9.0	31.7	40.9	16.0	1.2	1.2

A2.13 And please tick one box for each statement below to show how much you agree or disagree with it.

PLEASE TICK ONE BOX ON EACH LINE

n = 986

	Agree strongly	Agree	Neither agree nor disagree	Disagree	Disagree strongly	(DK/NA)
[PENOSOLC] a. The police should be allowed to question suspects for up to a week without letting them see a solicitor	% 1.6	6.9	8.0	49.7	33.0	0.8
[REFUGEES] b. Refugees who are in danger because of their political beliefs should always be welcome in Britain	% 5.2	20.3	29.8	32.9	11.1	0.7
[PCCOMPLN] c. Serious complaints against the police should be investigated by an independent body, not by the police themselves	% 39.6	52.1	3.6	3.2	0.6	1.0
[IDCARDS] d. Every adult in Britain should have to carry an identity card	% 17.4	35.2	20.5	17.7	8.4	0.9
[CRIMSLNT] e. If someone remains silent under police questioning, it should count against them in court	% 11.1	31.9	24.4	23.1	7.8	1.6
[NINPRISN] f. The prisons contain too many people who ought to be given a lighter punishment	% 4.3	23.9	30.5	33.2	6.5	1.4
[NOWARPNT] g. The police should not need a warrant to search the homes of suspects	% 3.8	15.0	10.6	50.3	19.6	0.7

OFFICE USE ONLY

3

A2.09 As long as there is no threat to security, should prisoners be allowed to ...

PLEASE TICK ONE BOX ON EACH LINE

n = 986

	Definitely	Probably	Probably not	Definitely not	Can't choose	(NA)
[PRISBKS] a. ...have as many books as they wish to read?	% 60.9	28.4	2.6	3.6	2.2	2.3
[PRISVIST] b. ...visit home occasionally, say one weekend a month?	% 6.2	18.3	20.8	47.7	3.6	3.3
[PRISCONG] c. ...have their wife or husband occasionally stay overnight with them at the prison?	% 6.3	17.0	16.2	53.9	2.8	3.8
[PRISJOB] d. ...earn a little money in prison?	% 28.0	43.3	7.9	15.9	3.0	2.0

A2.10 [CSSILENT] Suppose a cabinet minister gives false information to parliament about an important national issue.

PLEASE TICK ONE BOX

%

Should the law allow civil servants in the minister's department to reveal the correct facts,   80.7

OR

should civil servants be required by law to keep silent?   7.6

Can't choose   11.2

(NA)   0.5

A2.11 [LAWSAY] Some say that the courts in Britain should have the power to overturn laws made by parliament. Others say that parliament should always have the final say. Which comes closest to your view?

PLEASE TICK ONE BOX

%

The courts should have the power to overturn laws made by parliament,   43.2

OR

parliament should always have the final say?   39.2

Can't choose   17.0

(NA)   0.6

OFFICE USE ONLY

6

A2.16 How much do you agree or disagree...?

n = 2957

PLEASE TICK ONE BOX ON EACH LINE

	Strongly agree	Agree	Neither agree nor disagree	Disagree	Strongly disagree	Can't choose	(NA)
[WWXPTEMP] a. ... mothers of young children should not expect employers to make special arrangements to help them combine jobs and childcare %	6.7	22.5	19.7	30.1	16.0	3.6	1.4
[GOVCCARE] b. ... the government should provide money for childcare, so that mothers of young children can work if they want to %	20.1	34.1	14.1	21.8	6.3	2.4	1.2

A2.17 Think of a child under 3 years old whose parents both have full-time jobs. How suitable do you think each of these childcare arrangements would be for the child?

PLEASE TICK ONE BOX ON EACH LINE

	Very suitable	Somewhat suitable	Not very suitable	Not at all suitable	Can't choose	(NA)
[CHDCARE1] a. A state or local authority nursery? %	32.6	36.9	13.8	6.3	7.8	2.6
[CHDCARE2] b. A private creche or nursery? %	34.2	41.4	9.5	3.9	7.7	3.2
[CHDCARE3] c. A child-minder or babysitter? %	23.2	41.7	19.4	6.3	6.5	3.0
[CHDCARE4] d. A neighbour or friend? %	10.8	34.9	33.0	11.7	6.2	3.4
[CHDCARE5] e. A relative? %	38.6	39.8	10.8	3.8	4.7	2.4
[CHDCARE6] f. A workplace nursery or creche? %	47.1	31.3	8.3	4.9	6.3	2.1

A2.18 Now a few questions about local government. Which of the four statements on this card comes closest to the way you generally vote in a local election?

[LGREVOTE]

PLEASE TICK ONE BOX ONLY

n = 1957

	%
I vote for a party regardless of candidate	51.5
I vote for a party only if I approve of the candidate	28.2
I vote for a candidate regardless of his or her party	5.5
I do not generally vote at all	13.9
(NA)	0.8

A2.19 [PARTCNSL] In most areas all councillors come from one of the political parties and councils are organised on party lines. There are some areas where most councillors are independents and the council is not organised on party lines. Which do you personally think is the better system ...

PLEASE TICK ONE BOX

	%
... the party system,	33.6
OR the non-party system?	32.9
Can't choose	32.5
(NA)	1.0

5

A2.14 From what you know or have heard, please tick a box for each of the items below to show whether you think the National Health Service in your area is, on the whole, satisfactory or in need of improvement.

PLEASE TICK ONE BOX ON EACH LINE

n = 2957

	In need of a lot of improvement	In need of some improvement	Satisfactory	Very good	(DK)	(NA)
[HSAREA1] a. GP's appointment systems %	11.2	31.8	43.9	12.1	0.1	0.9
[HSAREA2] b. Amount of time GP gives to each patient %	7.9	23.6	53.7	13.5	0.1	1.2
[HSAREA3] c. Being able to choose which GP to see %	7.1	19.6	54.5	17.5	0.1	1.2
[HSAREA4] d. Quality of medical treatment by GPs %	5.2	18.4	51.8	23.3	0.1	1.2
[HSAREA5] e. Hospital waiting lists for non-emergency operations %	35.2	42.7	18.0	1.2	0.4	2.5
[HSAREA6] f. Waiting time before getting appointments with hospital consultants %	39.1	41.6	15.4	2.0	0.3	1.5
[HSAREA7] g. General condition of hospital buildings %	15.4	35.8	38.0	8.9	0.3	1.6
[HSAREA9] h. Staffing level of nurses in hospitals %	30.3	39.6	24.2	4.2	0.3	1.5
[HSAREA10] i. Staffing level of doctors in hospitals %	30.4	39.4	24.8	3.4	0.4	1.6
[HSAREA11] j. Quality of medical treatment in hospitals %	6.1	26.8	48.4	16.7	0.4	1.5
[HSAREA12] k. Quality of nursing care in hospitals %	4.8	22.7	45.0	25.5	0.4	1.6
[HSAREA13] l. Waiting areas in accident and emergency departments in hospitals %	17.7	36.5	38.1	5.7	0.5	1.6
[HSAREA14] m. Waiting areas for out-patients in hospitals %	14.3	36.2	41.8	5.8	0.3	1.6
[HSAREA15] n. Waiting areas at GPs' surgeries %	4.4	18.7	57.3	17.9	0.1	1.7
[HSAREA16] o. Time spent waiting in out-patient departments %	22.5	48.0	25.2	2.1	0.2	1.9
[HSAREA17] p. Time spent waiting in accident and emergency departments before being seen by a doctor %	28.6	42.8	23.3	2.6	0.4	2.2
[HSAREA18] q. Time spent waiting for an ambulance after a 999 call %	9.2	27.6	47.5	10.8	1.4	3.6

A2.15 In the last two years, have you or a close family member ...

PLEASE TICK ONE BOX ON EACH LINE

	Yes	No	(DK)	(NA)
[NHSDOC] a. ... visited an NHS GP? %	95.2	3.7	0.0	1.1
[NHSOUTP] b. ... been an out-patient in an NHS hospital? %	71.8	26.2	0.0	2.0
[NHSINP] c. ... been an in-patient in an NHS hospital? %	49.5	47.7	0.0	2.8
[NHSVISIT] d. ... visited a patient in an NHS hospital? %	74.8	23.5	0.0	1.7
[PRIVPAT] e. ... had any medical treatment as a private patient? %	12.6	85.3	0.0	2.0

A2.20 [COUNSIL1]
When deciding how to make up his or her mind about a local issue, which of the following do you think is the most important for a councillor to take into account?

PLEASE TICK ONE BOX ONLY

n = 1957

	%
His or her own views	1.3
The interests of the ward he or she represents	40.0
The interests of all the people in the council's area	52.3
His or her party's views	1.7
Can't choose	3.9
(NA)	0.7

A2.21 [COUNSIL2]
And which of the following do you think is the more important for a councillor to do?

PLEASE TICK ONE BOX

	%
To take up problems and complaints people have about the council's services	39.3
OR To help manage the council's services so that they are run as well as possible	49.5
Neither	1.8
Can't choose	8.7
(NA)	0.6

A2.22 Most people don't stand for election as councillors. How common would you say it is that people are put off because ...

PLEASE TICK ONE BOX ON EACH LINE

	Very common	Fairly common	Fairly uncommon	Very uncommon	Can't choose	(NA)
a. [CNSLRES1] ... they don't feel they have enough time? %	38.1	42.9	5.2	4.0	8.0	1.9
b. [CNSLRES2] ... it just doesn't occur to them to think of standing? %	46.9	34.7	5.5	4.0	6.5	2.4
c. [CNSLRES3] ... they think local government has too little power to change things? %	21.7	42.2	20.0	5.6	8.0	2.5
d. [CNSLRES4] ... they don't feel they have the skills to do the job? %	36.6	42.4	9.4	3.4	6.3	1.9
e. [CNSLRES5] ... they cannot afford it financially %	31.9	34.6	15.6	6.4	8.9	2.6
f. [CNSLRES6] ... they don't think enough people would support them? %	27.9	45.8	11.4	4.1	8.5	2.3
g. [CNSLRES7] ... they think local government is influenced too much by party politics? %	31.7	38.2	12.9	4.0	11.0	2.2

A2.23 Please tick one box to show how much you agree or disagree with each of the following statements.

PLEASE TICK ONE BOX ON EACH LINE

n = 1957

	Agree strongly	Agree	Neither agree nor disagree	Disagree	Disagree strongly	(NA)
[LGEFFIC1] a. The way that people decide to vote in local elections is the main thing that decides how things are run in this area %	10.2	45.6	25.9	14.1	1.8	2.3
[LGEFFIC2] b. There is no point in voting in local elections because in the end it makes no difference who gets in %	6.7	18.1	17.1	44.4	11.8	1.8
[LGEFFIC3] c. Private companies can always run things more efficiently than local councils %	5.6	17.8	30.1	34.6	9.9	2.0
[LGEFFIC4] d. Generally speaking, those we elect as councillors lose touch with people pretty quickly %	9.1	37.9	27.9	21.8	1.6	1.8
[LGEFFIC5] e. Local council elections are sometimes so complicated that I really don't know who to vote for %	5.1	24.5	19.6	39.0	9.7	2.0
[LGEFFIC6] f. People like me can have a real influence on politics if they are prepared to get involved %	5.4	33.7	31.1	24.6	3.0	2.3
[LGEFFIC7] g. I feel that I could do as good a job as a councillor as most other people %	6.2	28.7	28.8	29.2	4.5	2.6
[LGEFFIC8] h. Councillors don't care much what people like me think %	7.3	28.2	28.4	30.8	3.1	2.2
[LGEFFIC9] i. Private companies cannot be trusted to run important public services like rubbish collection and street cleaning %	10.3	19.5	25.2	35.5	7.6	1.8

A2.24 Britain controls the numbers of people from abroad that are allowed to settle in this country. Please say, for each of the groups below, whether you think Britain should allow more settlement, less settlement, or about the same amount as now.

PLEASE TICK ONE BOX ON EACH LINE

	More settlement	Less settlement	About the same as now	(DK)	(NA)
a. [AUSIE/MM] Australians and New Zealanders %	9.5	30.0	58.1	0.3	2.1
b. [ASIA/MM] Indians and Pakistanis %	3.4	60.1	34.2	0.2	2.0
c. [EEC/MM] People from European Community countries %	8.6	39.9	48.4	0.2	2.8
d. [WI/MM] West Indians %	3.9	54.2	39.2	0.2	2.4
e. [EEURO/MM] People from Eastern Europe %	6.6	47.5	43.2	0.2	2.5
f. [CHINA/MM] People from China and Hong Kong %	5.9	51.8	39.8	0.2	2.2

OFFICE USE ONLY

9

A2.25 [RELCONTL]
Now thinking about the families (husbands, wives, children, parents) of people who have already settled in Britain, would you say in general that Britain should ...

PLEASE TICK ONE BOX

n = 1957

	%
...be stricter in controlling the settlement of close relatives	53.3
OR be less strict in controlling the settlement of close relatives	8.7
OR keep the controls about the same as now	36.6
(DK)	0.2
(NA)	1.3

A2.26 Here are some ideas about sending people to prison. Please tick one box on each line to show how much you agree or disagree with each of these statements.

PLEASE TICK ONE BOX ON EACH LINE

	Strongly agree	Agree	Neither agree nor disagree	Disagree	Strongly disagree	Can't choose	(NA)
a. [PRISSEN1] People who get sent to prison have much too easy a time	% 27.7	35.9	18.6	10.3	2.4	3.9	1.2
b. [PRISSEN2] Prisons should try harder to reform prisoners, rather than just punishing them	% 23.6	52.3	9.7	9.3	2.8	1.4	0.9
c. [PRISSEN3] Prisoners who behave well should usually be released before the end of their sentence	% 5.2	30.3	17.5	33.6	9.5	2.7	1.2
d. [PRISSEN4] Courts should give longer sentences to criminals	% 28.8	37.2	21.0	7.0	1.8	3.1	1.1
e. [PRISSEN5] Only hardened criminals, or those who are a danger to society, should be sent to prison	% 11.6	19.1	10.0	40.1	16.8	1.1	1.3
f. [PRISSEN6] Life sentences should mean life	% 58.8	27.7	5.4	4.3	1.5	1.5	0.9

A2.27 There are a number of ways of dealing with criminals who are not a big threat to society, other than sending them to prison. How strongly do you agree or disagree with each of the following?

PLEASE TICK ONE BOX ON EACH LINE
More offenders who are not a big threat should be....

	Strongly agree	Agree	Neither agree nor disagree	Disagree	Strongly disagree	Can't choose	(NA)
a. [OFFEND1] ...kept out of prison but made to report regularly to probation officers	% 15.8	43.7	10.6	22.1	4.5	2.1	1.2
b. [OFFEND2] ...kept out of prison but made to spend a certain amount of time helping people in the community	% 28.2	44.3	7.8	13.6	3.2	1.7	1.2
c. [OFFEND3] ...kept out of prison but made to do military service for a period of time	% 29.5	32.4	12.0	17.6	6.1	1.5	0.9
d. [OFFEND4] ...kept out of prison but made to get training and counselling	% 22.7	40.9	12.6	15.7	5.3	1.7	1.2

OFFICE USE ONLY

10

A2.28 Here is a list of predictions. For each one, please say how likely or unlikely it is to come true within the next ten years?

PLEASE TICK ONE BOX FOR EACH PREDICTION

n = 986

	Very likely	Quite likely	Not very likely	Not at all likely	(DK)	(NA)
[PREDICT1] a. Acts of political terrorism in Britain will be common events	% 17.9	50.0	28.0	1.7	0.5	1.9
[PREDICT2] b. Riots and civil disturbance in our cities will be common events	% 12.1	40.4	41.2	4.1	0.5	1.7
[PREDICT3] c. There will be a world war involving Britain and Europe	% 2.6	12.4	54.5	28.1	0.5	1.9
[PREDICT4] d. There will be a serious accident at a British nuclear power station	% 8.3	34.7	45.4	8.5	0.5	2.6
[PREDICT5] e. The police in our cities will find it impossible to protect our personal safety in the streets	% 16.8	42.9	32.2	5.4	0.5	2.2
[PREDICT6] f. The government in Britain will be overthrown by revolution	% 1.8	8.5	46.7	40.0	0.8	2.2
[PREDICT7] g. A nuclear bomb will be dropped somewhere in the world	% 6.6	27.2	46.0	17.8	0.3	2.0

A2.29 [PROPREP]
How much do you agree or disagree with this statement? Britain should introduce proportional representation so that the number of MPs each party gets matches more closely the number of votes each party gets.

PLEASE TICK ONE BOX ONLY

	%
Strongly agree	18.8
Agree	30.0
Neither agree nor disagree	16.5
Disagree	13.8
Strongly disagree	4.4
Can't choose	15.4
(NA)	1.0

A2.30 There are many ways people or organisations can protest against a government action they strongly oppose. Please show which you think should be allowed and which should not be allowed by ticking a box on each line.

PLEASE TICK ONE BOX ON EACH LINE

	Should it be allowed?					
	Definitely	Probably	Probably not	Definitely not	Can't choose	(NA)
[PROTEST1] a. Organising public meetings to protest against the government	% 48.1	35.4	6.6	3.0	5.6	1.3
[PROTEST2] b. Publishing pamphlets to protest against the government	% 41.3	39.0	9.0	4.1	5.1	1.5
[PROTEST3] c. Organising protest marches and demonstrations	% 29.5	38.7	16.8	8.5	4.9	1.5
[PROTEST4] d. Occupying a government office and stopping work there for several days	% 2.1	6.2	34.2	50.0	6.0	1.5
[PROTEST5] e. Seriously damaging government buildings	% 0.4	1.7	9.3	82.6	4.6	1.5
[PROTEST6] f. Organising a nationwide strike of all workers against the government	% 12.1	18.7	22.9	38.6	6.4	1.3

OFFICE USE ONLY

12

n = 986

A2.32 Some people say that British governments nowadays - of whichever party - can actually do very little to change things. Others say they can do quite a bit. Please say whether you think that British governments nowadays can do very little or quite a bit ...

PLEASE TICK ONE BOX ON EACH LINE

		British governments can do: Very little	Quite a bit	(DK)	(NA)
a. [GOVTDOPR]	... to keep prices down?	% 36.0	61.6	0.1	2.2
b. [GOVTDOUN]	... to reduce unemployment?	% 34.4	63.9	0.1	1.6
c. [GOVTDOSL]	... to improve the general standard of living?	% 28.3	69.5	0.1	2.1
d. [GOVTDOSS]	... to improve the health and social services?	% 17.4	80.2	0.1	2.2
e. [GOVTDOPV]	... to reduce poverty?	% 27.8	69.9	0.1	2.3
f. [GOVTCRIM]	... to cut crime?	% 32.2	65.7	0.1	2.0

A2.33 Listed below are some of Britain's institutions. From what you know or have heard about each one, can you say whether, on the whole, you think it is well run or not well run?
PLEASE TICK ONE BOX ON EACH LINE

		Very well run	Well run	Not very well run	Not at all well run	(DK)	(NA)
a. [NHSRUN2]	The National Health Service	% 3.0	29.8	50.7	15.1	0.1	1.3
b. [PRESSRN2]	The press	% 2.7	43.8	40.3	10.4	0.2	2.5
c. [LGOVRUN2]	Local government	% 1.2	38.0	52.9	5.3	0.2	2.3
d. [CSRUN2]	The civil service	% 1.7	45.5	41.6	7.4	0.4	3.4
e. [MANUFRN2]	Manufacturing industry	% 3.0	55.6	32.6	5.0	0.4	3.4
f. [BANKRUN2]	Banks	% 8.3	54.5	27.2	7.5	0.3	2.2
g. [UNIONRN2]	The trade unions	% 2.5	44.9	41.9	6.9	0.2	3.6
h. [BBCRUN2]	The BBC	% 8.9	52.6	28.5	7.2	0.3	2.5
i. [POLICRN2]	The police	% 7.2	60.3	25.1	4.9	0.1	2.3
j. [UNIVRUN]	Universities	% 7.2	65.7	20.7	1.9	1.0	3.6
k. [SCHLRUN]	State schools	% 3.3	48.1	38.5	7.5	0.5	2.1

A2.34 [VOTEDUTY] Which of these statements comes closest to your view about general elections?

PLEASE TICK ONE BOX ONLY

%

In a general election : It's not really worth voting 8.8

People should vote only if they care who wins 21.1

It is everyone's duty to vote 68.2

(DK) 0.2

(NA) 1.8

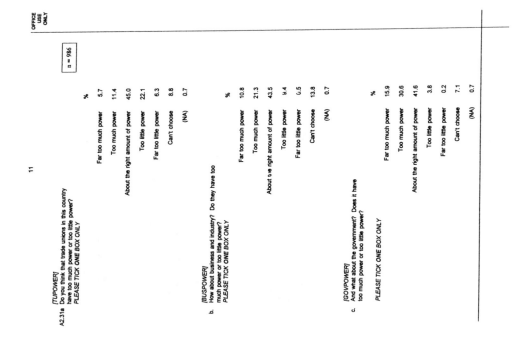

11

n = 986

A2.31a [TUPOWER] Do you think that trade unions in this country have too much power or too little power?
PLEASE TICK ONE BOX ONLY

%

Far too much power 5.7

Too much power 11.4

About the right amount of power 45.0

Too little power 22.1

Far too little power 6.3

Can't choose 8.8

(NA) 0.7

b. [BUSPOWER] How about business and industry? Do they have too much power or too little power?
PLEASE TICK ONE BOX ONLY

%

Far too much power 10.8

Too much power 21.3

About the right amount of power 43.5

Too little power 9.4

Far too little power 6.5

Can't choose 13.8

(NA) 0.7

c. [GOVPOWER] And what about the government? Does it have too much power or too little power?
PLEASE TICK ONE BOX ONLY

%

Far too much power 15.9

Too much power 30.6

About the right amount of power 41.6

Too little power 3.8

Far too little power 0.2

Can't choose 7.1

(NA) 0.7

14

OFFICE USE ONLY

n = 2957

A2.38 Now a few questions about the area where you live.
[AREAHELP]
In some areas people do things together and try to help each other, while in other areas people mostly go their own way.
<u>In general</u>, would you say you live in an area where ...

PLEASE TICK ONE BOX

	%
... people help each other,	24.5
OR ... people go their own way?	27.0
Mixture	45.6
Can't choose	1.9
(NA)	1.0

A2.39a *[BURGHELP]*
Do you think you live in the sort of area where people who thought a house was being broken into would ...

PLEASE TICK ONE BOX ONLY

	%
... do something about it,	62.1
OR ... just turn a blind eye?	6.1
Mixture	25.8
No burglaries in this area	2.4
Can't choose	2.5
(NA)	1.1

b. *[BURGAREA]*
And do you think burglaries in <u>this area</u> are ...

PLEASE TICK ONE BOX ONLY

	%
... mostly done by people from around here?	19.0
OR ... mostly done by people from other areas,	31.7
Mixture	35.7
No burglaries in this area	5.2
Can't choose	7.2
(NA)	1.3

A2.40 Please tick one box on each line to show how likely you think it is for any of these things to happen to you in, say, <u>the next year or so</u>.

PLEASE TICK ONE BOX ON EACH LINE

		Very likely	Fairly likely	Not very likely	Not at all likely	Can't choose	(NA)
a.	*[RISKCAR]* ... To have something stolen from a car?	% 18.8	39.0	23.0	12.8	4.3	2.1
b.	*[RISKBURG]* ... To have your home burgled?	% 9.2	36.7	41.1	5.9	5.4	1.7
c.	*[RISKROB]* ... To be robbed in the street?	% 4.4	17.9	53.4	17.8	4.6	2.0
d.	*[RISKVIOL]* ... To be attacked?	% 4.5	17.0	52.7	17.8	5.9	2.0

13

OFFICE USE ONLY

n = 986

A2.35 Please show how much you agree or disagree with each of the following statements.

PLEASE TICK ONE BOX ON EACH LINE

		Strongly agree	Agree	Neither agree nor disagree	Disagree	Strongly disagree	Can't choose	(NA)
a.	*[APATHY1]* I wish it were easier for people like me to get their views across to politicians	% 21.0	48.7	21.1	2.8	0.1	4.4	1.8
	[APATHY2] Politicians are in it just for themselves	% 14.5	32.4	27.6	19.9	0.6	3.1	1.9
b.	*[APATHY3]* Politicians these days are simply not good enough to do the job they have to do	% 11.8	31.4	32.4	19.2	0.3	3.2	1.7
c.	*[APATHY4]* Even the best politicians cannot have much impact because of the way government works	% 11.2	42.1	21.1	19.8	0.7	3.2	1.8
d.	*[APATHY5]* It doesn't really matter which party is in power, in the end things go on much the same	% 11.0	36.7	13.7	25.5	8.4	3.4	1.4

A2.36 Are you in favour of or against the death penalty for ...

PLEASE TICK ONE BOX ON EACH LINE

		In favour	Against	(DK)	(NA)
a.	*[CAPPUN1]* ... murder in the course of a terrorist act?	% 70.2	26.3	0.4	3.2
b.	*[CAPPUN2]* ... murder of a police officer?	% 67.4	28.4	0.4	3.7
c.	*[CAPPUN3]* ... other murders?	% 58.7	37.8	0.5	2.9

A2.37a *[PORNO1]*
Which of these statements comes <u>closest</u> to your views on the availability of pornography - that is, sexually explicit magazines and films?

PLEASE TICK ONE BOX ONLY

	%
They should be banned altogether	32.4
They should be available in special adult shops but not displayed to the public	43.7
They should be available in special adult shops with public display permitted	10.2
They should be available in any shop for sale to adults only	10.4
They should be available in any shop for sale to anyone	0.4
(DK)	0.2
(NA)	2.6

b. *[VIOLENCE]*
Which of these statements comes <u>closest</u> to your views on the availability of magazines and films that contain very violent scenes and actions?

PLEASE TICK ONE BOX ONLY

	%
They should be banned altogether	39.7
They should be available in special adult shops but not displayed to the public	31.0
They should be available in special adult shops with public display permitted	10.4
They should be available in any shop for sale to adults only	15.7
They should be available in any shop for sale to anyone	0.8
(NA)	2.5

OFFICE USE ONLY

15

A2.41 Here are a number of opposite statements.

For each pair, first of all decide which one you agree with more.
Then tick a box to say if you 'agree strongly' with the statement, or 'just agree'.
If you don't agree with either statement, tick the middle box.

n = 986

	This statement ↙	I agree with: OR →	This statement ↗				
	Strongly agree	Just agree	Don't agree with either statement	Just agree	Strongly agree	(DK)	(NA)
[WELTHDS5] a. Ordinary people get their fair share of the nation's wealth — A few rich people get too big a share of the nation's wealth	0.5	8.3	22.8	17.9	38.6	0.2	11.8
[NOTRUDS5] b. There is no need for strong trade unions to protect employees' working conditions and wages — Employees will never protect their working conditions and wages without strong trade unions	2.5	9.1	30.9	24.5	24.8	0.2	8.1
[PBOWNDS5] c. Major public services and industries ought to be in state ownership — Major public services and industries ought to be in private ownership	22.4	22.5	32.9	13.0	3.6	0.1	5.5

OFFICE USE ONLY

16

A2.41 For each these pairs of opposite statements, first of all decide which one you agree with more.
Then tick a box to say if you 'agree strongly' with the statement, or 'just agree'.
If you don't agree with either statement, tick the middle box.

n = 986

	This statement ↙	I agree with: OR →	This statement ↗				
	Strongly agree	Just agree	Don't agree with either statement	Just agree	Strongly agree	(DK)	(NA)
[TRADVDS5] d. Young people today don't have enough respect for traditional British values — Young people today should keep on challenging traditional British values	24.8	25.1	24.6	10.4	6.0	0.1	9.0
[GVJOBDS5] e. It is the government's responsibility to provide a job for everyone who wants one — It is everyone's own responsibility to find a job for themselves, and nothing to do with the government	16.7	15.7	30.5	17.2	11.8	0.1	8.1
[PRENTDS5] f. Private enterprise is the best way to solve Britain's economic problems — State intervention is the best way to solve Britain's economic problems	10.2	16.7	44.8	15.9	8.0	-	4.4

A2.41 For each these pairs of opposite statements, first of all decide which one you agree with more. Then tick a box to say if you 'agree strongly' with the statement, or 'just agree'. If you don't agree with either statement, tick the middle box.

n = 986

I agree with:

| | This statement | OR | Don't agree with either statement | OR | This statement | | |

g. [RCHLWDS5] There is one law for the rich and one for the poor ↔ Rich or poor, everyone gets treated the same

	Strongly agree	Just agree		Just agree	Strongly agree	(DK)	(NA)
g.	32.8	25.8	19.8	12.7	3.0	0.1	5.8

h. [CENSRDS5] Censorship of films and magazines is necessary to uphold moral standards ↔ Censorship of films and magazines has no place in a free society

	Strongly agree	Just agree		Just agree	Strongly agree	(DK)	(NA)
h.	30.3	23.2	16.3	9.6	4.6	0.1	5.9

A2.42 Please tick one box for each statement to show how much you agree or disagree with it.
PLEASE TICK ONE BOX ON EACH LINE

n = 2957

		Agree strongly	Agree	Neither agree nor disagree	Dis-agree	Disagree strongly	(DK)	(NA)
a.	[WELFRESP] The welfare state makes people nowadays less willing to look after themselves	% 9.5	34.2	21.1	28.9	4.3	-	1.9
b.	[WELFSTIG] People receiving social security are made to feel like second class citizens	% 9.3	41.3	23.1	22.9	1.6	0.1	1.8
c.	[WELFHELP] The welfare state encourages people to stop helping each other	% 2.7	28.4	29.8	34.0	3.3	0.1	1.7
d.	[MOREWELF] The government should spend more money on welfare benefits for the poor, even if it leads to higher taxes	% 10.1	39.6	25.3	21.1	2.0	-	1.9
e.	[UNEMPJOB] Around here, most unemployed people could find a job if they really wanted one	% 5.4	26.9	21.7	35.0	9.1	-	1.7
f.	[SOCHELP] Many people who get social security don't really deserve any help	% 3.7	22.5	24.4	38.3	9.0	-	2.1
g.	[DOLEFIDL] Most people on the dole are fiddling in one way or another	% 7.1	26.8	28.6	28.3	7.3	-	1.9
h.	[WELFFEET] If welfare benefits weren't so generous, people would learn to stand on their own two feet	% 5.4	21.3	22.6	36.5	12.4	-	1.8

A2.43 Please tick one box for each statement below to show how much you agree or disagree with it.
PLEASE TICK ONE BOX ON EACH LINE

n = 2957

		Agree strongly	Agree	Neither agree nor disagree	Disagree	Disagree strongly	(NA)
a.	[WEALTH] Ordinary people get their fair share of the nation's wealth	% 0.7	12.4	19.8	51.4	13.8	1.8
b.	[NOTRUNS] There is no need for strong trade unions to protect employees' working conditions and wages	% 1.6	14.7	21.3	46.7	13.9	1.7
c.	[PUBOWNST] Major public services and industries ought to be in state ownership	% 11.0	33.8	27.4	22.4	3.4	2.0
d.	[TRADVALS] Young people today don't have enough respect for traditional British values	% 11.9	46.3	24.1	14.0	1.9	1.7
e.	[GOVJOB] It is government's responsibility to provide a job for everyone who wants one	% 7.8	28.4	24.8	33.8	3.5	1.7
f.	[PRENTBST] Private enterprise is the best way to solve Britain's economic problems	% 3.7	24.9	36.4	27.3	5.3	2.3
g.	[RICHLAW] There is one law for the rich and one for the poor	% 24.3	44.9	14.7	13.1	1.5	1.5
h.	[CENSOR] Censorship of films and magazines is necessary to uphold moral standards	% 19.3	47.3	14.9	12.3	4.9	1.4

A2.44 Please tick one box for each statement below to show how much you agree or disagree with it.
PLEASE TICK ONE BOX ON EACH LINE

		Agree strongly	Agree	Neither agree nor disagree	Disagree	Disagree strongly	(NA)
a.	[REDISTRB] Government should redistribute income from the better-off to those who are less well off	% 13.1	37.6	22.6	22.5	2.5	1.8
b.	[BIGBUSNN] Big business benefits owners at the expense of workers	% 13.0	47.1	24.3	12.7	0.9	1.9
c.	[INDUST4] Management will always try to get the better of employees if it gets the chance	% 13.4	50.0	19.7	14.1	0.9	1.9
d.	[STIFSENT] People who break the law should be given stiffer sentences	% 27.5	49.4	16.4	4.7	0.4	1.5
e.	[DEATHAPP] For some crimes, the death penalty is the most appropriate sentence	% 35.2	32.9	8.9	12.4	9.1	1.5
f.	[OBEY] Schools should teach children to obey authority	% 27.8	53.7	11.6	4.7	0.7	1.5
g.	[WRONGLAW] The law should always be obeyed, even if a particular law is wrong	% 7.6	32.3	28.8	25.9	3.9	1.5

OFFICE USE ONLY

17   18

19

n = 2957

[QTIME]

A2.45a To help us plan better in future, please tell us about how long it took you to complete this questionnaire.

PLEASE TICK *ONE BOX ONLY*

%

Less than 15 minutes	3.7
Between 15 and 20 minutes	20.1
Between 21 and 30 minutes	32.0
Between 31 and 45 minutes	26.4
Between 46 and 60 minutes	10.2
Over one hour	6.5
(NA)	1.1

b. And on what date did you fill in the questionnaire?

PLEASE WRITE IN

DATE   0   1994
       MONTH

THANK YOU VERY MUCH FOR YOUR HELP

Please keep the completed questionnaire for the interviewer if he or she has arranged to call for it. Otherwise, please post it as soon as possible in the pre-paid addressed envelope provided.

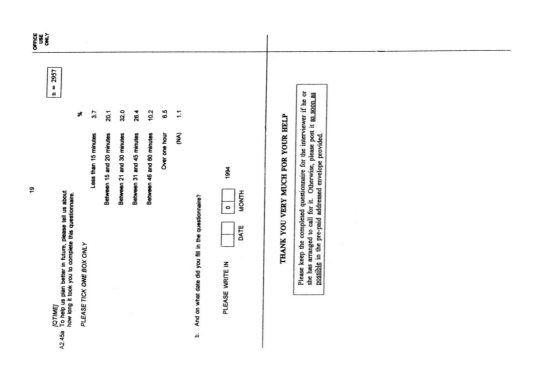

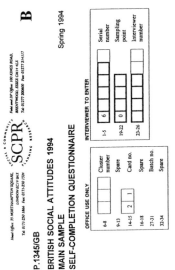

SCPR

Head Office, 35 NORTHAMPTON SQUARE,
LONDON EC1V 0AX
Tel: 0171-250 1866   Fax: 0171-250 1524

Field and DP Office, 100 KINGS ROAD,
BRENTWOOD, ESSEX CM14 4LX
Tel: 01277 200600 Fax: 01277 214117

B

P.1345/GB

BRITISH SOCIAL ATTITUDES 1994   Spring 1994
MAIN SAMPLE
SELF-COMPLETION QUESTIONNAIRE

OFFICE USE ONLY

6-8		Cluster number
9-13		Spare
14-15	2 1	Card no.
16-18		Spare
27-31		Batch no.
32-34		Spare

INTERVIEWER TO ENTER

1-5	6	Serial number
19-22	0	Sampling point
23-26		Interviewer number

To the selected respondent:

Thank you very much for agreeing to take part in this important study - the tenth in this annual series. The study consists of this self-completion questionnaire, and the interview you have already completed. The results of the survey are published in a book each autumn; some of the questions are also being asked in twenty-one other countries, as part of an international survey.

Completing the questionnaire:

The questions inside cover a wide range of subjects, but each one can be answered simply by placing a tick (✓) or a number in one or more of the boxes. No special knowledge is required: we are confident that everyone will be able to take part, not just those with strong views or particular viewpoints. The questionnaire should not take very long to complete, and we hope you will find it interesting and enjoyable. **Only you should fill it in, and not anyone else at your address.** The answers you give will be treated as confidential and anonymous.

Returning the questionnaire:

Your interviewer will arrange with you the most convenient way of returning the questionnaire. If the interviewer has arranged to call back for it, please fill it in and keep it safely until then. If not, please complete it and post it back in the pre-paid, addressed envelope, AS SOON AS YOU POSSIBLY CAN.

THANK YOU AGAIN FOR YOUR HELP.

Social and Community Planning Research is an independent social research institute registered as a charitable trust. Its projects are funded by government departments, local authorities, universities and foundations to provide information on social issues in Britain. The British Social Attitudes survey series is funded mainly by one of the Sainsbury Family Charitable Trusts, with contributions also from other grant-giving bodies and government departments. Please contact us if you would like further information.

1

B2.01 Some say that more decisions should be made by the European Community. Others say that more decisions should be made by individual governments. Do you think decisions about taxes should mostly be made by the European Community or mostly by individual governments?

n = 971

PLEASE TICK ONE BOX ON EACH LINE

		Mostly made by the EC	Mostly made by individual governments	Made by both equally	Can't choose	(NA)
a. [ECDEC1]	Decisions about taxes?	% 4.4	77.3	13.0	4.6	0.7
b. [ECDEC2]	And what about decisions about controlling pollution?	% 29.3	28.9	36.9	3.0	1.9
c. [ECDEC3]	Decisions about defence?	% 13.1	49.0	31.7	4.0	2.2
d. [ECDEC4]	Decisions about the rights of people at work?	% 20.3	48.0	26.5	3.2	2.0
e. [ECDEC5]	Decisions about immigration?	% 11.3	59.6	21.8	5.8	1.5

B2.02 All countries have a 'foreign policy', that is a policy to promote and look after their interests abroad. Here are a number of possible aims of British foreign policy. Please tick one box to say how important each aim is for Britain.

PLEASE TICK ONE BOX ON EACH LINE

		Essential	Very important	Fairly important	Not very important	Not at all important	Can't choose	(NA)
a.	To help Britain sell more goods abroad [FORPOL1]	% 53.2	33.1	10.4	1.0	0.2	1.5	0.6
b.	To promote Britain's link with Commonwealth countries like Canada and Australia [FORPOL2]	% 14.5	35.3	31.7	12.6	1.7	3.2	1.0
c.	To promote the best of British arts and culture, that is things like plays, films, music and the English language [FORPOL3]	% 14.3	29.1	37.1	13.2	2.5	2.6	1.2
d.	To ensure Britain keeps good relations with the USA [FORPOL4]	% 16.8	35.7	34.0	7.7	2.2	2.4	1.2
e.	To help poor countries in Asia and Africa improve their standard of living [FORPOL5]	% 11.2	31.4	38.1	11.3	5.0	1.7	1.3
f.	To encourage more people to visit Britain to help the tourist industry [FORPOL6]	% 20.5	40.8	29.4	5.9	1.5	1.0	0.9
g.	To strengthen Britain's role in a successful European Community [FORPOL7]	% 30.3	36.0	22.6	4.9	2.3	2.8	1.1
h.	To support the United Nations as the world's peacekeeper [FORPOL8]	% 41.2	34.3	16.9	2.6	1.4	3.0	0.7

OFFICE USE ONLY

2

B2.03 Here are a number of countries. For each please tick one box to say how much influence it currently has on world events compared with Britain.

n = 971

PLEASE TICK ONE BOX ON EACH LINE

		More influence than Britain	About the same influence as Britain	Less influence than Britain	Can't choose	(NA)
a. [FRANCINF]	France	% 15.0	54.3	20.1	8.5	2.1
b. [CHINAINF]	China	% 22.0	19.6	42.5	12.2	3.7
c. [GERMINF]	Germany	% 45.6	38.3	7.3	6.6	2.2
d. [AUSTINF]	Australia	% 3.4	26.4	57.9	9.2	3.0
e. [ISRLINF]	Israel	% 8.3	17.5	57.9	13.1	3.3
f. [INDIAINF]	India	% 1.1	8.2	75.0	12.8	2.8
g. [RUSINF]	Russia	% 29.7	32.8	23.8	11.1	2.7
h. [JAPANINF]	Japan	% 44.4	29.3	12.9	10.6	2.8

B2.04 Please tick one box to say how serious a threat to world peace you think each of these countries is likely to be over the next ten years or so?

PLEASE TICK ONE BOX ON EACH LINE

		A very serious threat	Quite a serious threat	Not a very serious threat	No threat at all	Can't choose	(NA)
a. [PEACERUS]	Russia	% 8.0	33.0	44.9	7.3	4.9	1.9
b. [PEACEGER]	Germany	% 4.1	15.2	49.5	23.3	5.3	2.6
c. [PEACECHI]	China	% 10.4	35.2	35.8	10.0	6.1	2.6
d. [PEACEUSA]	The USA	% 6.1	15.4	35.2	35.0	4.2	4.0
e. [PEACEIRA]	Iraq	% 28.1	45.7	14.8	4.3	4.8	2.3
f. [PEACEJAP]	Japan	% 2.7	10.2	47.8	29.9	6.9	2.4

OFFICE USE ONLY

9

[DAMAGE]

B2.21a Which one of these two statements comes closest to your own views?

PLEAS: TICK ONE BOX

	%
Industry should be prevented from causing damage to the countryside, even if this sometimes leads to higher prices	89.2
OR Industry should keep prices down, even if this sometimes causes damage to the countryside	8.9
(DK)	0.2
(NA)	1.6

[CTRYJOBS]

b. And which of these two statements comes closest to your own views?

PLEASE TICK ONE BOX

	%
The countryside should be protected from development, even if this sometimes leads to fewer new jobs	70.8
OR New jobs should be created, even if this sometimes causes damage to the countryside	25.9
(DK)	0.1
(NA)	3.3

B2.22 Please tick one box for each statement below to show how much you agree or disagree with it.

PLEASE TICK ONE BOX ON EACH LINE

	Agree strongly	Agree	Neither agree nor disagree	Disagree	Disagree strongly	(NA)
[GOVENVIR] a. The government should do more to protect the environment, even if it leads to higher taxes	% 15.8	42.6	27.1	11.8	0.7	2.0
[INDENVIR] b. Industry should do more to protect the environment, even if it leads to lower profits and fewer jobs	% 18.6	46.1	22.8	9.6	0.4	2.4
[PPLENVIR] c. Ordinary people should do more to protect the environment, even if it means paying higher prices	% 19.0	52.5	17.4	7.9	1.1	2.0

[TOWNTRAN]

B2.23a Thinking first about towns and cities. If the government had to choose ...

PLEASE TICK ONE BOX

	%
It should improve roads	37.0
It should improve public transport	62.2
(DK)	0.1
(NA)	0.8

[CTRYTRAN]

b. And in country areas. If the government had to choose ...

PLEASE TICK ONE BOX

	%
It should improve roads	33.8
It should improve public transport	65.0
(DK)	0.1
(NA)	1.1

8

Note: Questions B2.05-B2.18 are the same as questions A2.14-A2.27 of Version A of the questionnaire

B2.19 Listed below are various areas of government spending. Please show whether you would like to see *more* or *less* government spending in each area.

Remember that if you say "much more", it might require a tax increase to pay for it.

PLEASE TICK ONE BOX ON EACH LINE

n = 971

	Spend much more	Spend more	Spend the same as now	Spend less	Spend much less	Can't choose	(NA)
[GVSPEND1] a. The environment	% 10.1	38.4	42.8	2.9	0.3	2.6	2.9
[GVSPEND2] b. Health	% 37.8	49.8	9.9	0.7	0.3	0.8	0.9
[GVSPEND3] c. The police and law enforcement	% 24.6	47.4	23.4	1.5	0.3	1.0	1.7
[GVSPEND4] d. Education	% 29.1	44.4	22.2	1.5	0.4	1.0	1.4
[GVSPEND5] e. The military and defence	% 5.0	14.1	44.6	23.5	8.2	2.1	2.4
[GVSPEND6] f. Old age pensions	% 27.4	47.0	22.0	1.1	0.3	0.8	1.4
[GVSPEND7] g. Unemployment benefits	% 9.4	26.9	42.9	12.8	4.2	2.3	1.4
[GVSPEND8] h. Culture and the arts	% 3.7	8.5	41.7	28.8	13.0	2.9	1.4

[POWER1]

B2.20a. Which of these three possible solutions to Britain's electricity needs would you favour most?

PLEASE TICK ONE BOX ONLY

	%
We should make do with the power stations we have already	54.1
We should build more gas, oil or coal power stations	34.7
We should build more nuclear power stations	9.0
(DK)	0.3
(NA)	1.9

[POWER2]

b. If we *did* make do with the power stations we have already, do you think ...

PLEASE TICK ONE BOX ONLY

	%
OR ... they would produce enough electricity for Britain's future needs	37.0
... that homes, businesses and industry would be forced to cut down on how much electricity they use?	38.5
Can't choose	22.9
(NA)	1.6

[NUCPOWER]

c. As far as nuclear power stations are concerned, which of these statements comes closest to your own feelings?

PLEASE TICK ONE BOX ONLY

	%
They create very serious risks for the future	44.5
They create quite serious risks for the future	31.4
They create only slight risks for the future	17.3
They create hardly any risks for the future	4.7
(DK)	0.4
(NA)	1.7

10

B2.24 Please tick one box on each line to show how much you agree or disagree with each of the following statements.

PLEASE TICK ONE BOX ON EACH LINE

n = 971

	Agree strongly	Agree	Neither agree nor disagree	Disagree	Disagree strongly	(NA)
a. [HOUSBUIL] New housing should be built in cities, towns and villages rather than in the countryside	% 25.7	50.1	16.7	8.4	0.3	0.8
b. [KEEPBELT] It is more important to keep green-belt areas than to build new homes there	% 30.6	47.3	14.1	6.2	0.7	1.1
c. [PLANLAWS] Planning laws should be relaxed so that people who want to live in the countryside may do so	% 4.8	23.4	24.1	38.7	7.9	1.4
d. [FARMRSAY] Compared with other users of the countryside, farmers have too much say	% 5.0	25.0	40.0	25.0	3.5	1.5
e. [LESSVISIT] The beauty of the countryside depends on stopping too many people from visiting it	% 2.3	21.6	31.1	40.5	3.1	1.4
f. [CNTRPEOI] People should worry less about protecting the countryside, and more about those who have to make their living there	% 2.5	18.1	31.0	42.7	4.5	1.3
g. [CNTRPOPI] Some parts of the countryside are now so popular that it's no longer a pleasure to visit them	% 7.6	46.7	21.9	20.9	1.7	1.2

B2.25 Here are some statements about the countryside. Please tick one box for each to show whether you agree or disagree with it.

PLEASE TICK ONE BOX ON EACH LINE

	Agree strongly	Agree	Neither agree nor disagree	Disagree	Disagree strongly	(DK)	(NA)
a. [COUNTRY1] Modern methods of farming have caused damage to the countryside	% 17.5	54.0	25.4	1.1		0.4	1.6
b. [COUNTRY2] If farmers have to choose between producing more food and looking after the countryside, they should produce more food	% 4.2	29.6	58.6	5.4		0.3	1.9
c. [COUNTRY3] All things considered, farmers do a good job in looking after the countryside	% 6.8	67.0	22.0	1.7		0.3	2.2
d. [COUNTRY4] Government should withhold some subsidies from farmers and use them to protect the countryside, even if this leads to higher prices	% 7.5	45.9	39.8	3.0		1.0	2.8

11

B2.26 [FARMERS] Which of these two statements comes *closest* to your own views?

PLEASE TICK ONE BOX

n = 971

%

Looking after the countryside is too important to be left to farmers - government authorities should have more control over what's done and built on farms ... **43.9**

OR

Farmers know how important it is to look after the countryside - there are enough controls, and farmers should be left to decide what's done on farms ... **39.4**

Can't choose ... **15.9**

(NA) ... **0.8**

B2.27 [MEMBENV] Are you a member of any group whose main aim is to preserve or protect the environment?

PLEASE TICK ONE BOX

%

Yes ... **7.7**

No ... **91.6**

(NA) ... **0.7**

B2.28 In the *last five years*, have you ...

PLEASE TICK ONE BOX ON EACH LINE

	Yes, I have	No, I have not	(NA)
a. [PETITENV] ... signed a petition about an environmental issue,	% 47.7	50.0	2.3
b. [MONEYENV] ... given money to an environmental group,	% 24.3	66.2	9.4
c. [DEMOENV] ... taken part in a protest or demonstration about an environmental issue?	% 3.5	86.7	9.8

B2.29 Please tick one box for *each* of these statements below to show how much you agree or disagree with it.

PLEASE TICK ONE BOX ON EACH LINE

	Agree strongly	Agree	Neither agree nor disagree	Disagree	Disagree strongly	Can't choose	(NA)
a. [RAILSHUT] Local rail services that do not pay for themselves should be closed down	% 1.5	13.5	17.1	46.8	15.6	4.6	0.9
b. [BUSPRIOR] Buses should be given more priority in towns and cities, even if this makes things more difficult for car drivers	% 14.2	46.7	14.2	19.1	3.4	1.5	0.9
c. [CARCNTRY] A visitor to the countryside these days really needs a car to get around	% 13.9	61.8	7.4	13.2	2.2	0.7	1.0
d. [CAREASY] Car drivers still are given too easy a time in Britain's towns and cities	% 5.9	24.4	23.4	35.6	6.9	2.4	1.3
e. [BUSSHUT] Local bus services that do not pay for themselves should be closed down	% 2.1	11.1	13.7	50.4	18.1	3.6	1.0
f. [IMPTRP] Britain should do more to improve its public transport system even if its road system suffers	% 19.9	35.5	17.8	19.1	2.4	4.3	1.0

OFFICE USE ONLY

OFFICE USE ONLY

14

n=971

B2.35 Here are a number of opposite statements. For each pair, please tick one box to show which you agree with more.

a. [WELTHDS2]

	%
Ordinary people get their fair share of the nation's wealth	9.7
OR	
A few rich people get too big a share of the nation's wealth	78.4
Can't choose	10.9
(NA)	1.0

b. [NOTRUDS2]

	%
There is no need for strong trade unions to protect employees' working conditions and wages	24.3
OR	
Employees will never protect their working conditions and wages without strong trade unions	56.5
Can't choose	17.9
(NA)	1.2

c. [PBOWNDS2]

	%
Major public services and industries ought to be in state ownership	56.0
OR	
Majo public services and industries ough't to be in private ownership	20.9
Can't choose	21.6
(NA)	1.5

d. [TRADVDS2]

	%
Young people today don't have enough respect for traditional British values	60.6
OR	
Young people today should keep on challenging traditional British values	21.8
Can't choose	16.6
(NA)	1.1

OFFICE USE ONLY

12

n = 971

B2.30 Please tick one box for each statement to show how much you agree or disagree.

PLEASE TICK ONE BOX ON EACH LINE

	Agree strongly	Agree	Neither agree nor disagree	Disagree	Disagree strongly	Can't choose	(NA)
[CARTAXH] a. For the sake of the environment, car users should pay higher taxes %	5.8	17.6	16.8	44.0	12.8	1.9	1.2
[MOTORWAY] b. The government should build more motorways to reduce traffic congestion %	4.9	26.5	19.2	34.5	11.3	2.2	1.4
[CARCONV] c. Driving one's own car is too convenient to give up for the sake of the environment %	5.0	36.1	24.9	22.0	6.3	3.8	1.9
[BUILDTRA] d. Building more roads just encourages more traffic %	12.4	41.2	17.3	23.8	2.7	1.0	1.6
[CARALLOW] e. People should be allowed to use their cars as much as they like, even if it causes damage to the environment %	2.4	14.3	29.7	34.6	13.7	3.6	1.6

B2.31 Please tick one box on each line to show whether you would like to see more or less government spending on each of these

Remember that if you say 'more', everyone's taxes may have to go up to pay for it.

PLEASE TICK ONE BOX ON EACH LINE

	Spend much more	Spend more	Spend the same as now	Spend less	Spend much less	Can't choose	(NA)
[TRPSPND1] a. Improving local bus services %	11.7	41.7	35.3	5.2	1.1	3.4	1.6
[TRPSPND2] b. Building more roads %	3.6	14.8	44.2	22.0	8.7	4.6	2.1
[TRPSPND3] c. Improving local rail services %	14.5	41.2	32.7	4.7	1.0	4.1	1.7
[TRPSPND4] d. Improving and widening the roads we have already %	8.0	33.9	37.9	9.9	4.6	4.2	1.6

Note: questions B2.32-B2.34 are the same as questions A2.38-A2.40 of Version A of the questionnaire

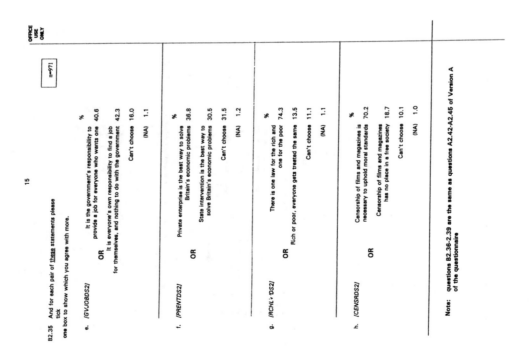

15

OFFICE USE ONLY

n=971

B2.35 And for each pair of these statements please tick one box to show which you agree with more.

e. [GVJOBDS2]

	%
It is the government's responsibility to provide a job for everyone who wants one	40.6
OR	
It is everyone's own responsibility to find a job for themselves, and nothing to do with the government	42.3
Can't choose	16.0
(NA)	1.1

f. [PRENTDS2]

	%
Private enterprise is the best way to solve Britain's economic problems	36.8
OR	
State intervention is the best way to solve Britain's economic problems	30.5
Can't choose	31.5
(NA)	1.2

g. [RCHLʼvDS2]

	%
There is one law for the rich and one for the poor	74.3
OR	
Rich or poor, everyone gets treated the same	13.5
Can't choose	11.1
(NA)	1.1

h. [CENSRDS2]

	%
Censorship of films and magazines is necessary to uphold moral standards	70.2
OR	
Censorship of films and magazines has no place in a free society	18.7
Can't choose	10.1
(NA)	1.0

Note: questions B2.36-2.39 are the same as questions A2.42-A2.45 of Version A of the questionnaire

C

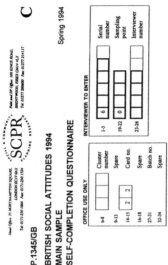

Head Office: 35 NORTHAMPTON SQUARE,
LONDON EC1V 0AX
Tel: 0171-250 1866   Fax: 0171-250 1524

Field and DP Office: 100 KINGS ROAD,
BRENTWOOD, ESSEX CM14 4LX
Tel: 01277 200600   Fax: 01277 214117

SCPR

P.1345/GB   Spring 1994

BRITISH SOCIAL ATTITUDES 1994
MAIN SAMPLE
SELF-COMPLETION QUESTIONNAIRE

OFFICE USE ONLY

6-8			Cluster number
9-13			Spare
14-15	2	2	Card no.
16-18			Spare
27-31			Batch no.
32-34			Spare

INTERVIEWER TO ENTER

1-5	6	Serial number
19-22	0	Sampling point
23-26		Interviewer number

To the selected respondent:

Thank you very much for agreeing to take part in this important study - the tenth in this annual series. The study consists of this self-completion questionnaire, and the interview you have already completed. The results of the survey are published in a book each autumn; some of the questions are also being asked in twenty-one other countries, as part of an international survey.

Completing the questionnaire:

The questions inside cover a wide range of subjects, but each one can be answered simply by placing a tick (✓) or a number in one or more of the boxes. No special knowledge is required: we are confident that everyone will be able to take part, not just those with strong views or particular viewpoints. The questionnaire should not take very long to complete, and we hope you will find it interesting and enjoyable. Only you should fill it in, and not anyone else at your address. The answers you give will be treated as confidential and anonymous.

Returning the questionnaire:

Your interviewer will arrange with you the most convenient way of returning the questionnaire. If the interviewer has arranged to call back for it, please fill it in and keep it safely until then. If not, please complete it and post it back in the pre-paid, addressed envelope, AS SOON AS YOU POSSIBLY CAN.

THANK YOU AGAIN FOR YOUR HELP.

Social and Community Planning Research is an independent social research institute registered as a charitable trust. Its projects are funded by government departments, local authorities, universities and foundations to provide information on social issues in Britain. The British Social Attitudes survey series is funded mainly by one of the Sainsbury Family Charitable Trusts, with contributions also from other grant-giving bodies and government departments. Please contact us if you would like further information.

OFFICE USE ONLY

n = 1000

1

C2.01 To begin, we have some questions about women. Do you agree or disagree ...?

PLEASE TICK ONE BOX ON EACH LINE

	Strongly agree	Agree	Neither agree nor disagree	Disagree	Strongly disagree	Can't choose	(NA)
[WWRELCHD] a. A working mother can establish just as warm and secure a relationship with her children as a mother who does not work	% 18.9	44.0	12.1	18.0	4.3	1.8	0.8
[WWCHDSUF] b. A pre-school child is likely to suffer if his or her mother works	% 5.7	32.2	17.1	33.6	8.2	1.8	1.4
[WWFAMSUF] c. All in all, family life suffers when the woman has a full-time job	% 5.9	26.5	14.9	37.1	12.6	1.6	1.4
[WANTHOME] d. A job is all right, but what most women really want is a home and children	% 5.8	18.9	23.0	34.8	13.6	2.6	1.4
[HWFEFFL] e. Being a housewife is just as fulfilling as working for pay	% 8.3	33.1	21.4	26.6	6.4	3.0	1.2
[FEMJOB] f. Having a job is the best way for a woman to be an independent person	% 10.8	48.4	16.5	19.8	2.1	1.2	1.2
[VOMENWRK] g. Most women have to work these days to support their families	% 18.9	56.2	12.5	8.8	0.8	1.2	1.6

C2.02 And, do you agree or disagree ...?

PLEASE TICK ONE BOX ON EACH LINE

	Strongly agree	Agree	Neither agree nor disagree	Disagree	Strongly disagree	Can't choose	(NA)
[BOTHEARN] a. Both the man and woman should contribute to the household income	% 16.9	43.6	24.2	12.2	1.0	1.0	1.1
[SEXROLE] b. A man's job is to earn money; a woman's job is to look after the home and family	% 5.0	18.7	16.3	40.5	17.5	0.9	1.1
[TRADROLE] c. It is not good if the man stays at home and cares for the children and the woman goes out to work	% 5.0	16.5	20.8	43.0	12.2	1.5	1.0
[FAMLIFE] d. Family life often suffers because men concentrate too much on their work	% 4.9	54.1	18.5	17.7	2.7	1.2	0.9

2

C2.03 Do you think that women should work outside the home full-time, part-time or not at all under these circumstances?

PLEASE TICK ONE BOX ON EACH LINE

	Work full-time	Work part-time	Stay at home	Can't choose	(NA)
[WWCHLD1] a. After marrying and before there are children	% 79.5	8.7	2.3	8.2	1.3
[WWCHLD2] b. When there is a child under school age	% 5.3	28.3	55.2	9.6	1.7
[WWCHLD3] c. After the youngest child starts school	% 16.3	65.2	8.0	9.0	1.6
[WWCHLD4] d. After the children leave home	% 62.6	20.9	1.5	13.0	2.0

C2.04 Do you agree or disagree ...?

PLEASE TICK ONE BOX ON EACH LINE

	Strongly agree	Agree	Neither agree nor disagree	Disagree	Strongly disagree	Can't choose	(NA)
[MARVIEW1] a. Married people are generally happier than unmarried people	% 3.8	20.3	37.4	27.2	6.2	4.1	0.9
[MARVIEW3] b. The main advantage of marriage is that it gives financial security	% 3.3	17.7	20.8	47.6	8.6	0.8	1.2
[MARVIEW4] c. The main purpose of marriage these days is to have children	% 2.4	14.5	17.7	51.2	11.1	1.8	1.3
[MARVIEW5] d. It is better to have a bad marriage than no marriage at all	% 0.6	1.3	3.6	49.3	43.0	0.9	1.3
[MARVIEW6] e. People who want children ought to get married	% 17.9	39.2	14.0	20.9	6.0	0.9	1.2
[MARVIEW10] f. One parent can bring up a child as well as two parents together	% 5.6	29.3	16.6	36.5	9.7	1.4	0.9
[MARVIEW11] g. It is all right for a couple to live together without intending to get married	% 14.2	49.9	14.8	12.5	6.1	1.2	1.2
[MARVIEW12] h. It is a good idea for a couple who intend to get married to live together first	% 12.2	45.7	22.0	13.1	4.6	1.6	0.8
[MARVIEW13] i. Divorce is usually the best solution when a couple can't seem to work out their marriage problems	% 8.1	44.6	22.8	16.5	3.7	3.5	0.8

C2.05 [IDLNCHLD]
All in all, what do you think is the ideal number of children for a family to have?

PLEASE WRITE THE NUMBER IN THE BOX

Median: 2

%
(DK) 1.8
(NA) 5.3

OFFICE USE ONLY

3

n = 1000

C2.06 Do you agree or disagree ...?
PLEASE TICK ONE BOX ON EACH LINE

	Strongly agree	Agree	Neither agree nor disagree	Disagree	Strongly disagree	Can't choose	(NA)
[CHDVIEW2] a. Watching children grow up is life's greatest joy	% 28.9	46.1	16.0	4.7	0.9	2.8	0.6
[CHDVIEW3] b. Having children interferes too much with the freedom of parents	% 1.0	9.2	20.7	55.3	11.4	1.8	0.6
[CHDVIEW6] c. People who have never had children lead empty lives	% 3.7	14.4	21.6	43.5	13.5	2.8	0.5
[CHDVIEW7] d. When there are children in the family, parents should stay together even if they don't get along	% 3.6	17.2	19.6	46.3	10.0	2.7	0.6
[CHDVIEW8] e. Even when there are no children, a married couple should stay together even if they don't get along	% 1.2	4.1	9.9	55.9	25.9	2.5	0.6

C2.07 [PREPCHLD]
Which of these would you say is more important in preparing children for life ...
PLEASE TICK ONE BOX

%
... to be obedient, 25.7

OR

... to think for themselves? 65.5
Can't choose 8.5
(NA) 0.3

C2.08 [MTHRWRKD]
Did your mother ever work for pay for as long as one year, after you were born and before you were 14?
PLEASE TICK ONE BOX

%
Yes, she worked 52.9
No 44.7
Did not live with mother 2.0
(NA) 0.4

OFFICE USE ONLY

4

n = 1000

C2.09a [MUMALIVE]
Is your mother still alive?
PLEASE TICK ONE BOX

%
Yes 57.4 → PLEASE ANSWER b. BELOW
No 41.7 → GO TO Q2.10
(NA) 0.9

IF YOU ANSWERED YES AT a.
b. [MUMVISIT]
How often do you see or visit your mother?
PLEASE TICK ONE BOX ONLY

%
She lives in the same household 8.5

I see or visit her: ... daily 4.3
... at least several times a week 9.5
... at least once a week 13.0
... at least once a month 7.4
... several times a year 10.2
... less often 4.5
(NA) 1.0

EVERYONE PLEASE ANSWER
C2.10 [DIVORCED]
Have you ever been divorced?
PLEASE TICK ONE BOX

%
Yes 16.4
No 71.1
Never married 12.3
(NA) 0.3

C2.11 [MARDNOW1]
Are you married or living as married now?
PLEASE TICK ONE BOX

%
Yes, married 62.9 → PLEASE ANSWER Q2.12a & b BELOW
Yes, living as married 6.6 → PLEASE ANSWER Q2.12a ONLY
No 29.6 → GO TO Q2.13
(NA) 0.9

5

PLEASE ANSWER THIS QUESTION IF YOU ARE MARRIED OR LIVING AS MARRIED
[SDIVORCD]
C2.12a Has your husband or wife or partner ever been divorced?
PLEASE TICK ONE BOX

	%
Yes	15.0
No	81.9
(NA)	3.1

IF YOU ARE LIVING AS MARRIED PLEASE GO TO Q2.13

n = 704

PLEASE ANSWER THIS QUESTION IF YOU ARE MARRIED
[COHABITM]
b. Did you live with your husband or wife before you got married?
PLEASE TICK ONE BOX

	%
Yes	26.7
No	63.6
(NA)	9.7

n = 637

EVERYONE PLEASE ANSWER
[NOTMARRY]
C2.13 Did you ever live together with a partner you didn't marry?
PLEASE TICK ONE BOX ONLY

	%
Yes, with a previous partner	8.5
Yes, with my present partner	5.7
Yes, both with a previous partner and with my present partner	3.0
No, never	81.6
(NA)	1.2

n = 1000

C2.14 Do you agree or disagree ...?
PLEASE TICK ONE BOX ON EACH LINE

	Strongly agree	Agree	Neither agree nor disagree	Disagree	Strongly disagree	Can't choose	(NA)
[MATLEAVE] a. Working women should receive paid maternity leave when they have a baby	% 34.2	48.4	8.1	6.3	1.6	0.8	0.7
[CHLDCRBN] b. Families should receive financial benefits for child-care when both parents work	% 11.0	31.3	18.4	29.8	5.5	3.1	0.9
[ABORTION] c. A pregnant woman should be able to obtain a legal abortion for any reason whatsoever, if she chooses not to have the baby	% 13.6	34.3	15.3	18.7	12.5	4.6	0.9

6

n = 1000

[PMSWRNG]
C2.15a Do you think it is wrong or not wrong if a man and a woman have sexual relations before marriage?
PLEASE TICK ONE BOX

	%
Always wrong	9.6
Almost always wrong	4.4
Wrong only sometimes	12.1
Not wrong at all	65.3
Can't choose	8.1
(NA)	0.4

[TNSWRNG]
b. What if they are in their early teens, say under 16 years old? In that case is it ...
PLEASE TICK ONE BOX ONLY

	%
... always wrong,	61.8
almost always wrong,	20.1
wrong only sometimes,	9.2
or, not wrong at all?	3.1
Can't choose	5.5
(NA)	0.4

[EMSWRNG]
c. What about a married person having sexual relations with someone other than his or her husband or wife? Is it ...
PLEASE TICK ONE BOX ONLY

	%
... always wrong,	63.8
almost always wrong,	22.6
wrong only sometimes,	7.1
or, not wrong at all?	2.0
Can't choose	4.2
(NA)	0.4

[HMSWRNG]
d. And what about sexual relations between two adults of the same sex? Is it ...
PLEASE TICK ONE BOX ONLY

	%
... always wrong,	48.4
almost always wrong,	5.5
wrong only sometimes,	8.6
or, not wrong at all?	22.2
Can't choose	14.8
(NA)	0.5

Page 8

OFFICE USE ONLY

C2.19a *[BOTHWORK]* **PLEASE ANSWER IF YOU ARE MARRIED OR LIVING AS MARRIED**
Do you and your husband or wife or partner both have paid work at the moment?
PLEASE TICK ONE BOX

n = 704

	%	
Yes	54.8	→ PLEASE ANSWER Q2.19
No	43.1	→ PLEASE GO TO Q2.20
(NA)	2.1	

b. *[EARNMOST]* Who earns more money?
PLEASE TICK ONE BOX ONLY

	%
The man earns much more	31.2
The man earns a bit more	10.6
We earn about the same amount	6.1
The woman earns a bit more	2.7
The woman earns much more	3.4
(NA)	2.8

PLEASE ANSWER Q2.20 AND Q2.21 IF YOU HAVE EVER HAD CHILDREN. IF YOU HAVE NEVER HAD CHILDREN, PLEASE GO TO Q2.22.

n = 754

C2.20 Did you work outside the home full-time, part-time or not at all …
PLEASE TICK ONE BOX ON EACH LINE

		Worked full-time	Worked part-time	Stayed at home	Does not apply	(NA)
a.	*[RMARWRK1]* After marrying and before you had children? %	71.2	6.7	8.4	6.6	7.1
b.	*[RMARWRK2]* And what about when a child was under school age? %	37.9	15.9	31.4	5.6	9.2
c.	*[RMARWRK3]* After the youngest child started school? %	36.1	25.5	13.5	15.6	9.2
d.	*[RMARWRK4]* And how about after the children left home? %	29.5	15.9	5.4	39.4	9.8

C2.21 What about your spouse/partner at that time - did he/she work outside the home full-time, part-time or not at all …
PLEASE TICK ONE BOX ON EACH LINE

		Worked full-time	Worked part-time	Stayed at home	Does not apply	(NA)
a.	*[SMARWRK1]* After marrying and before you had children? %	74.8	4.7	6.4	6.1	8.0
b.	*[SMARWRK2]* And what about when a child was under school age? %	52.3	9.0	22.9	6.5	9.3
c.	*[SMARWRK3]* After the youngest child started school? %	47.6	15.8	11.2	16.5	8.8
d.	*[SMARWRK4]* And how about after the children left home? %	35.7	9.7	4.9	40.4	9.3

Page 7

OFFICE USE ONLY

n = 1000

C2.16 *[HARASSCW]* Sometimes at work people find themselves the object of sexual advances, propositions, or unwanted sexual discussions from co-workers or supervisors. The advances sometimes involve physical contact and sometimes just involve sexual conversations. Has this ever happened to you?
PLEASE TICK ONE BOX

	%
Yes	23.6
No	75.2
Never have worked	0.7
(NA)	0.5

PLEASE ANSWER Q2.17 TO Q2.19 IF YOU ARE MARRIED OR LIVING AS MARRIED. IF NOT MARRIED OR NOT LIVING AS MARRIED, PLEASE GO TO Q2.20.

n = 704

C2.17 *[CPLINCOM]* How do you and your spouse/partner organise the income that one or both of you receive? Please choose the option that comes closest.
PLEASE TICK ONE BOX ONLY

	%
I manage all the money and give my partner his or her share	10.4
My partner manages all the money and gives me my share	12.6
We pool all the money and each take out what we need	52.7
We pool some of the money and keep the rest separate	13.0
We each keep our own money separate	8.7
Not married or living as married	-
(NA)	2.5

C2.18 PLEASE ANSWER IF YOU ARE MARRIED OR LIVING AS MARRIED
In your household, who does the following things?
PLEASE TICK ONE BOX ON EACH LINE

		Always the woman	Usually the woman	About equal or both together	Usually the man	Always the man	Is done by a third person	Can't choose	(NA)
a.	*[HHJOB1]* The washing and ironing %	46.6	31.9	17.8	1.0	-	0.7	-	1.9
b.	*[HHJOB2]* Small repairs around the house %	1.6	3.0	18.3	49.3	25.2	0.9	-	1.7
c.	*[HHJOB3]* Looking after sick family members %	21.8	25.9	44.9	0.4	0.4	0.4	4.1	2.0
d.	*[HHJOB4]* Shopping for groceries %	20.2	21.0	51.6	4.4	1.1	0.1	-	1.4
e.	*[HHJOB5]* Deciding what to have for dinner %	27.2	32.2	35.1	3.3	0.8	-	-	1.4

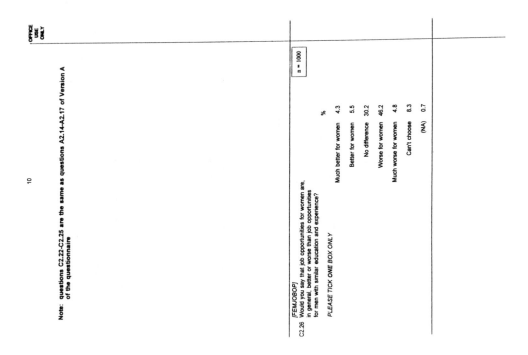

OFFICE USE ONLY

10

Note: questions C2.22-C2.25 are the same as questions A2.14-A2.17 of Version A of the questionnaire

n = 1000

[FEMJOBOP]
C2.26 Would you say that job opportunities for women are, in general, better or worse than job opportunities for men with similar education and experience?

PLEASE TICK ONE BOX ONLY

%

Much better for women	4.3
Better for women	5.5
No difference	30.2
Worse for women	46.2
Much worse for women	4.8
Can't choose	8.3
(NA)	0.7

OFFICE USE ONLY

11

n = 1000

[FEMEDOP]
C2.27 Would you say that opportunities for university education are, in general, better or worse for women than for men?

PLEASE TICK ONE BOX ONLY

%

Much better for women	1.0
Better for women	2.6
No difference	78.8
Worse for women	5.7
Much worse for women	0.7
Can't choose	10.5
(NA)	0.6

[FEMINC]
C2.28 And how about income and wages; compared with men who have similar education and jobs, are women in general paid better or worse than men?

PLEASE TICK ONE BOX ONLY

%

Women are paid much better	0.1
Women are paid better	0.7
No difference	25.3
Women are paid worse	58.8
Women are paid much worse	4.4
Can't choose	10.2
(NA)	0.5

[FEMPROM]
C2.29 And would you say that promotion opportunities for women are, in general, better or worse than promotion opportunities for men with similar education and experience?

PLEASE TICK ONE BOX ONLY

%

Much better for women	0.5
Better for women	3.1
No difference	24.1
Worse for women	57.5
Much worse for women	6.8
Can't choose	7.5
(NA)	0.5

n = 1000

C2.32a *[SINGMUM1]*
Thinking about a single mother with a child under school age. Which one of these statements comes closest to your own view?

PLEASE TICK ONE BOX ONLY

	%
She has a special duty to go out to work to support her child	8.8
She has a special duty to stay at home to look after her child	21.3
She should do as she chooses, like everyone else	59.7
Can't choose	9.4
(NA)	0.8

b. *[SINGMUM2]*
Suppose this single mother did get a part-time job. How much do you agree or disagree that the government should provide money to help with child-care?

PLEASE TICK ONE BOX ONLY

	%
Agree strongly	26.3
Agree	39.1
Neither agree nor disagree	16.7
Disagree	11.1
Disagree strongly	2.6
Can't choose	3.6
(NA)	0.6

C2.33a *[SMUMSCH1]*
And what about when the child reaches school age? Which one of these statements comes closest to your view about what the single mother should do?

PLEASE TICK ONE BOX ONLY

	%
She has a special duty to go out to work to support her child	5.5
She has a special duty to stay at home to look after her child	60.2
She should do as she chooses, like everyone else	5.7
Can't choose	0.7
(NA)	

b. *[SMUMSCH2]*
Suppose this single mother did go out to work. How much do you agree or disagree that the government should provide money to help with child-care outside school?

PLEASE TICK ONE BOX ONLY

	%
Agree strongly	14.9
Agree	37.0
Neither agree nor disagree	20.6
Disagree	18.4
Disagree strongly	2.2
Can't choose	6.2
(NA)	0.8

---

n = 1000

C2.30 Please tick one box for each statement below to show how much you agree or disagree with it.

PLEASE TICK ONE BOX ON EACH LINE

		Strongly agree	Agree	Neither agree nor disagree	Disagree	Strongly disagree	Can't choose	(NA)
a. A woman and her family will all be happier if she goes out to work *[WWHAPPIR]*	%	1.7	12.5	44.9	31.0	4.8	4.3	0.8
b. Women shouldn't try to combine a career and children *[WOMWKKID]*	%	2.7	19.5	22.4	43.3	9.6	1.4	1.0
c. In times of high unemployment, married women should stay at home *[FEMHOME]*	%	4.2	16.2	15.6	46.7	13.8	2.3	1.2
d. If the children are well looked after, it's good for a woman to work *[WOMWKGD]*	%	9.7	61.2	18.3	7.4	1.2	1.1	1.0
e. Most married women work only to earn money for extras, rather than because they need the money *[MWEXTRAS]*	%	4.8	24.6	13.3	43.6	10.9	1.7	1.1
f. If a woman takes several years off to look after her children, it's only fair her career should suffer *[WOMSUFFR]*	%	2.4	21.3	20.0	43.3	8.5	3.4	1.1
g. Married women have a right to work if they want to, whatever their family situation *[WOMRIGHT]*	%	19.8	56.7	10.2	8.5	2.2	1.6	1.1

C2.31 For each of the jobs below, please tick a box to show whether you think the job is particularly suitable for men only, particularly suitable for women only, or suitable for both men and women equally.

PLEASE TICK ONE BOX ON EACH LINE

		Particularly suitable for men	Particularly suitable for women	Suitable for both equally	(DK)	(NA)
a. *[JOBMF1]* Social worker	%	0.5	11.3	87.2	-	1.1
b. *[JOBMF2]* Police officer	%	32.2	0.2	66.7	-	0.9
c. *[JOBMF3]* Secretary	%	0.9	49.1	48.8	-	1.2
d. *[JOBMF4]* Car mechanic	%	57.1	1.4	40.3	-	1.2
e. *[JOBMF5]* Nurse	%	0.4	26.8	71.9	-	0.9
f. *[JOBMF8]* Bank manager	%	17.5	0.6	80.7	0.1	1.1
g. *[JOBMF9]* Family doctor/GP	%	4.7	1.8	92.5	-	0.9
h. *[JOBMF11]* Member of Parliament	%	7.8	0.8	90.1	-	1.3
i. *[JOBMF12]* Director of an international company	%	19.6	0.7	78.4	-	1.3
j. *[JOBMF13]* Airline pilot	%	44.3	0.6	53.9	-	1.2
k. *[JOBMF14]* Local councillor	%	5.4	1.1	92.0	-	1.4

14

C2.34 Please say how much you agree or disagree that ...
PLEASE TICK ONE BOX ON EACH LINE

[SMARMUM1]

	Agree strongly	Agree	Neither agree nor disagree	Disagree	Disagree strongly	Can't choose	(NA)
a. ... unmarried mothers who find it hard to cope have only themselves to blame	7.5	20.4	19.9	33.7	13.4	3.6	1.5
[SMARMUM2] b. ... unmarried mothers get too little sympathy from society	5.7	23.1	31.8	26.0	5.7	3.6	4.2

(%)

C2.35a [DUTYHOSP] Which of these two statements comes closer to your own view?
PLEASE TICK ONE BOX

%

People have a duty to help their local hospitals raise money for essential equipment patients need	6.9

OR

It's the government's duty to provide hospitals with all the essential equipment that patients need	86.5
Can't choose	5.9
(NA)	0.6

b. [DUTYSCHL] And which of these two statements comes closer to your own view?
PLEASE TICK ONE BOX

%

Parents have a duty to help raise money for some of the essential equipment at their children's school	13.9

OR

It's the government's duty to provide schools with all the essential equipment that pupils need	80.3
Can't choose	4.9
(NA)	1.0

C2.36a [CHARPAST] Over the last ten years, do you think that the number of people in Britain who would find it hard to survive without help from charities has ...
PLEASE TICK ONE BOX ONLY

%

... gone up,	72.5
gone down,	3.0
or, stayed about the same?	14.1
Can't choose	9.7
(NA)	0.6

b. [CHARFUT] And what about over the next ten years? Do you think that the number of people who would find it hard to survive without help from charities will ...
PLEASE TICK ONE BOX ONLY

%

... go up,	65.4
go down,	3.3
or, stay about the same?	19.5
Can't choose	11.1
(NA)	0.7

15

n = 1000

C2.37 Using this card, please say how much you agree or disagree with each of these statements.
PLEASE TICK ONE BOX ON EACH LINE

[CHARITY1]

	Agree strongly	Agree	Neither agree nor disagree	Disagree	Disagree strongly	Can't choose	(NA)
a. The smaller the charity, the more likely it is to put its money to good use	5.0	34.5	35.1	15.5	1.3	7.7	0.9
[CHARITY2] b. Nowadays charities can only do their job properly if they are run by paid professionals, not volunteers	2.5	17.4	20.5	48.9	4.4	5.2	1.1
[CHARITY3] c. The more money people give to British charities, the less the government will spend on people in need	15.4	51.0	13.7	13.6	0.9	4.3	1.1
[CHARITY4] d. Too often charities don't bother to say how the money they get is being spent	11.6	58.7	15.0	8.6	0.6	4.5	1.1
[CHARITY5] e. The bigger a charity becomes, the more out of touch it gets with those it is trying to help	8.3	40.3	25.8	17.5	2.2	4.8	1.1
[CHARITY6] f. Doing voluntary work is a good thing for volunteers because it makes them feel they are contributing to society	12.6	70.3	11.5	2.4	0.6	1.5	1.1

(%)

C2.38 Please tick one box to show how much you agree or disagree with each of these statements about secondary schooling.
PLEASE TICK ONE BOX ON EACH LINE

[SECSCHL1]

	Agree strongly	Agree	Neither agree nor disagree	Disagree	Disagree strongly	Can't choose (DK)	(NA)
a. Formal exams are the best way of judging the ability of pupils	9.2	45.2	15.5	25.9	2.9	-	1.3
[SECSCHL2] b. On the whole, pupils are too young when they have to decide which subjects to specialise in	9.0	53.8	19.0	16.3	0.7	0.1	1.2
[SECSCHL3] c. The present law allows pupils to leave school when they are too young	3.0	22.7	27.5	44.0	1.4	-	1.3
[SECSCHL4] d. So much attention is given to exam results that a pupil's everyday classroom work counts for too little	10.8	48.2	19.7	19.1	1.1	0.1	1.0

(%)

C2.39 Please tick one box to show how much you agree or disagree that ...
PLEASE TICK ONE BOX ON EACH LINE

[SKILLIMP]

	Agree strongly	Agree	Neither agree nor disagree	Disagree	Disagree strongly	Can't choose	(NA)
a. ... when recruiting school-leavers, employers pay too much attention to practical skills and training, and too little to exam results	1.9	14.9	25.8	44.8	4.0	7.4	1.2
[EXAMIMP] b. ... when choosing students, universities pay too much attention to exam results, and too little to practical skills and training	6.5	45.9	20.7	17.1	0.6	7.8	1.4

(%)

OFFICE USE ONLY

16

C2.40 Please tick one box to show how much you agree or disagree with each of these statements.

PLEASE TICK ONE BOX ON EACH LINE — n = 1000

	Agree strongly	Agree	Neither agree nor disagree	Disagree	Disagree strongly	Can't choose	(NA)
[MORALTH1] a. Teaching children the difference between right and wrong should be left to the family and kept out of schools %	7.6	15.8	9.8	50.0	15.1	0.5	1.3
[MORALTH2] b. Schools should spend more time teaching children right from wrong, even if it means less time is spent on basic subjects like reading and arithmetic %	5.7	21.8	18.6	44.1	6.4	1.3	2.0

C2.41 Here are some things that universities might make public, so that people can see how well they are doing. In your view how important is it that they should publish details of ...

PLEASE TICK ONE BOX ON EACH LINE

	Essential	Very important	Fairly important	Not very important	Not at all important	Can't choose	(NA)
[UNIVPUB1] a. ... How many students complete their degree? %	13.6	29.6	34.8	11.5	2.8	6.0	1.8
[UNIVPUB2] b. ... How many students get a first class degree? %	9.3	22.8	37.5	18.4	3.7	6.3	1.9
[UNIVPUB3] c. ... How many students get a job when they finish? %	18.9	38.8	22.3	8.5	2.9	6.5	2.0

C2.42 Here are some qualities that students may have developed by the time they leave university. In your view how important is it that universities aim to develop such qualities in their students?

PLEASE TICK ONE BOX ON EACH LINE

	Essential	Very important	Fairly important	Not very important	Not at all important	Can't choose	(NA)
[UNIQUAL1] a. Self-confidence %	31.1	46.3	18.0	0.7	0.3	2.4	1.2
[UNIQUAL2] b. How to live among people from different backgrounds %	22.8	43.2	25.7	4.1	0.7	2.2	1.3
[UNIQUAL3] c. Skills and knowledge which will help them get a good job %	37.0	50.5	8.7	0.3	-	1.7	1.7
[UNIQUAL4] d. A readiness to challenge other people's ideas %	14.4	38.0	35.5	7.2	0.6	2.9	1.5
[UNIQUAL5] e. An ability to speak and write clearly %	47.5	38.7	10.3	0.5	0.1	1.5	1.4
[UNIQUAL6] f. Knowledge that equips people for life in general %	38.4	42.6	14.0	1.5	-	2.3	1.2

17

C2.43 How much do you think universities in general actually develop these qualities in their students?

PLEASE TICK ONE BOX ON EACH LINE — n = 1000

	Very much	Quite a lot	Not very much	Hardly at all	Can't choose	(NA)
a. **[UNIDVQL1]** Self-confidence %	13.4	51.4	19.9	2.9	11.1	1.4
b. **[UNIDVQL2]** How to live among people from different backgrounds %	11.1	44.7	26.9	3.4	12.1	1.8
c. **[UNIDVQL3]** Skills and knowledge which will help them get a good job %	14.3	48.6	22.8	2.2	10.3	1.9
d. **[UNIDVQL4]** A readiness to challenge other people's ideas %	12.2	51.0	19.8	2.4	12.7	1.9
e. **[UNIDVQL5]** An ability to speak and write clearly %	18.2	44.1	22.4	4.0	9.6	1.9
f. **[UNIDVQL6]** Knowledge that equips people for life in general %	12.6	37.5	30.4	6.8	11.0	1.6

[NMARBABY]

C2.44a Imagine an unmarried couple who decide to have a child, but do not marry. What would your general opinion be?

PLEASE TICK ONE BOX ONLY

%

It would always be morally wrong	26.3
It would sometimes be morally wrong	16.5
It would rarely be morally wrong	4.2
Their decision would have nothing at all to do with morals	46.1
Can't choose	5.9
(NA)	1.1

[SMUMBABY]

h. What if a 30-year-old single woman who does not have a permanent relationship decides to have a child. What would your general opinion be?

PLEASE TICK ONE BOX ONLY

%

It would always be morally wrong	32.8
It would sometimes be morally wrong	20.0
It would rarely be morally wrong	4.7
Her decision would have nothing at all to do with morals	35.4
Can't choose	6.1
(NA)	0.9

OFFICE USE ONLY (columns for NA)

21

C2.50 Please tick one box for each statement below to show how much you agree or disagree with it.

PLEASE TICK ONE BOX ON EACH LINE

n = 1000

	Agree strongly	Agree	Neither agree nor disagree	Disagree	Disagree strongly	(DK)	(NA)
[WELTHOPP] a. A few rich people get too big a share of the nation's wealth	% 42.9	38.3	10.6	6.0	0.9		1.3
[NOTRUOPP] b. Employees will never protect their working conditions and wages without strong trade unions	% 15.8	41.4	22.5	17.8	1.2		1.3
[PBOWNOPP] c. Major public services and industries ought to be in private ownership	% 2.7	12.5	28.3	43.0	12.1		1.4
[TRADVOPP] d. Young people today should keep on challenging traditional British values	% 6.6	36.3	31.9	19.6	3.3		2.3
[GVJOBOPP] e. It is everyone's own responsibility to find a job for themselves, and nothing to do with the government	% 6.0	31.7	19.0	36.2	5.7		1.4
[PRENTOPP] f. State intervention is the best way to solve Britain's economic problems	% 5.2	31.6	38.3	20.0	2.3	0.1	2.5
[RCHLWOPP] g. Rich or poor, everyone gets treated the same	% 5.8	12.9	8.2	44.7	27.2		1.3
[CENSROPP] h. Censorship of films and magazines has no place in a free society	% 7.3	15.4	16.6	46.0	12.1	0.2	2.5

Note: questions C2.51-C2.54 are the same as questions A2.42-A2.45 of Version A of the questionnaire

---

18

C2.45 Here are a number of circumstances in which a woman might consider an abortion. Please say whether or not you think the law should allow an abortion in each case.

PLEASE TICK ONE BOX ON EACH LINE

n = 1000

Should abortion be allowed by law?

	Yes	No	(DK)	(NA)
[ABORT1] a. The woman decides on her own she does not wish to have the child	% 54.4	41.6	0.5	3.5
[ABORT2] b. The couple agree they do not wish to have the child	% 63.6	32.4	0.4	3.6
[ABORT3] c. The woman is not married and does not wish to marry the man	% 53.6	41.8	0.4	4.2
[ABORT4] d. The couple cannot afford any more children	% 61.1	34.5	0.4	4.1
[ABORT5] e. There is a strong chance of a defect in the baby	% 84.7	11.9	0.2	3.2
[ABORT6] f. The woman's health is seriously endangered by the pregnancy	% 91.7	5.3	0.2	2.9
[ABORT7] g. The woman became pregnant as a result of rape	% 92.6	4.8	0.3	2.3

C2.46a [EXIT1]
Suppose a person has a painful incurable disease Do you think that doctors should be allowed by law to end the patient's life, if the patient requests it?

PLEASE TICK ONE BOX

%
Yes 82.3
No 15.3
(DK) 0.4
(NA) 1.9

b. [EXIT3]
Still thinking of that person with a painful incurable disease. Do you think that someone else, like a close relative, should be allowed by law to help end the patient's life, if the patient requests it?

PLEASE TICK ONE BOX

%
Yes 53.4
No 44.4
(DK) 0.4
(NA) 1.9

Note: questions C2.47-C2.49 are the same as questions A2.38-A2.40 of Version A of the questionnaire

Subject index